$7

Three Hundred Eminent Personalities

A Psychosocial Analysis of the Famous

Mildred George Goertzel
Victor Goertzel
and Ted George Goertzel

Three Hundred
Eminent Personalities

 Jossey-Bass Publishers
San Francisco • Washington • London • 1978

THREE HUNDRED EMINENT PERSONALITIES
A Psychosocial Analysis of the Famous
   by Mildred George Goertzel, Victor Goertzel, and Ted George Goertzel

Copyright © 1978 by: Jossey-Bass, Inc., Publishers
                     433 California Street
                     San Francisco, California 94104
                     &
                     Jossey-Bass Limited
                     28 Banner Street
                     London EC1Y 8QE

Library of Congress Catalogue Card Number LC 78-1149

International Standard Book Number ISBN 0-87589-370-8

Manufactured in the United States of America

JACKET DESIGN BY WILLI BAUM

FIRST EDITION

Code 7817

A joint publication in
The Jossey-Bass Series
in Social and Behavioral Science
& in Higher Education

Preface

The eminent are not a random sample, representative of a larger population; they are, by definition, unique. Yet uniqueness does not mean that eminence is an individual trait. Rather, it is a social distinction. The subjects in this book are eminent because Americans have recognized them as such. In our society no central governmental authority chooses heroes for us to worship. Instead, heroes are chosen via the commercial media—by newspapers, magazines, and television and radio stations that bring celebrities to our attention; by publishing houses that decide which biographies to publish; and by bookstore owners and librarians who choose which books to stock. To the extent that this cultural apparatus responds to the preferences of the consuming population, the eminent are chosen by the reading and viewing public.

This book is a study of the lives of 317 eminent people, each of whom has been the subject of a biography. Their lives are fascinating and troubled, frequently titillating, and even sometimes scandalous. Still, as subjects of biography they are an important part of American society and thus merit serious study as well as our curiosity, for they serve as models of behavior for the rest of us or as surrogates acting in ways that we wish we could. They express talents, abilities, and feelings that less gifted people keep buried within themselves or display in less effective or notorious ways. It is one of our purposes, therefore, to explore the function these individuals have played in influencing the thinking and behavior of others of this generation.

Eminence is often ephemeral. Although some people are famous for long periods of time, others have only a brief moment in the spotlight. As the climate of the times changes, different people are chosen for eminence. Studying these changes gives us a way of assessing changes in American culture, changes in the values that make people worthy of social recognition.

A primary aim of this volume is to discover what a large group of eminent personalities were like as children, what kind of adults they became, and what some of the factors are that influenced their development. Psychology, the science of personality, does not tell us a great deal about the eminent personality. Psychologists usually study either the normal or the abnormal, the healthy or the mentally ill. Yet the eminent do not fit clearly into either category. Some have experienced mental illness, but as a group they have little in common with the psychopathological. They are often healthy psychologically, yet it is their remarkable deviation from the average, or "normal" in the correct sense of that term, which qualifies them as eminent. A psychology based on a concept of normalcy may help people to adjust to the world as it is, but it would be nothing less than an obstacle to the person who is driven to make his or her mark on the world. To the extent that we can isolate the eminent personality as a distinct type of individual, we may provide an alternative benchmark for people seeking to shape their own lives or those of their children. Study of these eminent personalities broadens our understanding of the varieties of human experience and the alternatives open to us as human beings.

The anecdotes described in this book are not to be regarded as miniature biographies, nor as literary essays, but as attempts to add the human dimension to the data. The task is to find, by observation or by analysis, important factors that are harmful or helpful to the child's development. How is it that boys and girls are so repeatedly and inevitably channeled into their respective slots? If you were to read the unidentified childhood histories of a number of these writers and scientists, there would be no confusion about which children became the writers and which the scientists. Among the various elements of what is called the "new life style" (which was familiar decades ago to a significant number of the 317 personalities) are a turning away from the rational and cognitive and a turning toward the emotional and intuitive; a growing acceptance of individual and small group violence to effect political change; and the right of the individual, whether female or male, to give top priority to her or his own sexual, creative, and vocational fulfillment.

The 317 men and women in our study are people who have lived into this century and are the subjects of biographical volumes published since 1962. In 1962 we published a previous study on the same area, *Cradles of Eminence,* which covered over 400 people who had achieved eminence prior to that year. In the present book, this earlier sample is used as a point of comparison to enable us to detect changes and continuities in the type of people who are considered eminent in America. In our first survey, biographies could be divided into those written in pre- and post-Freudian times. In the early books, "momism" was in; in the later volumes, "momism" was out. In 1978 it is completely discredited. What is in is the outpouring of information about the subjects' sex lives, including sexual divergency and marked unconventionality. Tennessee Williams, for instance, indexes in his *Memoirs* specific references to his homosexuality and his hospitalization for mental illness. This kind of candor did not exist prior to 1962. In those days, sex was out except for a few comments by women who reported that they were never told about conception and childbirth.

For purposes of statistical analysis, we have divided the 317 personalities into four areas of eminence, reflecting the fields in which they had made their major impact: *literary, political, artistic,* and *others* (a catch all). The ninety-two persons in the literary category include authors of fiction, drama, nonfiction, poetry, and a few editors and publishers. The seventy-seven persons in the political category include politicians and officials of all systems and persuasions, reformers, insurgents, military leaders, spies, and assassins. The seventy-five persons in the artistic category include graphic artists, musicians, performers, and directors. The category "others" includes scientists, persons who are subjects of biography primarily because of their personal association with an eminent person, mystics and psychics, athletes, religious leaders, philosophers, business leaders, psychotherapists, labor leaders, explorers, and a surgeon.

There were a number of statistically significant ($p < .05$) differences between the experiences of people who achieved eminence in each category. These are given at the beginning of Chapters Eight through Eleven and are summarized in the last chapter.

This has been a collaborative book, although there are those who ask how a mother, father, and son can collaborate. In a sense, we are more like children of ten months who enjoy parallel play. There are vast spaces in our togetherness. Ted was not included in the original plans to write this book. He came from Philadelphia to Palo Alto to visit when he was between books of his own and made the classical error of being critical of the limited scope of our proposed investigation. He made suggestions that we readily accepted, provided he would help. Consequently, he did the data analysis and considerable editing and writing.

The first reading was done by and the first rough drafts of the life stories were written by Mildred George Goertzel, who is not employed "outside the home." These drafts were rewritten by Victor Goertzel. Subjects who are described in some detail and who hold conflicting points of view or are well known to specific segments of the reading public were read by all three authors. These subjects include Simone de Beauvoir, Niels Bohr, Leonid Brezhnev, Rachel Carson, Hermann Hesse, Lyndon Johnson, Carl Jung, Robert Kennedy, Henry Kissinger, Doris Lessing, Ralph Nader, Anaïs Nin, Sylvia Plath, and Wilhelm Reich. Ted checked the libraries in New York, Chicago, Atlanta, and Philadelphia for the number of books about the subjects ranked as the top twelve (see Table 1 in Chapter One). His parents checked the libraries at Berkeley, California, and Ashland, Oregon. Anita Kramer, who was very helpful when we were all living in New Jersey and working on the survey that resulted in *Cradles of Eminence,* checked the Montclair library.

It is the 317 subjects and their biographers to whom we owe the most. We are especially indebted to authors who write meaningfully and explicitly about their childhood experiences: W. H. Auden, Andrei Codrescu, Christopher Isherwood, Jomo Kenyatta, Violetta Leduc, Jan Myrdal, V. S. Pritchett, Jean-Paul Sartre, Jessamyn West, Emlyn Williams, and Yevgeny Yevtushenko. Among the biographers who are exceptionally informative about the childhood experiences of their subjects are Michael Holroyd, who writes about both Lytton Strachey and Augustus John; Rudolph Binion, who writes about Lou Andreas-Salomé; Eugene Lyons, who writes about David Sarnoff; and R. M. Williams, who writes about the Bond family.

Finally, we express our appreciation to members of the staff of the Menlo Park, California, library for their helpfulness and interest.

February 1978   MILDRED GEORGE GOERTZEL
VICTOR GOERTZEL
Palo Alto, California
TED GEORGE GOERTZEL
Philadelphia, Pennsylvania

Contents

The Authors

MILDRED GEORGE GOERTZEL, formerly a high school teacher and director of the Forum School for Emotionally Disturbed Children in Paterson, New Jersey, now devotes full time to writing. She received her bachelor's degree in English from Ball State University and did graduate work in English at the University of Chicago and Northwestern University and in child development at the University of California, Berkeley.

She is coauthor, with Victor Goertzel, of *Cradles of Eminence* (1962), a chapter on gifted children in *The Clinical Psychology of Exceptional Children* (C. M. Louttit, Ed., 1957), and several journal articles on gifted children and eminent adults. She lives in Palo Alto, California, with her husband, Victor, and has three sons and three grandchildren.

VICTOR GOERTZEL is a psychologist specializing in group and individual psychotherapy in Palo Alto and San Jose, California. After receiving his B.A. and M.A. degrees in psychology from the University of California, Berkeley, he was awarded the Ph.D. degree in clinical psychology from the University of Michigan in 1953. He is a member of the American Psychological Association, the Society for the Psychological Study of Social Issues, the American Orthopsychiatric Association, and is a past president of the National Association for Gifted Children.

Victor Goertzel's professional experience began as assistant psychologist with the National Youth Administration of Illinois and the Chicago Board of Education Bureau of Child Study. After ten years as chief psychologist at the Wayne County Hospital and Mental Health Clinic in Detroit, he served as research director at Fountain House in New York City and as research psychologist with the California Department of Mental Hygiene at Camarillo, California, State Hospital, the San Mateo County Mental Health Services, and the San Mateo County probation department. In addition to *Cradles of Eminence*, Goertzel has written numerous articles for professional journals, including several articles co-authored with H. Richard Lamb on the community rehabilitation of psychiatric patients.

TED GEORGE GOERTZEL is associate professor and chairperson of the Department of Sociology and Anthropology at Rutgers, The State University, Camden, New Jersey. Prior to joining the Rutgers faculty in 1973, he taught at the University of Oregon (1968–1973) and the University of São Paulo (1967–1968). He was awarded the Ph.D. degree in sociology from Washington University in 1970.

Ted Goertzel is the author of *Political Society* (1976) and *Sociology: Class, Consciousness, and Contradictions* (with A. Szymanski, forthcoming). He has also published research on social class and political attitudes, generational conflict, and social movements. He is currently living in Philadelphia.

Three Hundred
Eminent Personalities

*A Psychosocial Analysis
of the Famous*

❦ 1 ❦

Who Are the Eminent?

*Each human being is a more complex structure
than any social system to which he belongs.*
                              Alfred North Whitehead

Identifying the eminent personalities of our age requires a systematic methodology. Although there is no one official standard of eminence, we decided that the number of biographies on the shelves of the public library was a good index. The fact that a biography has been published and purchased by a public library indicates that the person who is the subject of the book is of considerable interest to the reading public. It also ensures that some information is available on that person's personality, both for the reading public and for us as researchers. Some eminent persons may be missed (perhaps because their intimate lives were too dull to merit a biographical work), but the 317 people included in the sample are, by our working definition, eminent. For it is through the biographies, as well as through shorter pieces in magazines and newspapers and on television, that the eminent personalities became known to the people who make them eminent.

1

Definition of Eminence

In our original study, *Cradles of Eminence* (1962), about people who became eminent prior to 1962, we used the following criterion for including an individual in the sample:

> Include each person who has at least two books about him or her in the biography section of the Montclair (New Jersey) Public Library if that person was born in the United States and all persons who have at least one book about them if they were born outside the United States. Include only those who lived in the twentieth century.

This method of selection ensured a plentiful supply of people from many countries, which we felt was necessary to discover how universal certain habits of childrearing and educational practices are. We limited the number of Americans to those who had two or more books about them. Otherwise, the survey sample would have been overwhelmed with books about Americans who were of only temporary interest to the public. We were restive under this rule at times because it meant putting aside some excellent biographies of men and women whom we personally admire. Still, our purpose—the gathering of a great amount of data about what happens in homes that rear high achievers—was well met by our selection criterion.

The present sample was selected in the same manner, except that we used the Menlo Park (California) Public Library as our source and limited the selection to persons who have been subjects of volumes published since 1962 and who were not included in *Cradles of Eminence*. This procedure resulted in a completely different list of subjects to be surveyed.

The time a researcher knows best how a specific investigation should be done is *after* it is finished. We completed the inquiry on the Four Hundred (as we called our first sample) over fifteen years ago. While reading, we took data on all the items which we considered important at that time. In the present survey, we increased by over one third the items selected for each person among the Three Hundred (as we shall call them for convenience). In some

instances we can compare the two samples—the number of dominating mothers, for example. In some instances we cannot—for
example, we took no information on birth order for the Four
Hundred, and we now recognize that this was an unfortunate over-
sight. However, since the present project was unfunded, unlike some
other projects we have done, and since only three closely related
persons were involved, we are able to accept new concepts in mid-
stream—for instance, the significance of certain sibling relationships,
which we did not perceive until the project was well under way. We
feel strongly that much is lost in many surveys because the param-
eters are completely predetermined.

Our move from New Jersey to California in 1961 made it
necessary to change the qualifying library. We are convinced that
had we used Montclair again it would have made no substantial
difference. Nevertheless, our friend Anita Kramer, who helped with
the previous book, checked the names of the twelve most popular
subjects of biography in the Menlo Park sample with those in the
Montclair library and found a roughly similar pattern. We also
checked six other libraries and found that libraries, like chain stores,
have much the same stock of biographical volumes everywhere. The
top two among the Three Hundred, Robert F. Kennedy and Lyndon
Johnson, were the top two everywhere, although their relative positions varied. Table 1 shows the tallies in each of our sample libraries
for the twelve people who have the most biographies in Menlo Park.

As Table 1 shows, there is some variation from library to
library, perhaps reflecting regional differences in public interest or
merely random differences in the judgment of librarians. We cannot use the number of books in any given library as a precise index
of the degree of eminence of a person. We are, however, confident
that the people in our sample deserve to be there. If there are errors
in the sampling, it is in excluding some eminent people who for one
reason or another did not have a biography on the Menlo Park
shelves. There are, for example, no astronauts among the Three
Hundred. The journey to the moon is not celebrated by an outpouring of biographies, neither of those who first stepped onto the moon
nor of the scientists who made the trip possible. As Anaïs Nin says,
the inward journey to seek the identity of the individual is of more
importance than the journey to the moon. Incidentally, she is, as the

Table 1

Number of Biographies, Autobiographies, and Memoirs in Selected Public Libraries for Twelve Most Eminent Personalities Among the Three Hundred.

Person	Public Libraries							
	Menlo Park, Calif.	Montclair, N.J.	New York (53rd St.)	Chicago	Atlanta	Philadelphia	Berkeley, Calif.	Ashland, Oreg.
Robert F. Kennedy	14	11	15	24	13	23	16	9
Lyndon B. Johnson	11	13	19	32	21	28	22	8
Simone de Beauvoir	5	5	4	5	5	5	6	6
Anaïs Nin	9	2	2	1	3	4	8	6
Sidonie Colette	8	7	6	4	7	7	9	6
T. S. Eliot	7	9	6	4	7	7	9	6
Ché Guevara	7	7	8	2	5	10	4	6
Carl Jung	7	6	2	6	5	6	7	5
Edgar Cayce	6	7	4	6	7	5	5	4
Cesar Chavez	6	3	3	7	3	6	7	6
Hermann Hesse	6	6	5	7	3	6	5	4
Ezra Pound	6	10	8	11	11	14	7	6

table shows, much more popular on the West Coast than on the East Coast and is the least well known in Chicago, the heart of the Midwest. This seems a significant distribution of the books of the passionate exponent of the "inward journey," the godmother to encounter groups, to all those who are staunchly apolitical, and to women who prefer being mistresses, not wives.

The Three Hundred are not selected by the authors of this volume but represent those to whom the contemporary society has given recognition as subjects of biography. They are a varied lot. Some people become subjects of biography because they enhance our lives; please us with their poetry, paintings, or performances; or are competent and honest public servants. Others are innovators, loved by some and hated by others. It is they who invent, discover, and prod and become the agents of change. Others are exciting because they are disturbing and dangerous. Readers are curious about them and seek to know so they can protect themselves against them. Biographies of Adolf Hitler, for instance, are still popular.

Origins of the Eminent

The sample is truly international, with forty-five countries represented among the 317 subjects. But the nations and continents of the world are by no means equally represented. Half of the sample (165 subjects) were born in Europe in twenty-three different countries, ranging from forty-two born in England to two born in each of four countries and one born in each of six countries. One third of the sample (107 subjects) were born in the United States. This proportion would have been much higher had we used the same criterion for selection of American-born persons as we did for foreign-born and included Americans with only one biography. Only one subject in seven (forty-five persons) represents the rest of the world. They include persons from twenty-one different countries in Asia, Africa, and the Americas outside the United States, headed by seven from India and six from Canada. The most populous nation on the globe, China, has only three subjects: Chou En-lai, Han Suyin, and Henry R. Luce (an American born in China of missionary parents).

The 107 subjects born in the United States come from

thirty-three states and the District of Columbia. The leading states are New York (fourteen subjects), Pennsylvania (eleven), Massachusetts (seven), and five each from California, Nebraska, and New Jersey. Eleven states have one subject each, and seventeen states are not represented in the survey population at all.

Speculation as to the significance of the geography of eminence could be a lifetime inquiry, toward which the biographical notes included with the annotated bibliography at the end of this volume can make only a miniscule contribution. The simple task of ascertaining the place of birth of a well-known person is not as easy as it might seem if one is concerned with the relationship between the place of birth and the place where the child is reared. In our mobile society, children often are not reared near where they are born. Consequently, to merely state the place of birth may be quite misleading. Nureyev was born on a moving train far from his home. John Foster Dulles was born in his grandparents' home in Washington, D.C., and soon went home to live in a small town. Mothers from the farm or small town may go to the city hospitals to be delivered. Persons born on a farm stop trying to tell exactly where they were born and name the nearest town whose name is likely to be known to the questioner. Lyndon B. Johnson, we discovered after much searching, was born on the Sam Johnson farm on the Pedernales River near Stonewall, Gillespie County, Texas. He is sometimes called the "man from Johnson City," but that is because he was born on a farm that was somewhere between Stonewall and Johnson City. Children with English names who are born in foreign lands are often sent back to England or the United States to be reared and educated, sometimes as early as two years of age.

With these reservations, we find, taking a global view, that it is still the small town or the farm that produces 51 percent of the subjects. In the United States they come from such communities as Avon, South Dakota; Winstead, Connecticut; Sun Prairie, Wisconsin; Peru, Indiana; Lock Haven and Chadd's Ford, Pennsylvania; Clio, Alabama; Titusville, Florida; Anamosa, Iowa; Hailey, Idaho; and Hopkinsville, Kentucky.

Outside the United States they come from such communities as Woodbridge and Grand Calumet, Canada; Chislehurst, England; Bressanone, Italy; Rheine Fawr, Wales; Turkeve, Hungary; Kikl and Lwów, Poland; Uzlian and Kislovdsk, Russia; Zima Junction, Siberia; Ejarsea Gora, Ethiopia; Nyanirid Kango, Kenya; Kinlien, Annam; and Tipperary, Ireland.

Among medium-sized cities there are many, the world over, that are not great cultural centers or the site of a prestigious university; rather, they are industrial or they serve the agricultural areas around them. These are cities like Hoboken, New Jersey; Birmingham, Alabama; Duluth, Minnesota; Kalamazoo, Michigan; Nottingham, England; Augsburg, Germany; or Kiev, Russia. Omaha, Nebraska, surprisingly, is the birthplace of five of the Three Hundred: Fred Astaire, Marlon Brando, Henry Fonda, Gerald Ford, and Malcolm X. No other medium-sized city approaches this record.

One fourth of the Three Hundred were born in the great cities, such as New York, Boston, Tokyo, Paris, London, Moscow, Vienna, and Philadelphia. Often they were the children of immigrants who lived in the ghettos, where they were reared in what was essentially a small city within the city: Harlem or Brownsville in New York City, the Armenian section of Paris, or the Italian section of London. The great cities have also been the mecca for those born in the small towns and on the farms who sought more recognition of their talents.

There is no one from Chicago or San Francisco. There is also no one from Dublin. The glory that was Joyce, Yeats, Shaw, O'Casey, and Behan has faded away without a proper wake. However, there are men and women from other parts of Ireland, from Cork and Tipperary.

The Three Hundred Compared with the Four Hundred

How do the Three Hundred individuals who achieved eminence since 1962 compare with the Four Hundred who were eminent prior to that date? Among the earlier sample, five people had by far the largest number of biographies. They were Franklin D. Roosevelt with twenty-eight books; Mahatma Gandhi, twenty-one; Sir Winston Churchill, twenty; and Albert Schweitzer and Theodore Roosevelt, seventeen each. After them came a sharp drop to names almost as familiar but the subjects of only five or six volumes each when the data were gathered prior to 1962: Albert Einstein, Sean

O'Casey, Nelson Rockefeller, Leo Tolstoy, Mark Twain, and William and Henry James.

Some members of the Four Hundred continue to be popular subjects of biography. We checked the shelves at Menlo Park to see which of the top twelve of the Four Hundred have had new biographies published about them. Freud topped the list with twelve biographical volumes since 1962, to say nothing of many works about his theories. We found eight new volumes about Franklin D. Roosevelt, three of which are the popular revelations about the marital life of Franklin and Eleanor Roosevelt. Two of these were written by their sons James and Elliot. Winston Churchill has fourteen new biographies, one an adulatory, dull book by his son Randolph.

The men who believe in nonviolence are dwindling, if not in influence, certainly in the number of biographies. Gandhi has only three new biographies and Schweitzer has only two. (Indira Gandhi has four as a member of the Three Hundred.)

Six of the nine new studies of Tolstoy are informative about his rearing, including one written by his son Ilya, *Tolstoy, My Father*. Sean O'Casey is the subject of a book about him by his wife Eileen O'Casey. Only two of the nine new studies of the life and writings of Henry James are classified as biography. There are seven new volumes about Mark Twain. William James has two new biographies. Nelson Rockefeller has none, although there is one book about the Rockefeller family.

We found fifty-five biographical volumes published since 1962 about the top twelve of the Four Hundred. There are ninety-six books about the top twelve of the Three Hundred in the library in Menlo Park.

Interest in historical figures continues from one generation to another, but we see readers in the new sample relinquishing some values while holding others. Human nature itself, as Montaigne said, never changes. However, customs do, and although marital infidelity was certainly not unknown in the sixteenth century, when Montaigne lived, it was not common for sons to write books about their parents' sex life, as do Nigel Nicolson and the Roosevelt sons. (No parent, to our knowledge, has yet written a book about the less savory, intimate details in the life of a daughter or son, but the time may come.)

Although the top two among the Three Hundred are Robert Kennedy and Lyndon Johnson, they also are closely associated with the Four Hundred and are as well known as the most prominent of the Four Hundred. When we think of them, we think of John Kennedy, Dwight Eisenhower, Harry Truman, Nikita Khrushchev, all of whom were among the Four Hundred. Robert Kennedy and Lyndon Johnson were both loving husbands and devoted fathers to their children. Each was married only once. Perhaps they represent the ideal nuclear family and the democratic system.

Most of the Three Hundred represent some one segment of a fragmented society and have a strong, but not universal, appeal. For instance, Cesar Chavez represents those who believe in non-violent political struggle, which he uses in an attempt to bring economic security and dignity to the lives of farm workers. Non-violence was strongly represented among the Four Hundred by such people as Schweitzer, Gandhi, and Tolstoy; by Mark Twain in his whimsical fashion; and by Martin Luther King, Jr. As judged by its importance to the Three Hundred among subjects of biography, nonviolence is no longer a major cause in our world society. We found a volume published since 1962 on an apostle of nonviolence who might have been among the Three Hundred, John Luthuli, recipient of the Nobel Peace Prize, but he was in the children's section of the qualifying library. So was the only reference to pacifist-activist A. J. Muste. It is one of the signs of our times, then, that the books about the peaceable and impeccable are often for children only. Although there are other pacifists among the Three Hundred—including Danilo Dolci and the artists Oskar Kokoschka and Käthe Kollwitz—nonviolence is not as strongly espoused by the Three Hundred as it was by the Four Hundred.

Insurgency is on the rise among the Three Hundred. Ché Guevara, who was killed by his captors in Bolivia, was young, personable, and a victim. He is an appealing and popular example of the substantial number of revolutionaries. Moreover, yesterday's revolutionary is often tomorrow's head of state, as was the case with Fidel Castro, Ho Chi Minh, Chou En-lai, and Leonid Brezhnev.

Sexual revolution, political revolution, the "turning in and turning on" people are all found in quantity in the new biographies.

The casualties suffered in the pursuit of extraordinary achievement can be brutal. Ché Guevara, as noted, was killed while being held prisoner. Robert Kennedy was assassinated. Cesar Chavez receives frequent death threats. Lyndon Johnson left his high office an ill and disappointed man. Carl Jung, Hermann Hesse, Ezra Pound, and T. S. Eliot had serious "breakdowns."

The top twelve of the Three Hundred represent the factions into which our society has been fragmented. Two speak for the democratic-capitalist system and the nuclear family. Four speak for the burgeoning sexual revolution and for the welfare of the sexually divergent. One speaks for the efficacy of nonviolence as a way of effecting social change and solving conflicts. One speaks for revolution through armed struggle. Five choose the inward journey, are deliberately apolitical, prefer the intuitive to the coldly rational, and look for answers in mystery and myth and in primitive cultures. Most of the rest of the Three Hundred sort themselves into these same categories.

The failure of T. S. Eliot and Ezra Pound to qualify for inclusion among the Four Hundred, and their being among the top twelve of the Three Hundred, is a result of the reluctance of publishers and authors to use some persons as subjects during their lifetimes and also of the successful efforts of some celebrities to avoid becoming the subject of biography while alive. T. S. Eliot—who is variously described by present-day biographers as either impotent or homosexual and who was an unhappy boy and a miserable adult—requested in his will that his literary executor try to prevent the publication of any biography about him. Since his death there have been many such volumes.

Another talented poet, Ezra Pound, because of his violent anti-Semitism and his close relationship with the Italian Fascists during World War II, was unpopular in the United States and had no biographies. Now that he is part of the historical past and can be written about dispassionately, there has been a proliferation of writing about him by literary critics and biographers. Although he is one of those who antedate the current sexual revolution, he was part of a ménage à trois and persuaded both women to let others rear the two children they bore him.

Although the ways in which eminence is achieved have changed, we find fewer differences when we look at the family backgrounds that produce these eminent personalities. In many respects the major findings from both surveys agree. The firstborn, wherever they are found and regardless of the number of biographies about them, are favored as biographical subjects. In addition, we still read that young collectors of specimens become scientists, that little boys and girls who make up stories in their heads write fiction or drama when they are grown, that mothers who feel superior to their neighbors rear children with problems in social adjustment. Sons of widows do well. So do daughters of famous fathers. Children of immigrants are advantaged in the scramble for fame.

Among the like findings common to the Three Hundred and the Four Hundred are the following: most of the eminent are not born in the great metropolitan centers but drift to the larger centers from the farms, villages, and smaller cities. In almost all homes there is a love of learning in one or both parents, often accompanied by a physical exuberance and persistent drive toward goals. Many of the homes are quite troubled by quarreling parents, divorce, financial ups and downs, and parental inability to cope with the children's delinquencies, school failures, and what seems to be a wrong career choice.

Creativity and contentment are not compatible in the homes of the Three Hundred and the Four Hundred. The progeny who grow up to be writers almost all come from homes where, as children, they see tense psychological dramas played out by their parents. Nearly half of the fathers are subject to traumatic vicissitudes in their business and professional careers. Wealth is more frequent than is abject poverty, but most eminent personalities come from the business and professional classes.

The future subjects of biography are very likely to show strong dislike of school, especially of their secondary school. They love learning but not school. They like being tutored. Many are quite precocious, especially those who are to achieve fame in the fine arts and writing. Almost half are early, omnivorous readers. An important adjunct to achievement is a close, satisfying, intellectual and emotional relationship with a loving and concerned adult in the preschool years.

Neither sex, race, place of birth, parental occupation, nor level of education, then, can prevent certain family practices from having a predictable impact on the children in the family. It is these commonalities we shall discuss as we invade the homes of the Three Hundred to find out how it felt to be reared there and to leave home and go to school.

2

The Love of Learning

*The Grey family, root and branch, was a
bookish one, with whom reading was an
addiction. An uncle of mine once carried a book
to his brother-in-law's funeral lest he become
bored and be stranded without anything to read.*

Elizabeth Grey Vining

A captive bird that never hears the songs of its ancestors never sings them. An infant monkey fed by a surrogate mother of wool and wire does not develop sexually or socially. A human infant, however well fed and clean, if casually cared for in an institution, is not likely to survive its infancy, and if it does it probably will not thrive or will be retarded.

The boy or girl reared in a home where there is not a strong love of learning is not likely to become the subject of a biography or to write an autobiography, although that occasionally can happen, as we shall see. Still, in 90 percent of the homes in which the eminent personalities were reared, there was a love of learning.

There is a universal concern for the disadvantaged child in whose home there is not this love of learning, who does not have the cultural advantages of most of the Three Hundred. Consequently, no federally funded educational experiment was better received than Head Start. At its peak moments it resembled a large, warm extended family, and thousands of children from homes with a low-income breadwinner were given a crash course in the love of learning and the joy of creativity.

Early evaluations of Head Start were encouraging. Vocabularies increased. IQs, once thought to be quite stable, rose appreciably. Later evaluations, however, were disappointing. When the Head Start graduate remained in the same culturally disadvantaged home, lived in the same low-income area, attended a public school in the same economically depressed school district, when the total environment was unchanged, the gains the child made in Head Start were not maintained.

A group of four Australian educators had a similar experience in rural Bourke, New South Wales, Australia. They selected forty-five markedly disadvantaged, five-year-old white and aboriginal children for a compensatory program designed to prepare them for first grade in the public school. These children scored lowest among a group of over 100 in vocabulary, auditory association, grammatical closure, and operational thinking. They were the children who needed help most.

Eight months later, when the children were in the first grade, the test results, like those of many Head Start programs in the United States, were gratifying. The children had made the hoped-for gains. A retest at the end of the school year showed considerable erosion. The children were still disadvantaged and had begun to forget.

The Australian project director, P. R. Delacey, was not apologetic. His program had done what it planned to do. What was necessary, he said, was to do something about the *lack of intense parental involvement* in the learning process. Delacey (1970) brings us back to a contemplation of the role of a love of learning in the parental home in actualizing the potential of the offspring.

In the homes that nurtured the Three Hundred, most parents were psychologically incapable of *not* taking an "intense interest" in the education of their children. The Head Start program loses its funding. The exciting, beloved teacher goes away and never comes back. Fathers lose their "funding" too, sometimes, but when they move to a new location to find another job, the family moves with them. For better or worse the family provides continuity. If a love of learning is endemic in the family, the child absorbs, retains, and passes it on to the next generation.

The Parent as the Bone

Parents are inescapable, even when they die. Mature adults, though world famous, describe internal dialogues with deceased parents, explaining themselves, defending themselves, boasting about themselves, justifying themselves, measuring themselves against the well-remembered parental expectations.

Peter Ustinov—playwright, actor, producer—was the only son of two gifted and emotionally and intellectually complicated human beings. His father was a noted journalist; his mother an artist. Although his father frequently annoyed him, Peter says, "The most painful function of a parent is to be the bone on which the young may sharpen its teeth. I am forever grateful to my father for supplying such a resolute bone" (Ustinov, 1973, p. 13).

The Carter family of Archery, Georgia, was a reading family and a hardworking family. When Lillian Gordy Carter was not working or doing household chores, she read. She read at breakfast, at dinner, and at supper. Jimmy, who was the only child in the family for thirteen years, read as omnivorously as she. When his sisters Gloria and Ruth were born, they too were readers. To read was relaxation for Lillian, who, as a registered nurse during the Depression, sometimes worked up to twenty hours a day.

Jimmy's father, James Carter, whose eyesight was poor, was not a great reader, but he was a driving, striving, physically energetic man who could outwork any ordinary farmer. Since the family lived in the country, Jimmy's closest companion when he was growing up was his father, and they worked for long hours on the farm together. James Carter was a kindly man; he laughed easily and was well liked in the neighborhood. He was the leading citizen in his community—president of the school board, organizer of a fund-raising drive for a new hospital, Sunday school teacher, and was one of the first directors of the local Rural Electrification Administration that brought electricity to the Carter home when Jimmy was sixteen. (Until then, they had had no electric lights or plumbing.)

When Jimmy Carter was a presidential candidate, his small daughter, Amy, continuing in the family tradition, made a tidy sum selling lemonade. Like her grandmother Lillian, she is also an omnivorous reader. The press has been critical because Amy, while attending public functions with her parents, sometimes reads at the table. This criticism, it would seem, is a reflection of a generation accustomed to seeing children excluded from adult affairs. If Amy's busy parents want her to be near them and she enjoys the pleasure of sitting by them in adult company, she should be commended and so should they. Amy is the stuff of which highly achieving children are made. A great many of today's children, who have so little experience being close to adults, would run noisily about or try to attract attention or whine or complain. Reading quietly at a state dinner, we postulate, is quite permissible behavior for an eight-year-old.

Children absorb much that is positive from being in the company of accepting adults, even if they seem to be preoccupied with a storybook. There are 150 among the Three Hundred who, like Amy Carter, were early omnivorous readers. In addition, 35 percent were also precocious in writing, acting, painting, and composing. They also spent many more hours in the company of adults than do most children today, for whom the television set is too often the surrogate parent.

Isaac Bashevis Singer and His Father. The love of learning has no national boundaries, race, creed, or color. Writer Isaac Bashevis Singer says that neither poverty, war, nor the disdain of other relatives diminished his family's love of learning. At a time when about the only way a Jewish woman could be associated with scholarship was to marry a scholar, Singer's father, Rabbi Pinchas Singer, exceeded the accepted norms, not only in scholarship but in piety. He was so pious, so otherworldly, so unemployable, in fact, that his parents had difficulty finding a wife for him. Bathsheba Zylberman preferred him above all others the matchmaker recommended since she always had wanted to marry a scholar. How could her well-to-do parents be so irreligious as to deny her the honor of marrying a poor Hassidic rabbi? They reluctantly consented.

The marriage fulfilled Pinchas' in-laws' gloomy expectations. They had almost no furniture. Their fare was plain. Only the poorest congregations kept him very long. Pinchas was hopelessly charitable; Bathsheba was loyal. The rabbi had little satisfaction in the careers of his sons, Isaac and Israel, because they were secular writers, not the religious writers he would have liked them to be. Still, this family, which lived at a subsistence level, reared two sons who became internationally known.

The Jewish father often plays a very dominating role when a son's, especially an oldest son's, education is at stake. No sacrifice is too great if it will ensure the young male's future as a scholar or, if not a scholar, a cultured man of affairs. This interest in education, unfortunately, did not extend to the daughter. It was good for her to be "accomplished" in certain arts and be a good cook, and she needed to count and read. When Jewish girls were fortunate enough to marry a scholar, a rabbi possibly, they had to know enough to keep a tight budget. To keep shop, to help support a pious scholar, was considered an honor, as was rearing a scholarly son.

Abba Eban and His Grandfather. The discrepancy between a Jewish boy's training and a girl's is seen in the family that reared Israeli diplomat Abba Eban. There was never a Jewish grandfather as obsessed by a love of learning as Eliahu Sacks. His desire to pass on his knowledge to his grandson Abba was not extended to his granddaughter Ruth, who retaliated by making life miserable for her brother and for his indefatigable tutor. Eliahu saw his daughter Alida's gift for languages only as a social asset, as a novelty to enhance her femininity. He did not take her seriously as a scholar.

A Jewish merchant with little formal education can be as devoted to Hebrew and Talmudic law as any rabbi. Eliahu Sacks came to London an emigrant from Russia and could have been a very wealthy man from his wholesale egg business had he not also been a compulsive scholar, haunting bookstores, buying books, reading books. The father of four, Eliahu hired a poor Hebrew scholar, Benzion Halper, for a pittance to live in the house and teach the children Hebrew and respect for their Jewish heritage. Happy with having a responsible man in the house, Eliahu once went off to Cape Town on a business trip and his emotional, excitable, lovely oldest daughter, Lina, only two years younger than Benzion, began a romance with him. Benzion and Lina married and went to Philadelphia, where the bridegroom was hired to be a teacher of Hebrew in the newly organized Dropsie College for Hebrew and cognate learning.

A merchant of means can afford one scholarly son-in-law, but, not wanting to risk a second, Eliahu chose the husband of his youngest daughter, Alida, himself. This was a bright, able employee, Abraham Solomon, thirty-four, who married Alida when she was twenty-two. Abraham accepted the engagement arranged by his employer, and Alida fell in love with him after they exchanged letters and consented to marry him. Words had always delighted Alida, and she had begun learning languages as a little girl. To her father, her facility with language was amusing, a parlor trick, and she performed for his friends to please him. As a young woman, she no longer entertained others with her erudition, but she never stopped being a student of languages.

Abraham Solomon became the branch manager of his father-in-law's firm in Cape Town. However, he became ill with a disease that puzzled Cape Town doctors and so he was brought home to London, where he was found to have terminal cancer. One morning he asked to have the morning paper brought to him at once. He was going to die that day, he said. Did he have time to read the paper? He did, and he did die that day, January 26, 1916. His son, Abba Audrey, who was to become a world-famous diplomat in a country that did not yet exist, was one year old the following week. His daughter, Ruth, was fourteen months older than Abba.

Alida Sacks Solomon and the children moved into the Sacks family's London townhouse. However, Alida found being a young widow in her parents' home a dreary, confining experience, for her father and mother were eager to take over supervision of the children. Still, she had one exciting day in 1917 when Abba was still an infant. A call came from a family friend in Lord Balfour's office. Could she come quickly? The Balfour Declaration (which created a Jewish national state in Palestine) had been signed, and someone was needed to translate the fifty-six words into French, German, and

Russian. She performed the task with accuracy and dispatch and was rewarded by being taken that evening to the mass demonstration celebrating the event, where she saw the Zionist celebrities on the platform.

Grandfather Eliahu could scarcely wait until Abba was old enough to learn Hebrew and identify the Hebrew characters he had cut so painstakingly from sheets of brown wrapping paper. But when Abba was three, and already starting to read both Hebrew and English, his sister Ruthie became a problem, racing through the house, shouting and interrupting, so exasperating her grandfather that he told his wife to take her to the family house in Ireland for a long visit so that Abba and his grandfather could have peace and quiet.

This probably happened during the year Alida had returned to South Africa. Ordinarily her parents were quite competent in their care of the children, but Grandmother Sacks became quite ill and needed her husband's full attention. Grandfather could not endure seeing the four-year-old Abba waste days that could be more advantageously spent, and since he was doing well in his studies Abba was sent to study in a boarding school for small boys. When his mother came home and went to see Abba at the school, she found him sitting atop a warm radiator in a cold room reading aloud to a group of boys below him, just as he often read to Ruthie at home. Alida was told that Abba had been quite lost at school, had wandered about, silent, unsmiling, uncomplaining, unquestioning.

It was six-year-old Ruthie who was indirectly responsible for the family's move to a house in Kensington and for her mother's changed status. Ruthie went (or was sent) to Edinburgh to visit her uncle, Samuel Sacks, a physician, and there she became devoted, little-girl fashion, to her uncle's friend and colleague, Dr. Isaac Eban. Her mother paid no attention to Ruthie's girlish babblings until she too met Isaac, and eventually the two married and moved to Kensington, where he set up a new practice. Isaac Eban was fond of the children, and it was agreed that they should take his name. Alida bore two more children. Abba liked his half-sister Carmel because she loved words and so did he, and he had no animosity for his little half-brother; however, he and Ruthie were never close.

It was his grandfather Eliahu to whom Abba was closest.

When Abba was eight, Eliahu arranged for him to go to an excellent English preparatory school, where he studied the traditional subjects suitable for a boy who was college bound. In addition, every Friday after school Abba took a bus across London to his grandfather's house and spent two full days closeted with him in his study, learning Hebrew, Jewish history, and Talmudic lore. They did not waste time on Jewish religious ritual or regular attendance at the synagogue for Eliahu's interests were scholastic, not ritualistic. In the long sessions, Abba absorbed his grandfather's love of books—the touch of them, the smell of them, the magic of them.

In her unending campaign to break up the entente between her grandfather and his favorite grandchild, Ruthie acquired a fellow conspirator. Benzion Halper had died in America, and his wife Lina Sacks Halper had come home with two small sons to live in the family's London townhouse. Her younger son, Neville, joined Ruthie in pestering Eliahu and Abba when they closeted themselves in the study every weekend by playing ball under the study window or banging the ball on the wall, or by pounding on the study door and begging plaintively for Abba's release. There was never any response, and Abba's relationship with his grandfather lasted until Eliahu died, shortly before Abba was to attend Cambridge.

At Cambridge Abba won scholarships and was respected by his peers. However, having been a little old man since the age of eight, he never became any younger. Once he was heard to remark that he sometimes wished he had sown a wild oat or two while at the university, but he did not.

In an excellent biography published in 1972, Robert St. John reported interviews with Eban's colleagues and his staff in Israel. They stated they respected his intelligence, his learning, his sagacity, his understanding of international affairs, his knowledge of Arabic, and his genuine feelings for peace and for international harmony. But, they said, he was not an easy man to know as a person. To a remarkable degree, the colleagues sounded like Ruthie and Neville, who also would have liked to have been closer to him. He could not respond to their approaches. He had no small talk. He never spoke about his charming wife or his son and daughter. At times his employees found him pompous, selfish, self-centered, too fond of listening to himself on tape. He could not take criticism.

A colleague suggested that perhaps his mother had never scolded him, never punished him, never let him know that he, Abba Eban, was capable of making a mistake. It is doubtful indeed that Alida Sacks Solomon ever thought of correcting her son in any way. She was a warm, outgoing, intelligent woman, who loved her son and respected him, but he was never hers to rear. They had an adult relationship, almost like that of brother and sister.

His colleagues said Abba was happiest working alone, writing a book, preparing a position paper, studying his lecture notes . . . or alone with the ghost of his grandfather, who he said was the person most responsible for shaping his career.

Love of Learning in a Southern Black Family: Julian Bond

One southern black family that was intensely learning-centered for four generations, and that also encouraged female as well as male achievement, was the one from which Julian Bond, Georgia state legislator, is descended. Born in Nashville, Tennessee, in 1940, Bond, one of the youngest of the Three Hundred, came from a family that collected degrees as other families might collect blue ribbons at a county fair. The Bond family also showed other qualities not always evident in the Three Hundred in that the girls shared educational opportunities with their brothers. The wives also collected degrees as eagerly as did the men. When a Bond man married, it was to a woman who was extraordinarily intelligent and, in most instances, successful in becoming a scholar as well as a wife and mother.

Despite the strong family traditions in these directions, Julian Bond chose not to take the academic route to success. He dropped out of school a short time before completing his junior year at More-house College in Atlanta. This made him out of step with his parents, but not out of step with his generation, for he invested his genuine love of learning and strong physical, intellectual, and ethical drives to making a significant contribution to social change. He thus became a civil rights leader and later, at twenty-five, was the first black man to be elected a member of the Georgia State Legislature. Being black gave him almost no chance for election; being young gave him an almost insurmountable handicap. Yet he broke both barriers.

There is no other family among the Three Hundred families surveyed about whom four generations are so painstakingly described. Since the family of Julian Bond illustrates many of the findings obtained for the entire Three Hundred, let us try to trace their love of learning through the four consecutive generations.

Julian's Parents. Horace Mann Bond, born 1904—an educator, researcher, and himself the subject of a biography—once said at an invitational lecture at Harvard, "If we could give to every child in the land the same opportunities for intellectual stimulation now enjoyed by the children of the professional, technical and kindred workers, we would increase our talent pool five-fold" (Williams, p. 175).

As the fifth son of a Congregational minister and a mother who was a college professor, Horace had all the advantages he wanted all children, regardless of race, to have. He was an exceptionally precocious child. He read at three, was reading books on human anatomy at four, and was avidly reading the writings of a family friend, W. E. B. Du Bois, at six.

At fourteen he was sent to Lincoln Institute in Pennsylvania, the first institution in the world to offer black male students higher learning. Most of his classmates were nineteen or twenty years old and laughed at the grinning boy in knee pants, but when they taught him poker and blackjack, they stopped laughing because the first lesson was hardly done before he had emptied their pockets. The rumor was circulated that this was no boy, no prodigy, but a cardsharp disguised as an adolescent. Horace lived down that rumor but created other legends. He learned to hold his own at drinking moonshine whiskey, forgetting his mother's leadership in the Women's Christian Temperance Union. Water wars between dormitories were the rage, and he was an imaginative general. Still, zestful participation in extracurricular activities did not prohibit him from graduating with honors. He was accepted as a graduate student at the University of Chicago, where he earned a Ph.D. degree in education. Twenty-seven years after entering Lincoln Institute, he became its first black president. When he and his wife drove to the school for the first time, sure enough, a water war was in progress, with a student being held upside down from an upper-story window while another played a hose on him.

As president, Horace hired a Jewish professor and proposed permitting the registration of white, Jewish, Catholic, and even atheist students. However, his board of trustees, made up of Protestant and Christian fundamentalists, was recalcitrant. When Horace and other black faculty members used their children as plaintiffs in a suit to break segregation in the Chester County school system, the trustees were much annoyed, and eventually he was fired. (The suit was won, and Julian, who had been in Lincoln's segregated laboratory school, spent three unhappy years in the Chester County school system.) Horace then became dean of the school of education at Atlanta University and held that post for ten years.

Horace's wife, Julia Washington Bond, whom he had met when he was a new professor at Fisk University in Nashville, Tennessee and she was the most popular student on campus, was loyal, resourceful, and a tactful companion to her sometimes abrasive, dynamic, unpredictable husband. She had two master's degrees and worked as an educator and librarian.

Julian's Grandparents. Julian's grandfather, James Bond, was born a slave in 1863. When he was fifteen he walked from his home in Jarvis' Store, Kentucky, carrying his possessions in a pillowcase to Berea College fifty-five miles away, farther than he had ever been. He also brought with him a young steer, which he sold to pay his fees and other expenses.

Berea College was founded in 1855 by fundamentalist northern missionaries for the poor and culturally isolated, both black and white. All who came were admitted. The entrance fee was only two dollars, and room and board was eighteen dollars for each term. Those with little school learning were kept in a preparatory school until they could qualify for the collegiate program. In James' intermediate class there were twenty-two students from eighteen different states. Terms were short (three months) because many students often had to drop out for a term to work on nearby farms to earn money. On campus James split wood and rang class bells. When he was graduated he was one of the five students chosen to give a valedictory address. Later he took a degree in divinity at Oberlin College and became a Congregational minister.

James met his wife, Jane Browne, when she was a student at Oberlin and he was doing his graduate work. She was a tall, energetic woman who was president of the literary society and secretary to a professor. As husband and wife, James and Jane advanced each other's careers—hers as a college professor, his as a minister—and worked together on interracial projects.

As a minister, James was an important spokesman for his people. He opposed the Jim Crow law segregating Nashville's streetcars. He protested a law forbidding Berea from continuing as an interracial educational experiment and another law that tried to rule out high schools for black students.

For Jane and James, books came before new clothes and new furniture, and they were constantly buying books they could not afford for themselves and their six children. They also took the children to museums, concerts, and plays. All the children went to college, and four graduated. Two went on to earn Ph.Ds—Horace Mann Bond and his brother Max, a sociologist. (Two of Max's sons were later to earn doctorates in the sciences.)

When James died at sixty-five of a heart attack, Jane was left empty of purpose. She therefore joined her daughter Lucy, her youngest child, who was entering Oberlin as a freshman student, and enrolled in the Oberlin graduate school and earned a master's degree in history. A granddaughter remembers Jane as a matriarchal figure—rather rigid, competent, and quiet—who was "always taking care of everybody and everything."

Julia Washington Bond's father, W. E. Washington (Julian Bond's maternal grandfather), was principal of a Nashville high school and had either four or five degrees. His mother-in-law—much of whose physical attractiveness, poise, self-assurance, and friendliness Julia inherited—was the most prestigious matron in black Nashville; she was the widow of the well-to-do florist Joe Brown. Although she had no degrees, when she died at ninety she left Fisk University $150,000.

Great-Uncle Henry Bond, 1865–1929. Another branch on the family tree had its own impressive collection of diplomas. These were earned by the descendants of James' brother Henry. James was two years older than Henry and very much the typical oldest son; aggressive, self-confident, well oriented toward goals. Henry was like other youngest sons: unsure of himself, close to mother, unpredictable, cautious, less oriented toward goals.

James walked the winding mountain road to Berea alone. Henry, when he followed his brother to Berea two years later, brought with him two close friends from Jarvis' Store. James stayed four years and went on to Oberlin. Henry stayed two years and went home to mother.

Henry Bond was not at all confident about what he should do. He read law, but the clients were too few and his financial rewards too small. He went to Harlan County, Kentucky, to be a YMCA secretary but did not stay. When he married a staunch and supportive wife, Ann Lee Gibson, who was from his home community, Henry became the principal of the only black school in his county, a one-room country school. His wife was his only assistant.

Neither Henry nor Ann had a college diploma and his salary was small, but they scrimped and saved and did without for years to send three daughters and six sons to Knoxville College. Each son and daughter earned a diploma; five had master's degrees, and two became physicians.

Henry and Ann also made a home for Henry's mother, the ebullient woman who had started the family on its determined quest for college degrees. They also shared their home with Aunt Mary, the sister of Henry's mother. Later Ann left the older children in charge of the family home and went to keep house for her sons and daughters in college, who were living under one roof to save money.

Great-Grandmother Jane Bond, 1828–1920. The Bond family has always resented any implication that it was the white blood in the family that accounts for its high achievements. Preston Bond, the white father of James and Henry Bond, was a poorly educated farmer and preacher of no particular distinction—nor were his ancestors or his white descendants. Like many other preachers of his time, he had "answered the call," and his messages were emotional rather than intellectual.

Jane Bond, who was black, came into Preston's household when he married the daughter of Edward Arthur, a Kentucky gentleman of wealth and learning. Jane was a wedding gift from Arthur to his daughter, Preston's wife, and became Preston's property. Jane had no children during her first fifteen years as a slave in the Bond home. She was freed by the Emancipation Proclamation at age forty-one; her son James was then three and Henry one. What prompted the late-in-life liaison between Preston Bond and Jane is not known, but she left his household when she was free to do so. Like most slaves, she took the name of her owner and called herself Jane Bond. Although Edward Arthur, her former master, was dead, his son Ambrose still lived in the old home, and so did Jane's sister Mary and her husband. Ambrose Arthur welcomed Jane's return, since she was a practical nurse and a good housekeeper, and gave her a part-time salary, which she augmented by working in the community wherever she was needed. Her learned, liberal first master was the role model for her sons.

Jane soon was economically independent and could send her sons to a small private school in a mountain cabin that was run by another ex-slave. It was a "blab" school, since they had so few books, and students chanted in unison what the teacher said to them. Even so, by the time James was ten he was spelling long words such as "incomprehensibility."

Thinking that Emancipation had given her boys all the advantages other American citizens had, Jane believed there was nothing her sons could not do if they tried. Thus, when James started on his walk to Berea, she reminded him that there was no reason why he might not become President of the United States some day. Although she was illiterate at forty-one, she studied while the boys studied. In her old age, her sons were often impatient with her for reading what they called "mother's romances." Nothing wonderful that her sons or grandchildren did surprised her. It was, she thought, all because of their being free.

Julian Bond, 1940– . Jane Bond had a dream of a son in the White House. Julian Bond, her great-grandson, was another kind of dreamer and something new on the family tree—namely, a politician with a dream of a color-blind, egalitarian, nonviolent world for his children. Between Jane and Julian are two striving, driving generations who hoped that educational excellence would bring them security and recognition. Julian was a part of the new life-style of his generation—an apathetic schoolboy in a northern preparatory school in the 1950s and a college-student activist in the 1960s.

Quakers have a wry saying about themselves: "Quakers are people who stand up to be counted, then sit down for fear they will rock the boat." In 1952, a Quaker preparatory school in Philadelphia, with the best of intentions, recruited twelve-year-old Julian as a token black. But the administration and the white students were too self-conscious, too tender, too aware of his being different and so they inadvertently humiliated him. For instance, although only older honor students were permitted to live in a faculty home, Julian, even though he was young and a mediocre student, was also sent to live in a faculty home. In another case, he began dating white girls as an upperclassman. Although nothing was said as long as the dates were casual, when he and a white girl became serious about each other, he was told not to wear an identifying school sweater when he walked with her off-campus.

In the all-black, all-male Morehouse College in Atlanta he disliked being a student even more. Not only did he hate the implied segregation, but the school's academic level made him wonder if higher education ever would save the human race after all—a startling revelation, since his father was Morehouse's dean of education and research and his mother one of its librarians. Julian even found the distinguished Martin Luther King, Jr. poorly prepared and tedious. The student-faculty relationships, Julian said, were those of a drill sergeant and his charges (Williams, p. 195).

Thus, Julian was ready for the nationwide revulsion that stirred the college students of his generation—against war, against segregation, and against irrelevant teaching. The Quaker institution had schooled him in nonviolence. His family had fought segregation for years. As a college junior, he already had been published as a poet in four college anthologies. Ready for activity in the public sphere in the cause of integration, he did not graduate from college.

Much later, Julian was given an honorary degree by Lincoln College—to his father's wry amusement, since it had fired him as its first black president. Quite obviously, the Bond family has done more than its share in replenishing the nation's talent pool.

Two Eminent Women: Elizabeth Grey Vining and Nadezhda Krupskaya

Author Elizabeth Grey Vining was born into a book-loving, well-to-do family in Germantown, Pennsylvania, in 1902. She wrote her first poem at five and was a good student and had good peer relationships. In her home were two intelligent, loving, female adults to whom she could relate, her mother and her sister Violet, the latter nineteen years older than she.

A girl from a white Anglo-Saxon family, Elizabeth had to convince her father to send her to college by promising she would not lose status by using her education to go to work as a paid employee. Her father had refused to let Violet train to be a teacher because he felt that having an employed daughter would ruin his good standing in the business community. However, he finally did permit her to be a librarian for the Society of Friends. He was also not much concerned about his brilliant wife's intellectual life. Consequently, each of the three females in the house wrote in her own room. The mother wrote a novel that was never published and she eventually burned it. Violet wrote four children's books, which were published, and two rather pale novels. She remained a spinster and a second mother to Elizabeth all her life. It was Violet who insisted on her sister's having college training at Bryn Mawr, from which she was graduated at twenty.

Quite the opposite, Nadezhda Krupskaya was a Russian girl whose parents did approve of girls who worked. The woman who was to become the wife of V. I. Lenin and a central figure in the Russian Revolution, Nadezhda (meaning Hope) was born in Warsaw, Poland, on February 26, 1869, and grew up in a home remarkable for its love for learning, for girls as well as boys. Her mother, Elizaveta, was an emancipated, well-educated woman, and, except for one school year in Kiev, was her daughter's teacher until she went to secondary school. Her father, Konstantin Krupsky, was a Russian infantry officer who was sent to Poland to administer the politically important Warsaw district, where the Poles were pacified although not reconciled to their status as an occupied country.

Both father and mother were impoverished, landless members of the hereditary Russian nobility, but both were well-read, seeking, searching, learning-centered individuals. Elizaveta was the ninth and youngest child in her family and was educated as a governess in a government-sponsored educational institution for young gentlewomen in economic distress. Konstantin's parents died when he was nine, but he was well educated by relatives. They were self-reliant young people who had to be responsible for themselves.

For the ten years prior to her marriage, Elizaveta had taught other people's children and was weary of being snubbed and overworked by their wealthy parents. She eagerly assumed the task of educating her only child. Both mother and daughter learned Polish, and Elizaveta wrote a children's book in Polish to encourage Polish mothers to read to their children just as she read to hers. There was help in the house, the family had status, and they lived comfortably and happily. Both parents delighted in their small daughter and in each other.

However, when Nadezhda was five, Konstantin was discharged from his position under circumstances that made it impossible for him to ever have a similar position again. As a result of losing this privileged, reasonably well-paid position, his daughter's biographer says, he "became a traveling disturbed failure" (Mc-Neal, 1972, p. 9). More than twenty charges were brought against him by his superiors that he had not conducted the duties of his office properly. He had fraternized too much with the Polish people. His four-year-old daughter spoke Polish. He had danced a mazurka at a Polish social function. However, the charge for which he was formally discharged was that he had ordered employers to register their workers, part of his plan to find out who were unemployed and what could be done about unemployment. In her old age his daughter said that he became part of the early revolutionary underground and he knew, for example, that the czar was to be assassinated.

After Konstantin's dismissal, Elizaveta began working as a governess and thenceforth became the principal wage earner in the family. Konstantin once found a job as an inspector in a factory, but his report of the low wages and poor working conditions angered his employer and he was again discharged. The family wandered from town to town, almost fugitives.

During this difficult period, Elizaveta continued to be her daughter's teacher. Nadezhda read omnivorously—Pushkin, Lermontov, Tolstoy, translations of *Little Women* and *Ten Thousand Leagues Under the Sea*. She had few playmates. She made friends with a woodcutter, who let her drive his horse. She became acquainted with peasant women who sorted rags for making paper in the factory employing her father. Her parents encouraged her to play with working-class children, but she was often lonely because the family moved so often. Much later, when she had tremendous authority over educational practices in the Soviet Union, she encouraged activities for children that provided them with many playmates. She also encouraged the establishment of communes because she did not want other children to be as lonely and wandering as she had been.

When Nadezhda was old enough for secondary school, she found the two schools in which she was enrolled intolerable, and she was looked down upon because her parents were poor. Eventually she went to the Obolensky Gymnasium for female students in Petersburg and spent the years 1881 to 1891 there as a student and part-time teaching assistant. The love for learning in her home and her mother's able tutoring during the hours she had to spare had prepared her well, and she held an A − average in her studies of Russian, German, French, geography, history, science, and arithmetic.

As a young girl she had absorbed more of her father's humanism than his radicalism. For a time after her graduation, she was so impressed by Tolstoy's ideas about education that she tried out his methods with her students at the Obolensky Gymnasium and wrote to him describing her experiences. Later, in her twenties, she turned to radicalism when she and some of her ex-classmates became seriously involved in the underground movement. When she had tremendous power as Lenin's wife, she occupied herself with the education of the children and adults in the revolutionary regime and also with the rights of women to education, employment, and child care for working mothers.

Henry Luce

Missionary parents are often very close to their children. Publisher Henry R. Luce was born in Tengchow, China, where his father and mother were Presbyterian missionaries. His father, although a Yale graduate, came from a socially well-connected family, felt poor and was often ill. The household was Spartan but was enlivened by a fondness for stories and games. Ambitious for their four children, the parents spent considerable time with them, taught them word games, and read to them. The father was a sunny, energetic, independent evangelist with a gift for words. He spanked his sons when he thought they needed such punishment, but Henry's mother, a good-natured woman, often showed her sympathies for them by bursting out laughing when they played boyish pranks. At four Henry was dictating sermons that were quite clever and original, collected postcards, and studied French. He was also motivated quite early to do something tangible about the family's constant precarious financial standing and resented its reputation for being the poor branch of the Luce family.

Sent to Hotchkiss in Connecticut at age 15, he was called "Chink," started to stammer, and became surly and aloof. Though not popular, since he had been academically well prepared for secondary school, he made all A's. At Yale, where he also was an A student, he learned social techniques that made him respected, but he still remained aloof and was still not popular. Even so he became editor of the college paper and conquered his stammer by participating in the debating society.

The Precociousness of the Eminent

When one thinks of love of learning in the home, one may visualize a proper child who brings home a report card with A's and B's yet is also a part of his or her own peer culture. However, this does not describe the Three Hundred as children, who as adolescents were often performing at a level most adults never reach. Eminent personalities who as children could entertain others, who could sing, dance, or act, were well accepted. Children who read adult books, on the other hand, and who talked like adults but often did not act with the emotional maturity of adults, were sometimes upsetting to others. The following are some unusual achievements some of the Three Hundred showed in childhood and early adolescence. They may help us to understand the negative reaction of parents, teachers, and peers, who, of course, do not know that they are living in close proximity to a future celebrity.

When Peter Ustinov, actor, was nine months old, he astounded his fellow passengers on London trains by calling out "Oxo" when an advertisement for that beverage flashed into view.

John Foster Dulles, diplomat, at age one could pick out the letter o on his building blocks.

Rachel Carson, scientist-author, read storybooks at age two.

C. S. Forester, novelist, had been reading quite well for some time when he was sent to school at age three and one-half.

When Shirley Chisholm, U.S. Congresswoman, was three, she would shout, "Look at me!" to other children, who obeyed her because she was always saying something exciting. She read at four and began to keep a record of her thoughts at five. She spent much of her school time teaching other children.

Helen Hayes, actress, played her first professional role on the New York stage at age eight.

At ten, Laurence Olivier, actor, played Brutus in a school play after the manner of a professional actor. Ellen Terry heard him and said so.

Dag Hammarskjöld, UN Secretary-General, was never equaled by any other student in his classroom. At eight he wrote in a classmate's notebook a description of an idyll as a "lamb with a blue silk ribbon and a bell."

Arthur Rubinstein, pianist and composer, when he was three, listened to his sisters being taught the piano and screamed when they made an error. When the teacher left, he mounted the piano bench and played the melodies he had just heard. At eight he was giving charity concerts.

Paul Muni, actor, although he never went to school at all and learned what he knew from traveling with his actor parents, at age five, when he came to the United States, could read the travel brochure about the Statue of Liberty. At eleven, he was playing old-man parts professionally in the Yiddish theater. (Even New Yorkers were nonplussed to see an old man taking his constitutional on roller skates outside the theater.)

Eric Hoffer, longshoreman-author, also never went to school, not even for a day, but was taught by his German carpenter-scholar father to read both German and English before he was five. At seven he was blinded by a fall and did not regain his sight until age fifteen. During this period his father read to him for hours on end. When Hoffer regained his sight, he began to read omnivorously, fearing the blindness might come again.

George Kaufman, playwright, wrote (with a friend) a serious drama at fourteen, a tragic story of a father who disowned his son.

Doris Lessing, novelist, wrote some novels (not very good and unpublished) while in her teens.

At thirteen Vladimir Mayakovsky, Russian poet, could converse freely with college students on learned matters. His widowed mother and older sisters deferred to him as an adult.

Conclusion

Horace Mann Bond, after a long study of his family tree, decided it was environment rather than heredity that made so many of Jane Bond's descendants contributors to the talent pool. He saw nothing different in the Bonds other than the kind of learning-centered homes that his ancestors had maintained. It was this family pattern he wished other disadvantaged families to adopt. It had worked for his ordinary family, he said, so why not for others?

Psychologists have since corroborated his observations. Head Start pupils, it was found, made remarkable gains when they were given the kind of enrichment the Bond children had all their lives. In fact, Wallace A. Kennedy reports that black children seem slightly superior in intelligence to white children during their first two years. According to Bayley, ghetto children, who are responsive infants, experience a 20 percent deficit in their mean IQ by the time they are five unless they are given cultural enrichment in the community. For children who receive enrichment, the drop is only 10 percent. Children from middle-class and well-to-do families do less well today on achievement tests than such privileged children once did. We feel that television, broken homes, and other changes in life patterns have resulted in fewer child-centered homes. There are indications that Horace Mann Bond was seeing clearly about what kind of child rearing fills the talent pool.

Geneticists have their evidence as to the importance of heredity to offer, the most telling of which is the information that one-egg twins are more alike than two-egg twins. Also, siblings have been found to be more like each other than to stepsiblings reared in the same household. Identical twins reared apart resemble each other more than do brothers and sisters reared together.

Horace Mann Bond, as some of his family reminded him, may not have given enough credit to the women his father and his grandfather married or to the effect of heredity. Both Jane and Julia Bond were unusually intelligent, capable, well-educated women. An interesting study by Moss and Kagan on middle-class children studied in Yellow Springs, Ohio, and in Berkeley, California, found that the *mother's* educational level is superior to the father's in predicting the IQ of the child. Presumably this is because the mother is closer to the child in its formative years. Many geneticists, however, believe that intelligence is inherited to the same extent as are bodily characteristics.

We can deliberately breed dull rats or bright rats in the laboratory, but we cannot, of course, restrict human beings in their matings. However, the evidence is clear that children need physical and intellectual stimulation, lovingly and judiciously given in an appropriate fashion, in their preschool years. What is not known is how to extend the advantages of the learning-centered home to children everywhere. Until we learn to do so adequately, it will continue to be learning-centered middle-class and well-to-do families that will rear men and women who will enhance, advance, or sometimes painfully disturb the conditions of the world.

3

Failure-Prone Fathers

*When [Pop] talked about a new scheme he went
on for hours, painting a glorious picture and
giving all the objections and then batting them
down, as if six or seven people were discussing
the matter instead of one. [My brother] and I
never got over being entranced when Pop sold
himself on something new. But as time went on
my mother's eyes became less and less starry.*

Bill Mauldin

Among the Three Hundred, four out of ten had fathers who were
poor or erratic providers. Among the Four Hundred, six out of ten
had such fathers. The higher percentage of failure-prone fathers
in the second group compared with the first is due to the inclusion
of twice as many women—and women are not as likely as men to
have failure-prone fathers.

These failure-prone fathers were not lazy or stupid—indeed,

35

they often worked harder at being failures than do many other
moderately successful fathers. They are the Micawbers for whom
fame and money is just around the corner. They are the ebullient
father in Arthur Miller's *Death of a Salesman*. They are the idealists
who sacrifice security for conscience, the compulsive scholars who
get lost in the library stacks and never get the degree that would
have brought advancement, they read the Torah while the wife
sells meat patties to support the family. They are the charming
alcoholics, the physically and mentally ill with brilliant minds, the
sociopaths who try to substitute manipulation for honest work, the
displaced artisans who want to go on making carriages after the arrival of the automobile.

To be a person with the one chance in a million of having a
book written about himself or herself, it should not be necessary that
one's father be the kind of man who would desert his family, lose
money in foolish speculations, never hold a job very long, be a fugi-
tive, or be physically or mentally ill, yet having a failure-prone
father seems to motivate a son or daughter to be creative. Creativity
has been defined as the willingness to let go of certainties. Calculated
risks have to be taken. A high tolerance for frustration must be
maintained. In a conventional, comfortable family where the father
provides well for his children, the years of immaturity and dependence are extended. Why leave the nest when the branch is not
bending?

As mentioned, it is famous sons more often than famous
daughters who emerge from the chaos caused by their fathers'
ups and downs. Eminent women are more likely to come from well-
to-do homes. Twenty-eight percent of the women in our sample had
fathers with very successful careers, compared to 16 percent of the
men. There is no woman in our sample who also had a mother with
a successful career of her own; the concept of mother failure is not
valid in a financial sense.

Imaginative, striving, driving, but failure-prone fathers seem
to imbue in their offspring the eagerness to be innovative, a known
essential of the creative process. Creativity does not thrive in an am-
bience of smugness and contentment. After all, if John Shakespeare
had not had a catastrophic fall from favor and respectability, his
son William might not have left the thriving town where his father

had once been mayor and gone to London to make a name for himself. Thus, it is the intensity of the father's drives toward failure that seems significant.

There are two ways to react to a father who subjects his family to financial insecurity, and particularly to the dramatic ups and downs that give the child experience in being both poor and affluent. One is to opt for a civil service or other secure position; the other is to be a compulsive taker of risks like the father. Subjects of biography more often take the latter course.

The child who becomes accustomed early to traumatic ups and downs in the family fortunes matures early and learns to be helpful and/or independent. These families often produce the writers, artists, and performers who know when they enter these fields of endeavor that only a very few of their number ever will become well known or financially independent.

The other eminent in our Three Hundred who do not have failure-prone fathers are likely to be those who depend on higher education for possible eminence and who often achieve fame incidentally while pursuing their careers. They are the scientists, other professional people, editors, businessmen, explorers, and, as noted, the women, most of whom come from well-to-do families.

As we examine in detail some homes where there were acute financial ups and downs, of which there are 106 in the sample, observe the creative, but unfulfilled, nature of the father. The important difference between these families and ordinary poor families is the drive, the love of learning, and the intensity with which the father tries and fails to be "different."

Fathers Who Failed in Business

The father of Oskar Kokoschka, the Austrian pacifist-painter, was cheated by a business partner, and so lost his own business. Thereafter, he refused to have a friendly relationship with his well-to-do brothers since it disturbed him so much to be poor. One Christmas season, when he had no money to buy his children gifts, he sold his gold-headed cane to get cash, and from then on he hated Christmas.

After his father died, Oskar was very tender with his mother (who still continued to speak of her husband as if he were alive) and also felt responsible for his younger sister and brother. To Oskar, wealth was not all-important, and he reacted against his father's anxieties about money, rather devoting his life to expressing his revulsion at what he had seen on the World War I battlefield.

Some among the Three Hundred did not forgive their fathers their failures. Psychotherapist Carl G. Jung, for example, had such contempt for his father—a quiet, sickly, melancholy Lutheran pastor who had lost money in poor investments—that, although he married a rich wife, he was avid for money from his rich American patients. Playwright George S. Kaufman likewise worried about money, although his father Joseph had a different attitude toward it.

Joseph Kaufman was an erratic provider who needed continual drama and change in his life, and so the family sometimes found itself living in fine houses with servants and at other times in cheap boardinghouses. To this creative, eccentric man making money was a game, not a serious matter, and so his family seldom knew if it were rich or poor.

Himself a middle child in a very large family, Joseph had little financial support from it, yet he had such contempt for making money that he could not bring himself to go into his family's lucrative meat-packing business. He was a scholar who liked reading Darwin and Voltaire, an adventurer who once fought Indians and worked in a silver mine.

After he married (to an extremely neurotic and hypochondriacal woman), he tried manufacturing and did very well at it since he was clever at initiating new techniques, though he had no patience with any business once he had learned how to manage it. Despite himself, he did well in the steel business, and even better at making ribbons. Because he believed a business really belonged to the men who worked in it—not to its innovator—he would quickly abandon an enterprise and turn to another. Thus he introduced the forty-hour week in the textile industry.

Unlike his father, George—traumatized early by his mother's pathological anxieties about his health and his father's disdain of big business—worried about money all his life, though he became quite a successful playwright.

The Father of V. S. Pritchett. The most explicit description of a failure-prone father is told by critic, short story writer, and novelist Victor Sawdon (V. S.) Pritchett, author of two bittersweet autobiographies: *A Cab at the Door* and *Midnight Oil*. Born in 1900 in Ipswich, England, Pritchett in *A Cab at the Door* (p. 23) tells of "this cocksparrow, my father . . . dressy and expansive with optimism, walking in and out of jobs with the bumptiousness of a god."

Sawdon Pritchett made his four children, of whom Victor was the oldest, feel that he was a millionaire, yet they wondered at how their mother could be so poor when their father was so rich. Somehow, they thought, it must be their mother's fault if she went about in a coarse apron, moody and sullen. Victor's mother once had hoped for a happier home life with her husband, whom she met in a big department store while she was an apprentice in millinery and he was a floorwalker. As newlyweds they opened a stationer's store in a lower middle-class neighborhood in Ipswich. Her husband impulsively ripped out the worn fixtures, painted the shop walls with bright paint, and bought new shelves and display cases, but did not save enough money for stock. Thus the shop soon failed. However, he did not seem to mind, and blithely left his wife and baby at his parents' home while he went to London to find something else to do. He pursued this self-defeating pattern all his life.

In 1936, when V. S. had become a well-established writer and happily married, his father's needlework factory failed. This threw the three Pritchett sons into panic: their father, with his debt-creating genius, was about to be let loose on the world. One son had become wealthy and could afford to support his parents but not to finance his father's fantasies. Roles were reversed. Now it was the son V. S. who resembled the stern, worried father going to see an unmanageable son.

The old man talked more incessantly than ever, but no one but his admiring grandchildren still thought he was a wonder or listened to his endless stories about himself. He quarreled continually with his wife, and one time, when he found 300 pounds of her life savings hidden, he laughed at her, appropriated her painfully acquired money, and bought a cottage in the country. But when she died he was inconsolable.

"I felt sad," V. S. Pritchett wrote in *Midnight Oil* (p. 262) when he was nearing seventy, "that my father's ambitions . . . had come to failure. And this led me to think that, for all my travels and books, I was a failure, too, trapped in a character I could not escape. Was I, in my own way, as self-deluded as he?"

The Father of Lady Astor. In Chiswell Dabney Langhorne, father of Lady Nancy Astor, the first woman to sit in the British Parliament, we have an example of the impulsive, imaginative, sometimes creative father whose personality problems were his undoing. An American southerner, he experienced his first bitter failure as a young Confederate soldier, and for the rest of his life he hated Yankees—a prejudice his daughter inherited (even requesting that, at her death, her coffin be covered by a Confederate flag).

When the Civil War was over, Chiswell (known as Chillie) had only a wife, two children, and a barrel of whiskey. He never became a good provider, but by trading on his charm and tremendous vitality he always could find some kind of employment. He peddled pianos and pictures, became a tobacco auctioneer (inventing the "gobble, gobble" style of auctioneering), and at one time, although he knew nothing about building railroads, acted as a subcontractor for a firm that wanted a railroad built.

Yet his judgment was poor and his behavior unpredictable. Once, for example, when he was working as a night watchman in a tobacco warehouse, he became so bored that he turned in a false fire alarm. At another time, when his second daughter, Irene, wanted to marry a Yankee artist named Charles Dana Gibson, Chillie called him a "damned charcoal artist" and the marriage was delayed for a year because he would not give his consent. Later he accepted Gibson, who made Irene and her sisters the models for his famous Gibson Girls.

Chillie's wife, the former Nancy Witcher Langhorne, kept her youth and dignity because she had a sense of humor and because her husband, although a poor provider, never looked at another woman. When a gushing acquaintance eulogized her handsome husband's beautiful eyes, she cooled the woman's enthusiasm by telling her that he looked at a batter cake in the same romantic fashion.

The seventh and youngest living child of the eleven born to the Langhornes, Nancy was born in 1879 in Danville, Virginia.

Despite her dissatisfactions with her father, Lady Astor was always much like him in temperament and thinking. She was an unpredictable, emotional woman who relied on her charm and presence to gain wealth and fame. Like her father, she alienated her own children by being overly possessive and by not accepting their ideas when they differed from her own. Her judgment about world affairs was dubious.

Because Chillie had demanded obedience and fealty from his family, his male arrogance made a suffragette of Lady Astor. As a member of the British Parliament, she was sympathetic with any law that favored poor women and children whose husbands and fathers could not provide for them. She never forgot how poor she was as a child, and during her lifetime married two very rich men.

Poverty is experienced in a relative sense. In one family it may mean hunger; in another it may mean having three servants instead of eight. Yet the boys and girls who experience father failure and become subjects of biography often use the experience creatively. Since the father has failed, they know failure is not the end of life and are not afraid to take the risks necessary for exceptional achievement. They have experienced periods of poverty, or comparative poverty, in their youth and have learned to cope with deprivation. Consequently, it does not frighten them to contemplate failure. There are no family traditions to violate, no stable, provident elders to be shamed if they fail. They do not have ancestors who have to be emulated. They are on their own early, have already had experiences coping with their own and family needs.

By contrast, the young man and the young woman from comfortable middle-class or wealthy families who have not known panic and frustration, whose parents are willing and able to help them in times of crisis, have less incentive to be experimental in lifestyle and also are much more likely to be criticized by their fathers if they do not succeed in an innovative endeavor.

The Immigrant Father

A joke among New York Jews goes as follows: "What is the difference between a garment worker and a social worker?" Answer: "One generation."

The fathers who came to the United States during the peak of the East European Jewish emigration often experienced failure, sometimes again and again, in a heartbreaking effort to find a place for themselves and for their families in their adopted country. Fourteen percent of the Three Hundred are Jewish, and most are immigrants or second-generation immigrants. Between 1881 and 1914 almost one third of the East European Jews left their homelands. They fled mostly from Russia, Poland, and Rumania into Germany or Austria, from where they traveled by train to a major port of embarkation—Hamburg, Bremen, Rotterdam, Amsterdam, or Antwerp—and then to New York's Ellis Island, which in those years processed about 1,500 immigrants a day.

Steerage passage was brutal. The passengers were crowded into small spaces near the ships' engines, water was rationed, and the quarters stank of stale food and vomit. Once ashore the immigrants, both Jews and non-Jews, were victimized by landladies, sold goods they did not need, made to bribe petty officials, and forced to sell off possessions for extra cash. Most of the immigrants were simple people from small villages where their families had lived for generations and were unused to crowds and suspicious of strangers.

Generally, the father emigrated first. Usually he had the address of a relative, a former neighbor, the friend of a friend and could sleep on a cot or pallet on the floor in another immigrant's house. Some fathers never sent for their families; others, like the fathers of Golda Meir and Jules Masserman, were not eager to see them when they came. When Edward Steichen's mother did not hear from her husband for months, she came without an invitation and found him very ill. When the wives and children finally arrived, the father was often ashamed of the accommodations he could provide. Wives wept for their own mothers. A few went insane. Children who had been exceptional scholars in their own country were put in the first grade, teased on the playground, and beaten on the streets, as were the artist twins Moses and Raphael Soyer.

These were families who came because they were poor and wanted to better themselves. Among the Three Hundred, twenty-eight (9 percent) were first-generation immigrants and thirty (9.5 percent) were from the second generation.

Immigrants who came later because they wished to exploit

their talents more remuneratively or to escape a political regime that did not offer them freedom of thought or movement were often already adult and welcomed because of their talents as actors, performers, or scientists. Among these immigrants are people like Rudolph Nureyev, Vladimir Nabokov, Ingrid Bergman, and Greta Garbo. Such later immigrants did not come as children nor did their fathers emigrate. Some, such as Nabokov and Peter Ustinov, came from homes where the father was wealthy or a successful professional man.

To a remarkable degree, the immigrant has replaced the first- and second-generation pioneers in achieving eminence in the United States. Crossing the plains was replaced by coming over by steerage.

Benny Bufano's Father. The sculptor Beniamino (Benny) Bufano was born in San Fele, Italy, in 1898. His father, Canio Bufano, fled from Italy to the United States after his hero, Garibaldi, for whom he had fought, had been defeated. Four years later Canio sent for Benny and his mother, Lucretia, to join him in New York City, where he was employed making artificial flowers. They moved into a railroad flat, where the senior Bufanos were to spend the rest of their days, and Lucretia bore thirteen more children.

Canio never learned English, never made a good living for his overwhelmingly large family, and never stopped telling his fellow Italian immigrants about the days when he knew Garibaldi. When his oldest son began to draw and model with clay, Canio beat him unmercifully and destroyed his sketches and models; his first-born son would be a soldier or a politician, never a maker of mudpies.

When Benny was fourteen years old, his mother and two younger brothers helped him move into and furnish a studio of his own, and they were nearby to see that he did not starve. He survived by selling his art works. News of the Italian boy-artist reached wealthy Gertrude Vanderbilt Whitney, and she began paying his $12 a month rent. She induced him to try a sculpture she envisioned by drawing him a sketch, but when his finished work did not resemble her sketch at all she became so angry she broke it into bits. Just as Benny's father could not subvert his conscience or his creative impulses, neither could Gertrude Vanderbilt Whitney or anyone else. He was remarkably independent.

In 1914, Benny was asked to go to San Francisco to help an

older artist who had a contract for making sculptured figures for the Panama-Pacific International Exposition. Though he believed himself to be a coworker, he was paid a laborer's wage and made to do routine tasks. When he came home broke and disappointed, his father told him he had made a fool of himself and should know enough to stop trying to be an artist. However, Benny won the next round when a wealthy New York society woman paid him $2,000 to make a bust of her son.

Benny's mother was faithful and loving, but not because she appreciated his work. Indeed, she wished he had a "proper" job where he could wear a suit and tie. Her contribution to his art was to involve him emotionally with her idol, St. Francis of Assisi, a commitment that continued all his life. He also became committed to living simply and without pretense and to an abhorrence of war. When World War I began, he cut off his trigger finger and sent it to President Wilson. During the Vietnam War he gave sculptures of St. Francis and other figures glorifying peace to anti-war organizations to be auctioned off to raise money.

Beniamino Bufano could be quarrelsome and unpredictable and made friends and enemies without trying to make either. Yet his work was distinctive and self-fulfilling, and once he had established his independence from his father at fourteen he was his own man.

When Benny became well known, his father was still unable to praise him directly, although he was known to boast of his son to his old friends. Canio is almost a stereotype villain of biographies, a father who does not want to have a son who is an artist. Perhaps he was jealous of his son. Canio made artificial flowers all his life. Did he have artistic talents that were wasted in the repetitive making of a tawdry product? In addition, as an infant Benny had his mother's whole attention for his first four years. It would be natural for the son and father to compete for her affection when the family was reunited. Since Benny's mother encouraged him to leave home and defy his father, Canio may have become even more jealous and rejected.

Upton Sinclair's Father. Novelist and social reformer Upton Sinclair was born in 1878 in Baltimore, Maryland, in a family with three major problems: the Sinclairs were "poor relations," the father was an alcoholic, and the mother could not cope.

The father, Upton Beall Sinclair, was a dandy with a waxed moustache who would rather vote for a "nigger" than a Republican and who took his vacations in a charity ward being treated for delirium tremens. A one-time whiskey salesman who sampled his own wares, the senior Sinclair came from an aristocratic southern family with a reputation for hard drinking. (One brother died an inebriate in an old soldiers' home; another was an alcoholic who put a bullet through his head at age forty.) In his autobiography (p. 7), the younger Upton wrote, "When he was not under the influence of the Demon Rum, the little 'drummer' dearly loved his family! So the thirty years during which I watched him were one long moral agony."

Upton's mother, the former Priscilla Harden, who was a tight-lipped southern woman with a mind closed to the social evils her son would later write about, felt she had married far beneath her position as daughter of the secretary-treasurer of the Western Maryland Railroad, and she never forgot it. The Sinclairs lived in cheap hotels and boardinghouses, although a flat would have been cheaper; however, Southern ladies were not supposed to do menial labor. They economized by renting only one room and letting Upton sleep across the foot of their bed or on a bedbug-infested couch. Despite this enforced intimacy, any reference to sex was taboo in the Sinclair household, and Upton was in college before he found out how it was that the human infant was conceived.

Still, Upton was extraordinarily precocious. As a toddler he spoke in pedantic sentences. At five he taught himself to read by pestering his elders about words and the sounds of letters. A doctor told his mother that his mind was growing too fast for his body and he should not be sent to school. As a result he stayed home and read omnivorously. After he started school at age ten, he was able to complete all eight grades in two years. He was only thirteen when he went to college—at that time the College of the City of New York (CCNY) gave its students the entire secondary school and undergraduate college curriculum in five years—but he had already read all of Carlyle, Browning, Thackeray, Goethe, and Zola.

Sparked by one of his CCNY classmates, Simon Stern, who had had a story published in a Jewish publication for young people, Upton decided to try his hand at writing and sent a short story about a black boy whose pet bird proves him innocent of arson to *Argosy* magazine. He was astounded when he received a check for $25.

At that time his father had been drinking heavily and his mother was in severe financial stress. Usually this meant an enforced visit to rich relatives again. His later concerns with the painful contrast between the lives of the poor and the rich came from his childhood experiences. "I have one favorite theme," he wrote in his autobiography (p. 9), "the contrast between the social classes. . . . The explanation is that as far back as I can remember, my life was a series of Cinderella transformations; one night I would be sleeping on a vermin-ridden sofa in a lodginghouse, and the next night under silken coverlets in a fashionable home."

The *Argosy* check showed him that he could spare his mother these embarrassments, and he set about writing children's stories and jokes for money. He specialized in jokes and had a card file of them, alphabetized under various headings, and later wrote reams of them for pulp magazines. He also wrote about the unwashed and unlettered. As a boy he had played and fought with the gangs in his slum neighborhoods, stole potatoes from the vegetable man, and was passed over by trucks and knocked into the gutter by bicycles. (He once recalled fourteen instances when, as a small boy, he narrowly averted being killed in a street accident.) He knew both the world of wealth and the world of poverty, and both interested readers.

At age thirteen he was contributing substantially to the family income, and by seventeen he was still supporting his parents, even though he was living in his own apartment. By the time he was twenty-one he had written as much as Sir Walter Scott had written all his life, yet he was also studying literature at CCNY.

When as an adult Upton started writing social commentary, his first five serious novels paid him only $1,000. His most monumental work, *The Jungle*, his passionate denunciation of the working conditions in the Chicago stockyards that resulted in the passage of the first Pure Food and Drug Act, made him world famous. His exceptionally able biographer, Leon Harris, says that *The Jungle* is generally regarded as one of the three most effective muckraking novels in American history, along with *Uncle Tom's Cabin* and *Grapes of Wrath.*

Upton's early, intense involvement with his mother, whom he once called "my sweetest" in letters, cooled after his father died in 1908 when Upton was twenty. His mother lived for twenty-four more years but saw very little of her famous son, whose writings she disapproved of. For a long time he continued to send her a monthly check, but eventually these stopped and her care was assumed by her rich sister, the wife of a banker.

David Sarnoff's Father. No other immigrant son among the Three Hundred responded so early and so efficiently to being needed by an ill and helpless father as did young David Sarnoff. He is also unique in that he is one of only two male representatives of the business world—the other is German car manufacturer Emil Jellinek-Mercédès, born in 1853—among the Three Hundred. (We do have three wealthy businesswomen, Coco Chanel, Elizabeth Arden, and Helena Rubinstein, all involved in cosmetics and all from failure-prone fathers.) Why the lack of biographies about those who administer large multinational corporations? Fear? Resentment? Reluctance to understand? There is a plethora of serious nonfiction volumes about corporations and their influence but not about those who head them. This was not true in our Four Hundred biographies, when we examined the childhood lives of John D. Rockefeller, John D., Jr., and Nelson, along with Henry Ford, Edward Bok, Charles P. Steinmetz, Andrew Carnegie, and Austen Chamberlain (a wealthy manufacturer as well as a politician).

David Sarnoff, whose father was an ill and miserable invalid, was, as his biographer and first cousin, Eugene Lyons, puts it, an immigrant boy who became a great industrial giant. As head of RCA and a pioneer in electronics and communications, Lyons believes Sarnoff probably affected our daily lives more than anyone since Edison. For instance, it was he who pressured his company, much against its will, to build television sets and battled to produce color television. He stayed with RCA doing what he wanted to do even though a rival firm once offered him $5 million a year for five years, much more than he earned at RCA.

David was born in 1891 in Uzlian, an ugly, backward Russian village in the interior of the province of Minsk where a few families lived for generations. Although Uzlian had nothing to recommend it except its humanity, wherever there are human beings there is the exciting possibility of uniqueness, and the Privins and Sarnoffs produced that uniqueness in David Sarnoff.

The Privins were one of the "best" families. Samuel Privin, David's grandfather, was a pious, erudite man who was an unsuccessful teacher of small boys whom he strapped too often. Because the classes he organized seldom lasted very long, it was the indomitable Grandmother Rebecca who peddled meat patties and sweet syrups to keep her nine children fed. Eight of the nine were girls, who married common workingmen because their mother could not provide them with dowries. Leah Privin married Abraham Sarnoff, a handsome, religious, but unlettered and unrobust house painter. David was the first of five children, the last two of whom were born in New York City.

Letters about the fabulous lives of immigrants to the United States were passed from hand to hand in the *shtetl*, and David's father caught the emigration fever. Figuring he could not do worse than he did in Uzlian, in 1896 he kissed his wife and children goodbye and set out for America. His letters from New York City, however, were few and discouraging and money came in driblets.

Life went on at home as if no one were ever to leave. David, who was five when his father left, was sent away to Grandmother Privin's rabbi brother, 100 miles away, for what turned out to be an agonizing three years of unremitting tutoring and study and during which time he never went home. He was poorly fed, there were no other children in the household, and he sometimes studied for fifteen hours at a stretch; as a result he was able to memorize 2,000 words a day. While David struggled with the Talmud, his father was denying himself food to send money for tickets. Often he was too ill to work.

David was nine when the tickets came, and Leah Sarnoff and her three children traveled to Minsk. Minsk was the first big city he had ever seen, and young David clung to his mother's skirts while he watched Cossacks charging into a political demonstration, trampling women and children as well as men under the hooves of their horses. They sailed from Libeau on the Baltic Sea, and transferred to another ship at Liverpool.

David was the man of the family on the journey and felt terribly responsible. At one point in Liverpool, as he saw the family's hamper of kosher food being lowered into the ship's hold where they would not have access to it, he impulsively jumped into the hold, landing fifty feet below on some bundles, and seized the hamper. A watching sailor, Lyons reports, shouted, "You'll do alright in America!" (p. 24).

"The memory of that sordid crossing," Lyons writes, "would remain with them always—the human freight packed in like animals, the stench of unwashed bodies and vomit, the endless retchings and groaning. No immigrant by steerage could ever quite erase the horror from his mind, no matter how well he did in the adopted land" (p. 24).

As David looked up through the portholes he could see the first-class passengers, well dressed and comfortable, with their happy children running about playing. He daydreamed of what awaited him in America.

The family disembarked at Montreal, carrying their hamper and heavy bundles of bedding and linen. From there they traveled by train to Albany and then by Hudson River steamboat to lower Manhattan, where they arrived on a hot July day, still wearing heavy Russian clothing. Although a Montreal travel agent had been asked to wire Abraham Sarnoff to tell him when they would arrive, no one met them. Their message had been garbled or he could not read it, and Abraham was waiting on the wrong dock. The only address Leah had was that of the family with whom Abraham had been staying, and he found them there late that evening. From there they moved into a three-room railroad flat in a decrepit slum.

Abraham was ill, poor, and terrified by the responsibility of having to provide for a wife and three children. The family was often hungry. Leah wept for her mother and the friendly village of Uzlian where they were known and respected. The neighbor children mocked David and called him a greenhorn, and within two days after his arrival he was selling newspapers on the streets, at ten the only wage earner in the family.

To augment his income he built a wagon of packing cases

and discarded bicycle wheels and offered quick deliveries to stands
and stores for only 15¢ a week per customer. Selling newspapers
was a competitive business, and speed in delivery was crucial. He
also made quick deliveries to six other newsboys for a bonus of 10¢
per week and sang in the synagogue choir for another $1.50 a week.
When his brother Irving and his sister Ede were born, he had even
more mouths to feed, and so he worked evenings, nights, Saturdays,
and Sundays. Yet during this period he also was in school and
doing well.

At thirteen David saw that if he only had $200 he could
buy a newsstand and the family's economic problems would be solved.
He talked so freely about his newsstand idea to everyone that his
story reached the ears of a woman who had been commissioned by
a wealthy man to seek out and reward promising youths. Hearing
that David was only thirteen and had been supporting his family for
several years, she visited him and after only a few minutes gave him
the $200. With this Horatio Alger beginning, David bought the
newsstand and it did as well as he had hoped.

When David was graduated from grammar school he was
not able to go on to high school because his father was housebound
and could not help at the newsstand. Even so, David had a contempt for the unlearned, no doubt reflecting his rabbi uncle and
Grandmother Privin. He read omnivorously, attended evening
classes at the Educational Alliance, and joined a debating club.
Whenever he had a spare fifty cents he went to the opera. While
hanging around the newspaper office he taught himself to use a
wireless set to send and receive messages. He bought books about
electricity and telegraphy. He thought vaguely of becoming a reporter, of writing news stories instead of delivering them.

One day, when the newsstand had reached the point where
it could function without him, he walked into the Marconi company
and asked to be hired as a pony operator. Instead, since he was only
sixteen, he was hired as an office boy at $5.50 a week. Unknowingly,
however, he had started his life work in earnest.

To further his education on the job David chose men he
respected, invited himself to their laboratories during his off hours,
and helped them in order to learn from them. Then and later he
was not always welcomed, and he worked too hard and thereby

made other employees seem lazy. He also made suggestions for improvements that were not always appreciated, and indeed might have got himself fired had he not always been right. A year later he was promoted to pony operator, at a salary of $7.50 a week.

When David was seventeen his father died. David then sold the newsstand (at a profit) and the family moved to Brownsville where they rented a $9-a-week walk-up and Leah, no longer fearful about her surroundings, started taking odd jobs to help support the family.

By this time other relatives, including Grandmother Privin, had followed them to the United States. Grandmother Privin was as dominating a figure in her new country as she had been in Uzlian. More than anyone else in the family, David inherited her drive and uniqueness. She was inordinately proud of David and exploited him happily for the benefit of others. When she died, on the evening of the day she set for her death, she left jewels and other mementoes to other descendants. However, her debts she left to David. She knew they would not burden him.

When David and his well-to-do brothers were in mid-life, they set up a trust fund for relatives who needed help. David's sense of responsibility included his whole extended family and friends who were in need.

Victims of Circumstance

There are other fathers who are victims of circumstances seemingly beyond their control—war, drought, illness, a new law, an invention. They do not invite misfortune; it comes to them. For instance, artist John Sloan's father, who was a fine cabinetmaker, was made a pauper by the popularity of factory-made furniture. Novelist Phyllis Bentley's father had to close his textile factory in England because of a tariff act passed by the McKinley administration in the United States. Novelist Joyce Cary's father lost his estate in Ireland because he was a beneficent landlord who did not collect his rents from his tenants. A tenant law devised by the English parliament to punish evil landlords left him with bad debts he could not collect.

Doris Lessing's Father. Novelist and critic Doris May Lessing, born of English parents in Persia in 1919, gives an unexcelled description of a failure-prone father in her 1974 book, *A Small Personal Voice*. Her father, Alfred Cook Taylor, was born in 1896 at Saint Mary-at-the-Wall, Colchester, Essex. His father and he and his older brother were bank clerks. His mother was a practical, plain woman, a head cook, an able person like the woman he eventually was to marry.

Alfred's older brother was a much more clever student and able wage earner and became quite wealthy, but Alfred could not compete and was dark and introspective. As a youth he enjoyed only ten years of just being plain happy, singing, dancing (he thought nothing of walking to a dance fifteen miles away), flirting, playing billiards, cricket, and football. He was vigorous, sensuous, and compassionate. He almost married a girl when he was young but broke off his engagement when she was rude to a waiter, someone he viewed as defenseless. Such strong notions about what was ethical doomed Alfred to economic failure.

Offered a commission in World War I, he at first refused, preferring to take his chances with the common soldiers. But after some experiences with drunken buddies dragging him off to brothels and offending his pious and straightlaced sensibilities with tawdry jokes about girls, he changed his mind and became an officer. However, he valued the comradeship of the Tommies on the front lines and grieved intensely when they were killed. He often wished that the generals on both sides could be forced, for just one day, to endure the life of a common soldier, and he recalled how a certain brutal officer was killed by his own men. Once he met a German face to face in no-man's land; they lowered their rifles, smiled at each other, and walked away. He knew many men who had seen the angels on the battlefield at Mons.

Alfred also knew, because a fortune-teller had told him so, that he was to be a casualty of war. Later he was to tell his daughter that he was lucky to lose only one leg above the thigh ten days before his whole company was destroyed. He also was lucky to have a nurse, Sister Emily Maud McVeagh, who later became his wife.

Alfred told these war stories to his daughter over and over during her childhood, always with the same gestures and intonations, as contrasted with the stories of his youthful prewar days, which he told in a spontaneous and nonrepetitive way. After the war he found civilian life in England intolerable, as he saw that his hedonistic nation had no intention of making the world safe for democracy and ending war forever. He craved a change of scene, so he and his wife went to Persia, where he was manager of an English bank. They lived in a lovely house with high ceilings and a garden filled with roses and tropical flowers, and his wife enjoyed the social life centered around the British embassy, but Alfred was once more irritated by the corruption and indifference he saw around him to values he held dear. There was no more honesty or human decency, he decided, in Persia than in England. Thus, on a sudden impulse he put his life savings, 800 pounds, into a 3,000-acre farm in Southern Rhodesia. On his own land, he thought, he might determine his own destiny and live the honorable life for which he had a deep craving.

Emily, their two small children, and a governess followed him to Southern Rhodesia, taking along a piano, Persian rugs, and other household items she thought would help make entertaining pleasant on the farm. However, there were no near neighbors. The family lived high on the veldt in a thatch and mud house. Moreover, the farm was not nearly as profitable as Alfred had expected it to be. Although labor was cheap and Alfred paid more than the going wage, the workers were resentful at having been turned off the land the Taylor family now lived on and at being forced into reserves. Alfred's crops failed, and farm prices were low. Emily became increasingly depressed and neurotic, and her husband even more so. His hair turned gray, he became diabetic, he had stomach ailments, and he was no longer fastidious about his appearance. He made frantic attempts to do something about his failing finances, and for ten years he experimented with a gold-divining invention that came to nothing. Emily pretended to comfort herself that one of his schemes would work and that someday they would go back to England, where guests would come to supper and they could go to the theater.

As the years passed, Alfred became misanthropic. He was resentful of his worsening illnesses and made brews from plants growing on his farm, hoping they would cure his diabetes. He became angry about what he saw as the next great war, which he felt would punish those still unaware of the causes and evils of war. Perhaps it would be just as well, he told his listening daughter, if the people of the earth were destined to blow themselves to bits. There might be plenty more people, wiser and more advanced, on other planets. He read the Bible and saw both the Germans and Russians as the anti-Christ, believing that the Jews were God's chosen people. He read ancient prophecies predicting that 10 million dead bodies would soon surround Jerusalem. He came to believe in the Mosaic law of an eye for an eye and approved of flogging and hanging criminals.

When the Second World War, which he had predicted so long, finally came and his son, Doris' young brother, became a soldier, Alfred became very ill, both physically and emotionally. His wife moved him into a little house near the hospital in Salisbury, where Doris had got a job as clerical worker and telephone operator. Alfred's wife nursed him through two years of painful illness.

The legacy that Alfred Taylor left his daughter was an independence of mind and a stubborn commitment, similar to his, to a set of values. When Doris was seven she was sent to Salisbury to boarding school. At fourteen, however, she refused to go any longer, preferring the privacy and freedom of the veldt to the boredom of school. She read the classics and began writing novels, and she still rereads Tolstoy, Stendhal, Chekhov, Balzac, Turgenev, Zola, and Dostoevsky when she needs to renew her own commitment to humanism. These authors, she says, have nothing in common except their commitment to something. (She finds modern writers who have no belief in anything to be inconsequential, although they may be entertaining.)

For a time during the 1930s, after she went to England to live, she was drawn to communism, but she found it to be superficial since it did not distinguish the point at which the individual must make his or her own decision, even if it meant refusing to submit to the collective conscience.

Like her father, Doris fears the self-destructive tendencies of the human race and was outraged by the Vietnam War. She also was exasperated when her 1975 novel, *The Grass Is Singing,* about the psychic breakdown of the wife of a poor white farmer in Southern Rhodesia, was claimed by women's liberation extremists as a useful weapon in the "current sex war" when she had been writing about a mental breakdown and of self-healing rather than about man's inhumanity to woman. Although she wants women to have their rights and privileges, she feels the world is being shaken into a new pattern by present-day cataclysms and that if we live through these the "aims of Women's Liberation will look very small and quaint."

As the self-educated daughter of a poor man, Doris Lessing had no family traditions or expectations to break in her experimenting with life. She has tried mescaline (but only once), investigated Sufism and ESP, and contemplated the creative qualities of madness. She writes with passion and clarity about the continued exploitation of the native inhabitants of Southern Rhodesia and of the Union of South Africa.

In an essay on Olive Schreiner, to whom she acknowledges a debt as a mentor, she (1974, p. 108) writes about Olive's father what applies with equal force to her own father and also to the father of another woman writer she admires, Isak Dinesen:

> To the creation of a woman novelist seem to go certain psychological ingredients; at least, often enough to make it interesting. One of them, a balance between father and mother where the practicality, the ordinary sense, cleverness and worldly ambition is on the side of the mother; and the father's life is so weighted with dreams and ideas and imaginings that their joint life gets lost in what looks like a hopeless muddle and failure.

These three women novelists, who lived in and wrote about Africa, were strongly influenced by unsuccessful fathers.

To a remarkable degree Doris is fortunate to have had a father who was a failure for she uses the concerns he brooded about as the substance of her novels and as a reason for her existence.

Malcolm X's Father. Impulsive, irresponsible, restless, passionate, irate, uninhibited, idealistic, outgoing, angry, and ebullient are terms frequently used to describe fathers whom we classify as failure-prone. The mood swing of the failure-prone father is often as erratic as his income. He is neither passive nor indolent nor a nonentity. Certainly this describes Malcolm X's father.

No father was as abysmal a failure as was the Reverend Earl Little, who earned so little money that his wife had to feed her eleven children jackrabbit stew to avoid starvation. He was a failure as a husband too for he resented his wife's being better educated so much that he would beat her when she "put smooth words upon him."

As a passionate follower of the Garveyite tradition, he advocated that Negroes go back to Africa to keep the race pure, and he angrily and openly denounced discrimination in the United States. Since he stood six feet four and had only one eye, his very presence was intimidating, but he was such an "uppity nigger" that unknown assailants murdered him and left his body on the railroad tracks, where it was found cut in two. Only one of his irate, restless six brothers was not also murdered.

These and other experiences placed too great a burden on his widow, who became a patient in a mental hospital for twenty-six years. Her son Malcolm Little (who later became known as Malcolm X) believed she was driven there by insensitive social workers who took her children away from her and placed them in institutions or foster homes.

Despite the troubles at home, however, the young Malcolm X did well. As a seventh grader he was president of his class. In the eighth grade a teacher told him that, because of his race, he should not consider becoming a lawyer and suggested he be a carpenter instead. It was not a teacher but an older half-sister who loved and encouraged him. His eminence was quite clearly built on the ashes of his father's failures. Like Doris Lessing, he, too, was committed.

An Example of Determinant Concepts: Henry Moore

One subject who fits so neatly into the concepts that evolved from our research—so neatly that he seems almost to have been invented for that purpose—is the English sculptor Henry Moore, who was born in 1898 in Castleford, Yorkshire, a coal-mining town a few miles out of Leeds. Henry's mother was forty and his father fifty when Henry was born.

Although Raymond Moore, Henry's father, went to work at age nine, scaring crows in the fields, he was the perpetual earnest scholar. He went into the coal pits as a boy, but he spent his leisure hours studying, read all of Shakespeare, bought books and gramophone records for his children, studied algebra and geometry with his older children, and was able to tutor young Henry in all of these subjects. Raymond also enjoyed playing the violin and insisted that Henry take lessons, although Henry hated all the sounds he was able to make. When Raymond's first child was born, he vowed that none of his children would ever have to work in mines, and none of them ever did.

Raymond took part in a strike for two years and food was scarce in the household. Raymond worked as a shoemaker and his wife became a washerwoman. During the evenings there were strike meetings in the house, which leaders attended, and young Henry listened to talk about labor economics and the necessity of supporting a labor party. Henry Moore was a Liberal, never a Tory. No award pleased him as much as the key to Castleford given him by his townfolk.

Raymond's real father-failure came later. He worked very hard to qualify himself for a higher position in the mines, first as a deputy, then as an undermanager, but his eyes were injured in an accident and he was not permitted to continue working underground. Turning to his children to achieve his own lost ambition, he studied with and encouraged Henry.

In the Moore family, as in many other families, the highly achieving child, especially the youngest one, was not viewed as the most promising. In this case, of the five of the seven Moore children who lived to maturity, the oldest girl married young and had children, grandchildren, and great-grandchildren, all during Henry's lifetime. Another daughter, the middle child, became headmistress of a school and made a home for her parents in their old age. (Note the common negative effect of being a middle child.) Still another girl became a schoolteacher who married a schoolmaster. Henry's oldest brother became a schoolmaster, which was his father's ambition for all his children. A second brother went to Canada and was never heard of again.

Henry was the youngest son and was very close to his affectionate mother. Sixteen percent of the Three Hundred, like Henry, were born to mothers over thirty-five. Only one (Ethel Waters) was born to a mother of eighteen or younger. Henry is also one of fourteen disadvantaged boys who had unstinting help from secondary school teachers, usually spinsters. Like other subjects, Henry's siblings were upwardly mobile and gave as much or more satisfaction to their parents than he.

Henry's mother, unlike her somewhat aloof, authoritarian, and sober husband, was warm, loving, strong, and vital, though a bit vain, and lived to be eighty-four and savored life. It was she who unknowingly nourished Henry's enjoyment of life, his appreciation for textures and sights and sounds. She was given to severe bouts of rheumatism, and it was Henry who rubbed her back with strong liniment and felt her body's structure as he massaged away her pain.

A Miss Gostick, a remarkable young French-English woman, went far beyond the call of duty of an art teacher in the ugly mining town and organized pottery and weaving classes for the adults. Henry was not the only student who made a name for himself in art. One boy became a school inspector of art; another became a theatrical scene designer. Miss Gostick encouraged friendship among the three boys and invited them and other promising students to Sunday tea, where they could browse through her art books and listen to talk of a wider world than they ever had imagined. It was she who persuaded Henry's father to let him accept a scholarship to the art school in Leeds rather than to go to the university, although Raymond was afraid his son might not be successful as an artist and begged him to take a teacher's training course first. However, with three schoolteachers in the family already, the family could accept an artist.

When Henry was forty-seven and his wife was thirty-nine, after a series of miscarriages, a daughter, Mary, was born. (Note that, like Henry's own parents, they too were older parents.) They doted on the child, ordinarily took her with them when they traveled, and encouraged her very evident artistic talent. Mary started painting as soon as she could hold a brush and decided that she wanted to go to art school. After letting her go to the Slade in London one day a week for one term, Henry persuaded her to go to a university, saying that if she went to art school she would never learn anything else. His will prevailed and Mary went to St. Ann's College at Oxford.

Mary Moore, to our knowledge, has not fulfilled her talent in art. Henry, having had a poor, failure-prone father and being male and the youngest, was less vulnerable to parental pressure. He had the opportunity and freedom that he denied his daughter.

Comments and Conclusions

According to Detroit psychiatrist Louis Koren, the three most important needs of children are to be loved, enjoyed, and needed. In this chapter it is shown that it is the need to be needed that is particularly important. Children want to help, to set the table, to push the elevator button, and loving parents gratify this need to be useful.

In a world economy in which there is overcrowding in the cities, rapid depletion of fossil fuels, the stench and poison of pollution, and chronic unemployment, the need of each secondary-school graduating class to be put to good use is a burden to the parent and to the economy. We can love the baby, enjoy the growing child who is still dependent, but we often fear the adolescent who wants to be used and to be independent and whose maturational needs we cannot meet.

During the 1960s in the United States, some older citizens like Lillian Carter, the mother of the President, and thousands of young people found an outlet for their desire to be needed in the Peace Corps or VISTA. Others volunteered to go South to tutor disadvantaged students and to register voters. They marched and demonstrated to effect social change, thereby satisfying a fundamental need to be noticed and effectual. Some college graduates who found no market for their services returned to the land and used their muscles building and farming. Others among the unneeded responded to their plight with violence. It is the young, the aged, and the minority groups who feel the least needed. The youth are more restive than are their elders when their untapped potential is thwarted. They reject their elders, who seek to shield them, prolong their dependency, or are fearful of being vocationally displaced by them. When the economy does not provide work for all, it is the middle-aged, not the youngest or oldest, who are favored.

In the 1970s there have been sporadic efforts here and there in the world to help people help each other. Currently David Werner, a biology teacher from Palo Alto, is the recipient of a Guggenheim Fellowship that will permit him to describe his work in a remote area of Mexico. The Piaxtla Project began inadvertently, about twelve years ago, because of his own need. He resigned from his teaching position at the experimental Peninsula School in nearby Menlo Park to go to a remote area in Mexico to make paintings of rare birds and flowers. His physician had told him he had only about eighteen months left before his muscular dystrophy would disable him. He wanted to spend that eighteen months making a journey that would fulfill a long-time daydream. He went into a remote mountainous area famous for its exotic birds, where there were no roads or doctors and where most inhabitants had never been to the outside world. Werner backpacked in with his paint box and a first aid kit for his own use.

He soon won the affection of the people with the repeated use of his first aid kit. Soon he began teaching adolescents to do things they were not sophisticated enough to know they were not expected to be able to do—they built a medical center, a recreational center, a learning center, and other simple but architecturally beautiful buildings. He taught them to be quite adequate "barefoot" doctors, to fill cavities and make dentures, to dig deep wells to get clean water, to be agricultural experts, to be nurses, and to teach others what he taught them. Increasing numbers of college students, medical students, practicing physicians, and experts in various fields came to help him during their vacation periods. With a minimum of outside help and a shoestring budget, the whole area was changed.*

The State of California has recently established an experimental Youth Corps that has completed its first rugged period of

---

* Unfortunately, according to Werner, big-business "dope dealing" has found that isolated area. Dope peddlers from the United States have found good sources for marijuana and crude opium for heroin. Although most campesinos have no interest in using the products themselves, Werner reports, the lure of easy money that they offer has created a cultural and economic crisis that has disrupted or destroyed countless lives and entire communities.

work-training in what was once a Civilian Conservation Corps (CCC) camp. Young men and women from ages 18 to 22 who never in their lives have had a job have dug ditches, made compost heaps, learned to use a chain saw. For this work they were paid what amounted to a minimum wage. At the close of their three-month period of being "needed," they wept over having to leave each other. A great feeling of camaraderie had developed among these young men and women from the city. Now they are going their separate ways in smaller groups. One group will build hiking trails and picnic facilities on the grounds of a mental hospital; another group will build a small zoo for retarded children. There are many other such projects in progress.

It is this exhilarating feeling of being useful and productive that emerges in 106 homes of the Three Hundred. Here family members were close because they needed each other, and the son or daughter who was to become eminent was able to respond to a parental need with early maturity and self-confidence. Not every youth can support a family by delivering newspapers, like David Sarnoff, or by writing jokes, like Upton Sinclair, but still the 106 demonstrate the unquenchable human need not only to know but to be put to use. When the love for learning in the home is implemented by this feeling of being well used, there is a strong possibility that the boy or girl will not only enhance but may advance the status quo.

Among the 48 percent of the Americans in the sample who are not immigrants or the children of immigrants, there are fewer than a score of families who came to the United States during the expansionary period between the Revolutionary War and the Civil War, or whose parents were homesteaders in the West. Henry Fonda's family originated in Italy, where they were well known in the days before Columbus. A nobleman in the family left Genoa in the fifteenth century to escape political persecution and went to the Netherlands, from which Henry's branch of the family emigrated to New York (then New Amsterdam) in 1828. Cesar Chavez' family homesteaded on government land in New Mexico, having come originally from Old Mexico. R. Buckminster Fuller came from an old English family and is the grandnephew of Margaret Fuller. Ezra Pound's family tree includes Henry Longfellow. Other old

American families are the Calders, the Carters, the Dulles family, the (Norman) Thomas family, the Lardners, the Luces, the Lodges, the Kinseys, the Hepburns, the Humphreys, the Vinings, the Fulbrights, the Iveses, the (Lyndon) Johnsons. Ladybird Johnson is descended from a Spanish-Scottish family, the Patillos, who were one of the first families of Texas, with their own small kingdom of 18,000 acres of grazing land.

But, interesting as these old families are, they now take second place to the recently arrived in producing subjects of biography. The westward movement across the country, which led to the flowering of excellence after the Revolutionary War, has been replaced in the United States by the trans-Atlantic passage, which led to a similar flowering of excellence among first- and (mostly) second-generation immigrants. Among the 113 Americans in our survey, 52 percent are either first- or second-generation immigrants. Two of these, Israeli politician Meyer Weisgal and Israeli prime minister Golda Meir, emigrated twice—once to the United States and the second time, when still young adults, to Israel. Among the American-born, Lady Astor and T. S. Eliot, from old-time American families, became English citizens.

The rather large number of Jewish emigrants to the United States is due to historical events, mainly the frequent pogroms in Russia and the persecution by the Nazis. Presumably because of their well-known love of learning, Jews have always been higher in percentages than other ethnic groups in the number of eminent men (although not women), and we find this true in our sample, in which they make up 14 percent of the Three Hundred.

Religious preferences are difficult to discover, since a great many biographers and autobiographers do not mention the religion the family prefers, or they designate them as agnostic or atheist. Writers seem to assume that all English are Anglican, all Germans Lutheran, all Russians Greek Orthodox, and all Latin Americans and French Catholic, although they do not say so. Sometimes a father, as was true in author Simone de Beauvoir's family, is agnostic, and the mother is a devout Catholic. Children do not always follow the family religion, especially when the father is a minister. Ingmar Bergman, Carl Jung, Laurence Olivier, Norman Thomas, Lord Beaverbrook, Sir Francis Chichester, Dorothy Thompson,

Hermann Hesse, and Malcolm X were all sons of Protestant ministers, and all deviated from their fathers' faith.

The count of all families in the Three Hundred shows that 45 percent were Protestant, 20 percent Catholic, 14 percent Jewish, 12 percent atheist or agnostic, and 7 percent Moslem, Hindu, or "other," including African religions practiced by a particular tribe. There were no statistically significant differences in economic status or in the number of failure-prone fathers in families of the various religions.

The fluctuation in family fortunes would not seem so important if it were restricted to fathers of the twentieth century. Like a Cinderella theme, it is common in biographies of historical figures from centuries back. By the very nature of things, more fathers fail than become well-to-do. However, it is the ebullient, experimental quality of the failure that is memorable. Charles Dickens' father was Micawber incarnate. Thomas Edison's father, a failed revolutionary, ran thirty miles to reach the American border and find sanctuary. Tolstoy's father, a fop and a gambler, married a rich wife who refused to pay his gambling debts. Abraham Lincoln's father was a genial rolling stone who always hoped to better himself. Albert Einstein's father, who was the poor relation in his family, had to leave Germany and go to Italy to find work because relatives had grown tired of helping him.

William Shakespeare's father, John, had a dramatic failure that reduced him from an ermine-clad bailiff of Stratford who led civic processions to a defeated failure who dared not go to church or attend meetings of the town council, of which he was a member, because he might be imprisoned for debt. William's wealthy son-in-law, Dr. John Hall, and William's favorite daughter are buried beside him, as is his wife. But his father, John, and his other daughter, who married a ne'er-do-well tavern keeper, are buried elsewhere. The impressive home of Dr. John Hall is one of the tourist sights of Stratford-on-Avon, as is the impressive birthplace of William Shakespeare, built during his father's affluent period.

The house where John Shakespeare was born, on a side street in nearby Snitterfield, is still intact—a clean-lined, two-story, stone building with cobwebbed windows. It was privately owned by a retired schoolteacher in the early 1970s. There is no marker to designate that this is the birthplace of the father of William Shakespeare, the world's most talented poet and playwright. Although any villager can tell a curious visitor where this father who failed so spectacularly was born, no tourists come to see it. The descendants of the Ardens (Shakespeare's mother was an Arden) are still more highly respected in the larger community than are the descendants of the Shakespeares. Branches of both families have descendants, although the direct Shakespeare line has died out. (None have achieved as literary figures.) Memories are long in rural areas. John Shakespeare has not yet lived down his catastrophic failure.

❦ 4 ❦

Famous Fathers

> *Children begin by loving their parents. After a*
> *time they judge them. Rarely, if ever, do they*
> *forgive them.*
>
> Oscar Wilde

If having a creative father who fails to give adequate financial support to his offspring contributes to eminence and the likelihood of becoming the subject of biography, then the opposite should be true for the offspring of famous parents. Some who felt it was a handicap to be overshadowed by a famous parent or parents, but who overcame it, are Michael Chaplin and Charles Chaplin, Jr., Jane and Peter Fonda, Ring Lardner, Jr., Jan Myrdal, Dag Hammarskjöld, and Svetlana Alliluyeva. Robert and Edward Kennedy are silent about how they felt about being the sons of Joseph Kennedy. Women who took well to having had famous fathers are Mary de Rachewiltz, daughter of Ezra Pound; Evangeline Booth, daughter of William Booth; and Indira Gandhi, daughter of Jawaharlal Nehru. Like the well-known daughters of Marie Curie, Tolstoy, Alfred Adler, and Freud, they also extended the parental career.

Robert and Edward Kennedy are among those present in biographical material written about their grandfathers, their father, and their mother, two of their brothers, a sister-in-law, and a brother-in-law. Jan Myrdal shares his listing in *International Who's Who* with his mother and father. Alva Myrdal is the most prestigious mother in the survey sample. Famous people are not ordinarily expected to have famous sons and daughters. Yet there are eighteen such among the Three Hundred, and four of these families have two or more offspring who also have biographies. Take a random group of 300 persons. If asked to name any relative, past or present, who ever has been the subject of biography, they would be most unlikely to produce even one such name. Contrary to myth, eminence in the family does encourage eminence. Such eminence, however, comes hard and is not without trauma and bitterness. A number of the second generation of the eminent in this sample are not nearly as productive, as yet, as were their ancestors, and may never be. A few are more so. What is useful is their descriptions of the interactions between themselves and their parents in homes complicated by the pressures of parental success and affluence. People in artistic families, for example, live well together, as in Kipling's paradise, "each on his separate star, drawing the thing as he sees it, for the God of things as they are." For instance, members of the Wyeth, Calder, and Renoir families enhance each other's productivity. In the other homes, however, being overshadowed by a father is intolerable or emasculating to the sons.

In this chapter we shall examine how these families differ from those in which the father fails to provide. We shall also present, in the conclusion, a statistical evaluation of career choices of the parents and of their economic status. We will now describe parents who are among the most influential men and women of our times and see what they and their offspring have contributed.

Michael Chaplin and Charlie Chaplin

I Couldn't Smoke the Grass on My Father's Lawn by Michael Chaplin, published in 1966, documents the turbulent sixties and the rebellions of a nineteen-year-old rebel born in 1946 in Beverly Hills. It also documents the oppositional tendencies that having a much-publicized father can arouse in an offspring, for

Michael says that when his father told stories around the swimming pool Michael could have fallen in and drowned and no one would have noticed. Many of Michael's younger days were spent having to keep out of the way of the photographers and newspaper reporters who followed his father wherever he surfaced.

Most of his classmates at school thought living with Charlie Chaplin would be one long circus. Michael found *The Gold Rush* very sad for he did not like seeing his father being kicked around and being "conned out of his mind." He also found his father "quite a handful," a complex and frightening man: "kindly, volatile, moody, gay, self-absorbed, inventive, funny, affectionate, stern, sad, brilliant, autocratic, irrational, snobbish, splendid, silly, unjust, loving, perceptive, indifferent, sensitive, cruel, jolly, extension-in-reverse of my own flesh and thought and feelings" (p. 2).

His mother, the former Oona O'Neill, had a relatively simple personality. Married in her late teens, she wanted to have ten children. She enjoyed being mistress of a large establishment and entertaining guests but was supersensitive about her children and hated conflict. When he wrote his autobiography at nineteen, Michael had deep resentments toward his parents. Although his father had in one survey been named the most widely known person in the world, his parents refused to be financially responsible for Michael and his wife, Patrice, after Michael's runaway marriage at age eighteen. After Michael had written his autobiography and turned it over to the publisher, he repented some of the harsh things he had said in it about his father, and took legal action to prevent publication. Although he lost the suit, his publishers permitted him to modify some of his statements.

Michael says the whole world knows how it was with his father, and we do: put in an orphanage, earning his own living at age five, knowing what it was to be cold and hungry. "But," Michael asks, "does that entitle him to give *me* a hard time because I have found it difficult to adjust to the kind of posh education he decided was best for me?" (p. 3).

Indeed, Michael had altogether too much too soon. In Beverly Hills his life was one birthday party after another, with chauffeurs and nannies dragging bored children from one great

Hollywood house to another, each small fry bringing huge packages to prove his or her family was more important than any other. Few children enjoyed such comforts, entertainments, and luxuries.

Later, as an adolescent living away from his parents' home, he reduced his needs to a roof, a mattress, blankets, a few cans of soup, a crust of bread, and some raw carrots. All he wanted was books, music, a place to sleep, some marijuana and LSD, and people to talk to who shared his interests.

He disappointed his parents by being an indifferent student, but they tried to please him. One of Michael's persistent irritations was the closeness of his father and mother, which shut him out; they did not seem to need words, he said, but communicated to each other by "telepathy." He felt that his parents were more important to each other than he was. Still, he complains only of lack of understanding and perceptiveness, not lack of love. Indeed, he had two mothers—Oona, his biological mother, and a servant, "Kay-Kay," to whom he was also devoted. He had no horror stories to tell of sadistic or rejecting servants, although a chauffeur, Mario, encouraged him in some of his delinquencies. In fact, he preferred his home to school so much that he would pretend to be ill in order to be permitted to stay home.

When he was fifteen, his parents took him and his older sister Geraldine on an around-the-world trip. Michael found it a bore. One luxurious hotel was like every other luxurious hotel. Wherever they went there were official receptions for Charlie Chaplin, and he was surrounded by cameramen and reporters. His mother sneaked the children through side entrances to avoid their being trampled by their father's fans. Still, what little he saw of native populations fascinated Michael. Even close by the hotels he saw people living in "primitive hell" and would loved to have talked with them and gotten to know them. He resented being fed strawberries flown in from Portugal when he saw people begging. He wanted to get closer to the sweat, smells, hungers, and real necessities of life.

During this period Michael's one other interest was in animals, particularly bats and rats. Michael's parents were so disturbed by his obvious lack of interest in his holiday that his father planned as a diversion a trip to a bat cave. When they arrived at the cave, Michael was in ecstasy. He loved the smell of the decayed bat excrement that had piled up for centuries, and father and son stood ankle deep in the slime and slush while overhead bats urinated on them. Charlie was nauseous but stuck it out until Michael was ready to leave, delighted that at last Michael had found a special interest.

All in all, this book is a perceptive documentation by Michael of the generation gap that affected thousands of other families during this period. Neither the author nor the parents emerge as villains.

Michael's two older half-brothers grew up in different circumstances and felt less antagonistic toward their father than he did at nineteen. Charlie Chaplin, Jr., and Sidney Chaplin were children by Chaplin's second wife, actress Lita Grey. From the beginning the marriage between the sixteen-year-old girl, who had not yet finished high school, and the thirty-five-year-old moody, sophisticated star was a nightmare. Their divorce, with its complaints and countercomplaints, competed with the Lindbergh trans-Atlantic flight for the headlines. In the settlement, Charlie established a $200,000 trust fund for his infant sons, and they did not see him again until after they were three or four and then only infrequently.

Sidney was the outgoing, emotionally healthy boy. Charlie Chaplin, Jr., was, as he described himself in *My Father, Charlie Chaplin* (1960), a gentle, docile boy who had nightmares and broke out in hives when he went to the ocean; he was never able to initiate a new venture and always felt insecure and dubious about the future.

Both older sons became actors and, had they not been in competition with Charlie, might have been reasonably satisfied with their not inconsiderable achievements. Charles, Jr., for instance, played in the Circle Theatre group in Hollywood, and in New York he played with Fredric March in *Now I Lay Me Down to Sleep.* Although Sidney enjoyed being an actor, when asked his profession he always called himself a businessman so he would not be compared with his father, and in fact he was successful in his business ventures.

Michael says his father and Sidney got along well together, and they would talk happily for hours when the latter came by to visit, but Charles Chaplin, Jr., was too timid to drop in on his father casually and always called ahead to make sure he was welcome.

Besides his insecurities he had other troubles. He became a periodic
drinker, which hindered his career. During the McCarthy period,
he was often blacklisted for supposedly having been a Communist
like his father, though in fact neither was. Charlie went abroad to
live, but Charles, Jr., stayed in the United States and took the brunt
of animosity intended for his father. He was quite willing not to try
to compete with his father, but other people would not permit him
to. Once, after cooling his heels in a New York producer's waiting
room for half an hour, he was admitted to the inner office where he
found the producer sitting with a newspaper up in front of his face.
After a long time the producer asked from behind his paper, "Are
you as great as he is?" As Charles, Jr., wrote later (p. 336), "What
kind of answer could you give to a question like that? I just turned
and walked out without a word. I heard him calling after me, but I
didn't once look back."

Jan Myrdal and Gunnar Myrdal

Like Michael Chaplin, Jan Myrdal developed oppositional
tendencies very early. However, these were not from a negative reaction to a famous father's constant publicity but from the frustrations of having to submit to school regulations he found intolerable,
partly because both his parents, during his school days, were busy
with their own demanding careers. All three Myrdals—Jan; his
mother, Alva; and his father, Gunnar—have had considerable influence on contemporary society, and all are concerned, in their own
way, with the human condition, the social order, and politics.

Jan, born in Stockholm in 1927, is a novelist, dramatist,
screenwriter, and author of nonfiction about Afghanistan, Soviet
Central Asia, and China. He is best known in the United States for
his volume *Report from a Chinese Village,* but his most recent
volume is *Albania Defiant.* As a Sunday columnist he writes about
current history and culture. He is also a Marxist.

His mother, Alva, is a sociologist, writer, politician (Social
Democrat), diplomat, and professor whose publications are about
as numerous as those of her husband and son. Her most recent book
is a study of disarmament. As a Swedish cabinet member and diplomat, she has interests in peace, cooperatives, the role of women, edu-

cation, and the handicapped. Among other things she has been secretary of the Swedish Commission on Women's Work (1935–38), principal director of the United Nations Department of Social Affairs (1949–50), director of the Department of Social Sciences (1951–55), and minister to India, Burma, and Ceylon (1955–56)' and is presently in the Swedish Foreign Office.

Gunnar is a famous economist who is well known internationally for his classic study, *The American Dilemma*, about black-white relationships in the United States, as well as for many other publications. As a Social Democrat, he too has been influential in Swedish politics, has served in the Ministry of Foreign Affairs, and was Secretary to the United Nations Economic Commission for Europe (1947–1957).

There is only one other family among the Three Hundred in which a father, mother, and (in this case) two sons are, like the Myrdals, listed in *International Who's Who:* Lady Sackville-West, novelist; Harold Nicolson, diplomat; and their two sons, Lionel and Nigel, both authors and publishers. There was one such family also among the Four Hundred: Marie Curie, her husband, her son, two daughters, and a son-in-law, all of whom are or were eminent and can be found in various standard reference works.

Jan Myrdal was a school rebel, but though he may have deep resentments toward his parents, he does not express them in his *Confessions of a Disloyal European* (1968). (He also has not one but two autobiographies in Swedish, which we cannot read.) Michael Chaplin said the more money parents spent sending their children to expensive secondary schools in Switzerland, the more they were cheated, and Jan's secondary-school experience in Sweden and the United States seems to bear this out.

Until ten his life was pleasant. He lived with his parents and played with neighborhood boys, watching older bullies forcing younger children to fight each other—a spectacle that prejudiced him forever against physical violence. He circulated more or less unnoticed among his parents' talkative guests and made cynical judgments about some of the politicians that they never dreamed he was capable of making. He loathed organized sports, but he was an omnivorous reader, and at ten his favorite book was Strindberg's *Inferno*. In particular, he liked Strindberg's description of the sen-

sation of walking between two persons speaking to each other as
being like a thread being snapped. Jan was observant and perceptive
and had an early ability to deal with abstract concepts.

At twelve, however, he was sent to Lincoln High School of
Columbia University in New York City, where he was very unhappy. Although the administration was proudly progressive and
devoted to developing the well-rounded personality and actualizing
the unique potential of each student, Jan was not considered an
"all-around boy," and so he was sent to a psychologist. This gentle,
kindly person told him that she wanted to see him grow freely like
roses grow, by which she meant that the overweight Jan should play
more outdoors and not spend so much time in the library. After all,
tests indicated he was not "group-minded" and thus must be suffering from some deep, unhappy disturbance.

Jan nonplussed the psychologist by reminding her that the
principal and teachers all said that the students were free to be
different, that the playground was a gloomy corner lot, and that he
didn't want to go there to play baseball. However, he did enjoy the
exceptionally well-stocked library, he said, and he could be group-
minded, if she liked, about organizing other students who preferred
the library to baseball, but he saw no reason to play baseball when
he was not group-minded about that. "For two years," he writes,
"teachers and psychologists with understanding and tenderness
fought to drive me out of the library. I emerged victorious because
I was stubborn. But it was very unpleasant. . . . After all, I was
but twelve years old, and they were a collective of tender and group-
minded grownups" (p. 39).

When World War II began, Jan and his sisters were sent
back to Sweden to live with his paternal grandparents. The Myrdal
children had not been baptized in the traditional Lutheran faith
because their parents wanted them to make their own decisions
about a religious preference when they were mature; however, this
perturbed many of his relatives. Thus, the two sisters, ages five and
seven, were forced to be baptized. They resisted and had to be held
down; fourteen-year-old Jan was furious.

Jan was no happier in the Bromma Secondary School in
Sweden than he had been in the United States. He was expelled
from gym class before he even had time to enroll because he walked

on the polished gym floor wearing hobnailed boots. But no one tried to keep him from going to the library, and no one tried to tinker with his personality and its development. Still, at one point he blundered, as gifted students often do, when he tried to convince an intolerant, elderly teacher that the whole Euclidian geometry was false. After lecturing to the teacher and his snickering classmates about Möbius, Jan was ordered expelled from class.

While riding his bicycle after this humiliating event, he fell and was so severely injured that he had to have a minor operation on his knee, which, happily, for awhile prevented his going to school. During his recovery he went to the school and to the hospital on alternate days, but when he improved to the point where his doctor said he needed to see him only once a week, Jan deliberately neglected to tell his grandparents or teachers about the change and so gained two free days a week of uninterrupted reading at the public library. For a time, when it seemed his knee might recover entirely, he exercised it violently so he would still have an excuse not to go to school. His surgeon, puzzled over the slow recovery, performed a second operation. By this time Jan had become so practiced in deceit and so rejecting of the classroom that he managed never to have to go to school again, and from then on he was self-educated.

At seventeen he lost his virginity and, like other young men, thought he had invented sex. At eighteen he was working as a cub reporter earning a minimal wage and eating only one full meal a day, but he had four girl friends.

Jan celebrated his new sexual way of life with what a Swedish literary friend called "the talent of a new Rimbaud" by writing a slim volume of poems. It was inevitable that he should think of publication since he came from a family in which publishing was a routine performance. Naïvely, he thought a publisher would judge his poetry entirely on its merits, but all the major publishers in Sweden knew his parents and, like them, were people of moderately radical traditions, serious about civil liberties, censorship, and freedom of speech but not about free love. The first publisher answered him with a long, avuncular, friendly letter praising the intensity and passion of the writing but refusing to publish it. He pointed out that since Jan's father was then a member of a government coming up for reelection, enemies would use his son's divergent views on sexual

freedom to ruin his father and his party. The publisher advised Jan
to obtain his father's permission before he submitted it to another
publisher.

For ten years Jan papered his room with rejection slips as
word passed from publisher to publisher to beware of any offering
from young Jan Myrdal. Even when his father went to Geneva to
work for the United Nations, the taboo prevailed, but his parents
took no part in this ostracism, not being in Sweden most of the time.
For a long time Jan did not understand why his manuscripts were
always politely and evasively returned, but later, when he was well
established as a writer, a publisher told him in a friendly fashion
that he never had read his manuscripts because he had been told
that "Jan Myrdal was impossible." During this time the same publishers were very critical of the lack of freedom of the press, a
disparity that made Jan cynical.

When he finally became noticed, there were apologies, but
he was never placated. Toward the end of *Confessions of a Disloyal
European* he writes, "But of course I have forgotten and forgiven
nothing. I would rather fry in hell than stretch out my little finger to
help any of those men and women who for ten years stopped even
the possibility of my publishing an article under my own name.
. . . I have wished them dead since 1945 and I do still" (pp. 184–
185)'.

Mary de Rachewiltz and Ezra Pound

Daughters, more often than sons, emulate and admire their
prestigious fathers. It is Anna Freud—not Freud's sons, whom the
father forbade to be physicians—who shares her father's fame. The
daughters of Tolstoy and Adler were competent and well-known
disciples of their fathers. One of Alan Watts's daughters became interested in his ideas; the same is true of one of Jung's daughters.
Daughters find it much easier to accept eminence in an immediate
ancestor.

Mary Rudge de Rachewiltz is the illegitimate but adoring
daughter of American expatriate poet Ezra Pound, and like him is
a poet and writer of considerable consequence, writing in both
Italian and English. In her autobiography, *Discretions,* she is not

critical of him, even though he farmed her out to a poor, unedu-
cated, peasant family during her early childhood. Famous parents
seldom have any needs their offspring can fulfill, but Mary was a
notable exception, for when she was older she translated his poems
into Italian, twice gave him room and hospitality when he was ill,
and nursed his aged mother during her terminal illness. She gave
more than she took. At the time when she had two small children
and she and her husband, Boris de Rachewiltz, were attempting the
difficult task of turning an abandoned castle into a home for paying
guests, she still visited her hospitalized father in the United States
and nursed his invalid mother. Her rapport with her father was
always good, even during the brief periods when they were together
during her childhood.

Mary was born in 1925 in Bressanone, a town north of
Bolzano in the Italian Tyrol, the daughter of Pound and his mistress,
Olga Rudge, another American expatriate and a concert violinist.
Olga had a successful career and had no intention of giving it up,
and Pound was married. Thus, when at the hospital Olga met a
peasant woman who lived on a farm near the village of Gais, Ezra
and Olga asked her if she would rear their daughter in return for
payment for her keep. Since Klöcka Sâma and her husband, Joggl,
loved children and already had one foster child at home, they consented to care for Mary.

The Sâmas reared seventeen children, nine of them abandoned, the others—like Mary—children whose relatives for some
reason did not want to take care of them. After Mussolini came to
power, the keep for some of the children was paid for by the state,
although the sum was minimal since pious Catholics believed Mussolini fostered sin by this law. Mary's affectionate "big sister" was
the Sâmas' oldest foster child, Margit, left behind by a gypsy who
had asked Klöcka to mind the baby for an hour. Klöcka herself had
lost her own parents when she was fourteen and cared for her seven
younger brothers. Joggl Sâma, crippled in the hand during World
War I, was a kindly man who never minded when Mary asked to be
carried on his back.

Under the Sâmas' care, Mary was happy at home and at
school, where she excelled. By contrast, Omar Pound, Ezra's son by
his wife Dorothy and reared by his wealthy grandmother, was "in

purgatory" at his English boarding school. Neither child at that time knew of the other's existence.

Dorothy, who was quite aware of Olga's existence, and Ezra Pound lived in a cottage near the beach in Rapallo. Olga Rudge, when she was not traveling, lived nearby at Sant'Ambrogio, although she also had a house in Venice. For two weeks each summer, when Dorothy went to England to see Omar, Olga and Ezra would spend the same period entertaining Mary Rudge. During one early visit, however, Mary was so homesick for the Sâmas that she did not stay the entire time.

When Ezra's father, Homer, retired from his civil service post in Hailey, Idaho, he and his wife came to live near their son in Rapallo and began visiting Mary in Gais, which pleased the Sâmas, who were always uneasy about Mary's relationship with the strange gentleman and lady, her parents. After meeting her grandparents, particularly Homer, who had once lived on a farm and related to them easily, they felt comfortable about Mary.

Although Homer had advised Ezra that she be left on the farm, because she was so happily immersed in the life of the village, Mary was sent to a convent boarding school for her secondary-school training. There she was miserable and disobedient. When her father sent her copies of articles he had written, the nuns forbade her to read them because of the bad words they found in them. When told they were written by her father, the nuns replied that was impossible—the writer's name was Pound, hers was Rudge. Mary then told them Pound was not his real name, only a *nom de plume,* but they still punished her by segregating her in a small room for three days. She still continued to defend everything her father wrote and insisted on reading his letters and articles, and eventually they stopped trying to change her.

When she left the convent and stayed with her mother at her house in Venice, Olga asked her daughter to pretend to be her cousin, since if the press found out she was Pound's illegitimate child his reputation would be ruined. There was frightening talk of Pound's having to go back to the United States. Mary was very confused about her identity and her father's pro-Fascist, anti-Semitic activities. They moved back to Olga's house in Sant' Ambrogio, where they lived in almost complete isolation. Ezra rarely visited; he was in Rome broadcasting pro-Fascist statements. He told Mary he was exercising his rights as an American citizen to protest the policies of the President who, by promising American mothers that their sons would not be sacrificed yet actively preparing for war, was exceeding his rights and endangering the Constitution. Having been brought up in Gais as a loyal Italian, Mary was unable to evaluate what her father was doing.

When the Italian army cleared the beach where the Pounds lived, Dorothy and Ezra moved into Olga's home in Sant'Ambrogio, and at that point Mary learned that her father had a wife and a legitimate son, Omar. Pound and the two mothers of his children lived in Olga's house for over a year. Olga gave music lessons to defray Ezra and Dorothy's expenses. Neither Olga nor Dorothy was home when the Allied authorities came and took Ezra away for having been an outspoken traitor to his country. Mary had been sent to Gais and later worked as a secretary in a convalescent home for wounded German soldiers, who accepted her as simply a Tyrolian country girl. Still later, when the Americans took over the hospital, she returned to the Sâmas' house and found it full of polite American Hawaiians, who were delighted when she spoke American with them.

After the war, despite her affection for her father, Mary decided she wanted to be free of the emotional tensions she felt when she was with her parents. In *Discretions* she writes: "I was eager to start out on a life of my own, free, with clear and high ideals and, to be sure, an overdose of pride. I thought I was rejecting all of the lies and pretensions and compromises, Mamile's [mother's] dark resentment, grandmother's stubbornness, Dorothy and Omar, whatever and whoever they were. I was leaving everything behind. All I wanted to keep was something to believe in— the freedom to live the kind of life I thought Babbo [father] had meant for me to live—simple and laborious" (p. 266).

The Rockefellers

In homes where the father is a poor provider because he has financial problems or fails his family because of absence, illness, or personality problems, the sons and daughters have to learn early

to be self-reliant and helpful to each other, and this early responsibility leads to early maturity. However, in homes where the father
is famous and is often well-to-do, the sons and daughters are not
needed except to enhance the aura of success in the family and to
prove that the great man also is capable of producing healthy, pre-
sentable offspring. To those admirers who have made this famous
man a personal hero, the very existence of these children is an
affront. In their fantasies they are his children, and he is their own
ideal father. Emotionally, we are able to admire the poor widow's
achieving son, but we are not as enthusiastic about the achievements
of the son of a famous father. Michael Chaplin, for instance, mentions that other boys seemed to like him until they found out who
his father was, then they would be overly critical of him for not
being any better than they. The press also is quick to criticize any
deviation from the norm by the sons and daughters of the famous,
although daughters of the famous are less vulnerable to the pressure
of high expectations and the jealousies of their peers than are sons.
How many talented and creative children of highly achieving parents are thwarted in their development is important to know, since
society is the loser when the capable child is not well used. Still, the
fact that there *are* so many famous sons of famous fathers is a
tribute to the energy and persistence of these sons.

The Rockefellers are popular subjects for study. Nelson
Rockefeller reacted to his family's wealth by rearing his family as if
they were only moderately well-to-do, following the pattern of his
father, John D. Rockefeller, Jr., who required his children to swat
flies, clean shoes, weed gardens, and raise rabbits all for profit. In turn,
his father, John D. Rockefeller, Sr., was provoked by the thought-
less behavior of his father William (Big Bill) Avery Rockefeller, a
charlatan, who did such things as sell fake cancer cures to sufferers
for $25 a bottle. John D., Sr., felt sorry for his mother and deter-
mined early to become rich so he could reward her for her long years
of trying to bring up a family on insufficient means. During Big Bill's
long absences from home, his wife and children were shabbily
dressed and ill-fed, and when he was home he would cheat his sons
to teach them how to be clever about handling money. John D., Sr.,
learned responsibility early when his father sent him to bargain for
firewood at the tender age of ten and entrusted him with the task of

seeing that a house was built for the family when he was not much older.

The twenty-one great-great-grandchildren of Big Bill have different values. Seventeen of these fourth-generation Rockefellers, who are commonly known as the "Cousins" and who are between twenty and forty years old, were interviewed in depth by Peter Collier and David Horowitz for their 1976 book, *The Rockefellers: An American Dynasty*. When, for instance, some of the Cousins have sought psychotherapy for personal problems, the third generation, commonly known as the "Brothers," has not understood it; to the Brothers, therapy is "copping out." Nor is this all. As Collier and Horowitz state: "If the Brothers didn't understand how their children felt oppressed by the Rockefeller identity and all it portended, they also failed to calculate the extent to which the Cousins were children of their own time, an era of protest over imperial war, racial inequality, and social injustice. The generation they identified with was challenging exactly those powers and assumptions on which the family tradition was based" (p. 537).

As children the Cousins never felt really at home in the fine mansions in which they lived but in which the servants made the rules. For instance, over the protests of the gardeners on the family estate at Pocantico Hills, they would build shacks out of old orange crates. They could not ask for sympathy from anyone because they already had all the things that were *supposed* to make them happy. They dreaded having to tell their names since that was how they lost friends and became curiosities. At school and at summer camp, they were always on stage, were asked for autographs, and watched to see if they showed signs of selfishness or pride or artificiality. Acquaintances who invited them home with them kept apologizing for their chinaware or for some other fancied lack of luxuries.

The females, who represent two thirds of the Cousins, were the first to revolt against being simply philanthropists dispensing money. Fewer than a half dozen accept fully the pleasures of being merely the idle rich. Among the rest, one became a Marxist and radical feminist, another a psychiatrist, and another a psychologist. Still another lives with her student husband on an income of $700 a month and believes, like Thoreau, that a person is measured by the things he or she can do without. All complain about the social isolation of being from a rich, powerful, and famous family, with whose history they are not eager to be identified, and they have sought various ways to lose their identities, some marrying young and divorcing young, acquiring new names in the process.

As students some Rockefellers did social work in faraway places; one worked on London's East Side, another did research on the health problems of Navajo Indians, and another lived and worked in a Brazilian *favela* (urban slum). Michael went to New Guinea and presumably was killed there by cannibals. Jay Rockefeller, the most successful in creating a public image that identifies him as being a unique individual, left Harvard and spent three years living with a middle-class family in Japan.

Comments and Conclusions

Most of the Three Hundred come from the middle classes, and most of their fathers are or were businessmen or professional men, not as rich as the Chaplins or Rockefellers nor as poor as the father of Malcolm X.

The failed and famous fathers produced a great many of the most innovative and dynamic personalities among the Three Hundred. The challenges they presented were motivating. An almost equal number of fathers were competent but not outstanding professional and business men. Each father was only one individual in a nuclear family. Mothers, including those who could not cope, those who were dominating, and those who were rejecting, also played their definitive roles.

Before we begin segregating the achieving offspring into smaller categories based on their ordinal position, delinquency, mental illnesses, occupational choice, sexual preference, and so forth, it seems appropriate to take a global look at all the 317 families, at the occupation of both fathers and mothers, and the relationship of the achieving child in the family to both father and mother.

The distribution of occupations of the fathers shows the largest group to be proprietors of small, medium, or large businesses (17.5 percent). The next largest category is that of unskilled, semiskilled, or skilled workmen (14 percent). These are followed by government officials and politicians (11 percent), little and big farmers (10 percent), and clergymen (8 percent). No other occupation accounts for as many as 5 percent of the fathers. Among the fathers of the Three Hundred there are fourteen teachers, thirteen professors, and fifteen scientists. Other professionals among the fathers include thirteen lawyers, twelve military men, nine actors and performers, seven writers and publishers, six physicians, five salesmen, three artists, and three photographers.

In contrast to the fathers, the great majority of the mothers (71 percent) had no occupation outside the home. Many of those who had occupations in addition to being housewives and mothers held their positions prior to becoming mothers. Overall, there were eighteen unskilled workers, six actors and performers, and five clerical workers among them. There were a scattering of other occupations with one or two mothers in each. The most eminent mother is Alva Myrdal.

Yet the mothers of the Three Hundred were more likely to have careers of their own than are the mothers of the Four Hundred. They were also less concerned about the careers of their children, more likely to desert the family or to obtain a divorce, and were not self-sacrificing in the manner of the mothers of the Four Hundred. The mothers looked on most favorably by their offspring were those who were noncritical, good cooks, pleasant, and noninterfering. Children were more often exasperated than angry with their mothers, and the most severe conflicts were between fathers and sons and were usually provoked by the choice of a son's career.

There is no apparent desire on the part of biographers or autobiographers to enhance their subject's status by presenting an idyllic picture of the parents. Sometimes it seems as though even the opposite is true, as when a professional writer gets carried away while describing the interesting agonies of his youth. However, we have simply recorded what was said, noting the adjectives and direct quotations. The categories described here were not chosen a priori. They were derived from observations made and recorded after almost all of the reading of the biographical material upon which this book is based was completed.

The upbringing of the Three Hundred varied widely as to stability and as to the attitude of the father toward his children. In some homes there was no father. Approximately half of both fathers and mothers were perceived as being generally supportive (fathers 48 percent; mothers 52 percent). Other parents were perceived as being inadequate (fathers 18 percent; mothers 19 percent), rejecting (fathers 17.5 percent; mothers 12 percent), dominating (fathers 9 percent; mothers 7 percent), or smothering (fathers 1 percent; mothers 6 percent). The remaining 6 percent of the fathers and 4 percent of the mothers were classified as being inconsistent in their attitude toward their offspring.

The supportive mothers and fathers were those who encouraged their children to do what they wanted to do and helped them financially, often at some sacrifice. They were helpful but not interfering. They used good judgment and tact when the child experienced a crisis. Some of the subjects had only one supportive parent, but among those who had two supportive parents who lived to see their offspring grown and successful were Fred Astaire, Charles Aznavour, Niels Bohr, E. E. Cummings, Bernadette Devlin, John Foster Dulles, Otto Hahn, Hubert Humphrey, Julian Huxley, Lyndon Johnson, Frédéric Joliot-Curie, Estes Kefauver, Robert and Edward Kennedy, Ernest O. Lawrence, Louis Leakey, Francis Meynell, Edmund Muskie, Ralph Nader, Alan Watts, and Jessamyn West.

The inadequate parents were not demeaning or cruel and had sporadic impulses to be helpful, but they could not be counted on in a crisis and might not even have been around to do so. Children of British civil servants working abroad—like writers P. G. Wodehouse, C. S. Forester, and Rudyard Kipling—often have this kind of inadequate parenting. Perhaps the most inadequate of the inadequates were the parents of the humorist P. G. (for Pelham Grenville) Wodehouse, who took the fact of his parents' long absences nonchalantly and without criticism. The youngest of three boys, all of whom were born in China, the sons of a British civil servant, P. G. was taken to England at age two and left in the care of a stern and rigid spinster until he was old enough to enter boarding school. Every six or seven years the parents came to visit their sons, and during school holidays the boys stayed with various wealthy English relatives who did not much want them and relegated them to the servants' quarters. Consequently, P. G. was eventually to become famous as the author of Jeeves, the quintessential butler.

Parents were categorized as "rejecting" only when they were described as being blatantly and persistently so—when, for instance, they deserted the family, disliked the children intensely, or were given to ridicule or the use of physical violence and verbal abuse. The strongest expressions of rejection by both parents were found in the cases of Lord William Beaverbrook, Sir Francis Chichester, Henry Miller, Viscount Alfred Northcliffe, and Ethel Waters.

We found far fewer dominating mothers among the Three Hundred than among the Four Hundred. The capable, strong, persevering mother who might have done well as a career woman seems to be vanishing from biography. There is no mother among the Three Hundred who can match the dominating mothers of Pablo Casals, Mackenzie King, Yehudi Menuhin, Franklin D. Roosevelt, Frank Lloyd Wright, or of General Douglas MacArthur, whose mother roomed nearby her cherished youngest at West Point and complained so vigorously to Congress about other students hazing first-year men (among them her son, of course) that the practice was stopped. There are now not only greater opportunities for women to have careers of their own, but it is also less acceptable for mothers to become directly involved in their sons' careers.

There also are fewer smothering mothers—the kind who adore their sons to the exclusion of all other persons in their lives—among the Three Hundred than among the Four Hundred. However, Moshe Dayan, one of only two military leaders among the Three Hundred, is an excellent example of the mother-smothered son who grows up to enjoy the excitement of battle and to feel invulnerable when the bullets fly close to him or even to his children. Ché Guevara's mother was another overprotective, overpossessive woman who doted on her oldest and asthmatic son so extravagantly that his three younger siblings used to gang up on him and beat him soundly. Zelda Fitzgerald is an example of a mother-smothered daughter.

The inconsistent mothers, who numbered only 5 percent, were those who blew hot and cold, who were sometimes sympathetic, sometimes rejecting. Some were excellent mothers to their babies, but could not tolerate them as adolescents. These mothers often withdrew their affection when they were displeased. Divorce and family quarrels between the father and mother often created tensions that made the parents inconsistent in their behavior toward their offspring. In the parental homes of the Three Hundred, more than 8 percent were broken by divorce or separation. The divorce statistics suggest the coming of new life styles, since only 2 percent of the parents of the Four Hundred were divorced or separated (and all were the parents of actors, performers, or writers). Many couples in both samples quarreled hotly and continuously but were neither divorced nor separated.

✵5✵

Birth Order

I grew up telling people [eight brothers and sisters, all younger] what to do and spanking them, so that in some way I will always be doing that.

James Baldwin

Of the 306 subjects for whom birth order could be determined, 51 were only children, 92 were first children, 81 were middle children, and 82 were youngest children. However, 44 percent of the literary persons and only 7 percent of the political persons were only children, while 39 percent of the political figures and only 17 percent of the literary figures were middle children. The firstborn are found almost equally in the literary, political, artistic, and "other" areas of eminence. The youngest are somewhat more likely to become artists.

The Firstborn

The ninety-two firstborn for the most part are people with confidence and charisma. They have presence. We recognize them and remember them. Their art is distinctive and original, their

85

political beliefs strongly stated, they expect attention and get it. They often go through long periods of being frustrated or disliked and still maintain their faith in their own destiny. When they are on our side, we revere them; when they are not, we fear them. Among the Four Hundred firstborn were Clarence Darrow, Albert Einstein, Sigmund Freud, William James, Yehudi Menuhin, Benito Mussolini, Friedrich Nietzsche, John D. Rockefeller, Eleanor Roosevelt, and Harry Truman. Among the firstborn of the Three Hundred are James Baldwin, Simone de Beauvoir, Beniamino Bufano, Alexander Calder, Shirley Chisholm, Angela Davis, Ché Guevara, Lyndon Johnson, Carl Jung, Henry Kissinger, Henry Luce, Margaret Mead, Drew Pearson, Edson Pelé, Babe Ruth, David Sarnoff, Haile Selassie, Norman Thomas, George Wallace, and Andrew Wyeth.

The firstborn have the advantage of seldom being rejected or neglected. They gain authority by the early exercise of power over their siblings. They feel needed and accept what seem at times to be inappropriate responsibilities.

Their greatest single advantage may be in their close association with their parents during the early years. We have only begun to be aware of the importance of the first two or three years in the development of learning skills. New parents are eager to get responses from the firstborn. Subsequent children rarely experience as much attention.

Although there are a few who play the role of the eldest who are not actually firstborn—that is, firstborn sons who have an older sister—they are not included in our statistical count. We have seen that phenomenon in the family in which Abba Eban was reared. What happens to a boy who follows a girl depends very much on how much weight the family places on maleness. Margaret Mead had the full advantage of being the firstborn in her family. Eugene McCarthy, Estes Kefauver, and George McGovern, however, had older sisters whom they overshadowed.

Others of the high achievers become firstborn belatedly through the death of an older child. Harold Ellis Jones, a child psychologist at the University of California, Berkeley, cautions against not taking the death of a sibling into consideration when determining the effect of birth order. John Kennedy became the surviving oldest son when his brother Joseph died. Edward Kennedy now bears a tremendous burden as the youngest who has become the only living son. Golda Meir was born after three male siblings died. Spiro Agnew is the firstborn of his father but not of his mother.

When children are widely spaced, or where there are only two children in the family, each child in the family shares some of the advantages of being the firstborn.

Let us now consider four firstborns: Henry Kissinger, Drew Pearson, Margaret Mead, and Nancy Mitford.

Henry Kissinger. The forceful former U.S. Secretary of State was born in 1923 in Fürth, Germany, a Bavarian city long known for its religious and civic harmony. His father, Louis, thirty-six years old at the time of his first son's birth, was a gentle, competent schoolmaster in a high school for well-to-do girls. His wife, who was twenty-two when Henry was born, came from a respectable, middle-class Jewish family, was a practical, efficient woman and a superlative cook, a skill for which the women in her family were noted.

A second son, Walter Bernhard, was only a year younger than Henry. The two boys looked very much alike, rather unattractive but alert and healthy. Both were well behaved and good students.

For their 1974 book, *Kissinger,* Henry's perceptive biographers, Marvin and Bernard Kalb, interviewed a number of the old friends, neighbors, and childhood acquaintances in Fürth. To them Henry was a playful, outgoing child, prone to minor mischief and teasing. He liked girls and was often seen in the center of an admiring group of girls when he was in his early teens. He had a knack for choosing the prettiest.

Their elders were frightened by the rise of Hitler and the Gestapo. When Henry and a friend played in the park after dusk, his playmate's father strapped both to remind them of the risks they were taking. Both Kissinger boys were beaten by members of a Hitler youth group. Aggressive Henry was more vulnerable to attack than was Walter. A time came when they could not go to school and had to stay home in their comfortable but ordinary five-room flat.

It was Kissinger's mother who got the family out of Germany, taking them first to an aunt in London and after a few weeks going on to America. Henry does not like to talk about this period, saying that he scarcely noticed what was going on (although he was fifteen at the time). He says those experiences during his childhood are not the key to anything in his adult life, that nothing he has done as a diplomat is related to his last days in Fürth. This may be the bravado of the firstborn who sees himself as the one who has an impact on others and himself as the master of his emotions and his destiny.

The father found it impossible to use his teaching skills in the United States, where German was becoming increasingly unpopular as a language, and had to accept clerical work that did not make full use of his talents. However, his wife turned her cooking skills to good use and in due course had a small, thriving catering business.

Henry worked as a delivery boy during the day and went to evening high school, planning to become an accountant, and with his good grades he was able to get into tuition-free City College of New York. However, a few weeks before he turned twenty, he was drafted into the U.S. Army.

In the army he became a protégé of Fritz Kraemer, a refugee from Germany employed to brief soldiers on why they were drafted to fight, and he convinced his superiors that Henry was unbelievably gifted. Henry thus became the German-speaking interpreter for the commanding general of the 84th Infantry Division when it was ordered to Europe during the concluding weeks of the war. Later, at the age of only twenty-one, Kissinger was given the responsibility of putting Krefeld, a devastated city of 200,000, in order, and within three days the municipal government was again functioning. He made quick decisions, was fair and firm, showed kindness to women and children, and although he had the power to arrest without question, he was not punitive. However, he forbade the American soldiers to fraternize with the Germans, and made his own presence felt by confiscating a 1938 white Mercedes from a Nazi and by choosing as his living quarters a fine residence in a suburb named for Adolf Hitler. He exuded authority, and even won a medal for the speed with which he rounded up former Nazis. The Kalbs quote him as saying, "I merely put an ad in the local newspaper saying all Germans with police experience who wanted jobs should show up at company headquarters . . . the Gestapo people showed up" (p. 41).

Like his brother, Walter Kissinger also had exceptional managerial skills and executive ability. For instance, according to Charles Ashman, another of Henry's biographers, he efficiently reorganized the management of the coal industry in Korea after the Japanese management had fled, about the same time Henry was in Germany. Walter graduated from Princeton, went on to Harvard Business School (where he was not quite the important man on campus his brother was), then became a troubleshooter for industries in financial straits, and has since become a multimillionaire and head of his own company. When his brother Henry became Secretary of State, he refused further government contracts, lest his brother be accused of favoritism. (Or was it because he did not wish to be in any way associated with his brother?) He seems to be closer to Henry's first wife and to Henry's son and daughter than to his brother. Neither brother talks much about their relationship.

After being discharged from the army, Henry went to Harvard, a freshman at the age of twenty-three. Too driving and suspicious of the motives of others, he was not popular. He hated phrases like "family of man" and the "indivisibility of peace" and was tough, invulnerable, and caustic about "psychological junk." The Kalbs say that a school classmate described him as "an extraordinarily able person who was a prima donna, self-serving, self-centered" (p. 44).

His attitudes were solidified by the time he was ready to submit his undergraduate thesis, in which he stated his views on the role of statesmen. His thesis was that peace could come only from a balance of power and that to attain this balance statesmen had to use cunning and patience to manipulate events and people. As the Kalbs quote him:

They must play the power game in total secrecy, unconstrained by parliaments, which lack the temperament for diplomacy. . . . They must not be afraid to use force, when necessary, to maintain order. They must avoid ironclad rules of conduct; an occasional show of "credible irrationality" may be instructive. They must

not shy away from duplicity, cynicism, or unscrupu-
lousness, all of which are acceptable tools for statecraft.
They must never burn their bridges behind them. And, if
possible, they must always be charming, clever and visible
[p. 47].

This summary of Kissinger's thinking as of 1950 gives us the
feeling for the firstborn in his most aggressive, self-confident stance.
Drew Pearson. Andrew (Drew) Pearson, the late controversial, outspoken journalist and columnist, was born in Evanston,
Illinois, a lusty firstborn who weighed ten pounds at birth and was
sometimes called "The Lion" because of his capacity for roaring
both joyfully and wrathfully.

His father, Paul Pearson, a teacher of speech at Northwestern University, was an impulsive, energetic idealist. His mother,
Edna, whom Paul met when he was an upper-classman at Northwestern and she was a freshman student at Baker College in Kansas,
was an inquisitive, somewhat paranoiac woman who studied people,
questioned their motives, and sought hidden reasons for their behavior. Paul's father was a Methodist farmer turned storekeeper;
Edna's father was a Jewish dentist. Paul was a short, round-faced,
effusive young man; she was a shy, lovely blonde with two long
braids of thick hair. Both were from pioneer families. In fact, her
ancestors had arrived in America in 1730, and one of her remote
ancestors was captured by Indians as a young woman and came
home years later with a half-Indian son.

Twenty-two months after Drew was born his brother Leon
was born, a sickly baby who had whooping cough and nearly died
and who later had meningitis that left him with a crippled arm.
For years after Leon's birth, his mother was a semi-invalid, and so
Drew was very much needed. He was always protective of his invalid brother, nursing him, telling him stories, playing with him.

Facing any change was always hard for Drew's mother, who
when his father wanted to leave Evanston for a better job at
Swarthmore, Pennsylvania, initially resisted, fearing the Quakers
would not accept a Jewish woman. However, she soon felt comfortable in the college's liberal community, and both Pearsons became active members of the Swarthmore Friends Meeting. She

often planned dinners for 200 at Quarterly Meeting and visited newcomers.

When her health improved, she bore two more children, Barbara and Ellen. Drew was the ideal big brother, teaching the little girls their nursery rhymes and caring for them affectionately and willingly. He also continued to be close to Leon, and his frail, neurotic mother relied upon him as if he were adult.

Yet Drew himself was not always an easy boy to rear. He was happy when he was needed and busy, but rambunctious and rowdy when he was bored. At one point he put a skunk behind the radiator at school and was almost expelled. During summer vacations at his paternal grandfather's home in Kansas, he was happy when he could work in the garden, but when he had nothing else to do he skylarked in his grandfather's store, so that at one time a letter had to be written to his father, who advised shutting him up somewhere for a couple of days. One day Drew's father scolded him for not doing his chores, and that evening he did not come home for supper. Neighbors called to help search found him sulking under a tree on the Swarthmore campus. Since he was so able, willing, and reliable when he studied, worked, or took care of his siblings, he did not take criticism well—a familiar attribute of the bright and responsible oldest who feels adult although he is not, and resents authority.

Still, his mother could see no wrong in him. She admired his surefootedness when as a college student he risked his life scaling a tower to ring bells to celebrate an athletic victory. She complimented his driving skill when he exceeded the speed limit in the family car. She fretted, however, about his being away from home too much when his father took on the directing of Chautauqua programs during the summer and needed Drew's help as tent boy and advance manager.

One July morning during one Chautauqua trip, he and another member of the tent crew, a black youth, were bathing after work in seminudity from a spigot near the railroad tracks in Reisville, North Carolina, and were arrested (just as the sun was coming up) for indecent exposure. Drew was only sixteen at the time and the pair were acquitted, but years later, in 1968, Senator Thomas Dodd dragged up the incident on the Senate floor to show that Drew was a liar, devil, monster, and child molester. However, the adverse publicity was short-lived.

Drew went to Phillips Exeter Academy and later to Swarthmore, where he graduated Phi Beta Kappa in 1919. As a college student he was a star swimmer and soccer player, and he won the Pennsylvania state oratorical contest with an essay, "Our Debt to Humanity." However, he always felt he learned more from working with his father. His father often hired prestigious speakers, such as Judge Ben B. Lindsey, who advocated companionate marriage to shocked audiences and Senator Robert M. LaFollette, Sr., another ultraliberal. Drew assumed a variety of responsibilities and was very useful to his father. As his sisters grew older they also helped, and the Pearson family, mother excepted, worked well together.

After college, from 1919 to 1921, Drew joined a Quaker work group sent to help in famine areas of Siberia, Albania, and Montenegro. He received $10 a month in addition to transportation and board, and his ruggedness and physical strength kept him in the program after many others found the primitive conditions unbearable. Although he was one of the youngest members of the unit, he was soon asked to serve as director because of his tremendous drive, physical strength, and his knowledge of farm techniques.

At one point he wrote a long, sentimental letter to his family, a farewell letter that would solace them if he should die in Siberia. His mother, he said, had given him her love, more than he deserved. He told Leon to be worthy of his parents and to be tender with his mother. He recalled how much he enjoyed rocking his little sisters to sleep and told them how wonderful it had been to watch them grow into fine big girls. His father and mother saved and treasured the letter.

Deciding he no longer wanted to work in the Chautauqua circuit, Drew visited a number of newspaper editors in the United States and received several commissions as a free-lance foreign correspondent, his first important assignment being to interview the twelve most important men in Europe. Always thrifty—some people said "niggardly"—he came home a year and a half later with a profit of $714.

During the decades that followed as a muckraking columnist he made many enemies, among them Father Charles E. Coughlin,

General Douglas MacArthur, Huey Long, Jacqueline Onassis, and senators Joseph McCarthy, Theodore Bilbo, and Thomas Dodd. During the Vietnam War he rode presidents Johnson and Nixon particularly hard.

When he died suddenly from a heart attack, he was called a descendant of Lincoln Steffens and Upton Sinclair by the *New York Times* and a muckraker with a Quaker conscience by the *Washington Post*. Senator Wayne Morse called him a "citizen-statesman dedicated to the service of mankind" (Pilat, 1973, p. 311). He was always the aggressive, indomitable firstborn.

Margaret Mead. Firstborn females can be as assertive and dominating as firstborn males, and the famous anthropologist Margaret Mead is a case in point. Born in 1901 in Philadelphia, where her mother-smothered father was professor of economics at the University of Pennsylvania, Margaret was the oldest of four children. In her autobiography, *Blackberry Winter* (1972), Margaret reports her youngest sister, Priscilla, as describing the family relationships as follows: "Dick was Dadda's favorite, Elizabeth was grandmother's favorite, Margaret was everybody's favorite. I was Mother's favorite, but Mother didn't count for much in our house" (p. 29).

Margaret's mother, Emily Fogg, was a writer of articles for an encyclopedia and a Ph.D. candidate in sociology at the University of Chicago when she met and married Alfred Mead. When Margaret was born, her mother read about childrearing with the same avidity she used in her professional writing and was eager to be a perfect mother. Margaret turned out to be quite a handful, however—a beautiful, eager, inquiring child.

When two years later Richard was born, he disappointed Margaret, who had been promised a playmate, because he was sickly and could not talk or play and always stayed indoors while she went out to play. Thus, from earliest childhood Margaret felt superior to him and grew up believing boys could not do what girls did.

Being reared in a home where both her mother and grandmother were professional women also taught Margaret that women had brains. Her grandmother, who lived with them, had been widowed when her only son, Alfred, was eight. When her husband, a school superintendent, died she became a school principal. Alfred, who had watched his father die painfully, was afraid of illness thereafter, for himself and for those he loved, and was a fearful, dependent man.

His father had been a dynamic, active young man, so innovative in his educational reforms that school boards seldom had kept him more than a year at a time in any one school district. His son had a fear of death, for himself and for his children. When he tried to put restrictions on Margaret to protect her health by keeping her inside, she ran angrily through the house banging on doors, trying to get out. Whereas the sickly firstborn son, Dickie, permitted himself to be sheltered and coddled, the ebullient firstborn girl would not take restraint. Dick was always a good little boy who could not tell a lie without looking guilty, but this habit hampered his obstreperous big sister when she led him into mischief.

When Margaret was four, Katherine was born, and Margaret was very pleased with her little sister. When Katherine was three months old, Margaret decided that the three children could do very well on their own, and so, gathering together provisions and diapers, she locked herself and her siblings in the bathroom, where they were to live under her care and domination. It was an hour before her mother could coax her to open the door.

Katherine died when she was nine months old. Although Margaret could understand what had happened—indeed even as a young adult she still dreamed about her sister—Dickie simply wandered miserably about the house, and Alfred, to whom each tragedy or frustration became an excuse for self-defeating action, said he would never permit himself to love another child. He blamed his wife for not calling the doctor sooner, a statement with which the doctor, who became close friends with Alfred, agreed. The doctor also told Alfred that his Emily was emotionally inadequate, perhaps assuming that any woman who wrote articles for an encyclopedia could not be a loving, caring mother.

Emily was acutely unhappy. Although her mother-in-law always sided with her, especially when Alfred was unfaithful to her, and although Emily respected Grandmother Mead for her capableness and fairness, she wished she could have had her home to herself.

After a difficult pregnancy, during which the doctor sometimes threatened to abort the fetus, Elizabeth, the fourth child, arrived screaming—and kept on screaming, her hair standing on end with rage. Steel mitts had to be put on her hands to keep her from scratching her face. When Margaret was a baby, her mother had filled seven notebooks with data on her growth and development, and she had made four such notebooks about Dickie. Now she was too busy caring for children and being pregnant to keep further records. Alfred, as he had resolved, was indifferent to the new baby and to his wife, and Elizabeth, a stormy child who was to grow up to be an imaginative artist, became Grandmother Mead's special responsibility.

The grandmother, who called on Margaret to be a helper, used methods that in later years were written about as innovative in educational journals. Margaret, starting her life as a social scientist early, assumed the task of keeping precise notebooks, under her grandmother's direction, on the development of Elizabeth and Priscilla, the fifth and last of the Mead children, a quiet baby who caused no one trouble. After Priscilla was born, her mother had a serious postpartum depression and had to go away for rest and treatment. However, she was obliged to return when the children became ill with whooping cough.

At age eight, still being the social scientist, firstborn Margaret kept notes on the small natives in her own household. Protective and domineering with the best of intentions, she made plans for her siblings' futures. Dickie, who had a good voice, should be a fine singer. Elizabeth should be his accompanist and learn to dance. Little Priscilla, who was exceptionally pretty, should have fine clothes and display her beauty in a suitable setting.

The family moved often, living in rented houses, but the siblings were together often because Grandmother Mead took over most of their schooling, finding the various schools they tried wanting. Between the ages of five and seventeen, Margaret spent two years in kindergarten, one year of half-day sessions in fourth grade, and six years in high school. When she was home, she had lessons with Grandmother for an hour each day. The rest of the day she was free to run through the meadows and along country roads and to read uninterruptedly for hours. Her mother sought teachers for her in the neighborhoods in which they lived, finding people who could teach wood carving, painting, weaving, music, and graphic arts. She also welcomed her children's playmates. In the summer they went to a farm because Grandmother believed every child should learn to live on a farm. They learned to ride horses and to help when threshers came and had to be fed. All her life Margaret continued to be the protective, dictatorial big sister.

In *Blackberry Winter*, thinking over the differences between the three sisters, she says: "The differences between the three girls could not be attributed to sex. There was, of course, birth order. Elizabeth was neither the eldest or the youngest, and she used to remark bitingly, 'When I die I'm going to leave everything to the next-to-the-youngest' " (p. 67).

Nancy Mitford. Another assertive woman is the English novelist, Nancy Mitford. As a child, Harold Acton says of her, in *Nancy Mitford: A Memoir* (1975), "She used to scan Blor's *Daily News* for an account of a shipwreck in which her parents (who sailed every other year to Canada to prospect for gold) might be among the 'regretted victims.' In spite of what psychoanalysts might infer, she loved her parents—with comprehensible reservations in the case of her father—but at the age of seven she nurtured an enterprising ambition to 'boss the others.' The brood continued to increase, however, which she considered 'extremely unnecessary' " (p. 2).

The Only Child

Among the Three Hundred there are 51 who are only children. Although it is customary to combine the first and only born in ordinal studies, we chose not to do so, with puzzling but provocative results. When others have studied the only and firstborn as a unit, they found them to be high achievers, intelligent, highly verbal, anxious, independent, responsible, and close to their parents, whose maturity they emulate. V. D. Thompson (1974), for instance, says only children are not more arrogant, selfish, or socially inept than are other children and that the good relationship with their parents persists into adulthood.

However, when we isolated only children from firstborns, we

found the fifty-one only children intelligent, highly verbal, and anxious, but there the similarity ends. Good relationships with their parents, we discovered, are uncommon. Many subjects were exceedingly neurotic and troubled and had poor peer relationships as children and as adults. Only four were reared in homes that were relatively untroubled.

Since 44 percent of the only children are literary figures, it is clear that they do excel in verbal skills. Twenty-one percent are artists, performers, or directors. Three of the nine mystics or psychics are only children, as are three of the twelve philosophers. Only one only child in our sample is a scientist, only one is an athlete, only five are political figures. The fifty-one only children do not resemble the mature, accommodating only child found in other studies but do resemble writers we described in the Four Hundred. As we wrote in *Cradles of Eminence,* "Seventy-four of the eighty-five writers of fiction or drama, and sixteen of twenty poets, came from homes where, as children, they saw tense psychological dramas played out by their parents" (p. 272).

The fifty-one are often only children for very specific reasons that do not promote family harmony. For instance, nine of the only children were born to unwed mothers. Being an illegitimate child has never been much of a barrier to achievement, and in fact there is an aura of romance about the "love child," especially if he or she is the son or daughter of a member of the nobility. (One common daydream of rebellious adolescents is that of being not the child of ordinary parents but an adopted child from a much superior family.) Attitudes vary with social milieu, and in wealthy and unconventional circles, the fact of illegitimacy had minimal impact on the mother and child, whereas, in our sample, the two unwed mothers and their children in lower-class Catholic families were both severely rejected.

Let us now consider the various types of only children—typical only children, orphaned and half-orphaned only children, only children from happy homes, and only children from troubled homes.

Typical Only Children: Willy Brandt, Catherine Cookson, Violetta Leduc, Jean Genet, and Maurice Utrillo. German politician Willy Brandt, who was born in 1913, was illegitimate but was quite comfortable with it. His mother, who worked in a cooperative, was an active member of the Social Democratic Party, as was her father, a skilled laborer who acted as the boy's surrogate father until his daughter married. Willy's stepfather also was a Social Democrat. Father, mother, and stepfather were proud of Willy's early leadership in the party, and his being born out of wedlock did not make him a social pariah in his home or community.

For Catherine Cookson, an English novelist born in 1906 in a poor, largely Roman Catholic area of Simonside Bank, England, being an illegitimate child was torture—both at home and at school. Her proud, haughty, working-class mother, Kate, who strove to be upwardly mobile, had been courted by a fine gentleman wearing a top hat and a topcoat with a fur collar. He had exquisite manners and spoke with an upper-class accent. Kate was resistant to being seduced but when he finally succeeded and she became pregnant he disappeared. When she tried frantically to find him, she found he had given her a false address, a false name, and incorrect information about his place of employment. Kate's pride was so damaged, the criticism of her by her mother, sister, and all their friends was so vituperative that she became severely alcoholic and was a lifelong burden to Catherine.

To the teaching nuns and Catholic classmates, Catherine was the "devil's own." She retaliated by being brash and hostile. Her self-chosen guidebook to being upwardly mobile was a book reminiscent of her gentleman father—*Lord Chesterfield's Letters to His Son*. One of her most popular novels is *I Never Had a Da* [Daddy].

Reading *La Batârde* ("The Bastard"), the first volume of French novelist Violetta Leduc's autobiography, is a heady experience, like coming suddenly on a powerful, primitive African woodcarving among handpainted china teacups. She has her own rich, sensuous, harsh, personal idiom, especially when she is describing her sexual relationships with a fellow student and a schoolmistress at her girls' boarding school. In *French Novelists of Today* (1967), Henri Peyre, professor of French at Yale University, says that *La Batârde* and Jean-Paul Sartre's *Les Mots* were the two most remarkable French publications of 1965. (Sartre, another only child, won the Nobel Prize for literature presumably because of this autobiographical account of his unhappy childhood.) Violetta's autobiography was an immediate sensation in France and was widely translated.

Violetta's mother, Bertha Leduc, was a lady's companion in a wealthy home. There she was seduced by her mistress's son, a sickly student, and obligated to leave, although the mistress could not understand why her favorite servant left without any sensible explanation. Violetta was born in 1907; her mother attempted to rear her as if she were the legitimate daughter of a wealthy gentleman. She bought her frilly, expensive clothes and brushed her hair assiduously, trying to make a fairy princess of the homely, sickly child. She sent her to the Protestant church and to a Protestant boarding school because her father was a Protestant. In the lower middle-class Catholic neighborhood in which they lived, the mother's unusual treatment of her child set Violetta apart from her peers. Nor did she succeed in pleasing her mother. The only person Violetta ever really loved was her accepting, comfortable grandmother, and when she died Violetta was desolated. When Bertha married, Violetta was jealous and fearful, having been taught by her mother that all men were predators, that they followed women, and that she must never let them catch her. Until she was nineteen, Violetta believed that babies came from a mother's navel.

"I suffered my mother's humiliating experience too early," she wrote in *La Batârde*. "I dragged it behind me as an ox drags its plow. The wrong done inside her had become a universal wrong" (p. 26).

Having lost faith in her mother's judgment but not in her mother's teaching, she rejected her stepfather, and when she was sent away to boarding school, she was ready to be receptive to sexual approaches from other females. Peyre describes what happened:

> At school the other girls mocked her as "la bâtarde." Moreover, she was ugly and aware of it. She felt atrociously alone in the world as a child when she needed understanding and consolation. She grew sour, cynical, rebellious, but at the same time she desperately yearned for beauty in music, poetry, nature. She sought the love of other girls and occasionally attracted strangely innocuous males longing for an intellectual camaraderie.

. . . Her long narrative is a weird mixture of burning,
naïve, lucid and unadorned sincerity, and of a poetic
inner monologue [p. 385].

As a bisexual adult, Violetta made herself miserable by falling in love with homosexual males or straight females. One who did
not respond to her overtures was Hans Sachs, who taught her how
to write. Another was the homosexual Jean Genet.

French novelist and poet Jean Genet was a foundling and
therefore presumably illegitimate. According to his biographer,
Jean-Paul Sartre, in *Saint Genet: Actor and Martyr* (1963), Jean
was placed in a foster home in rural France. *Saint Genet* is not truly
a biography but a series of essays on Genet's writings. Sartre extrap-
olated the autobiographical data from Jean's works of fiction or
poetry and did not, as more meticulous biographers do, visit the
village, interview teachers and old acquaintances, and so on. Sartre
writes that Jean became a compulsive thief because his foster parents, who were so kindly that he often forgot he was a foster child,
called him a thief when he stole a household object. As a result, his
compulsion caused him to be sent at age fifteen or sixteen to a reform school. But this explanation seems too glib, for unless a traumatic experience is reinforced—unless the foster parents continued
to call Jean a thief on many other occasions—it seems improbable
that Genet could have been so seriously damaged.

In the reform school, Jean became a homosexual mainly because he was lonely and accepted advances from older boys, even
though they teased him and used him only for their own sexual needs
without tenderness. Sartre says: "But he became a homosexual because he was a thief. A person is not born homosexual or normal. He
becomes one or the other because of the accidents of his history and
his own reaction to these accidents. I maintain that inversion is the
effect of neither a prenatal choice nor an endocrinian malformation
nor even the passive and determined result of complexes. It is an
outlet that a child discovers when he is suffocating" (p. 78).

Jean, Sartre believes, was suffocating for attention, any
kind of recognition.

Another French only child, artist Maurice Utrillo, is easier
to comprehend. He was the illegitimate son of a famous Mont-

martre model who was also a minor painter of considerable talent (some of her pictures hang in the Louvre)'. A great many of the artists for whom she was a model are lightly suggested as the possible father of her child, but the gossip is idle and without venom.

As a boy Maurice was doted upon by his grandmother, who had most of the care of him. However, she fed him wine in ever increasing amounts because he liked it so much, and, consequently, he was an alcoholic before he was eleven. After a number of hospitalizations, a psychiatrist suggested that his mother teach him to paint as a therapeutic measure. Still, he did not become self-supporting as an artist until he married a dominating wife who watered his wine, kept his accounts, and managed the sale of his works.

Orphaned and Half-Orphaned Only Children: Eileen Garrett and Alesandr Solzhenitsyn. A frequent reason for being an only child is the death of one or both parents, and we found thirteen among the fifty-two who were orphaned or half-orphaned. The two that were fully orphaned are Eileen Garrett and Ingrid Bergman. The half-orphaned are Andrei Codrescu, Mazo de la Roche, Erik Erikson, George Gamow, Eric Hoffer, Aly Khan, Flannery O'Connor, J. B. Priestley, Maurice Sachs, Jean-Paul Sartre, and Alesandr Solzhenitsyn.

Psychic Eileen Garrett was orphaned when she was two weeks old. Her mother killed herself during her postpartum depression, and her father shot himself at work. Her aunt, who unwillingly assumed her care, beat her when she talked about playmates whom no one else saw and when she anticipated the death of a relative. Eileen killed her aunt's baby ducks in retaliation but was remorseful when she saw a thin, smokelike substance rising from the ducks' bodies as they died.

While the advantages of being fully orphaned are obscure, there are advantages to being a half-orphan, for a widower or widow may turn to the child or children for companionship. If the remaining parent is wise and perceptive, the children profit by the closer companionship and feel the warmth of being needed. In the Four Hundred the half-orphaned included Marian Anderson, Arthur Balfour, Stephen Crane, André Gide, Friedrich Nietzsche, Al Smith, and Joseph Stalin. Among the half-orphaned only children of the Three Hundred who had loving relationships with the remaining parent are de la Roche, Gamow, Hoffer, O'Connor, Priestley, and Solzhenitsyn.

Alesandr Solzhenitsyn was born during the Russian Revolution in 1918 in Kislovodovsk after his father had died for lack of medical care following a hunting accident. His father had been a student in the philology department of Moscow University when he left school to enlist in the Russian Army and was working as a forest ranger when he died.

Since Alesandr's mother came from a wealthy family, she was not able to get work commensurate with her education in the new regime. Though she could read English and French, she was forced to take a job as a typist. Tolstoyan in ideology, she was an idealist and was interested in internationalism and peace. But she could not get housing in those days of an acute housing shortage and was obliged to rent a broken-down hut from family friends.

Since she did not remarry, she remained a close companion to her son and extended to him her own love for literature. How much his intense drive to be at the top of his class and to write came from her is not clear, but he decided to become a writer when he was ten. Alesandr's first wife had been one of his classmates when he was in secondary school, and she says in her biography about him that he suffered intensely if his status as top student was threatened. As a result, his sympathetic classmates relaxed their own efforts in order to let him excel. Once when a history teacher bawled him out, he fainted and hit his head on his desk.

Only Children from Happy Homes: Alan Watts. Among the four supportive and generally happy homes with only children, the best described is that of the late popularizer of Eastern religions, Alan Watts, who was born to Lawrence Wilson Watts and Emily Mary Buchanan Watts in the village of Cheslehurst, Kent, England. Alan's mother had two miscarriages and lost another baby two weeks after birth, and so Alan was the only surviving child.

Although Emily was not pretty, her husband, Lawrence, adored her, and they often held hands under the table at mealtimes. An amateur entomologist and lover of the outdoors, Lawrence taught his son to be an expert archer and a crack shot with a rifle. Before her marriage, Emily had taught physical education and home economics to the daughters of missionaries left behind while their parents worked abroad, and she, too, was the daughter of missionaries. Their home was thus a little oasis of Eastern culture, filled with treasures and books from India, China, Samoa, and Japan. Alan's father read to him from Kipling and about the East, and made him feel closer to Buddhism than to Christianity. He also read the books his grandparents had collected on Zen and the Orient.

Alan felt he never had enough time with his parents. They hired nurses and nannies to cushion themselves against him from the time he was an infant until he was seven and a half. Still, he was close to his mother. It was she who taught him the magic of stained-glass windows, rose trees, speckled thrushes, and hop fields. She believed in him, so he believed in himself, and accepted that it was his destiny to do something special. When he was naughty, she did not scold but said, "It isn't like you to do that." In his 1972 autobiography, *In My Own Way,* he says of his parents, "There never was a more harmonious and unostentatiously virtuous couple, yet I feel I never quite gave them what they wanted. I don't know what that was, and perhaps they didn't either" (p. 9).

He promised himself never to be like his father, who was tied down to a regular job that often took him away from home, nor would he talk incessantly, as his father did. His mother's poor health and the loss of her first babies made her overanxious about Alan, and he reacted by being fearful about his own health. Yet he promised himself he would not worry about his own children's constipation—people were always asking him, "Have you been?" and dosing him with calomel and castor oil and syrup of figs.

At seven and a half he was sent away to the oldest boarding school in England, where young relatives of the royal family, rajas' sons, and descendants of the Imperial House of Russia were miseducated and made miserable at great expense. "There was even a boy who had been buggered by an Arabian prince," he wrote later. "And my parents knocked themselves out to send me to this amazing institution" (p. 44). His parents cautioned him about not making friends with the lower-class boys.

Long after other children gave up such "twaddle," Alan believed in fairies and magic. From the age of four to seven and one half, he ruled an imaginary kingdom on an island somewhere in the Pacific. At the age of twelve he had a penchant for the weird and fantastic. At seventeen he was reading Nietzsche, Lao-tze, the Upanishads, Blavatsky, George Bernard Shaw, and Havelock Ellis.

He was too interested in Oriental culture to do his usual school-work, so he was not recommended for higher training.

At twenty he fell in love with and soon married a girl much younger than he, Eleanor Everett. After their marriage in England they went to Chicago, where they were installed in a palatial duplex provided by her family. His mother-in-law was not only wealthy but also an eminent Buddhist, and it was she who gave him his start in life, accelerating his career as a student of Zen and as a lecturer and educating him further in the ways of Buddhism. But he was continually seeking. Although he had been ordained an Anglican priest, he was uncomfortable in that role. He liked the Quakers because they, too, practiced meditation, but he felt too many were moved to speak in Meeting and he came to believe that all Quakers were psychologically "constipated."

Alan and Eleanor had seven children, but he said that by society's standards he was a terrible father. He loved the children when they were voiceless, playful infants, but loathed the "Disneyland childhood" they and their mother and other relatives preferred. Eventually he left the family and followed the sun to California, where he found his childhood kingdom near Big Sur. In his last years he found the magic of his mother's favorite stained-glass windows again in the psychedelic world of the California drug culture, in LSD, in the Beatles, in Bob Dylan, in Timothy Leary's slogan "Turn on, tune in, drop out."

Only Children from Troubled Homes: T. H. White. Fourteen of the fifty-two only children in our survey came from homes in which there was separation, divorce, desertion, or constant incompatibility. They are Martin Buber, Erik Erikson, Indira Gandhi, Uri Geller, Helen Hayes, Howard Hughes, André Malraux, Pola Negri, Frank O'Connor, Cole Porter, Maurice Sachs, Upton Sinclair, Vita Sackville-West, and T. H. White.

O'Connor and Sinclair had alcoholic fathers. Buber's mother disappeared when he was three and no one told him why, and he did not see her again until he was thirteen, although his biographers make no explanation. Porter's mother and his millionaire grandfather assumed full responsibility for rearing him and made a sorry mess of the task; his father, a kindly and sensible man, was denied any meaningful relationship with his son.

Novelist T. H. White's biographer tells how he was made sexually inadequate by his mother. Terrance Hanbury White was born in 1906 in Bombay, of British parents. His father, Garrick White, was a superintendent of police and his mother, Constance Aston, the popular daughter of a judge. When Constance was thirty, her mother nagged her once too often about not being able to choose among her suitors, and she vowed to accept the next man who proposed to her. The result was a disastrous marriage.

The two quarreled violently, at one time struggling for possession of a pistol to see who would get to kill first Terrance, then the other parent. From the beginning, Constance was also an indifferent mother. On an ocean voyage to England, for instance, her infant would have died had not a ship's doctor asserted his authority and saved him. She dismissed a nurse to whom the little boy grew attached. Still, until he was eighteen, he was passionately in love with his mother, and as an adult he pitied and loved his father.

He was a fat little boy with thick lips. When he was in England, living with his mother's parents for six happy years, he sent his photograph to his mother in India. In her reply she was critical, saying his lips were too sensuous. As a result he became ashamed of his lips and as an adult grew a beard and moustache to conceal them. His parents were divorced when he was about fourteen, and his home and education collapsed about his ears. "Ever since then," he is quoted as saying in his biography, "I have been arming myself against disaster" (p. 25).

T. H. White was always an unhappy man. His intelligence was materialistic, he said, but his heart was tender. He often fell in love, but since he was impotent he did not marry. In *T. H. White* (1968), Sylvia Townsend Warner, a most capable biographer, quotes his saying of his mother, "I've always thought she was sexually frigid, which was why she thrashed it out of me. Anyway she managed to bitch up my loving women" (p. 25).

The Middle Child

Those who study birth order find the middle child hard to evaluate since there are so many ways to be a middle child. The middle of three? The middle of ten? The middle boy among sisters?

Brothers? Do sex distribution and spacing make a difference? Does a middle child who becomes a first child when an older sibling dies have a different role to play? Like other researchers, we designate everyone who has an older and a younger sibling a middle child.

Several students of the middle child believe that this position is favorable to being an executive or a politician. Only four of the youngest among the Three Hundred were practicing politicians. In this chapter we will limit ourselves to accounts of the life stories of four middle children who became United States Senators: George McGovern, Hubert Humphrey, Robert Kennedy, and Edmund Muskie.

The factors most often held in common—by these politicians and certain other eminent politicians whose life stories will be told later—other than birth order are the following: (1) supportive parents and an intact family, (2) strong influence of the father compared to the mother, (3) good sibling relationships, (4) good physical and mental health, (5) scholarship, (6) being helpful and well behaved at home, (7) good peer relationships, (8) heterosexuality, (9) ability to take frustration and postpone gratifications, (10) being a debater, (11) working on the school paper, (12) being hardworking and well-liked, (13) having a family that was respected in the community and participated actively in community affairs, and (14) marrying a woman who was loving and helpful.

George McGovern. During the years between his first year of school and his sophomore year in high school, George McGovern was distinguished only by being indistinguishable and was very shy in large groups. Indeed, when he was in the first grade the teacher thought him retarded, ignored him, and promoted him "on condition." His English teacher and school librarian, Rose Hofner, watching him go through the books in the library, enlisted the help of another teacher, young, charismatic Bob Pearson, in drawing out the potentials of the shy but exceptionally able student.

In South Dakota, where McGovern grew up, debate was the most popular school activity and rivalry between schools was intense. Pearson remembers that his top debater excelled in knowledge and in logic and was superb in noting weakness in an opponent's argument. However, George "didn't excel for the sake of being ahead of everyone else," Pearson told Robert Samanson in his

1972 biography, "He had a great deal of curiosity. He wanted to do well. To him it was a duty to fulfill himself. He never saw any kind of obligation to place himself in the forefront" (p. 29). What George lacked was what Pearson had: charisma and the ability to elicit emotional appeal. Thus, although he turned George into a Jeffersonian-style Democrat, he could not get him to use his hands or show enthusiasm.

Through his debating, George met someone who was to do what Pearson could not do, give him the freedom to express emotions in the intimacy of a warm, uncritical relationship. When George and his partner went to debate at Woonsocket High School, they discovered their opponents to be two pretty and delicate identical twins, not quite five feet tall, so openly happy and excited about just being debaters, yet mere novices just experiencing their first public debate. To the visitors' chagrin, the judges awarded the contest to the twins, Ila and Eleanor Stegeberg. George courted Eleanor for several years, and, despite the fears of their elders, who thought they were too young, they were married during World War II when George was on leave from Officers Training Camp. The marriage between the dynamic, affectionate, firstborn daughter and the inhibited, intellectual, middle-born son was a happy one that has lasted far beyond the graduate school years of economic deprivations and the quick succession of babies. The embarrassment of the initial debating defeat persisted in a way, for during George's campaign for the Presidency, his aides were uneasy because they feared Eleanor might overshadow him as a speaker.

Eleanor's home environment had been quite different from his. Her parents had been childhood sweethearts, and were married sweethearts until the mother died when the girls were eleven years old. Although George never knew the mother of the woman he was to marry, he appreciated her warm, creative qualities reflected in her daughter.

George's father, a strict Wesleyan minister, was forty-eight when he married a lovely, placid woman twenty years younger than he. The Reverend McGovern was not an unjust or cruel man, but his temper was explosive whenever one of his children violated principles he held dear. His wife, who was averse to violence or quarreling, kept her own counsel, and so did George. He was closest to his

older sister, Olive, who became a high school teacher. His younger
sister, Mildred, and the favorite of his parents, handsome and
affectionate Larry, were a twosome, though Larry became sexually
delinquent in adolescence and had to marry a pregnant schoolmate
and became alcoholic as a young adult. George did not rebel except
on Saturday afternoons, when he sneaked away to the movie mati-
nee. At home he read omnivorously and was obedient. His father
believed in healthy, outdoor play and did not prevent him from
roaming the countryside or playing games with his friends as he
grew older.

    Hubert Humphrey. The late Senator from Minnesota and
former Vice-President of the United States was born in Wallace,
South Dakota, in 1911, the second of four children of Hubert H.
Humphrey, Sr., a pharmacist who was elected Democratic mayor of
a Republican town. Hubert's father seldom stopped talking, mostly
of politics and civic affairs. When he laughed he shook all over.
When his son brought a barefoot friend into the drugstore and was
unhappy because his friend's feet were blue with cold, Hubert, Sr.,
went immediately to the till and gave him money for new shoes.
During the Depression he took food from farmers in lieu of the
money they did not have to pay for prescriptions. However, his
generosity was not based on his affluence, and young Hubert never
saw his father cry until the day he had to sell the family home in
order to pay the debts he had incurred during those lean years when
his customers could not pay.

    When Hubert was ten, he started helping his father in the
pharmacy, washing dishes and listening to the talk in the store. In
his 1976 autobiography, *The Education of a Public Man,* he re-
marks, "I've attended several good universities, listened to some of
the great parliamentary debates of our times, but have seldom heard
better discussions of basic issues than I did as a boy standing on a
wooden platform behind a soda fountain" (p. 27).

    Hubert was less enthusiastic about his mother, the former
Christine Sannes, a pretty, little woman with dark-brown hair and
twinkly blue eyes; she was a wonderful cook. She came from a small
seaport town at the southern tip of Norway. Grandfather Sannes, a
retired sea captain, had come to South Dakota and bought 300
acres of rich Dakota soil. His values were the honor of labor, the evil

of debt, and the pursuit of excellence. He was conservative in his politics. His daughter incorporated these values and added to them a love of poetry.

She was also Republican and a strict churchgoer, and the parents disagreed on politics and religion since Hubert, Sr., had been influenced by the charismatic agnostic, Robert Ingersoll. At forty, however, the father became a church member, largely because of his interest in social issues the church espoused. The Humphreys were descended from Pennsylvania Quakers, and one of Hubert's grandmothers was an intellectual who read the classics to her children and also was, Humphrey writes, "unselfish, unsparing of her strength and energy in behalf of others . . . and like her father before her, a free, fearless, analytical thinker of positive temperament and quick decision" (p. 22).

The four children—Ralph, Hubert, Fern, and Frances— grew up in Doland, a South Dakota town that Hubert says was admirably suited for the rearing of children. His youth was very happy. He accepted the precepts of his father, sold newspapers, starred in school plays, sports, and debating, had good peer relationships, was useful to his parents, and was always an outstanding student.

However, the Depression hit Doland very hard, and he and his brother dropped out of school to help their father. By means of a six-month crash course and independent study and the experience he already had had working in his father's store, Hubert passed an examination ordinarily taken by students who had had a four-year college course in pharmacy and became a registered pharmacist. At about that time he also married a hometown girl, Muriel Buck, who encouraged him after six years in Doland as a pharmacist to go back to school. While he was a graduate student, they suffered lean years, and she sold sandwiches and did typing to add to their income. At that time, Hubert, Sr., had considerable national status in the Democratic Party and would have liked them to stay in Doland to keep store while he campaigned for Congress, but they begged off, pleading Hubert's need for more education.

Hubert's autobiography is dedicated to his family—to his sisters, Frances and Fern; to his children, Nancy, Skip, Bob, and Doug; and to Muriel, "my partner and sweetheart who has made my life fuller and without whom I could not have reached out to be what I wanted to be."

Edmund Muskie. The Senator from Maine and unsuccessful Democratic Presidential candidate was born in Rumford, Maine, in 1914. His sister Irene was three years older, and he was followed by four other children—Eugene, Lucy, Frances, and Betty.

Their father was born Stephen Marciszewski in 1882 in northern Poland, in a small village near the Russian border. He was apprenticed to a tailor when he was twelve so that he might have a trade, emigrate, and escape being conscripted by the Russian czarist military forces. He emigrated to Rumford, a prosperous papermaking town where he had a sister, and did well as a tailor. His wife, a girl of Polish descent born in Buffalo, New York, was a hard-working, thrifty woman with a deep need to be financially independent. Indeed, even after Muskie became a national figure she insisted upon taking in wash to augment her income. She was, her son said, "a sparrow with a hawk's strength." She had a need to have the last word. When he asked her if she would vote for him, she told him she might if no one better came along.

Neither parent realized, Muskie told his biographer David Nevin in *Muskie of Maine* (1972), what agonies he suffered to overcome his shyness. For instance, when ice cream and cake were served at his fifth birthday, he took them to his bedroom to eat. After he entered the first grade, his sister Irene had to pull him along to school, and the teachers could not coax him to play with other children on the playground. His shyness was the result, in part, of being teased because he was Polish and Catholic. The Muskies were one of only three Polish families in Rumford and the Catholic minority was small, and for five years the Muskie children were called "dumb Polaks" by other children. However, Edmund was not shy with his brother and sisters and joined them in giving shows for the entertainment of their parents.

As a growing child he was intensely religious, and many family friends thought he surely would be a priest. His religious convictions have not lessened, and during his campaigns he managed to attend mass nearly every day.

Stephen Muskie had had little formal education but he took

an interest in everything—current events, politics, community affairs, world news. He was not easily cowed or talked down and had an explosive temper, which his son inherited or imitated. Once a wealthy Republican, who was one of Stephen's best customers, walked out when Stephen declared himself a Democrat and argued hotly about a controversial political issue.

His sophomore English teacher, observing that he had read nearly every book in the school library, suggested he become a debater, which might also help stop him from being so shy. During his junior year he became president of the student council and a member of the Latin and dramatic clubs, and during his senior year he was general manager of the school fair and was class valedictorian. He was still shy with girls and won respect rather than close friendship from boys. He consented to play basketball, although he had no interest in sports, since he was six feet four. During one basketball tournament when the coach called for him, he was found in the locker room reading a book.

After high school he obtained a scholarship to Bates College, a small, liberal arts college in Lewiston, Maine, and his parents sacrificed to pay the extra costs. Later he set up a law practice in Waterville, Maine, interrupted during World War II when he was called to active duty.

During lunch Edmund always ate at the same restaurant, always alone, always reading a book. Two sisters who ran a fashionable Waterville dress shop and who ate at the same place became self-appointed matchmakers; they decided their attractive bookkeeper, salesgirl, and model, Jane Gray, would make him the right wife. Like Edmund, Jane came from an upwardly mobile middle-class family, where her mother, who had lost her husband when her five children were small, had supported them by taking in college student boarders. Eventually Jane and Edmund were married; he was thirty-two and she was twenty-one.

Muskie can be very direct when his sense of right and wrong is involved. He called for halting the bombing of North Vietnam when it was not politically wise to do so, called Nixon a trickster, and spoke of "credibility." Some writers speak of him as Lincolnesque; others call him an impractical innocent. Very much the product of his upbringing and his father's child, he wept angry tears when political opponents circulated fabrications about his domestic life.

Robert Kennedy. The Kennedy home breaks one pattern we have noted: the love of learning is missing. However, formal education is valued, as is collecting information, and winning is all-important.

Even though Joseph Kennedy, Sr., was more conservative than his sons were when they matured, there is no criticism of him in print by his children or his wife, Rose. To both parents, maintaining a family cohesiveness was paramount. Sibling supportiveness is also strong. Despite their wealth, the senior Kennedys needed their sons to give the socially rejected Catholic family the status and recognition Catholic families did not have in Boston and to give their father what he craved, a son who would be President. Robert Kennedy was born in 1925 in Brookline, Massachusetts, the seventh child, following Joseph, Jr., John, Rosemary, Kathleen, Eunice, and Patricia, and preceding Jean and Edward. Robert was the runt of the family. His older brothers were too big to play with; he shivered with fear and kept out of the way when they quarreled or wrestled. His brother Edward was too young to be a companion, and his sisters pushed him around or ignored him. Although Rose feared Robert's being sandwiched in between sisters would make him effeminate, in a household in which the girls were fearless competitors in the family games he became more "macho" than girlish. At age four, for instance, he jumped repeatedly from a family sailboat into cold, deep water, determined to learn how to swim. His brother Joe, Jr., kept pulling him out, but he kept jumping in, until Joe, Jr., remarked that the kid had guts or was just plain dumb.

To love learning for the joy of knowing or savoring the sound of words was not a Kennedy trait. John Kennedy once said he did not remember ever seeing his father read a book. Although Joseph, Sr., had attended Boston Latin School and Harvard, he considered learning a tool to be used, not something to enjoy. He hired the men and women who read the books or wrote the books and used them to help him make money. Only John, who was so often ill, became the reader among the boys. Politics was the family game. They were taught current events at the table, heard talk about politics, and met politicians who came to the house as visitors.

Whereas Joseph wanted his sons to have power and status, Rose wanted all the children to be good Catholics and to be well-mannered. She taught the girls to be thrifty housekeepers and saw to it that they were sent to Catholic schools. In the interest of the boys' political futures, the father chose Protestant schools for his sons, so that they could grow up closer to other young men who could open doors for them.

Robert was the most devoutly religious Kennedy child, and because he was Catholic he walked out of an Anglican school in England when he was told he must go to chapel. He also revolted when he was in another Anglican school in New Hampshire. After his mother interceded, he was sent to the Priory, a Catholic school in Rhode Island. He made low grades and so his father withdrew him and sent him to Milton Academy, the Protestant, academically tough preparatory school for Harvard. There he worked very hard, but his grades were still discouraging, and had he not been on the varsity football team, his life would have been intolerable. He grew moody, argumentative, and unfriendly, which somewhat pleased his father, a man who could be very belligerent when crossed, since it showed, he said, that the boy was going to be like him. Robert's grades improved and he was graduated.

In November 1943, Robert volunteered for pilot training and was transferred to Officers Training classes being taught on the Harvard campus. During that time, his brother John was seriously injured and Joseph, Jr., was killed; in his anguish Robert went to Washington and volunteered for active duty. However, his father arranged through the Secretary of the Navy to see that Robert was suitably and safely placed, so he spent the war as a second-class seaman in the Caribbean on a renovated destroyer newly rechristened *Joseph P. Kennedy, Jr.* and never saw action.

After the war he was a foreign correspondent for one of the Hearst newspapers for a time but did not enjoy the experience and quit to enter Harvard. Already older than most other undergraduates, he did not care much for social affairs and chose as friends young men who were working their way through school. Whereas

Joseph, Jr., had been president of the student council and a good
student and John had written, as a senior, the book *While England
Slept*, Robert did not go to class much. Instead, he played football
obsessively—even playing with a fractured leg—and won his letter
at the annual Yale-Harvard game.

His sister Jean introduced him to her Manhattanville College
roommate, Ethel Skakel, and in 1950 they were married. Super-
ficially the Skakels and Kennedys had much in common. Ethel's
father, George, a Protestant of Dutch extraction, started work as a
poor boy earning $8 a week as a railway clerk and rose to head his
own company and become many times a millionaire. He married a
Catholic girl, Ann Brannack, a generous, jolly, devoutly religious
woman who bore him seven children. Ethel's birth order was, coin-
cidentally, much like Bobby's.

Ethel grew up in a three-story brick mansion on a heavily
wooded ten acres which had swimming pools, gardens, terraces, and
animals everywhere. Her mother loved company, and the house was
never too small for her children's friends; sometimes twenty or more
spent the night. Dogs wet on the rugs and children ran and wrestled.
Once Ethel's older brothers tied a rope around her middle and
dangled her from a second-story window. Sometimes the boys filled
an old-fashioned station wagon with unwary guests for a tour of the
estate and then deliberately drove it into a pond so that guests had
to wade ashore.

Whereas the Kennedys lived in a fortress, the Skakels lived
in a recreation center, zoo, and fun house. Whereas the Kennedys
gave their children smaller allowances than those given most upper
middle-class children, the Skakel children were indulged. Whereas
the Kennedys were not generous to others, the Skakels were exceedingly so. Whereas the Kennedy children could roam freely on
their fifty acres of land and take physical risks, they had to be inside
the house before dusk and were expected to be at the table five
minutes before the food was served. The Skakel children, by contrast, ran wild, though all grew up to be responsible, well-functioning adults.

Ethel resolved that she and Robert should always share the
same interests and she expected him to have a brilliant career. Thus,
she read about matters that interested him, welcomed his friends,

and shared his concerns about the victims of poverty and prejudice. As the parents of a large family themselves, they set more limits than the Skakels had, fewer than the Kennedys had. Robert's relaxation was roughhousing with his children, and guests were sometimes disconcerted to be dragged into the melee or asked to play hide-and-seek. He also heard the children's prayers and took them to church on Sunday.

The Youngest Born

In his 1973 book of essays, *Forewords and Afterwords,* poet W. H. Auden writes as follows about his friend Evelyn Waugh: "Mr. Waugh was the younger of two sons, I the youngest of three and the youngest of quite a number of grandchildren. I should be curious to know if this ordinal position in the family has had the same effect upon him that it has had upon me. It implanted in me the lifelong conviction that in any company I am the youngest person present, a conviction quite unaffected by the fact that now, at fifty-eight, I am often the oldest" (pp. 502–503).

Auden is not only right about himself but about most of our youngest-born subjects. They are the naïve, the gullible, the credulous, the inexplicable, the unexpected.

The youngest has less compulsion to please the family than does the earlier born. The baby in the family is the pet, the toy, or the nuisance, the final irritant in a household tired of diapers and dependence. The youngest also may be the captive companion of an older mother who has had too few satisfactions in her life and seeks to relive it through her youngest, the last link of her own youth.

Youngest children seem to have more freedom to do the unanticipated. Every time we turn on an electric light we are indebted to a youngest son, Thomas Edison. Every time we travel by plane we are indebted to Wilbur and Orville Wright, the youngest sons of a Church of the Brethren bishop who also was a college professor and had married one of his students. Whereas the three older children were college graduates, the parents were content to let the youngest two tinker in their bicycle shop and work at their inventions.

In this section, we will discuss four youngest born: Rachel Carson, Ralph Nader, Edward Kennedy, and Ho Chi Minh.

Rachel Carson. Author and zoologist Rachel Carson was born when her mother was thirty-seven years old and had already borne two older children, a girl, ten, and a boy, eight. Her mother was a musician and schoolteacher before her marriage and was living in the Presbyterian parsonage when a traveling quartet came to sing for her father's country congregation. Her husband, a quiet, rugged fellow, was one of the members of the quartet. After their marriage they settled down on sixty-five acres at the edge of Mayesville, Pennsylvania, although they had only a few animals and did not seem to farm intensively. Rachel's father was not a good provider.

Her mother, Maria, was not unfriendly, but she had little in common with the wives of other farmers. Her youngest daughter was to be especially precious to the aloof and lonely woman. Since so little is said about Maria's husband, in Rachel's biographies, we may wonder if the marriage was emotionally or physically satisfying. Maria found excuses not to send Rachel to school (the snowdrifts were too high; she might catch measles or whooping cough), and since Rachel started reading when she was two and was a superior student the teachers did not complain about her mother's displacing them.

Rachel and her mother also shared a passionate love for nature, and walked for miles in the Allegheny Valley, looking, touching, classifying. Their wanderings set them even further apart from their neighbors, who thought to walk when there was no need to walk seemed odd. Thus, like her mother, Rachel became accustomed to being "different" in childhood. She loved books and assumed very early that she would grow up to write them. When she was ten she received a Silver Badge from *St. Nicholas Magazine,* and she wrote for her high school and college magazines.

In her entire life she was never known to have a romantic interest for any male or female, and when she was teased about going to a women's college, where there would be no male students, she responded primly that she was going to college to learn, not to meet boys. At college she studied literature, and her recreation consisted in hiding herself in the book stacks to read. She was never unfriendly or unkind.

During her junior year she changed her major to zoology because of the influence of a teacher, and, even though she received a scholarship in that field, she still thought of herself as a writer. She took her master's at Johns Hopkins and did graduate work in marine biology at Woods Hole Oceanographic Institute and found a part-time teaching job. She wrote poetry, but soon had such a collection of rejection slips that she felt obliged to find a more remunerative occupation and so accepted a civil service job writing radio scripts about nature for the U.S. Department of Fish and Wildlife in Washington, D.C.

Her mother and father came to live with her. Then her father died and not long afterwards her sister Marian also, leaving two little girls who were in grade school. Rachel now had three dependents. Although her work was not pleasant, she did it conscientiously, this being the Depression, and her $2,000 a year was barely adequate. Still, she was cooperative and not unfriendly at work; and at home her little nieces found her jolly and loving. She was closest to her mother and to some married neighbors, Dorothy and Stanley Freeman.

She wrote an essay about the sea for her supervisor, but he found it quite unsuitable for his purposes and suggested she send it to the *Atlantic*. The magazine accepted her essay, and this started her writing again. It was years before she received much recognition or remuneration, but it gave her a great deal of pleasure to write about the earth and sea she loved so passionately.

Rachel wrote slowly, discarding fifty pages before one satisfied her. She saturated herself with knowledge about any aspect of nature she chose to describe and let the message of the material impose itself upon her. If she stayed quiet and receptive, she felt, the book or article would write itself. Although she never wrote about a living person, she could turn the sea and the desert into great living entities. Loneliness did not bother her, since she knew writing was a lonely occupation.

Her niece, Marjorie, died and left a small son, Roger, whom Rachel adopted. Before Roger was two she taught him to recognize a whelk, periwinkle, or mussel as they walked on the beach together, as she once had walked with her mother in the woods and meadows of the Allegheny Valley. She cherished her family obligations. The children she reared were as precious to her as she was precious to her own mother.

Rachel was not a strident or rebellious woman and did not seek out causes to espouse. It was only her passionate love for nature that set her to the difficult task of writing *Silent Spring*. She had to use the work of many specialists in various scientific fields, and she was not used to working with others in this manner. Ill, crippled with arthritis, and already slowly dying from leukemia, she had only a few years to endure, and sometimes enjoy, the furor *Silent Spring* created. Critics of her thesis about pollution tried to use her illness to discredit her, saying her leukemia made her oversensitive about pollutants. She died at fifty-six when Roger was only eleven.

No one is a better example of the unexpected youngest than the shy, socially withdrawn Rachel Carson, for who would have expected this reticent minor government employee to challenge such powerful government and industrial interests? She was as daring, in her own quiet fashion, as a shy only child, Charles Lindbergh, who crossed the Atlantic alone in a flimsy plane.

Ralph Nader. Another lonely child who has made a passionate concern his life's work is the consumer advocate Ralph Nader, youngest of four children. He learned his impatience with injustice from his immigrant father, a Lebanese restaurateur, who reacted passionately to official wrongdoing or organizational betrayals of American ideals. His wife, Rose, a sturdy but amiable woman, was the steadying influence in the dynamic family. The oldest son helped with the family business; the younger children were all college-trained, and one sister is a research scientist in Berkeley, California.

Ralph was graduated summa cum laude from Princeton, which he enjoyed and appreciated, and Harvard Law School, which he called a high-priced tool factory. As an extracurricular activity he learned Chinese, Portuguese, Spanish, Russian, and Arabic. Most Harvard law graduates find remunerative jobs as corporation lawyers or go into business or politics. Ralph lives simply, disdaining fashion and fads, and is indefatigable in his task of protecting the American consumer and of exposing bureaucratic bungling.

Edward Kennedy. Theo Lippman, Jr., in his 1976 book,

Senator Ted Kennedy, says of him as a new senator, "Ted Kennedy was a genius at getting along with older men. 'Ninth-child talent,' a friend put it. His mother said, 'As the last child, handsome and robust, he expects to like people and expects to be liked' " (p. 3).

Edward was a docile, cheerful little boy, and his father was so busy and away from home so often that he might have suffered from not having an adult male model had he not had a companion in his mother's father, whom the Boston citizens affectionately called "Honeyfitz." The aging grandfather, John Francis Fitzgerald, who was only five foot three inches tall, and young Ted took long walks in Boston, where "Honeyfitz" had once been mayor. He heard stories of how it was when his grandfather was mayor and met men and women who reminisced with him. Edward was also the favorite of his big brother, Joseph, Jr. It was Edward (Teddy) for whom Joe asked first when he came home from college.

The power drives in the Kennedy family had been diluted somewhat when Edward became an adolescent, because the Kennedys had begun to make their weight felt in Boston and Cape Cod, where they had been snubbed by the Protestant community. He was still a small boy when his father was named ambassador to the Court of Saint James.

The deaths of Joseph, John, and Robert, the illness and death of his father, and the Chappaquiddick affair may have rescued Edward Kennedy from what he once spoke of as the "extraordinary sense of expectation." Robert Sherrill, a perceptive biographer, says that Ted Kennedy has spoken out more freely since he gave up running for President—for instance, telling a Southern audience their hero, William Calley, the My Lai killer, got the punishment he deserved. He has also told an American Legion audience that full amnesty should be offered all Vietnam War resisters and told a near mob of Boston antibusing protestors to go home and obey the school laws. Neither his father nor his brothers were ever able to speak out as strongly for unpopular causes, and frequently changed their views as a matter of political expedience.

Ho Chi Minh. There are seventeen individuals who could be called political among the eighty-two youngest. Among the most elusive to biographers is Ho Chi Minh, who made no secret of his reluctance to talk about his personal life. As far as anyone can tell,

Ho had no wife, no mistress, no male lover in his life. Since Marxist doctrine sees the state rather than the family as the most powerful factor influencing character development, biographies in the form the Western world knows them are not written in the countries where Marxism is dominant. Customs do not change easily, and most subjects of biography who lived, or are still living, in these countries still come from what were upper-class, educated families. Ho Chi Minh was no exception.

Ho started life as Ngu Yen Thanh in 1890 in Kimlien, central Vietnam. His father had an advanced degree similar to that of a Ph.D. and was a teacher in his earlier years. His wife, who brought him a substantial dowry, died when their youngest son was nine. In 1905 the father received a civil service appointment as secretary in the ceremonial office of the Imperial Palace at Hue, but he lost his position because of his anti-French stance and for twenty years thereafter was a wandering scribe, storyteller, and seller of relics. He was a genial and welcome visitor in the villages of Vietnam and was popular with the young people. However, the family seems to have fragmented after the father's failure in high office.

Like their father, all three children were revolutionaries. Ho's brother, who died in 1950, taught the Vietnamese language as part of the protest against students being taught French in French-dominated schools. His older sister was imprisoned for a time because of her militant anti-French activities. When Ho was a national figure in Vietnam, she saw his picture in a newspaper and recognized him as her younger brother, lost years ago. He had changed his name many times but she remembered his face and journeyed to the capitol to see him. They had a brief visit that was not repeated. He pled the pressure of work on behalf of his people and did not attend his brother's funeral. Whether or not he ever saw his father after he quit school at fifteen is doubtful.

Despite Ho's alienation from his family, he repeated his father's style on a much grander scale. When he was nine he started his own revolutionary activities by acting as a messenger under the tutelage of an uncle. He was educated by his father and attended the best secondary school in Vietnam, which also was a source for a great many future revolutionary leaders. At fifteen he went underground and began to travel widely in France, England, China, and the USSR. He learned seven European languages and knew a number of Chinese and Vietnamese dialects. Once he visited the United States while a messboy for a French ship and resided in Harlem for a time. Although he was the perpetual scholar and took classes at the Sorbonne, he was self-supporting and kept close to the working classes by working as a laborer to earn his living, shoveling snow and being a gardener, cook, or handyman. Never without a book— Zola, Shakespeare, Hugo, Roland—he wrote for left wing papers.

It was not easy for the Communists to discipline him. Once he was accused of being a follower of Trotsky, and in 1948 he said that he used to be a Communist but that he no longer was one. He said he believed in freedom of worship, residence, and movement. As a guerrilla leader in Indo-China during World War II, he rescued American flyers downed by the enemy, and he naïvely expected the United States, since it was also born in revolution, to support him when he had driven out the French. In writing the constitution for an independent Vietnam, he relied heavily on the American Declaration of Independence.

Ho liked being called the "Universal Uncle." His roving revolutionary father had also been called "Uncle," a common term of respect for older men in Vietnam. Ho prided himself on having "no name, no family, no children, no possessions." When he came to power in Vietnam, he lived modestly in the gardener's cottage of the governor's palace. He was not given to destroying political opponents. He had the insouciance and lack of egotism, but not the self-defeating, turned-inward qualities of so many youngest-born.

He resembles other men of arms who have romanticized war and violence in poetry—Gabriele D'Annunzio, George Patton, Chairman Mao. One of Ho's biographers, Jean Lacouture, translates from one of Ho's poems as follows: "The poems of today must be clad in steel; poets, too, must know how to fight" (p. 82).

Conclusion

As in other studies of excellence, the only and firstborn combined are overrepresented in our Three Hundred. The mean number of siblings in our population is 3.6 while the firstborn and only children account for 47 percent of all the subjects. We have no quarrel with the numerous studies that show that the firstborn child, with siblings or without, will constitute approximately half of any highly achieving population, whether they be Merit Scholarship winners or famous scientists. However, as we have indicated, the firstborn with siblings are different in personality traits and in areas of achievement from the only children. The personality traits usually ascribed to the combined firstborn and only children are appropriate for the firstborn with siblings, who are more numerous than the firstborn without siblings. They do not describe the only child who is likely to be from a troubled home, is not close to the parents, is a "loner" and prefers occupations that do not require close interpersonal relationships. Therefore, it is not surprising that they abstain from politics and are likely to have literary careers. Studying the firstborn with siblings and those who have none is a disservice to the latter, which is the minority group.

Vaida Thompson, in her comprehensive review of the extensive research on family size, cautions against a too rigid insistence on the "Xeroxed two-child family," which as yet cannot be proven to be superior to another family size, when the child's development is the issue. In her 1974 article she says, "Obviously, only as decisions about childlessness and childbearing become completely informed and completely voluntary—as individual and not moral-normative responses—can there be a realization of the recommendation that families in the future *average* two children" (p. 118). Wide spacing, she says, is to be encouraged to give each child born an advantage of more close companionship with adults during its early years.

At an observational level it would seem that only couples who are eager to have children and can set aside the time to interact freely with them during their children's formative years, who can enjoy them and make them feel wanted and needed, will, in the more enlightened future, want to have children.

🌿 6 🌿

Mental, Physical,
and Behavioral Problems

*We must take a strong stand against the
implication, however it may creep in, that talent
is a disease and creativity a neurosis.*

Rollo May

To parents and counselors who are anxious about mental, physical,
and behavioral problems in families with which they are personally
concerned, it may be comforting to know that a child is not prevented from achieving distinction because he or she comes from a
home where there is delinquency, physical illness, or mental illness.
Though some children break under such strains, others do not, and
there is reason to believe that a child needs some experience with
frustration to be able to cope effectively with disappointment and
disillusionment as a young adult. While these frustrations occur
naturally in most families, some overconcerned parents manage to
protect their children from experience with injustice, deprivation,
discrimination, and even boredom. A number of these children,

123

especially the most precocious, become depressive when as adults
they find life disappointing.

There is no evidence that poor mental health is one of the
necessary characteristics of genius or that an occasional bout of
manic-depression or acute psychosis accelerates the creative process.
Physical illness, on the other hand, can provide the time out that
gives an introspective youngster time for reading and contemplation
and also serves to set him or her apart from a peer group, which
seems to be a necessary part of being set apart as a unique and
achieving individual.

Delinquency is no more common among the Three Hundred,
and may very well be less, than it is in the general population. Few
adults in any culture reach maturity without disobeying some regu-
lation or parental or community standard, especially in relation to
premarital sex. Most of the delinquencies among the youthful
females among the Three Hundred are sexual. Young males are not
regarded as delinquent when they lose their virginity and are more
likely than are women to boast of having been mischievous, destructive, or school truants. The aging achieving male, in his autobiography, likes to present himself as a lively young lad.

Mental breakdowns are limited to depressive neurosis or to
manic-depressive psychoses. No other form of emotional distress
seems to permit a young man or woman to function well enough to
become highly achieving. These episodes, as well as suicide, occur
frequently in homes where the boy or girl is lovingly reared according to the then popular concept of good childrearing practices.
Breakdowns can occur in homes where two loving parents are eager
to do the best they can for their children. They err, if they do, in
being overanxious and in expecting too much for their precocious
offspring.

The home environment of the Three Hundred is seen as
"usually quite happy" in only 28 percent of the homes. Some of
the causes of unhappiness are beyond the control of the family,
caused by war, drought, depression, discrimination, political changes,
unemployment, and so on. Other troubles are activated by disagree-
ments within the family—by divorce, desertion, death and illness,
child rebelliousness, or dominating or rejecting parents. Parents often
quarrel bitterly.

Twenty-seven percent of the Three Hundred remember their childhood home fondly and say they had a happy childhood. Forty-four percent are candid, or their biographers are, about the homes having been quite unhappy. The rest are in a gray area: the home was a roof and a bed and breakfast, but it was easy to separate from it. All homes, however, managed somehow to preserve the curiosity, the drive, and the desire to excel.

Eminent People Who Were Delinquent

Sixty-four of the Three Hundred were delinquent as children. For the most part, these delinquencies come from rejection or from a severely dominating father's trying too hard to impose his will. Sometimes the delinquent was the "odd child" who did not share the family talents and values. Perhaps the parents were unable to cope with a child who was hyperactive and brilliant, and the more conventional siblings were often quite well behaved and were a comfort to their parents.

Singer Al Jolson, who disliked his neglectful rabbi father, was a member of a street gang at age ten.When he was eleven, his father sent him to a Catholic-run school for incorrigibles.

Boxer Muhammad Ali once stole two iron shoe-rests from a shoeshine parlor and placed them on a railroad track. It took two days to clean up the mess.

When industrialist Emil Jellinek-Mércèdes was a small boy, he spit in a horse's eye to see what would happen. A nonacademic in a prestigious academic family, he was repeatedly expelled from school. When his scholarly father hired a tutor for him, he boxed the sleeping tutor's ears. After Emil was expelled from college, his father found him a job as a minor employee of a railroad company, but he was fired when he played engineer and took one of the trains out for a solitary joyride.

Playwright Enid Bagnold ran away from her exclusive school in Switzerland, nor was she well behaved in Prior's Field, the prestigious English boarding school whose headmistress was the mother of Aldous, Julian, and Trevenen Huxley—who were well behaved and conscientious and loved their parents but had serious problems as adults.

Entertainer Maya Angelou was an unwed mother at sixteen and a madam at nineteen. Ethel Waters was a wild girl of the streets. Singer Edith Piaf was a prostitute when she was very young, and by age fifteen could no longer remember who had been her first sexual partner.

Singer Bob Dylan ran away from home repeatedly when he was a young boy. Filmmaker Ingmar Bergman was often a school truant. Sculptor Benny Bufano was arrested for swimming naked in a public fountain. Photographer Cecil Beaton was beaten for drawing pictures of women in his classroom. Roger Riou, Babe Ruth, and Jean Genet were sent to reformatories.

Novelist Ilya Ehrenburg, born in Russia in 1891, was an exasperating and incorrigible child. His father was too busy with his brewery and the ups and downs of his financial career to be close to his youngest child and only son. When his neurotic, hypochondriacal mother took him with her to a resort where she was to have a "rest cure," the management soon asked them to leave because Ilya played jokes with itching powders, stink powders, sneezing powders, and toy snakes. Once an aunt grew so exasperated that she locked him in a coal cellar, whereupon he stripped himself naked and rolled in the coal dust.

The family had a peaceful interlude when a young tutor was hired, but later it was discovered, after he was fired for being too interested in one of Ilya's sisters, that he had bribed Ilya to be good by generous gifts of candy. The only peace the family ever had was provided by Ilya's omnivorous reading. He went to the library every day for a new book to read—Tolstoy, Dickens, Dostoevsky.

At fourteen, Ilya was more interested in politics and revolution than in the dull curriculum, although he was a good scholar. He joined the Social Democratic youth group and wrote and distributed leaflets. He also wrote messages on thin cigarette papers, which could be swallowed if the Cossacks caught the carriers. When they did arrest him at his home for his activities, his older companions were imprisoned, but he was released to the custody of his parents because he was a minor. He broke the heart of his bewildered mother, who was a cherisher of traditions, a fearful and tearful woman who was afraid Ilya would take after her side of the family, which included a poet and a circus owner.

At seventeen he was sentenced to a five-month term in prison for his political activities; there he developed a severe depression. He was diagnosed as suffering from neurasthenia and was released, but the police followed him continuously. He went to Kiev to escape them but could not find work or a legal place to live, since no one dared have him as a roomer, until a sympathetic prostitute took him in, as did a motherly midwife. Although he went openly and angrily to the police and demanded that they either stop following him about or put him back in jail, they did neither, and so at age nineteen he fled to Paris. His mother wept, not because of his political activities, which she did not understand, but because he might be led astray by the unconventional women of Paris.

Eminent People Who Suffered from Physical Illness

The incidence of serious or chronic physical illness among the Three Hundred is approximately one-fourth, the same as that of the Four Hundred. The proportion does not vary significantly between the four areas of eminence—political, literary, artistic, and other—although the psychics had the most illnesses. Interestingly, most of those who were chronically ill in childhood did not die young; indeed, many exceed threescore and ten. In the days when most of the Three Hundred were children or young adults, the new drugs that have lowered mortality rates were not yet in use. Thus, the eighty-four children who suffered from chronic or severe illnesses were necessarily isolated from their peers, at least for considerable lengths of time, and spent more time alone, which meant they had time for reading and introspection and often had close associations with intellectually stimulating adults.

Novelist Joyce Cary was almost blind in one eye. Assassin Friedrich Adler suffered from blinding headaches and poor eyesight. General Moshe Dayan had trachoma. Revolutionary Ché Guevara, musician Leonard Bernstein, and writer Isaac Babel were severely asthmatic. Psychiatrist Hélène Deutsch was quite ill and unhappy with digestive and respiratory problems as a child, which her mother blamed on the succession of nurses who came to care for her daughter. Among others who were sickly and unable to attend school regularly, or sometimes not at all, were Rachel Carson, T. S.

Eliot, Thor Heyerdahl, Violetta Leduc, Pope Paul VI, Elizabeth Grey Vining, and Andrew Wyeth. While in college, Jessamyn West developed tuberculosis and began to write her first novel. Daisy Bates, Enid Bagnold, and T. H. White also had tuberculosis. Ernest Lawrence and Henry Luce were set apart from their peers because they stammered.

Revolutionary Antonio Gramsci, though born normal, was injured by a fall and became a hunchback, and he never grew to be more than a meter and a half tall. When he was injured his anguished and impoverished mother massaged him for hours but could not help him. She then made him a small coffin and prepared a burial dress, but he survived. Although he lived to manhood, he was seldom free of pain.

Archaeologist Louis Leakey was kicked on the head while playing rugby in college. He lost his memory and was advised to leave school and spend a year in the open air to speed his recovery. It was during this interval that he spent eight months digging for dinosaurs in Tanganyika and developed skills and interests that determined the course of his future. He suffered from a mild form of epilepsy after the accident.

Edgar Cayce, Uri Geller, Peter Hurkos, and Carl Jung experienced personality and physical changes after head injuries and periods of unconsciousness. Mickey Mantle was kicked on the ankle, and when the boy developed severe osteomyelitis, a specialist advised amputation, but the operation was avoided. Actress Marlene Dietrich's well-to-do parents had expected her to become a violinist, but a tumor on her right wrist ruled out that career and she went to theatrical school instead. The childhood of choreographer Katherine Dunham was made miserable by colds, fevers, and aching bones.

Southern novelist Flannery O'Connor, author of the bitter first novel *Wine Blood*, was no doubt influenced by having the debilitating disease from which her father died, lupus erythematosus, and from which she herself died at age thirty-nine. The shy, lonely, only child of an aristocratic southern family, she had a penchant for the grotesque and made pets of genetic mutations among the chickens. When her father died, she told her mother that he was better off than they. Her mother was a withdrawn woman who praised her daughter for not making friends unless they came to her first.

Although Flannery was Catholic herself, she viewed her Catholic neighbors with cold and critical eyes. In her last years she retired to the family farm to raise swans, burros, and peacocks.

Eminent People Who Suffered from Mental Illness

Among the Four Hundred there were only five persons who had incapacitating mental illnesses. One of them, writer Van Wyck Brooks, tenderly reared in a home that was relatively untroubled, had an incapacitating panic and depression that kept him in a mental hospital for four years when he was an adult. However, he wrote very efficiently during his hospitalization. Virginia Woolf had painful and acute periods of mental illness and was a suicide. At the height of his career Vaslav Nijinsky became schizophrenic and was hospitalized. Toulouse-Lautrec and Friedrich Nietzsche, both said to be syphilitic, died mentally ill.

Among the Three Hundred, however, twenty-four were mentally ill at some period in their lives. Nine were hospitalized, and the other fifteen had long periods of inactivity because they were depressed. Why this rise in numbers of biographies about celebrities who are psychotic or incapacitatingly neurotic has occurred is difficult to determine. It may be due, as some people believe, to an increase in stress in the world during the advancing decades. Or it may be that the recorded increase in mental illness may not reflect an actual increase but may result from a new openness toward mental illness and also a more accepting attitude toward those who have "nervous breakdowns" than existed in earlier years. It also may reflect an increase in treatment facilities and professionals in mental health.

The current trend in biographies is toward frank and open discussion of mental illnesses and also sexual divergency. Artists, authors, or actors who tell the most intimate details of their personal lives are no longer handicapped vocationally. No playgoer ignores a new production of a Tennessee Williams play because the author conveniently indexes many references to his homosexuality and his mental illness in his *Memoirs*. Neither Marilyn Monroe's sex appeal nor her box-office appeal was diminished by her emotional problems. Van Gogh's attraction as an artist is heightened by his madness and suicide. Still, the converse is true of other professions, especially of politicians, who can be destroyed politically if it is found out they were once treated for depression.

We are grateful to the emotionally ill who write autobiographies and to their biographers, for persons with literary gifts often write case histories of emotional distress that are more insightful and informative than are the usual psychiatric case histories. An anthology taken from the writings of famous persons who have psychiatric problems and write so cogently and perceptively about themselves would be worth doing.

The twenty-four mentally ill among the Three Hundred, hospitalized and nonhospitalized alike, are likely to be manic-depressive rather than schizophrenic. Schizophrenics are said to be more likely to come from the less well-educated and less well-employed than are manic-depressives. Depression is the disease of the intellectuals and of professional men and women. Before becoming mentally ill manic-depressives are characteristically conforming, conscientious, and socially responsible. When they fall short of the high standards they have set for themselves or feel they have disappointed others who are important to them, they become guilt-ridden and self-deprecating.

Manic-depressives show extreme fluctuations of feelings. In the manic state they are euphoric, hyperactive, and noisy; they may be vulgar and make sexual allusions. In the depressive state they indulge in self-recrimination, cry easily and often, or laugh uncontrollably. They may talk of suicide or attempt suicide or succeed in committing suicide. Fortunately, there are now drugs to control these extreme manifestations, drugs that were unavailable when most of the Three Hundred needed them. There is, however, no known cure. Eventually a chemical or genetic cause may be found. Research on identical twins gives some indication that this may be true. If one of a pair of identical twins is a manic-depressive, the chances are seven out of ten that the co-twin also will be a manic-depressive. The rate is only two out of ten for fraternal twins (Rosenthal, 1970, pp. 242–45).

An unexpected finding is that the homes of the persons with severe emotional problems are frequently quite acceptable from the viewpoint of mental health and educational experts. That is:

1. The child has two apparently congenial parents.
2. The parents are seen as being more loving, supportive, and admirable than are most parents.
3. The parents are highly literate; there is a respect for learning and achievement, and reasonable but not excessive ambitions for the children.
4. The homes are comfortably middle-class or wealthy.
5. When a boy or girl has emotional problems, the parents are quick to seek professional help.
6. The children are not delinquent or rebellious and tend to be "too good" rather than troublesome.
7. The subject is precocious as a young child and shows exceptional talent in school.
8. The siblings usually make good social adjustments.
9. The parents are permissive rather than punitive.

The twenty-four mentally ill persons comprise only seven percent of the survey population. There are no valid figures on the prevalence of mental illness in the general population. Ten percent is often given as an estimate. It may well be that the seven percent frequency we find is, in fact, below that of the larger society. We do not know what causes most mental illnesses nor how to cure them. These observations about the homes in which our subjects were reared are not given as prescriptions or proscriptions; they are simply what we find in reading a vast amount of material describing these childhood homes as they were seen by the subjects themselves and by their biographers. The significance of the data is open to interpretation by others.

Angela Davis. When Angela Davis completed her graduate work at Brandeis University, she obtained a scholarship to study at the Institute for Social Research at Goethe University in Frankfurt, Germany. As a child Angela had been intensely serious and conforming. Her mother was a grade-school teacher with a master's degree from New York University. Her father was also a teacher, but quit to earn more money to support his family by operating a filling-station.

Nothing in the childhood home, except possibly high expectations for all of the children, can account for Angela's period of deep depression in Germany. She was the first-born child, was attractive, quite precocious, an excellent student, and had good relationships with her parents. Her mother took the children with her when she went to New York City for several summers to study for her M.A. degree so that they might enjoy the cultural advantages of the northern city. Angela herself had a tremendous capacity for self-discipline.

In Germany she studied hard as a graduate student, learned the language, and worked compulsively on her research, sometimes ten to twelve hours a day. But, her biographer, Regina Nadelson, writes, in *Who Is Angela Davis?*, there were also days when she sat huddled on her bed in the cold room doing nothing at all. She forgot to buy groceries. She lost her capacity to deal with practical matters. She could not remember to take her clothes to the cleaners. She could not make decisions. Her body movements became jerky and unsure, and she once awkwardly knocked over bookshelves, scattering books. She felt that she was an outsider in Germany, yet she also felt guilty for being an overprivileged black girl living abroad when Watts was burning in Los Angeles. For the next two years she was in psychotherapy, although at first it was hard to remember to go for her session and hard not to be late. However, after two years her friends observed that she "fit her skin better." She was more open with people, had no problem getting down to work, was less defensive and less guarded. "Even her gestures were more graceful," Nadelson writes, "she rarely dropped things, she seemed altogether more in control of her life" (p. 109).

Eminent People and Suicide

It is difficult to separate a discussion of emotional disturbance and suicide and attempted suicide, since there is a relationship between them in many of the lives. Nor is suicide easy to identify, since those who die of overdoses of drugs are likely not to be officially classified as suicides.

Since suicide follows accidents and homicide as the leading cause of death in persons from fifteen to twenty-four years of age in the United States, it seems important to observe the homes of subjects whose breakdowns came in their college days or younger.

Among the Three Hundred the breakdown often comes when there is a fear of failure. The student with exceptional intelligence uses it to conceal his emotional problems and to present a relatively untroubled façade to peers, teachers, and parents. Those who recover the most successfully are the students who break down under the stress of facing examinations such as the revolutionary Angela Davis.

Yukio Mishima. The Japanese novelist Yukio Mishima (his pen name; his real name was Kamatake Hiraoka) committed hara-kiri on November 25, 1970, at the age of forty-five. He had been nominated for a Nobel Prize three times and had written an incredible number of works: forty novels, eighteen plays, twenty volumes of short stories, and as many literary essays. He was also a movie director and an actor and had conducted a symphony orchestra.

One of his translators and biographers, American John Nathan, who came to know him well, writes in the 1974 biography *Mishima:* "Mishima wanted *passionately* to die all his life, and . . . he chose 'patriotism' quite consciously as a means to the painful 'heroic' death his lifelong fantasy prescribed. I don't believe necessarily that the ardent nationalism of his final years was a hoax. But it does seem to me that his suicide was in essence private, not social, erotic, nor patriotic" (p. xi).

All Mishima biographers agree about the horrors of his first twelve years. Being a poor relation is a circumstance that has spurred many of the Three Hundred to high achievement, and Yukio is no exception.

Yukio's maternal grandmother, oldest of twelve children, was a difficult child, given to fits of hysteria, and the well-to-do family, although it belonged to the feudal nobility, found it difficult to find a husband for her. She was brilliant, cultured, selfish, and so emotionally unstable that her family sent her away from home to live with another family with whom she might be more congenial. A husband finally was found for her, a young lawyer working for the Ministry of the Interior, the upwardly mobile son of a peasant who had become well-to-do and educated his sons. Unfortunately, Jotaro Hiraoka's opportunistic marriage into the upper classes did not turn out well. He lost the dowry his wife provided and became bankrupt. He misused public funds and was forced to resign his position. The family moved into a rented house, where their grandson was born. Jotaro became an alcoholic and womanizer and spent his declining years in a back room playing *go* and fraternizing with former associates who had fleeced him.

His wife hated him for his inability to manage his affairs and developed sciatic neuralgia. She dominated the household. As a young adult, Yukio believed his grandfather's "womanizing" destroyed his grandmother and that her illnesses and severe depressions were the result of a venereal disease she had contracted from him. These unhappy parents had an only son, Azusa Hiraoka, a practical, unemotional, phlegmatic man who supported his parents and his wife and three children as best he could as deputy director of the Bureau of Fisheries in the Agricultural Ministry. He married a quiet, submissive girl, Shizue Hashi, the daughter of a secondary-school principal. In accordance with the Japanese custom she became the obedient daughter-in-law. She and her husband lived upstairs; her mother-in-law, who dominated the household, lived downstairs. It was not an impoverished household. The family had six servants, but the grandmother was woefully extravagant and they felt poor because of what they had lost.

Yukio (Kamatake) was the firstborn son. There were two other children, a boy and a girl. His mother, Shizue Hashi Hiraoka, was an unhappy woman. Her mother-in-law was cruel to her, and her husband ignored her. When the baby tumbled down stairs and hurt himself rather severely, his grandmother took him from his parents and insisted that he spend his days and nights in her sickroom.

"On Kamatake's fiftieth day of life," his biographer, J. Nathan, writes, in *Mishima*, "Natsu took him away from his mother and moved him, crib and all, into her darkened sickroom downstairs. And there she held him prisoner until he was twelve, jealously, fiercely, hysterically guarding him against his parents and the outside world" (p. 8). She took no interest in the two other grandchildren. Yukio was five or six before his mother had permission to take him for a walk alone, and then only on sunny, windless days. The only playmates he was permitted were three older girls who were relatives. He played with dolls and folded paper into fanciful shapes (origami). When his mother did have the opportunity to spend a few hours with him, she was the overdevoted, loving mother, who crowded into a few minutes the affection she felt for him. The slightest noise made his grandmother ill, but he never seemed to resent living in her sickroom, never complained or made demands. He was the silent "good" boy, almost autistic.

His inevitable tensions were first evidenced by a sudden collapse when he was five. For no apparent reason he vomited until he was near death. The pediatrician, unable to find a reason, told the troubled family that this kind of illness happened only to children "who were sensitive and intelligent." Yukio's repeated similar attacks bound him closer to his grandmother, and his mother hated her husband when he would not free their son from his incarceration.

The grandmother preferred him to be her nurse, and so he bathed her, massaged her hip, and helped her to the bathroom. At six, when he started school, when he was permitted to play with a boy cousin, the experience frightened him. He missed his darkened room, his fantasies, and his self-identification as a female. His cousin expected him to play with guns and to play war. He comforted himself by convincing himself that even if he were ever struck by a bullet, there would be no pain for him. He enjoyed "playing dead." When he went to school, Yukio did his homework in his grandmother's bedroom, where her nurse often played obscene jokes on the compliant boy. When Mishima was twelve, his grandmother, then age sixty, was still his sweetheart. She brought him up to be what she had been—a brilliant and haughty and emotionally disturbed young girl.

When Yukio became an adolescent and was freed from his grandmother's domination, he fell in love with his mother in a nonphysical fashion. She felt that "he was now her lover returned to her" and he reciprocated her feelings. The relationship continued during his young manhood. She helped him with his writing and took his manuscripts to established writers for criticism. He bought her presents, sent her flowers, and took her with him on his holidays and to the theater. No other woman ever meant as much to him as his mother. His father, uneasily aware of his son's difficulties, disliked and rejected him, and when his son began to write, he was so disturbed by what seemed to him to be offensive subject matter that he tore up his papers.

At age thirteen he was sexually excited at the sight of male swimming teams. His first sexual emission was elicited by looking at a reproduction of Guido Reni's *Saint Sebastian,* a dying, naked young man tied to a tree, pierced by arrows. (Twenty-five years later, at his own request, he posed for a photographer as Saint Sebastian.) He liked to look at pictures of dueling scenes or of young samurai cutting open their bellies, and the thought of blood excited him sexually. He had homosexual feelings in boyhood, and his first physical attraction was to an extroverted, rude, athletic classmate whom he dared not approach. He felt ill at ease when other students talked about women, and the word "woman" meant no more to him sensually than the word "pencil." All during his life he was attracted to men who had the physical qualities of the animal, whose flesh was unspoiled by intellect, to young toughs, sailors, and fishermen.

At school he was seen as a puny, pale boy with a strange way of laughing. His few associations were with boys older than himself who appreciated his literary talent. He tells of his fantasies of cannibalism, of boy-sacrifice, of young bodies being carried to a banqueting room on a huge plate. As a college student he read Radiquet, Oscar Wilde, Maria Rilke, and Lou Andreas-Salomé, who fascinated him.

He was in law school and subject to the draft when World War II began, but developed a continuous fever, which caused him to be rejected as a soldier, much to his disappointment, since he had a craving for death and blood. He was quite an eligible young bachelor with a lucrative civil-service position, but he spent his leisure hours writing. His parents urged him to marry and he proposed to two women, but they rejected him. Finally a marriage was arranged with a suitable young woman, mainly to please Yukio's mother, who was diagnosed as having cancer and wanted grandchildren before she died. The couple had two children. Yukio became enormously successful as a writer, his works were widely translated, and he was honored as one of Japan's greatest contemporary literary figures. Intelligent, with a fine sense of humor, he made men he met casually feel that they alone mattered to him. Later he raised a small army and initiated a right-wing coup to take over the government to try to return it to the military status it had before

World War II, an ill-conceived move destined to failure. Having sent his wife and children out of the country (to the United States to Disneyland) and prepared to execute himself publicly if the coup failed. When Yukio Mishima committed hara-kiri, his death did nothing to diminish his popularity as a writer, and the income from his royalties during the year after his suicide was $250,000. Despite his success, however, Yukio had confided to his mother a few days before his suicide that he never in his life had done anything that he wanted to do.

Julian Huxley. Novelist Graham Greene and biologist Julian Huxley both came from privileged homes and had loving and concerned parents. Neither blames his parents for his emotional problems, although both are inclined to think their problems were hereditary and to blame their depressive grandparents. In the lives of these two gently reared Englishmen being thwarted in love, having a dislike for school, and having guilt feelings about sexual relationships were added to fear of failure.

When Julian Huxley was twenty-one he became formally engaged to a girl who was very much in love with him and whose family accepted him warmly. However, his own feelings toward her were quite ambivalent and he did not know how to tell her or her parents so. As a pre-World War I internationalist, he also was emotionally upset over the prospect of England going to war with Germany. As a research student in a German university, he had witnessed first hand the saber duels, chauvinism, and militarism there, and he hated war.

His anxieties about the war and his possible involvement and his impending marriage were too much for him. When he broke off his engagement he experienced his first serious breakdown. As he expressed it in his 1970 autobiography, *Memories,* "I relapsed into a real 'nervous breakdown' . . . in modern terminology, a depression neurosis. Whatever it is called, it was a horrible experience, a hell of self-reproach, repressed guilt, a sense of my own uselessness and the futility of life in general" (p. 97).

His uncle, who was a physician, advised hospitalization. Julian preferred hypnosis, which was found not to be helpful. Eventually he went for what was called a "rest cure" in a sanitorium, where he spent time lying in bed, being well fed, and taking tonics. He was soon able to go to the United States, where he had an academic appointment at Rice University and where he fulfilled his obligations well. But when he went home for a summer vacation in 1914, he had another mild fit of depression and another rest cure in Surrey.

His brother, Trevenen, had suffered a depressive breakdown also; they were at the same nursing home. Although Julian recovered and left, Trevenen did not; he hanged himself in response to an unhappy love affair. A handsome, athletic, brilliant youth, a superb mountaineer, and a good poet, Trevenen had fallen in love with Sarah, his mother's parlor maid, but such alliances between the gentlefolk and the commonfolk were not socially acceptable in those days. When Sarah left and found other employment, she wrote him a despondent letter while Trevenen was recovering from his depression. The letter was found in his pocket. His brother's tragic death exacerbated Julian's depression.

After two years of courtship, Julian married a charming, intelligent young woman named Juliette, who was governess of the daughters of the last white raja in northern Borneo. Juliette was not told of her young husband's tendency toward mental illness, but when he had a severe depression soon after their honeymoon, she behaved in a loving and mature fashion. At that point they were living in Oxford, where he had a teaching fellowship in zoology. As a beginning teacher he found he had forgotten certain factual material he was supposed to know. "Things came to a head," he reported in *Memories*, "while I was giving a demonstration; I found myself unable to answer the undergraduates' questions, and collapsed on the floor in a semi-faint" (p. 124).

The couple went to Switzerland to stay with Juliette's mother in Neuchâtel, and then to Lausanne, where he was to be treated by Dr. Vittoz, who was recommended by Lady Ottoline. At that time Julian could not make any decision, even about trivial matters. He was in anguish about the burden he was placing on his young wife.

His physician started his treatment by setting him to a simple task, such as visualizing a square or circle, and frequently examined his "brain impulse" to see if he could find evidence of being able to concentrate. Julian improved and they went back to stay with Juliette's mother. (Dr. Vittoz merely put his finger to the patient's temple. It was the patient's confidence in the prestigious physician, rather than his specific treatment, that helped.) However, he still had suicidal fantasies and felt weak, and everything was an effort. Finally, during the autumn term, he returned to teaching, and by borrowing a friend's notes was able to prepare for his classes meticulously.

It was not until years later, when he was a distinguished adult, that he had another acute period of depression. In 1941, he resigned his position as secretary of London's Zoological Society because it resented his going (on unpaid leave) to the United States at the invitation of the Rockefeller Foundation to give a series of lectures. Since he and Juliette had lived on the zoo grounds in an official residence, they had to find housing, which was very difficult during World War II, especially in the London area. He felt financially insecure, although there were continual demands for his services as a free-lance lecturer and scientist. While working as a consultant in Africa he contracted hepatitis. "I felt miserable as a result of my attack of fever," he wrote, "and also perhaps because of my forced resignation from the Zoo, having now to face earning my living as a freelance. I got home yellow with jaundice and deeply depressed" (p. 279).

When he was hospitalized in London, a bomb fell on a corner of the hospital and he was taken by ambulance to a nursing home, where his hepatitis was cured and where he also had electric-shock treatments. Within three weeks or so he was able to go for little walks. He had many productive years after this last breakdown.

Julian speculates that the reason he and Trevenen had such severe bouts of depression was that there were temperamental problems that skipped a generation in his family. His distinguished grandfather, T. H. Huxley, was cruelly subject to depression, and both of his maternal grandparents were also extremely temperamental. Indeed, his maternal grandfather was temperamentally unemployable, even though he had taken a first in "Greats" at Oxford, and repudiated Victorian England by emigrating to Tasmania, where he failed as a farmer. He married the daughter of the governor of Tasmania, the fiery-tempered, proud Julia Sorrell, but failed to support her and seven children adequately, partly because he changed his church affiliation from Anglican to Catholic and thereby lost his academic post as school inspector of Protestant Tasmania. When he was being received into membership in the Catholic church, Julia smashed the windows of the church with stones. On another occasion she threw dinner plates at visiting priests.

As far as his own father and mother, however, Julian had nothing but praise and no feelings but those of loving nostalgia for his childhood. "I adored my mother," he wrote. "She wore pince-nez . . . she used to throw back her head and explode with laughter when amused—but could pass from gay to grave as the mood took her . . . Her steady gaze was truth-compelling, but full of love, even when she had to reprimand us . . . she founded a girls' school near Godalming, Prior's Field . . . After her too early death at forty-six . . . her pupils told me . . . how uncannily understanding she had been with all their personal troubles" (pp. 18–19).

It was his mother who taught him to read when he was four, who took the children for walks, collecting and identifying flowers. His father was as delightful as his mother but less driving. Julian wrote: "My father Leonard was T. H. H.'s second son. He enjoyed life—whether at work or play, gardening, or on the tennis court, at skating, rambling or climbing mountains, botanizing, listening to music or entertaining his friends. Though he had great sorrows in his life, I never knew him to be depressed or ill-tempered . . . It seems as if the Huxley genes skipped a generation to assert their particular characteristics, which are perhaps best defined as temperamental, in his grandchildren" (p. 15).

Graham Greene. The English novelist says it was the interminable repetitions in his life that broke him down when he was a seventeen-year-old student in the preparatory school, for which his well-meaning father was headmaster. The repetitious schedule by which he lived seven days a week bored him. Classes he did not mind, but living in the dormitory was intolerable, and he was bullied by two boys whom he was honor-bound not to report.

He attempted suicide by slashing his leg with a pocketknife, but he was unable to hurt himself severely. He drank an entire bottle of his hayfever drops. He ate a bunch of deadly nightshade. He swallowed twenty aspirin tablets. These tactics did nothing but make him uncomfortable.

One morning he ran away and hid in the village commons,

where he could eat wild berries, intending to stay out until his parents were worried enough to give him permission to quit school. But after a couple of hours his older sister, while crossing the commons, happened to see him slinking about, and he went docilely home with her.

His father was certain that Graham was miserable because he was part of a ring of boys known to exist in the school who were masturbating together, which the headmaster and staff believed led to madness. Since Graham did not know what the word "masturbate" meant, he did not sufficiently reassure his apprehensive father, who sent for an older brother in medical school who in turn advised sending Graham to a distinguished psychiatric inpatient clinic in London. He was not told that there was insanity on both sides of the family or that his parents were fearful lest some of their children have a "hereditary taint."

Graham had the happiest six months of his life at the clinic, enjoying Freudian therapy, uninterrupted reading, and explorations of London. He met the poet Walter de la Mare and they became friends. When he came home, he was permitted to live at home while attending school, and life was quite tolerable. However, two years later he tried Russian roulette in a secluded spot on the same village commons.

While on summer holiday with his parents as a student at Oxford, he developed a hopeless, obsessive passion for the governess of his young brother and sister after he had glimpsed her thigh at the beach. She was unhappy and apprehensive about her forthcoming marriage to an engineer in the Azores because she had not seen him for a year. Graham and the twenty-nine-year-old governess kissed and cuddled unobserved in closets and dark corners, but he was too young to marry. Still, he could not bear to think of her marrying anyone else, and, like his grandfather who, he says, was a manic-depressive, he fell into a deep depression. To alleviate his pain, he tried Russian roulette. It worked wonders. When he pulled the trigger and no shot was fired into his head, he felt an instant rush of intense joy and an exhilaration with life. Later he tried Russian roulette again and again. By the fifth experience, however, he was bored; the thrill was gone. Since he never liked routine, he quit playing the game.

As he grew older, he found other ways to achieve the same exhilarating effect. When his spirits were low and life was dull, he exposed himself to danger in places where bullets were flying: Tabasco during the religious persecution, the Kikuyu reserve during the Mau-Mau insurrection, the French war in Vietnam, and many other such places.

Antonio Gramsci. A severely crippled boy, hunchbacked and small, from a small town in Italy, Marxist revolutionary Antonio Gramsci came from a poor but affectionate family and obtained an education only by the most stringent economy. His father, a generous and kindly man, had been jailed for years by political opponents who found a small discrepancy in his financial records when he worked as city registrar. Antonio himself was usually cold, hungry, and ill, and was always self-conscious about his crippled and ill-clothed appearance. As a student his small grant did not provide the necessities, and his parents and a brother sacrificed to help him, though they had little to give. Toward the end of his college course he found himself unable to face a final examination. He grew dizzy with fatigue, had severe headaches, suffered loss of memory, and, he said, "felt positively insane." He could find no peace, waking or sleeping; he rolled on the floor like a maniac.

He found it easy enough to get a school doctor to certify that he was unable to take the examination at the scheduled time, diagnosing him as having "acute neurosis," but unfortunately the school administration revoked his grant. Nevertheless, he was able to rest, renew his energies, and find money enough to complete his schooling.

Even so his life was singularly tragic. Imprisoned for his revolutionary activities, he did not break down emotionally, but his wife would not visit him and he had difficulties finding out what was happening to his children. He finally died in prison after suffering a number of painful, debilitating illnesses, any one of which could have ended his life.

Family Influences

Social workers and others who work with families where a dependent adolescent has a psychotic episode or a severe neurosis have observed that there is a difference in the attitude of the well-educated and poorly educated parents. The more intellectually sophisticated are likely to seek help quickly, to be less emotionally devastated, and to be more understanding of the ill youth. The less well educated family is fearful, shamed, emotionally distraught; intense closeness turns to revulsion and neglect when recovery is slow; parents and siblings become antagonistic both toward the patient and toward the physician. In the families that produced the Three Hundred, however, there are few illiterate families. Typically they are upwardly mobile, striving, driving, middle class.

There is, however, a difference in concern between the families accustomed to working with people and ideas and the families where the father is preoccupied with business and the mother with respectability. In the families of subjects whose breakdowns came in adult life, there was not the concern given Julian Huxley or Graham Greene, despite early signs of emotional instability. For instance, playwright Tennessee Williams's father was contemptuous of his "sissy" son, and Tennessee's insensitive mother was primarily worried about concealing the evidence of her bad marriage. Poet Theodore Roethke's father, though he rejected his precocious, non-athletic, sensitive son, also had his own problems: he quarreled with his partner-brother, exposing his misuse of funds, but was defeated in his revenge when the brother committed suicide. T. S. Eliot's father, Tom, a successful brick manufacturer, felt he had to take second place to his own father, a Saint Louis Unitarian minister who was the most positive contributor to social change and educational progress in his city, responsible, for example, for founding Washington University and other social and educational institutions. Tom Eliot seems to have had little to do with his youngest son, who was dominated by his older sisters and by his mother, who admired her minister father-in-law and wrote his biography. When T. S. made England his home and married without first telling his family, his father disowned him.

The Williams, Roethke, and Eliot families were not thought of poorly by their communities, but these parents also did not show the kind of concern and understanding of deviance shown by half the families who reared children with emotional problems requiring hospitalization or lengthy psychiatric attention. In particular let us look at the breakdowns of Tennessee Williams and T. S. Eliot.

Tennessee Williams. A robust, healthy boy until he was

seven, Tennessee (Thomas Lanier) Williams had diphtheria and was ill for nearly a year. When he was eight, his father began to earn more money as a shoe salesman, and the family moved away from the pleasant grandparents' home in Mississippi to a sordid apartment in Saint Louis. The antagonism between the sickly boy and the father, who was alcoholic, was intense. In early adolescence the young Williams was so shy that he blushed hotly whenever his eyes met the eyes of another person.

When he was sixteen his maternal grandfather, a Protestant minister, who was always close to him and quite helpful to him at times, took him to Europe. Here he had his first near-psychotic crisis. Suddenly, in the city of Cologne, the nature of the thinking process in humans became a terrifying complex mystery to him—so terrifying that he ceased to function and, drenched with sweat, stumbled into the Cologne cathedral, where he prayed until he was released from his anxiety. Later, when the terror returned, also in Cologne, he exorcised it by composing a poem. In the years that followed he abused his body with an intensity that was almost suicidal, becoming addicted to pills, liquor, and "feel-good" shots.

His relationships with his rejecting father and his insensitive, overprotective mother were never satisfying, and he was always jealous of his achieving brother, Dakin, who pleased his parents. But he was always close to his lovely, intelligent sister, Rose, though unfortunately she had a lobotomy when her mental illness made her too overtly aggressive, and thereafter she was pleasant but dull. When one of his homosexual lovers, Frankie, died of cancer, he went into a seven-year depression that was not lessened by success or a succession of other male companions.

In 1969, at the nadir of his depression, he was taken by ambulance to a private mental hospital, where he stayed for three months. While there he had a blackout, a great many painful convulsions, and a "silent coronary"—he remembers, for instance, walking down the corridor after a severe convulsion with the exaggerated, mincing walk of a drag queen, chanting a poem, the refrain of which was the word "Redemption!" As he walked, he says in his 1975 *Memoirs*, he also chanted an improvised poem about "the birth of my brother Dakin when I was eight and my first sight of him, suckling the bare breast of my mother in the St. Louis hospital" (p. 220).

When it became evident to him that he had to improve his condition or stay in the hospital forever, he decided to free himself and began to accept help, especially that of a neurologist named Levy, whom he found "less inhuman than the others." But, though he began to read books and to play bridge with other patients, he was not entirely acquiescent. When he was given his first outside pass, for instance, he went straight to a drugstore and bought a box of sleeping pills. And when his mother and brother came to visit him, he needled them so much that his brother retaliated by bringing him an unflattering *Esquire* article about him.

When he was released, he went home, reluctantly, to his mother. He found her intolerable. In one vivid scene in *Memoirs* he tells how she talked continuously while he tried to watch a movie on TV in which his old friend Vivien Leigh was playing. He and Frankie attended a party given by her on Frankie's last night out before he died. Tennessee was aware that Vivien Leigh had emotional problems even more incapacitating than his own. As his mother's chatter kept him from hearing the movie's dialogue, he watched the actress moving gracefully about on the screen—and consoled himself that she, too, knew how it was to be mad.

T. S. Eliot. The youngest child of a well-to-do Saint Louis family, T. S. Eliot could not have been more preciously reared, but in September 1921, his wife, Vivienne (who was actually more emotionally unstable than he and was eventually to be hospitalized), told him that he must see a nerve specialist. Lady Ottoline Morrell recommended Dr. Roger Vittoz of Lausanne. Julian Huxley, who had been his patient, was also consulted and agreed that they had made a good choice. Eliot's bank gave him a three-month leave to go to Switzerland to recover from his anxieties and depressions.

In Lausanne he was depressed, distracted, unable to write. A family reunion with his mother and a sister, whom he had not seen in years, had not been pleasant. His doctor told him that all that stopped him from writing was his fear of writing anything short of perfection, that he was thinking he was God himself. Eliot was speechless with rage, and instead of resting for the prescribed three months, he stayed on in Switzerland and wrote *The Waste Land.*

Drugs and alcohol are associated with the deaths of a number of the Three Hundred who also had severe emotional problems: singer Janis Joplin, novelist Malcolm Lowry, painter Jackson Pollock, actress Marilyn Monroe, F. Scott Fitzgerald's wife Zelda, and singer Judy Garland. Edwin S. Shneidman, in *Suicidology* (1977), says that some individuals who cannot bring themselves to destroy themselves by killing themselves do so by adopting a life-style that is self-destructive. He also speaks of the difficulty of determining whether someone who dies while intoxicated does so by accident or by intent. Jackson Pollock was very drunk when his car smashed into a tree and was killed instantly, as was one of two young women riding with him. They had begged him to stop the car when it was obvious he had lost his self-control and judgment. Shneidman calls him a suicide. A person's death from an overdose of sleeping pills while intoxicated is very often described as being accidental rather than intentional.

Janis Joplin. All that is known for sure about Janis Joplin's death is that she died following the injection of a large dose of heroin. Whether she intended to die is not certain. She seemed unusually "high" just before she injected the drug. (This is often reported by persons who have been extremely depressed and finally made a firm decision to end it all.)

Until she was fourteen, Janis was a "father's girl." She had two younger siblings, a sister who became a psychologist and a folk singer, and a brother who was a willful adolescent, artistic and unsure of his life goals. Her mother is described by Myra Friedman, one of Joplin's biographers, in *Buried Alive* (1973), as an industrious, disciplined woman who was the registrar at the local college in Port Arthur, Texas.

Janis was the firstborn. She sat up at six months and was handling a spoon and fork with dexterity at age one. She was well behaved, cherubic, docile, and adaptable. She sang herself to sleep. She began to draw as soon as she could handle a pencil. She had her own library card when she was still a toddler and could choose her own picture books. She read well before starting school. (She was a great reader all of her life but tried to conceal her intellectual interests from her public.) When she started writing plays in first grade, her proud father built her a puppet theater. The family backyard was the gathering place of all of the children on the block.

Janis accepted the births of her sister and brother with loving enthusiasm. The parents encouraged their children to voice their opinions and ideas. The children were not urged to excel. The gifted girl was closest to her father, whom she described as a "secret intellectual" in the dull oil town of Port Arthur, where an interest in books and culture was rare and suspect. A graduate engineer and manager of all of Texaco's enterprises, Seth Joplin was a man who loved his family and was close to his precocious daughter. But when she reached adolescence, he became fearful of her reactions to her maturation and tried to influence her to be closer to her mother and to be more like her mother, who was sensible and socially well adjusted. Janis' reading of Zelda Fitzgerald's biographies and her determination to be Port Arthur's "Zelda" was something he could not handle.

Janis remembered her childhood as idyllic and her adolescence as a disaster. "Then the whole world turned," Friedman quotes her as saying. "It just turned on me" (p. 13). Port Arthur was never proud of Janis, not even when she became nationally known, but one of the women teachers in town said, when interviewed, that Janis' problem was that the school did not recognize her exceptional abilities and failed to give her the kind of challenge and recognition she wanted and needed. She had her first clash with her peers when she was in the ninth grade and said that she favored racial integration. Two of the boys in the class followed her about and called her "nigger lover." Her mother felt she was too strident and belligerent in her response to teasing. Not a pretty girl, she began to drink, to dress oddly, and to act the buffoon. Her parents were not able to cope with the pent-up, angry adolescent who so recently had been a happy, gifted, docile child. Her father, however, was still the more permissive, less punitive parent. Her mother would not give an inch when her own values were contradicted, although Janis was the apple of her eye. The parents alternated between being quite liberal in some ways and very strict in others. The family conflicts soon became acute, frequent, and painful.

Janis aligned herself with five intelligent, adventurous boys from her high school who were also disdainful of Port Arthur. They read books they were told not to read, listened to jazz, climbed water towers, drank beer. According to her biographers, the relationship of the lone girl to the boys was not sexual. She tagged along as the lone jester. They liked her because she "raised such hell." She was loud, boisterous, and crude. Other students mocked her, threw things at her, called her ugly names, and she responded obscenely and went home to cry. Still, she was already selling her paintings, and the family expected her to be an artist.

After graduation from high school she lived at home and took courses at Port Arthur Business College. When she found Port Arthur more than she could bear, she went to visit an aunt in California. In Venice in Los Angeles she found some young people— so-called "beatniks"—and immediately identified with them. She then drifted into the nightclub circuit and became popular. The audiences liked her toughness, her bigger-than-life agonies, her lack of inhibitions, and they liked the way she strangled a song to death.

Biographer David Dalton, who followed her about on tour with a tape recorder, quotes her, in *Janis* (1971), as saying: "All my life I just wanted to be a beatnik, meet all the heavies, get stoned, get laid, have a good time, that's all I ever wanted, except I knew I had a good voice and I could always get a couple of beers off of it. All of a sudden someone threw me in this rock and roll band . . . it was better than it had been with any man, you know. Maybe that's the trouble" (p. 81). She died at the peak of her popularity at age twenty-seven.

Malcolm Lowry. On the day Malcolm Lowry died he drank heavily, which was not unusual. He was embarrassed by his wife's weeping in a pub because she was still grieving for the home they had lost in Canada when his publishers refused to give him an advance. They went home together to listen to a Stravinsky concert scheduled for 7:30 P.M. When he turned the volume high, she protested because he was drowning out selections from Bach that the friendly neighbor next door was playing on her radio. He reacted angrily and turned the volume even higher and sat huddled in a corner, drinking directly from a bottle. She snatched the bottle from him and broke it on a fireplace fixture. Infuriated, he chased her downstairs, and she fled to the home of the Bach-playing neighbor, where she stayed all night. In the morning, she found him dead. Two bottles of sleeping pills were missing. The coroner's verdict was "death by misadventure," which would permit Lowry a church burial.

The Sylvia Plath Story

The intentional death of an older person who already has enjoyed recognition is not as devastating a loss to society and the survivors as is the suicide of a young person. For instance, Thomas Chatterton (1752–1770) is remembered in the dictionary as a "young English poet who committed suicide." It is the tragedy of his death, not his poems, that keeps alive his memory. A suicide, especially a young suicide, does irreparable damage to the immediate survivors and to a considerable extent enhances the fame of the young person who dies by his or her own hand.

This has been true of poet Sylvia Plath, who died a suicide at thirty. Her novel, *The Bell Jar,* which sold only moderately well under a pseudonym before her death, became quite popular after her death. She has been the subject of an impressive amount of biographical and critical evaluation. A. Alvarez, a personal friend and critic for the London *Observer,* has written perceptively about his friendship with her while she was in England. Her roommate at Smith College, Nancy Hunter Steiner, has told what it was like to live with her during the period soon after her first suicide attempt at nineteen. Edward Butscher, a biographer who never knew her personally, interviewed a great many persons who did: grade school, high school, and college teachers; high school and college friends; English neighbors who knew her well when she and her husband lived in a farmhouse in Devonshire.

Her mother, Aurelia Schober Plath, who is herself a competent writer, edited *Letters Home,* selecting from among 696 letters by Sylvia to her mother and brother between 1950, when she entered Smith, and her death in London in 1963. In Thomas Chatterton's day there was no comparable outpouring of data about any poet's life. Now we can know Sylvia Plath more intimately than we know Shakespeare or even Elizabeth Barrett Browning or Emily Dickinson.

The Sylvia Plath story illustrates many of the findings concerning the Three Hundred: the positive effect on achievement of a love of learning in the home; good sibling relationships; the strong drive for achievement, upward mobility, and resistance to frustration of her immigrant parents and grandparents; the destructive effect of a death in the family; the greater tendency of girls to be conforming in school, (though Sylvia, like other writers, deeply disliked studying subjects she found irrelevant, such as science and mathematics); the devastating effect of being defeated and frustrated on children reared tenderly by idealistic parents.

The Bell Jar is a poorly written novel that Sylvia said she wrote as a quick potboiler, although feminists who take an extreme stance accept it as an authentic biography. However, her own letters, the biography by her Smith roommate, and the observations of her friend Alvarez all contradict the assumption that she was a lesbian or did not enjoy being a mother or a wife. The hurt people feel about her death demands a victim. One biographer blames her mother's assumed "religiosity" and speaks of her as being Puritan, Calvinistic, and worst of all, Unitarian. The ultra-liberal Unitarians, who are facetiously said to address their prayers "To Whom It May Concern," are not to be confused with the Puritans. He also blames her mother for having exposed her to the bourgeois perils of a small college town.

We would agree with George Slade, who writes the introduction to Nancy Hunter Steiner's *A Closer Look at Ariel* (1972), that "the image of the poet that rises out of the poetry and the memory of Sylvia Plath as recorded by her friends never quite came together, even when they did seem to cast a kind of light on each other. But [Steiner's book] increases the area of overlap considerably; and it helps us to understand why the poet in the poetry and the poet in the memoirs of her friends often seem like two different people" (pp. 3–4).

The best source of information about her is *Letters Home,* edited by her mother, Aurelia Schober Plath. Sylvia is another of the manic-depressives who was reared in what appears to have been an ideal home, although when she was four to eight years old her father was seriously ill and would not accept medical care, her mother became ill with an ulcer, and her brother had asthma. Still, to a considerable degree the home is the kind we have presented in previous chapters as being a good background for the encouragement of the creative potential: a middle-class, academic home in which the child was wanted and loved and in which early companionship with affectionate adults happily stimulated the child's artistic and intellectual interests.

The Plaths and Schobers. Sylvia's biology professor father, Otto Plath, was forty-three when he married his graduate student, twenty-two-year-old Aurelia Schober. He had grown up in Grabow, Germany, a little town in the Polish Corridor, where he spoke German and Polish and learned French in secondary school. Letters about his scholastic abilities prompted his grandparents, who had immigrated to Wisconsin, to offer to pay his college expenses if he would promise to prepare himself for the Lutheran ministry. Because his German father, a blacksmith, could not send him to college and because as a pacifist Otto wished to avoid military service, he eagerly accepted his grandparents' invitation. At sixteen he arrived in New York, lived for a year with an uncle, and spent the year auditing courses in a grade school. At the end of the year he could speak English without a trace of foreign accent. He handled many frustrations well.

At college he made A and B grades, but his pleased grandparents did not know that Otto was reading Darwin and consequently were not prepared for his rejection of his courses, his teachers, and his classmates when he was sent to a Lutheran seminary. When he told his grandfather he could not, in good conscience, become a minister, his name was blotted out from the family Bible and he was asked to leave his grandparents' home and never come back. For the rest of his life he was on his own. He worked at a great many menial jobs before he finally acquired a doctorate in biology from Harvard. At the time of his marriage to Aurelia, he was already a world authority on the social life of the bumblebee.

Otto was eager for fatherhood. When he insisted upon doing the marketing and planning the meals and was very much the head of the family, Aurelia, whose home was more matriarchal than patriarchal, conquered her negative reactions and let him enjoy his pleasure in being a husband and father. He was a kindly man—tall, handsome, learned, a confiding and friendly person, who had been very lonely for years.

Aurelia's parents were immigrants from Austria. Her father, a genial headwaiter, was only six years older than Aurelia's husband. After her father lost his savings in 1920 buying worthless stock, he left most major decisions to his wife. "Nevertheless," Aurelia says, "ours was a peaceful, loving home, and I assumed that all marriages were like that of my parents" (p. 4). Aurelia started work at fourteen, as an aide in a library, but her father insisted she take the two-year course at Boston University's College of Practical Arts and Letters instead of the four-year college course that would prepare her to teach English in high school. However, her jolly, easygoing mother, who loved books and learning as much as she, persuaded her father to let Aurelia transfer to the regular college division when she completed her commercial work. Actually, grandmother Schober's motives were somewhat ulterior, for she saw no reason why one tuition fee could not serve two, so she read her daughter's textbooks and novels. There was a resistance to frustration on both sides of the family which overprivileged Sylvia did not have.

The Schober grandparents lived in a house near the beach at Point Shirley, Massachusetts, with the sea on one side and the bay on the other, and were to be an important part of Sylvia's life. The Plaths lived nearby in Winthrop, an ordinary middle-class suburban town near Boston.

Sylvia Plath: The Early Years. When Aurelia Plath learned she was pregnant, she stopped reading Rilke and Emily Dickinson and began reading books about child psychology. Sylvia was also what her father wanted—a daughter, who would be more affectionate, he believed, than a son. Sylvia was kissed and cuddled and told nursery rhymes, and as the firstborn grandchild, with a young aunt and uncle also nearby, was the pet of an extended family. Quick to learn, at age one she handled her knife and fork with dexterity.

Before their marriage, the Plaths had planned to have two children to whom they would give all of the pleasures and advantages they themselves had lacked. When Aurelia became pregnant again, she began preparing Sylvia, who was then two and one-half years old, to accept her sibling, and Sylvia "helped" her mother prepare the accoutrement for the new baby, Warren.

The early years of the marriage were seemingly idyllic. Aurelia was proud of being a faculty wife and was useful to her husband, who was quite busy with new publications. They worked together at the dining-room table for hours, clearing it tidily before meals. The grandparents were eager babysitters. When Warren was a year old, Otto's health began to deteriorate. He was often fatigued, lost weight, had a chronic cough and severe cramps in his legs, and was certain he had lung cancer, though he refused to see a physician because he feared surgery. Four years later, in 1940, Otto developed gangrene in his little toe, and it developed he was diabetic. His leg was amputated, but he died, from an embolus in the lung.

Aurelia was left with the equity in the house and about $5,000. Her parents sold their beach house and moved in with her, because one roof was cheaper than two, and Grandmother Schober kept house while Aurelia reluctantly resigned herself to becoming a teacher of secretarial students at Boston University.

Six-year-old Warren reacted to the news of his father's death by hugging his mother and saying how glad he was that she was healthy and could care for him. Eight-year-old Sylvia was angry. She said she would never speak to God again.

Sylvia Plath: The Productive Years. When Sylvia was nine the family moved to Wellesley; there was profit in the move for everyone but grandfather, who had to stay over at the country club where he worked as headwaiter four nights a week because the drive was too far to make each day. They moved because Sylvia was having constant sinus infections and Warren had chronic asthma. Aurelia hoped the move away from the sea to a warmer, drier climate would help and also thought the schools had more to offer. She missed the intellectual life she had enjoyed with Otto, and in Wellesley, which was a college town, she hoped she could find stimulating friends at the Unitarian Church, having been a Unitarian before her marriage. Unitarians, since the days of Emerson, have provided a haven for people who are not theistic, who dislike dogma, and who are interested in life, literature, knowledge, civil liberties, and social reform. Aurelia was hungry for that kind of companionship. Grandmother Schober was happy wherever her family was, although she missed her beach house.

The Wellesley teachers were pleased with the neat, obedient, brilliant Plath children. Sylvia, who was ready for fourth grade, was double-promoted to sixth grade, but when her mother objected, because she felt her daughter would not be happy among older children, was demoted back to fifth grade. However, since the fifth grade work was not challenging to her, she had art, dancing, and music lessons. She also went to a sailing camp and to Girl Scout camp.

Throughout school and college Sylvia made straight A's without strain, and her whole academic life was a procession of awards, prizes, commendations, certificates of achievement, and scholarships. She enrolled in special high school English classes, belonged to honor clubs, acted in school plays, and wrote for school newspapers. She

dressed modestly and plainly, but in the latest fashion, was beautiful, but not too beautiful. She dated, petted with her boyfriends, but
never went "all the way."

Even before she went to college she established a reputation
as a writer, and at Smith other girls recognized her as "the girl who
wrote for *Seventeen*." To be an important, successful writer was
paramount in Sylvia's life, although she also wanted to find a tall,
talented husband whom she could boss, and to bear him sons. She
wanted to be a good mother, wife, and recognized writer. She
achieved these goals before she was thirty. When her exemplary
husband, whom she had cherished, left her for another woman, she
killed herself. Although she suffered from recurring bouts of exhilaration and depression, she was strong-willed and proud, and
feared lest an admission of any weakness would handicap her career.
Her defenses were strong. She was the perfectionist who had had
almost no experiences with failure.

Her feeling that she must constantly escalate the rate of her
achievements was encouraged by everyone—her mother, friends, her
casual acquaintances, scholarship sponsor. She had no defenses
against failure, having experienced so little of it (except for several
rejection slips from *Seventeen*, of which the world was not aware),
and whenever she felt she had failed those who expected much of
her she panicked.

We can feel these tensions in the letters she wrote to her mother
during the months before her first suicide attempt: the emotional
ups and downs, the ecstasy, the alternating joy and despair. On
November 19, 1952, Sylvia wrote her mother a long, emotional
letter stating she felt like killing herself because every time she
opened her physics textbook she felt as though her nose was being
rubbed in its own slime. She hated formulas and didn't give a damn
about valences, artificial atoms, and molecules. She had thought of
going to the school psychiatrist, but he would only suggest she drop
the extracurricular activities she enjoyed. Her whole life was being
ruined by having to take physics. "No rest cure in the infirmary will
cure this sickness in me," she said (p. 99).

On about December 1, 1952, Sylvia wrote her brother at Exeter that life was looking up and she was no longer in danger of
flunking her science course. She told him she had seen her more or

less steady boyfriend, Dick, who was in a tuberculosis sanitarium but that she had also met another man, Myron Lotz, first in his class at Yale, who had pitched for the Detroit Tigers that past summer and earned $10,000. She was fascinated by Lotz and begged her brother for information about the Detroit baseball team so that she could dazzle the "brilliant lug"—although, she said, she did not really want to get married, not for a few years anyway. She was on top of the world.

On December 15, 1952, she wrote that she was still seeing Myron Lotz and they had taken a ride in a small private plane with a pilot they met. Yet she said she was also going to the infirmary because of insomnia. Her mother was not to worry, if she got a notice from the college, however, since she had better news: A college trustee had recommended her for a Fulbright grant and for an instructorship in English at Smith.

During the Christmas holidays Sylvia broke her leg while visiting Dick, her wealthy but tubercular admirer whose parents were so pleased with her. She was foolhardy, having borrowed skis and without instruction tried to ski on a difficult slope. Still, the accident ended the long siege of depression that had plagued her. She had reached the bottom, thought every straw was her last, but now she was merry again. She even had found the courage to ask to audit the detested science course rather than take it for credit. If winter was so wonderful, how could she endure the joy of a green young spring?

In early 1953, she told her mother that February would go down in history as Sylvia Plath's Black Month. The sight of her leg coming out of its cast all hairy and yellow had once more thrown her into a deep depression. She was hopeless with misery. On February 28 she thanked her mother for her comforting letters and said she was a superlative mother and that she ached to make her proud, to repay her for all of the treats she had given her during the two decades of her life.

On March 17th she was high with joy. She felt violets sprouting between her fingers. Myron Lotz thought she was brilliant, creative, and beautiful all at once. On March 21 she wrote that she had heard the poet W. H. Auden speak and had found her God in him. She would like to touch the hem of his garment. On April 24th her birthday present to her mother was the information that *Harper's* had sent her a $100 check and *Mademoiselle* had sent $10. The Harper check represented her first professional acceptance (not a students' award). The *Atlantic* and the *New Yorker* were now her unclimbed Annapurna.

On April 28th, still high, she was elected editor of the *Smith Review*. On May 12th she wrote her brother, then a senior at Exeter, planning their summer vacations. She expressed her fears that her mother was not well and said she was writing for *True Story,* and even writing jingles for a Lucky Strike contest, to try to earn money to help her mother with their heavy expenses. Their mother, she told Warren, was an abnormally altruistic person, and her children must fight against her selflessness. Aurelia would kill herself if they went on accepting everything she wanted to do for them. Warren should remember not to let her fix his breakfast. She and her brother had had it good. She only hoped the world wouldn't blow up and queer it all.

Sylvia and Warren were both liberal in their views. They had worked together as migratory laborers, the *Christian Science Monitor* had published an antiwar poem by her, and she campaigned for Adlai Stevenson while a Smith student.

Both children had so far led a charmed existence, winning prizes, going to the best schools, eating and dressing well. As an example of good fortune, in May a telegram came inviting Sylvia to be one of twenty girls who would be guest editors of *Mademoiselle* for a month. The girls would be housed in a luxury hotel, would meet and interview famous people, be entertained, and escorted about town to see the sights. The stipend for the one month was more than Sylvia had received for the previous summer's hash-slinging at a resort. She accepted the invitation.

However, she was miserable in New York, depressed, worn-out by the heat and constant activity. Late in June she wrote her brother that the world had split open before her gaping eyes like a cracked watermelon. She had been ecstatic, horribly depressed, shocked, elated, enlightened, and enervated all in the course of four weeks. It was too much for her. All she wanted to do was to come home and sleep and sleep. Would he meet her at the station? She loved her brother more than the male hucksters and wealthy beasts she had met in New York. She would let him know what train her coffin would come in on.

The mood persisted after she came home. She talked endlessly of being a failure, of never being able to live up to the expectations of everyone she knew. She could not eat, sleep, or work. She had not been accepted for the creative-writing class for which she had applied at Harvard, a two-week course with writer Frank O'Connor to which she had assumed she would be admitted.

When she cut her legs purposely, to see if she "had the guts to do so," her mother took her to a psychiatrist. Shock treatment did not help. She was certain she would never amount to anything. She was agitated when the date for the opening of the fall semester at Smith drew near. One day she seemed to be herself, pink-cheeked and bright-eyed, and insisted her mother go see a film with a friend. When her mother came home Sylvia was gone, and so were the sleeping pills which her mother had been doling out to her from a locked box. For three days, hundreds of people searched for her, and she was finally found unconscious in a crawl space beneath the house. She did not return to Smith until the next winter semester. The rest of her young life was a repetition of these early experiences.

Mentally Ill Parents

Among the Three Hundred there were ten subjects who had mentally ill parents. The mothers of Lady Bird Johnson and Margaret Mead suffered depression because of their life circumstances and had periods of treatment away from home. Other parents were psychotic or brain-injured, were delusional, sometimes violent, or in a catatonic state for years. Among these were the mother of Allen Ginsberg and of Raphael and Moses Soyer, the mother (and also the grandmother and uncle) of Marilyn Monroe, and the mothers of Ethel Waters, King Hussein, Dom Moraes, and Friedrich Adler (whose sister also was mentally ill). The father of King Hussein was brain-injured.

Two of the Three Hundred lost both parents by suicide: Wilhelm Reich and Eileen Garrett. The fathers of Jean Cocteau and Isak Dinesen killed themselves. The mother of Peter and Jane Fonda was a suicide. The father of King Hussein had sudden fits of madness—possibly the result of epilepsy or brain injury—in which he became murderous; of his own volition he abdicated his throne and placed himself in the custody of others. The mother of Dom Moraes, who loved him very much when she was well, was also physically dangerous to her child when she was ill. His father, an intelligent and kindly man, handled the family tragedy well, and the son was not damaged by the experience.

Except in Marilyn Monroe's family, nothing in these family relationships justifies the extreme anxiety about a possible hereditary taint that haunted the families in which a young person was emotionally ill. With the possible exception of Allen Ginsberg, whose psychiatric treatment may have been chosen as an alternative to being arrested, the mentally ill parents did not rear mentally ill children. Nor did the Three Hundred who had emotional disturbances as adults or youths, as far as we can discover, bear emotionally disturbed offspring.

Conclusion

It is not the numerically small group of the mentally ill and the suicidal among the Three Hundred with whom we are primarily concerned but with what we can learn from their lives that may help to stem the rising suicide rates throughout the world in recent years. J. C. Coleman, in *Abnormal Psychology and Modern Life* (1976), says that the incidence of suicide among college students is twice as high as it is among young people in the same age range who are not in college. Ten thousand college students attempt suicide each year, and over 1,000 succeed. Three times as many females attempt suicide as do males, but males are more likely to succeed. Among the significant warnings of suicidal attempt, Coleman states, are change of mood, acute depression, lack of self-esteem, and loss of interest in studies.

"Students who manifest suicidal behavior," Coleman says, "are, as a group, superior students, and while they tend to expect a great deal of themselves in terms of academic achievement and to exhibit scholastic anxieties, grades, academic competition, and pressure over examinations are not regarded as significant precipitating stresses" (p. 609). During the period before the suicide attempt, they may be too depressed to prepare adequately for exams, may cut classes, stop studying, and sleep during the day, but it is ordinarily not their classroom experiences that have made them depressed. However, they may kill themselves when they are unable to study and know they would disappoint their parents. The most frequent cause of suicide, Coleman believes, is the breaking up of a romance, but students who kill themselves under such circumstances are more likely to be from homes where there has been separation, divorce, or the death of a parent.

E. S. Shneidman, in *Suicidology*, includes a chapter adapted from Hendin's *The Age of Sensation*, in which Hendin makes it clear that he does not believe that students attempt suicide because of classroom competition or overwork. In fact, he says, "far from being harmed by their work, many students used it as a barricade. 'Work,' as one student put it, was his 'main defensive army.' . . . Dull, demanding mental labor was often the nexus of the suicidal students' existence" (p. 324).

In observing the Three Hundred we came to several tentative conclusions that may be helpful and may suggest areas for further study:

1. The subjects of biography who become psychotic or commit suicide are almost all manic-depressives.
2. Creative productivity is hindered, not helped, by the emotional disturbance.
3. Parents of these manic-depressives and the suicidal are not often seen as punitive, rejecting, or insensitive.
4. The deeply depressed are often able to conceal their failures and are reluctant to seek help for fear of ruining their careers or losing social status. Their defenses are high.
5. The most frequent trigger to eminent persons' emotional breakdown or suicide or attempted suicide was failure to meet their own expectations and those of their elders, parents, or peers. The second most frequent trigger was grief or guilt over a love affair or unhappy marriage.
6. Symptoms of an impending suicide or breakdown often include

feelings of total inadequacy, inability to make even simple decisions, drastic disturbances of sleep patterns, and a rigidity and awkwardness in body stance.

7. When a person who has been deeply depressed is suddenly cheerful and overexcited, it may be because he or she has finally made the decision to end it all.

8. Bodily mutilation, such as cutting oneself, is a strong indication of suicidal intent.

9. The compulsive perfectionist who is reared by loving and conscientious parents, who inculcate in the child a strong sense of right and wrong, is especially vulnerable to depression when he or she first becomes acutely conscious of the iniquities and injustices of society.

10. Suicidal persons may try to relieve their tensions by undertaking physically dangerous activities.

11. The few mentally ill among the parents of the Three Hundred are not manic-depressives. They are more often schizophrenic, often violent, completely out of touch with reality at times. The children they bear and rear do not often become schizophrenic.

7

Sexuality and Marriage

The things most people want to know is none of their business.

George Bernard Shaw

Among the questions for which we seek answers in this examination of the adult life of the Three Hundred are those related to female-male relationships. Did they marry? Were they divorced? What was their sexual orientation? Were they notably unconventional?

The preponderance of the survey sample are heterosexual, or considered to be so by their biographers. Among the 317 there are forty-seven who are described as being notably unconventional in their relationships with the opposite sex, who belonged to a ménage à trois, had liaisons without the blessing of state or church, or were noted for the inestimable numbers of their sexual partners. Twenty-one are identified by themselves or by their biographers as being homosexual or bisexual (including three of those also involved in ménages à trois).

These forty-seven women and men were early participants in the sexual revolution and have influenced the women's liberation movement. They have had a powerful effect on attitudes toward the

161

sexually divergent by their unprecedented openness about their own psychosexual development. The sexual revolution as it affects both homosexuals and heterosexuals is anticipated in the lives of these subjects.

Among the Four Hundred there was only one individual, Oscar Wilde, whose sexual divergence was openly spoken of by his biographers, although there were a number of sexually divergent— Willa Cather, André Gide, Marcel Proust, Gertrude Stein—who are now casually described as being homosexual. It is possible that this century will be remembered not as the period when man (but as yet no woman) first stepped on the moon but as the century of the sexual revolution.

Eminent Women: Marriage, Motherhood, and Career

Pippi Longstocking has replaced translations of *Little Women* and *Alice in Wonderland* in Scandinavian children's literature and is internationally popular. The heroine of millions of little girls the world over, Pippi Longstocking, says Shari Steiner in *The Female Factor* (1977), "best personifies independence and brashness. And from the very first page those characteristics are offset by a thoroughgoing self-discipline. If she is so strong that no policeman can tell her what to do, Pippi also accepts the responsibility of making herself go to bed. No characterization of the Scandinavian woman could define more clearly her interlocking liberty and responsibility" (p. 244).

There are traces of Pippi Longstocking in many of the brash and independent women among the Three Hundred. Women constitute 51 percent of the general population, but they make up only 26 percent of the Three Hundred sample (although this percentage is almost double that of the Four Hundred). Moreover, despite the presence of Indira Gandhi and Golda Meir, women constitute only 13 percent of the people in politics, half as many as would be expected if they were evenly distributed in the various areas of eminence.

Since individual achievement and individual differences are not officially recognized in the Soviet Union and in the People's Republic of China, biographies describing the early lives of their prominent citizens are not often available. We do know that the new power structure in China includes no women. There was one Russian woman cosmonaut, but we have no biography of her. There also is no biography of Alva Myrdal, Swedish sociologist, who probably has done more than any other woman in the Western world to advance the status of women. In the 1930s she convinced the Royal Commissions that a career for married women should be viewed as being as normal as for married men. All four Scandinavian countries have women cabinet members. Women politicians totally control the city councils of Norway's largest cities—Oslo and Trondheim. The Soviet Union, China, and the Scandinavian countries all have more publicly supported child care facilities than do most other countries. Obviously, something more than being relieved of full-time child care during working hours is necessary to make men and women equal in eminence.

The eminent married men in our sample usually have children. Some have wives who are ill or barren, such as those of Felix Frankfurter and John Sloan; Charles Ives and his wife adopted a daughter. The eminent women do not find it easy to combine marriage, children, and career. Forty percent were divorced. Six percent were separated but not divorced. Thirty-two percent (including some of the homosexual women) were married. Twenty-two percent never married, but they included some very sexually active women, such as Edith Piaf, and some with open, longtime established liaisons, such as Lillian Hellman, Katharine Hepburn, and Han Suyin. Fifty-eight percent of the eighty-two women in our sample were childless.

Percentage figures do not transmit the quality of human relationships. Some of the women separated from their husbands, not because they did not love them but because of the inability of the husband to fit into the family life when the woman became absorbed in her work. Married women generally appreciate a hardworking husband who is successful in his career, but husbands frequently do not appreciate having a hard-working wife who is successful in hers. Elizabeth Arden, Daisy Bates, Mary McLeod Bethune, Indira Gandhi, Eileen Garrett, Golda Meir, and Helena Rubinstein are among those who regretfully separated from their husbands because their family life and career could not be reconciled. Strong, able women seem to marry men who are kindly, lovable, and loving and who are often cultured and intelligent but are less driving and ambitious than are their wives. They are often forced into the role in the family that the wife of the male politician or famous artist plays—a supportive and less prestigious role.

There are, of course, fewer adjustments to make when the married woman has no children. Among those who were divorced and were also mothers are Ruth Dayan, Jane Fonda, Lillie Langtry, Doris Lessing, Margaret Mead, and Elizabeth Taylor.

Only seven of the women in our sample had a lasting marriage and children as well as a career that made them celebrities. Most of these women had a husband who shared their values and was not competitive with them. There was no time in their lives when either had to sacrifice a career for the sake of the other. The husband accepted the wife fully as a working person but was not made to feel inferior to her or less important than she. There was help in the house to care for the children.

The seven women, whom we will discuss, are painter Grandma Moses, novelist Vita Sackville-West, psychiatrist Hélène Deutsch, artist Käthe Kollwitz, playwright Enid Bagnold, actress Helen Hayes, and writer Anne Morrow Lindbergh.

Grandma Moses. Not very many young women of today will be encouraged by the prospect of waiting until they are seventy-six years old to start a career. The popularity of biographies about the saucy and independent Grandma Moses probably represents a nostalgia of present-day readers for a vanished way of life—the close, intimate, rural family in which the children settled down close to the parents and in which the women in the family were sturdy, independent, and hard-working partners and not overawed by city collectors of folk art or by sudden fame.

Grandma Moses, born on a farm in 1860 and member of a large, close family, lived to be 101. She was once Anna Mary Robinson, the hired girl who married the hired man, Thomas Moses, and lived with him happily ever after. They had five active, noisy children, and their father liked to roughhouse with them. When they bothered her with their monkeyshines, she said "Ishkabibble" over and over to calm herself. She did not like scolding women.

In *Grandma Moses: My Life's History* (1952) she tells her

autobiography as a family story—of friends, relatives, children, a happy marriage, and of children who stayed close to the family. The two oldest boys built a two-family house on land given them by their provident parents, married sisters, and were near neighbors. Anna, the oldest daughter, became a nurse. When she died, Anna and Thomas Moses reared their grandchildren until the son-in-law married again. (One granddaughter became a nurse like her mother; the other was a biologist.) Winona, the second daughter, was given a fine wedding at home when she married an engineer. The youngest, Hugh, married at nineteen and after the wedding trip brought his wife, Dorothy, home to live with his parents. Grandma Moses was living with them when she was discovered.

Vita Sackville-West. English novelist Vita Sackville-West and diplomat Harold Nicolson had an unusual shared value, a mutual respect for each other's sexual divergency. In their declining years they also collaborated in renovating an estate they had purchased. Like some other husbands and wives among the Three Hundred who had stormy lives together during their sexually active periods, they became quite companionable in their latter years.*

The pair reared their two sons at Knole, the family estate, where Vita's mother had come as a bride and where Vita's father and Vita herself had been born. Vita's father was a country gentleman, and her grandfather had been an important diplomat, at one time ambassador to the United States. There is no other family among the Three Hundred in which the mother, father, and two sons (both authors and publishers) are all listed in *Who's Who*.

In *Portrait of a Marriage* (1973) Nigel Nicolson gives what is probably the only detailed account by a son of the marriage of a lesbian mother and homosexual father. Since the family history of Vita is much more spectacular than is the more distinguished and conventional family history of Harold, their son is more informa-

* The even more unconventional Lou Andreas-Salomé, and the distinguished philologist she married, with whom she never had conjugal relationships and who angrily refused her a divorce, were very close in their old age when she had diabetes and he had cancer. Augustus John and his mistress, Dorelia McNeill, were often estranged during their four decades of living together but were close in old age. Waiting forty years to attain conjugal harmony is also not one of our contemporary mores.

tive about the former than about the latter. (He edited the three-volume edition of his father's memoirs but tells little about his father's psychosexual development.) The father is the more celebrated, for Lady Sackville-West's voluminous writings have not lasted, whereas Sir Harold Nicolson played a definitive role in English history, especially in his work with the League of Nations.

In *Pepita,* Vita tells the story of her grandmother, a beautiful, impulsive, and adventurous Spanish woman, among whose lovers was Vita's grandfather, Sir Lionel Sackville-West. She bore him five children, one of them Victoria Sackville-West, whom Sir Lionel brought to Washington as his hostess, creating quite a stir since it was thought the ambassador was a bachelor. As Pepita and the ambassador were not married, their children did not inherit the title or the estate. The succession passed to "Young" Sir Lionel Sackville-West, who had no defenses against his dynamic first cousin Victoria, and married her despite the protests of the women of the family, who feared her Spanish influence and possible bad blood. This marriage was not a success, but it did save the estate, which had been badly managed. The ruthless Victoria took over entirely, managed well, played the stock market successfully, had a shop in London, and relegated her husband to an apartment on the estate.

The two had one child, Vita, a strange youngster who behaved and looked like a boy. At the age of nine she listed her toys as follows: a claret jug, a whip, some armor, swords, guns, soldiers, tools, a bow and arrow, a cricket set, and a football. The coachman's small son, who demonstrated to her how boys differ from girls, repelled and disgusted her, but she dressed like a boy when other girls were not doing so, wore a khaki bandage around her head, and called herself Julian. She was much closer to her father than to her mother, although he sometimes ridiculed her and often said he wished she were normal. At ten she had a passionate and erotic interest in a girl playmate; in adolescence she was tumbling happily in bed with another girl, Rosamund. Rosamund was her bridesmaid when she married Harold Nicolson.

For the first year or so of their marriage they had an unexciting but friendly and happy relationship, and she bore two sons, although she found conjugal relations unpleasant. Despite her relationship with Rosamund, when she married she did not know there were other women who were sexually attracted to women, and when Harold explained the lesbian experience to her she reproached him for not having told her sooner that such relationships existed. They continued to live amiably together, however, although she took no interest in his diplomatic career and never traveled with him.

When Vita had an affair with a woman friend, Violet Trefusis, and ran away with her to the Continent, Harold and Violet's husband followed them. After a stormy confrontation and period of indecision both came home. Following that episode Harold also turned to homosexuality. Vita seduced the novelist Virginia Woolf, upsetting her husband, Leonard Woolf, who felt the relationship was making Virginia more vulnerable to one of her periodic psychotic episodes.

Despite their sexual divergencies, Vita and Harold reared two children and remained married all their lives. Their relationship with their sons was friendly but not close, because the boys were cared for by servants, the father was often not home, or the boys were away at school. Though both sons were schoolboys when their grandmother told them about Vita's running away with a woman, they were not perturbed. As adults, they became writers and publishers, were married, had children, and were divorced. Nigel says they made better fathers than husbands.

Hélène Deutsch. A psychiatrist who married a psychiatrist as considerate of her career needs as of his own and as nurturing of their only son as she, Hélène Deutsch is the "new woman," unconventional in her younger days but happy in a long marriage.

Born in 1884 in Przemysl, Poland, Hélène Rosenbach was the gifted, unpredictable youngest child. Her sister Malvina was eleven years older, her sister Gizella seven, and her brother Emil ten. Emil disliked school, was an indifferent scholar, and had no ambitions, and it was hoped the baby that turned out to be Hélène would be the boy who would emulate the father, a successful lawyer, in ability and prestige.

Hélène's mother never forgave her for being the bright girl who could never be a bright boy, and Hélène disliked her. The mother was given to outrageous tempers, so that, for example, when Emil made a mess, Hélène was beaten. Her father, a passive man, tried to ignore these rages, since he could not cope with them, and was enchanted with the new baby girl, whom he regarded as a Rosenbach, his spiritual heir, regardless of her sex. Had it not been for her sister Malvina, who smothered her affectionately, and for her joyous, loving maternal grandmother, Hélène feels that her femininity would not have been saved, that she would have identified completely with her father.

Her father read Schiller and Goethe to her before she could read for herself and talked and walked with her, and soon she was reading in several languages. However, despite these accomplishments, he saw no reason why she should have a higher education and agreed with her mother that fourteen was the age at which a girl should consider her formal education completed. At fourteen Hélène ran away from home and would not return until her father promised to permit her to continue her studies and eventually go to the university. She also demanded that the promise be put in writing for fear her dominating mother would make him change his mind.

Hélène spent five years preparing for the examination required for admission to the university. Like many Przemysl youth, she also became a socialist activist, partly an expression of dislike for her mother, who judged people by their wealth, respectability, and conformity to upper middle-class rules. For years, until she was almost through college, she had an affair with the local socialist leader, a married man sixteen years older than she. When her mother found out, she went into a terrible rage, but her father defended her on the grounds that her lover was the best-educated, most charismatic man in town, and that there was no better man in that dull town with whom his gifted daughter could have fallen in love. Her relationship with her lover was broken while she was in medical school.

Hélène graduated from the University of Vienna's School of Medicine, one of only three of the seven women in her class to finish. An admirer of liberated artist Käthe Kollwitz (she had probably seen her stark black-and-white sketches of weary mothers holding ill children), she had decided she could best serve working-class women and their children by becoming a pediatrician. However, she married a brilliant young psychiatrist, Felix Deutsch, the same year she received her medical degree, and herself began her residency in psychiatry.

After a few years they decided to have a child. Because she had feared she might not be able to conceive, her joy when Martin was born was without bounds. Felix Deutsch was the ideal father and shared the care of the baby, but by then World War I had begun and both were overwhelmed as physicians taking care of war victims; Martin was taken care of by "Old Paula," a competent and faithful nurse. Later Hélène regretted this decision, when her professional work with other people's children convinced her that children do best when they have the full attention of their mother for at least the first two years.

Felix was never too busy to be tender; no flowers were too exotic a present. In *Confrontation with Myself* (1973), she says of her husband: "He was the most mature man I have ever known, and one of the few who could have claimed the superiority of the wise man . . . After Martin I had no other children, but he and his father filled my emotional life to the brim" (p. 126).

Felix encouraged her to continue her career, and she worked with Freud, studied problems of female sexuality, wrote the *Psychology of Women*, and taught. She was infinitely happier as a wife and mother than she ever had been in her younger days. Eventually, they fled the Nazis for the United States and were employed at the Boston Psychoanalytic Institute, from which they both retired at age seventy. Martin studied at M.I.T. and became a physicist and was devoted to his father.

Käthe Kollwitz. The love story of Käthe and Karl Kollwitz is one of the most moving in biography, comparable only to the love story of Lucretia and James Mott, who worked together so effectively in the cause of woman suffrage in the United States and were also loving parents. The Kollwitzes had strong shared values about social change, and Karl did not resent his wife's eminence but was able to do very well in his own career.

Born in 1897 to Katherine and Karl Schmidt of Königsberg, Germany, Käthe came from a family involved in the leadership of a new dissident pacifist group called the Free Religious Congregation, which resembled certain aspects of the Quaker or Unitarian groups in England and the United States. The group's founder, Julius Rupp, Käthe's maternal grandfather, had been the Lutheran chaplain at the military post at Königsberg, but resigned to establish the sect, which was deeply involved in social issues. Käthe's father, Karl, also sacrificed to become a member of the new sect, giving up the study of law and becoming a stone mason, which was work he could do without violating his conscience. When his father-in-law grew older, Karl became the leader of the group.

Thus, Käthe was born into a small, close community where each person lived according to conscience and was sensitive to the feelings and rights of others. Käthe herself exceeded the norm in sensitivity and frequently burst into loud crying spells that she could never explain. She was also restless, pale, sickly, and had unwarranted fears. She disliked any form of organized learning, but she steeped herself in the excellent books in the family library. The Schmidt children did not go to school but studied in small groups with their siblings and cousins, who were taught by the older members of the family. Her art talent was valued and encouraged, and at twelve she began her art lessons with a noted local teacher.

At seventeen she became engaged to Karl, a medical student, and attended art school, her only formal schooling, until Karl was established as a physician for a workers' health insurance fund in Berlin's poor section, and they married. Both shared the same values and the same social concerns, but whereas he expressed his values through giving service to the poor, she expressed them in her art. She set up her studio next to his office and many of her first models were her husband's patients, young working-class women who sat in the hallway, their ill children in their arms.

When her labor pains began for her first child, Hans, she worked in her studio until almost time for the delivery and completed an etching called *Greetings* for him. Hans was a lifelong joy and comfort to his parents and became a physician like his father. A second son, Peter, was born four years later.

Although as a child Käthe had been sickly and temperamental, as an adult she was like her own mother—strong, serene, tireless, sensible, and loving. Aided by a housekeeper, who stayed with them for fifty years, Käthe was able to spend many hours working in her studio. Although she worked hard at her art, she was devoted to her husband and children and tender and helpful to the battered women and troubled adolescent girls who came to her to tell her their personal problems after they had seen her husband about their medical needs. Her diaries are full of their stories.

From age thirty to forty Käthe was exceptionally fulfilled, achieving, and happy. Her family was complete. She became internationally known for her powerful paintings and sculptured figures. World War I destroyed this happiness. Her son Peter died at eighteen on Flanders Field; for five years she labored and sculptured figures showing herself and her husband kneeling in grief over Peter's death, to represent the grief of all parents who lost sons in war. She and Karl were not Jewish, but their views were well known and the Gestapo threatened them. They resolved to commit suicide rather than be separated and sent to concentration camps. However, fortunately, she was so well known internationally that the Nazi authorities only grumbled and threatened rather than risk the publicity her incarceration would provoke. For most of the war she was under what amounted to house arrest.

World War II brought new and devastating problems. Her works were taken from museums, stolen, lost, or stored in damp basements.

Karl died in 1940, leaving her to struggle through the deepest depression of her life, which was augmented by the death in battle of her oldest grandson, also named Peter. She commemorated his death by one of her best-known lithographs, *Seed for the Planting Shall Not Be Ground Up*. She died in 1945 just before the war ended.

In the introduction to his 1959 biography, *Käthe Kollwitz*, H. Bittner quotes Romain Rolland as follows: "The work of Käthe Kollwitz, which reflects the ordeal and the pain of the humble and simple, is the grandest German poem of the age. This woman of virile heart has looked on them, has taken them into her motherly arms, with a solemn and tender compassion. She is the voice of the silence of the sacrificed."

Enid Bagnold. Born in 1889 in Rochester, England, playwright Enid Bagnold had a new play in production in 1977, in which Katharine Hepburn played the leading role—that of an aged woman who still remembered her husband lovingly. Enid's husband, to whom she was married for forty-two years, was Sir Roderick Jones, chief of Reuters. Her best critic, he also gave her "unalterable, immutable love" and encouraged her to write.

She cherished her four children and seven grandchildren and enjoyed being a mother. Writing as an aged widow in her rambling, humorous *Autobiography* (1970), she is explicit about the new life-style that repudiates the nuclear family: "Family love. This is something everyone now is prepared to throw away. They are asses" (p. 374).

Helen Hayes. Born in 1900 in Washington, D.C., Helen Hayes had a husband she adored, two children, and a career that was remarkably uncomplicated by anything except success. When she was five years old, producer Lew Fields saw her doing an imitation of a Gibson Girl in a school dance recital and passed the word to look him up if she ever came to New York. When Helen was nine her mother took her to see him and her career began. She was an immediate success and continued to be so all of her life.

Her father had married for love and wanted a home. Her mother had married to escape home and wanted to be an actress. Out of this conflict came Helen, their only child, with the emotional stability of the father and the drive and talent of the mother.

However, she enjoyed being a wife and mother as much as she enjoyed being an actress. She and her playwright husband, Charles MacArthur, understood and accepted each other's career needs, both loved children, and were sentimental and outgoing. Her husband, she said, "was a man who knew how to lift a woman's heart."

There were no great griefs in Helen's life and few frustrations, until her daughter, Mary, died of polio in 1949.

Anne Morrow Lindbergh. Anne Morrow Lindbergh was born in 1907 in Englewood, New Jersey, and was graduated from Miss Chapin's school with honors in literature in 1927. An excessively shy girl who felt that she was not as lovely as her older sister, she married an excessively shy aviator, Charles Lindbergh, in 1929.

Charles shared her love of nature, solitude, and family life, and she was soon as avid about flying as he. A diarist since childhood, she wrote delicately, maturely, and insightfully about flying, the sea, the outdoors, and her personal philosophy.

When their firstborn was kidnaped and murdered, the attendant publicity was more than they could bear, and they sought sanctuary in England. Despite this early tragedy, they did not become overanxious or restrictive about their other children.

The Unconventional: Ménages à Trois and Others

The influence of the forty-seven unconventional and sexually divergent subjects on contemporary mores is augmented by the sheer volume of the biographical material they produce and its popularity, especially with women readers. Simone de Beauvoir has written six autobiographical volumes that total 2,673 pages. Anaïs Nin has written six diaries covering thirty-five years in 1,956 pages. Colette is a prolific author in whose pages fact and fiction are inextricably mixed. R. Binion takes 587 pages to tell about Lou Andreas-Salomé. The two-volume biography of Lytton Strachey by M. Holroyd is told in 600 pages. Holroyd's biography of Augustus John is 676 pages. There is a proliferation of books about Ezra Pound and his peripheral connection with the Bloomsbury group.

The amorphous Bloomsbury group, a mix of unconventional and sexually divergent people, was the arbiter of excellence in English literature. Martin Green's *Children of the Sun* (1976), a narrative of "decadence" in England after 1918, is an excellent source of information about many of the persons discussed in this chapter, including W. H. Auden and Evelyn Waugh. Green says, "I think I can show that a certain type of experience, appropriate to a certain mode of being, was cultivated by the young men who felt that they were *the* generation of English writers growing up after the War; who convinced most of their contemporaries who cared about books that they were right; and who, therefore, established a new identity for 'England,' a new meaning to 'being English,' in the world at large and in the privacy of individual minds" (p. 3).

Some of the unconventional, not primarily involved in social change, were self-absorbed and considered themselves as individuals, rather than as cooperative members of a nuclear family. Many were ruthless in placing their personal happiness and intellectual development above the needs of a parent, spouse, or child. Several of the women, for instance, demanded the right to an education, to sexual freedom, to being unmarried, to abortions, to financial independence, to the right to do "men's work." The wish to escape housewifely routines and motherhood did not start in the 1970s, and many of today's young women can find prototypes among the women of the Three Hundred.

Other unconventional people formed groups much like communes of the 1960s. There are ten instances of ménage à trois experiments in group living in which an unusual cast of characters create a family to their liking. In doing so they often imitate the conventional nuclear family against which they are in revolt. For example, a lesbian woman may fill the role of a dominating father. Ménages usually failed not because of outside pressures and lack of money but because of tensions from within; the participants became emotionally entangled with each other and often behaved in a very conventional way in a most unconventional setting. We have already described Ezra Pound's ménage à trois; two others involved artist Augustus John and poet Vladimir Mayakovsky. Six others who had similar living arrangements, and whom we will discuss, are Marguerite Radclyffe-Hall, Lou Andreas-Salomé, Simone de Beauvoir, Jean-Paul Sartre, Lytton Strachey, and Paul Tillich.

Marguerite Radclyffe-Hall. Born in 1880 in Westcliff, near Bournmouth, England, lesbian writer Marguerite Radclyffe-Hall had a most unhappy childhood. Her stepfather was a fat and irritable singing master and some of his young lady students boarded with the family. He and her jealous, shrewish mother quarreled incessantly and threw things at each other, so it was a noisy, turbulent household. Marguerite, who often hid in the garden, away from the noise, was drawn into lesbian relationships with some of her stepfather's students, who also were lonely and unloved.

When she was fifteen, her biological father, who had left Marguerite's mother when she was seven months pregnant, came to call. Handsome, rich, romantic, and cultured, he was touched by his daughter's resemblance to himself and as he left promised he would leave her "all his property." From that day on, she identified with him and daydreamed about him, but three years later he died and in fact *did* leave her wealthy and independent. She then left her mother's house forever, taking with her her grandmother, and bought a house of her own.

From then on she called herself "John" and emulated her father by wearing men's jackets. A slim, sensuous, seductive woman with ash-blond hair, she attracted many other women as lovers, the most notable being Una Troubridge, young wife of a distinguished admiral. Una and her daughter left her husband to live with "John," who never accepted the child as a stepdaughter; Una herself learned not to show affection for the child for fear of irritating her temperamental, demanding lover.

Una was the organizer, the helpful critic, the faithful, submissive partner, subordinating her every mood to Marguerite's needs, and was proud of her contribution to her lover's success as a writer. But after the excitement of the publication of Marguerite's *The Well of Loneliness* and the subsequent publicity, life was dull for the pair. Both were now middle-aged. "John" had always resented the presence of Andrea, who was now at Oxford. When the charming and friendly girl became engaged to a fine young man, "John" was excessively rude to the suitor's parents when they came to call and delighted in shocking them. Andrea, who was well accepted by her in-laws when she married, broke her relationship with Una and "John."

Middle age was hard on both of them. Marguerite was no longer attractive, and they were no longer popular with acquaintances, who had sought their company because they were eccentric, beautiful, famous, and rich. Una was often ill and nearly died after a hysterectomy. When Souline, a rather stupid, obstinate Russian nurse, came to care for Una following her surgery, "John," who always liked to flirt with other women, fell in love with her; indeed, she courted her as passionately as she once had courted Una. Una was very unhappy but still loved Marguerite and could not leave the household because she could not support herself. Finally Souline consented to be "John's" mistress, and when she developed a spot on her lungs and needed care—being a muddle-headed person who could not look after herself—Marguerite insisted on a ménage à trois. On one point she was firm, says her biographer, Lovat Dickson, in *Radclyffe-Hall at the Well of Loneliness* (1975): "Una is not to be displaced. She tries to persuade her young lover to accept Una, as she has succeeded in persuading Una to accept the fact of Souline. This must have been a bitter pill for Una to swallow" (p. 215).

Marguerite herself in turn became ill, of terminal abdominal cancer, but Souline left and went to live in Oxford, refusing to come home even for Christmas. Indeed, even when Marguerite was dying and Una wrote her and begged her to come, Souline did not answer the letter. Marguerite left her wealth to Una, who had been with her for twenty-eight years, with the understanding that Una would provide for Souline "with discretion."

Lou Andreas-Salomé. Born in St. Petersburg, Russia, in 1861, Lou Andreas-Salomé was the sixth and last child in the family. Her father wanted a girl, her mother wanted a boy, and this circumstance may have influenced her becoming a writer and psychoanalyst as well as a lover of and influence on an incredible number of famous men.

Her handsome, dominating father, a government official under Czar Nicholas, was descended from part of a conclave of liberal Lutheran Pietists in St. Petersburg. At thirty-seven he was a dynamic general who had won favor for storming and conquering Warsaw, and his twenty-two-year-old wife, Louise Wilm Salomé, worshipped him to the exclusion of her children. A cold, proud woman, she dreamed of raising six sons and was resentful of the baby daughter who foiled her and also usurped her as the most important female to her husband, who adored his baby daughter. Having come from an unhappy home—her father went mad and tried to kill his son, her mother kept her husband locked in a back room for the rest of his life—she wanted her home to be perfect and irreproachable.

As a child, Lou romped and played with her older brothers and was especially devoted to her father, who held her and caressed her and with whom she had "secret tenderness." Later, as an adult and disciple of Freud, she recalled how she cried and soiled herself so he would punish her, because, she said, she had sexual pleasure in being spanked. She also daydreamed of entering his bowels and discovering and appropriating his penis. Once he accidentally burned her with his cigarette and covered her with kisses. "I would now gladly let my arm be burnt off if only he would kiss me that way again," reports her biographer R. Binion in *Frau Lou* (1968, p. 6). When she was sent to school she disliked girls, whom she found foolish, was a poor student, and was called a "liar" because she did not distinguish fact from fantasy.

Her father died when she was seventeen, and because Lou was so troubled her mother asked the new, popular Lutheran minister, Hendrik Gillot, to speak with her. Having two daughters of his own, he understood the emotional problems of adolescent girls and was quite clever in his approach. He asked her to come to his office at certain fixed hours and relate her fantasies to him, then spend the rest of the day on a demanding course of advanced study. She loved him so much that she read day and night, absorbed the thinking of his favorites (Kant and Spinoza), and in a year's time was a well-educated young woman.

Her unexpected brilliance blinded him to the significance of her demands to be held on his lap, to be caressed and fondled, but by age eighteen she was a most attractive young woman and one day he embraced her impetuously, telling her he had decided to divorce his wife and planned to marry her. Angry, shocked, and repelled, she told her mother what had happened and her mother, despite her displeasure with her spoiled daughter, took her to Zurich to avoid scandal in the family.

Besides Gillot, the only person upset over her leaving was her brother, Eugene, who was three years older and who had been her closest companion. An effeminate, passive boy who took dolls to bed with him, he continued to live with his mother most of his life and had a lifelong love-hate relationship with her. Mother and son quarreled incessantly, but he said she needed something to fuss about.

In Zurich, the mother, who had always disliked her daughter was not concerned about what Lou did away from home and she permitted Lou to set up a platonic living arrangement with a young Jewish philosopher, Paul Rée, in an apartment where each had a separate bedroom. The living room, which they shared, became a popular salon where the intelligentsia met. Rée suggested they add another to the arrangement, his best friend, Friedrich Nietzsche, then an older man of thirty-eight who, Rée thought,

would make an excellent chaperone. Unfortunately, Nietzsche also
fell in love with her.

Lou's companionship with her father and with her three
older brothers (two others had died) had prepared her for male
roommates but not for marriage. The ménage à trois established
itself in Lucerne for a time, and the sexually frustrated men made
a joke of their relationship by having a photograph taken that
showed Lou riding in a cart pulled by the two men in her life.
Elizabeth Nietzsche, who considered her brother her private
property, was furious about these goings-on, even though Lou tried
to assure her she had no physical designs on her brother. The two
men, who had been best friends, became so jealous of each other
that a duel was narrowly averted. Rée never recovered from his
loss and after ten years of brooding fell or jumped from a cliff to
his death. Nietzsche always spoke of Lou as a cruel and dangerous
woman.

At twenty-one she married an extraordinary man, Friedrich
Carl Andreas, a philologist of Dutch, Malayan, and Armenian
descent who knew over twenty languages and the essential facts
about the folklore, geography, political history, and archeology of
all countries where these languages were spoken. He called her his
"Little Daughter," and she called him her "Oldster." However,
she was unable to have sexual intercourse with him and remained
his virgin bride for over six years. She tried hard to be a wife to her
scholarly husband, whom she admired, and even suggested he
force himself upon her while she was asleep; however, when he
tried this she awakened and tried to choke him. Lou was happy
to let her husband have a relationship with their housekeeper, who
bore him two children, one of whom lived with Lou in her old
age when husband and housekeeper were both dead.

At thirty-one she finally had a sexual relationship with the
effeminate and introverted poet, Rainer Maria Rilke, who had his
own psychosexual problems because of his relationship with his
mother, whom he adored, and his father, whom he hated. Andreas
was permissive with Lou because he did not want to lose her, but
he never permitted a divorce, not even when she was pregnant by
a lover and wanted to marry him. Too bourgeois to have a child

out of wedlock, she had an abortion, as she also did when she became pregnant by Rilke.

Her most informative biographer, Binion, describes her many love affairs meticulously. Her approach to men was always the same. Her primary need was to be close to a beloved teacher, but once he had taught her what she wanted to know, she broke the relationship, leaving behind broken hearts, ruined careers, suicides. If a man had weaknesses, she felt, that was not her problem. She could merge with a man intellectually but never emotionally.

In *Three Women* (1975) W. Sorell tells of Lou's relationship to Paul Bjerre, a Swedish psychotherapist, fifteen years younger, whose wife was an invalid and Lou's close friend. When Lou was fifty, the pair frequently traveled together. Paul Bjerre stated that Nietzsche was right in calling her an evil woman because she liked to triumph over men. She was passionate, he said, but only to satisfy herself and actually was cold emotionally and careless of the consequences of her effect on others.

During her later years she had sexual relationships with a number of young men and women, whom she called "brothers" and "sisters." We have discovered no other woman in this century who had so many relationships, sexual and nonsexual, with so many eminent men, among them Martin Buber, Sigmund Freud, Walter Gropius, Gerhart Hauptmann, Arthur Schnitzler, and Ferdinand Tönnies. However, Binion says, she was unpopular with the feminists of her day, who vehemently denied her characterization of women. Although she preferred the intellectual companionship of men, she thought women were superior in beauty, goodness, wisdom, health, reverence for life, both the eternal mother and the eternal child, a complement to man but never his rival. She predicted that women's best works would never compare with those of men, for men had more selfless devotion to a goal whereas women were always lolling within themselves. Still, she believed women were more sensuous than men because they reacted to sex with their whole being; men, she thought, had a cruder approach to sex.

Simone de Beauvoir and Jean-Paul Sartre. Simone de Beauvoir was born in 1908 and Jean-Paul Sartre in 1905, both in Paris. In 1929 they signed a conjugal pact that was a declaration of an intent to live together without making the relationship legally binding. The love they felt for each other was to be for life and was to be "the necessary love." However, within the framework of their lives, they were both to be permitted "contingent loves"; that is, either might have an affair without endangering the primary relationship.

They lived in Paris and saw themselves as superior people who rejected conformity, family life, children, and all the other bourgeois virtues. They lived simply, like students, disregarding the amenities of life. Their flat was untidy, full of dirty dishes, papers, books. Simone almost always dressed in black and made no attempt to attract Sartre or anyone else by her appearance. She scorned comforts and luxuries and liked testing her physical strength by going hiking with a heavy backpack, for example. Sartre, who was indifferent to exercise and the outdoors, puffed behind her goodnaturedly.

For years the relationship was not threatened by any "contingent loves." Then Sartre insisted that one of Simone's pupils, Olga, a discontented, rebellious girl, become a part of their circle. Simone was hurt and forced to realize for the first time in her life that other people did exist and that Olga's right to love and be loved was as justified as her own. Nine years younger than Simone, Olga did not make life easy for her teacher and was contemptuous of the plain, unadorned, older woman. The triad did not last long, however, because Olga did not want to be turned into a facsimile of her older companions and left them. Still, the incident led Simone to purge her resentment by writing her first successful novel, *L'Invité* [*She Came to Stay*], published in 1943, a thinly disguised account of the affair as it began, though not as it ended. In the novel, the hero, Pierre, is a stage director and the heroine, Françoise, is a novelist. Pierre is taken away from both women by the war, just as Sartre was mobilized at the beginning of World War II. Françoise is a mature woman, wise, patient, omniscient; Xaviere, the young girl whom they befriend, is crassly ignorant, rude, gauche, selfish. When Pierre leaves for the front, the two women are left together. Françoise is unable to tolerate her young rival and kills her by turning on the gas spigot. In the novel, the heroine is exhilarated and is proud of herself. A choice had to be made between her and the girl. She chose herself. This novel established Beauvoir as one of France's leading novelists.

Although Beauvoir and Sartre had tit-for-tat "contingent loves" (both had one American lover each), there were no more attempts at ménage à trois until much later, during a period when Simone's fear of growing old and her contempt for the aging bodies of women was already appearing in her memoirs. She was forty-four when she had an affair with a young Marxist journalist, Claude Lanzmann, seventeen years younger than she. She is unable to write about the sex act, but she does say, in her memoirs, that their bodies met happily. After they returned from a trip together, she and Lanzmann decided to live together. However, because she did not like giving up her annual two-month summer holiday with Sartre, yet also felt unhappy being away from Lanzmann during that time, she persuaded Lanzmann to join them for ten days or so in the middle of the period. In *Simone de Beauvoir* (1975) R. D. Cottrell says, "The attempt to work out a ménage à trois in the 1930s had been unsuccessful, largely, it seems, because of Beauvoir's jealousy of Olga. This time it was much more successful. Sartre, it would appear, was not at all jealous" (p. 131).

Simone de Beauvoir was born into an extended household in which there were adults festering with deep hurts, financial anxieties, and insoluble differences. She was an attractive, hyperactive child who received the attention she demanded because she was the only person in the household to whom all the others could affectionately relate. She could be both madly gay and madly angry. When crossed, she threw herself on the floor in raging tantrums. When disciplined she vomited. Her Uncle Maurice complained because she could not sit still, even for a minute. She craved sweets and would not eat bread and milk or shellfish or any meat with fat. She had to be coaxed to eat—a spoonful for grandmother, another for grandfather, another for mamma.

When a baby sister, Hélène, came along, she refused to be dethroned and felt superior to her. From infancy Hélène was tearful and peevish, albeit more affectionate and eager to please than was Simone, but Simone's nurse continued to cater to her every wish, even sleeping in the bedroom with Simone whereas Hélène had to sleep on a cot in the hall. It was Hélène, Simone believed, who was guilty of not being the son the parents and relatives had wanted.

Simone's mother, pretty, provincial, and a devout Catholic, married a handsome, freethinking Parisian lawyer who disliked his work and preferred being an amateur actor. Marriage did not interrupt his pleasure in his sophisticated mistresses, of whose existence his young wife was uneasily aware. He often did not come home until dawn, half-drunk, muttering about playing cards all night. Even on their honeymoon he was indifferent to his wife's wishes and insisted on attending the races. She was in love with him, however, and preferred to ignore his infidelities. Later she became more and more angry, nagging, and emotional, quarreling with him in front of guests over trivialities but not about her deepest hurts. She was inhibited by guilt feelings about her dowry or the lack of it, since her father had gone bankrupt soon after her marriage and the money was not forthcoming. She also resented having to share her home with her mother, who hid food about the house and ate it in secret, and her sister and was bitter about her mother's liking her youngest sister best. Simone says her mother could hold a grudge for forty years. Identifying her younger daughter, Hélène, with her own disliked sister, she was partial to Simone. Although the grandmother and aunt had much of the physical care of Simone, she felt contemptuous toward them because she knew her mother wished they were elsewhere. Until Simone was ten she had matters well in hand and felt happy, confident, and superior.

Writing when she was in her sixties, Beauvoir said she felt that having had a family of attentive relatives about her in her cradle was good for her. In *All Said and Done* (1974), she says, "I have always insisted on carrying my desires, refusals, acts, and thoughts right through to the end. One does not insist unless one reckons on obtaining what one calls for, both from others and from oneself: and there is no getting it unless one does call for it" (p. 4).

After World War I the Beauvoirs became "genteel poor" because the father had made bad investments. This calamity hurt Simone's pride because she did not have pretty clothes to wear and her parents were unhappy, but it freed her to prepare to go to the Sorbonne so that she could learn to earn her own living.

She was less unhappy than she might have been because of the close friendship she developed between the ages of ten and twenty with a classmate, Zaza, a radiant, intelligent, loving girl who was more feminine and outgoing than was Simone and who taught Simone how to dress so that other girls would not laugh at her. They met at Cours Désir, the Catholic girls' school both attended. There were considerable differences, however, between the two friends. Zaza still believed in God; Simone lost her faith at twelve. Zaza adored little babies; Simone could not understand why. Zaza could be flippant, disobedient, critical with impunity; Simone could not. Both were excellent students, although Simone does not describe any love of learning either in herself or in her parents at this period in her life.

Zaza and Simone went on to the Sorbonne together, but Zaza's mother later withdrew her because she disliked the company her daughter kept—including that of Simone, whom Zaza's mother rejected because Simone had lost her religious faith. When Zaza was twenty, she died from influenza followed by meningitis. Years later, Beauvoir wrote that Zaza was murdered by her bourgeois environment (although diseases often attack the poorly nourished proletariat more frequently than they do the well-fed bourgeoisie). "It was through Zaza that I discovered how odious the bourgeoisie really was," she said, in *All Said and Done*. "For me Zaza's murder by her environment, her milieu, was an overwhelming, unforgettable experience" (p. 10).

At the Sorbonne she met Sartre, the first person she had ever known, she said, who was more intelligent than she. She never again had an intense friendship with another woman, and Cottrell does not believe that she likes women, because the female characters she creates in her novels are egotistical, surly, defiant, and ill-mannered, bristling with rage when they suspect their freedom is being limited. However, they cannot get along without men, whereas the men, who are much superior in character, can get along remarkably well without women. The men are more often sincerely involved in some activity that promises positive social change.

Cottrell does not question the scholarship of Beauvoir's *The Second Sex*, which has been translated into nineteen languages and has been read by millions, but he does not see it as a tribute to women and questions whether she is a friend or foe of feminism. "Throughout all of her work," he says, "Beauvoir tends to view the self as unescapably locked in conflict with others . . . Indeed Beauvoir has always tended to divide mankind into two opposing camps: 'adversaries and allies' " (p. 40).

Sartre has said that Beauvoir's brief volume, *A Very Easy Death,* written in 1964 after her mother's lingering death from cancer, is her best literary work. Cottrell does not disagree with the literary quality of the work but says, "Beauvoir's inability to see her mother except through ideological lenses is chilling" (p. 136). He understands why the mother, as she lay dying, looked at her oldest daughter and complained of being frightened by her. The doctor also suggested to Simone that her presence in the room was not beneficial to her mother.

In *A Very Easy Death,* Beauvoir does not pity her mother because of her father's infidelities, although she does commend her for having been an independent working woman who took care of her own needs after her husband's death. Simone believes that marriage inevitably kills sexual desire, so her mother had no right to expect fidelity or affection from her father. As she watched her mother die, she remembered how her mother had tried to make companions of her daughters when they were adolescent. When she and Hélène had come back from an outing with friends and were cooking crayfish in the kitchen, her mother had joined them despite their remonstrances, saying she had a right to be in her own kitchen and a right to eat with them. She remembered how her mother had tried to keep her and her sister apart during this period because of Simone's antireligious beliefs. Cottrell believes the book is not an expression of genuine grief over her mother's death but "an elegy in which Beauvoir laments the dissolution of her own being" (p. 137). For many years Beauvoir has been primarily concerned in her memoirs with the loss of her sexual desires, with her aging body and a fear of death, and most recently with the dilemma of older women discarded by men in favor of younger women.

Cottrell is critical of Beauvoir as a person but not as a writer. Her biographer Jean Leighton, however, is even more caustic and in *Simone de Beauvoir on Women* (1975) criticizes both the philosophy and the scholarship of *The Second Sex.* Henri

Peyre, who writes an introduction to Leighton's book, says that Beauvoir and Virginia Woolf are the two best women novelists of the century but that the former's hasty reasoning shows a lack of plain common sense. Peyre also notes Beauvoir's intense dislike of female body functions and her description of the fetus as "carrion" and the "quivering gelatin which is wrought in the womb." He accuses her of branding her own sex as being inferior, incapable of self-criticism, and reminds us that Beauvoir's personal associations almost exclusively have been with men.

Unlike Cottrell, Leighton does not see *The Second Sex* as a scholarly work but as a diatribe against the female sex. Also unlike Cottrell, Leighton sees no contradiction between the thesis of *The Second Sex* and the characters of the women in Beauvoir's novels; the novel characters illustrate the types of women Beauvoir describes in *The Second Sex*. They are also much like Beauvoir herself. Leighton says Beauvoir never describes a woman she admires, and she finds her indictment of motherhood excessive. Simone holds that a mother does not do anything, that she is merely the passive receptacle of the egg, and in *The Second Sex* she speaks of the humiliation of the pregnant woman, whose distorted body frightens children and amuses young people. Motherhood also destroys the opportunities of close association with men, who are the real demigods, persons with ideas, people who are intellectually stimulating. Children, Beauvoir believes, are unfit companions for an adult female and menstruation an intolerable interruption in the life of a busy woman.

A different point of view is taken by Alice S. Rossi, in her excellent volume, *The Feminist Papers: From Adams to de Beauvoir* (1973). Rossi describes Beauvoir as "Europe's leading feminist" and notes that she was among some 300 Frenchwomen "who signed a ringing manifesto in the spring of 1971 which publicly announced that they had at one time or another undergone an abortion" (p. 672).

Beauvoir believes that women are potentially as strong as men (a theory students of anatomy and physiology do not corroborate) and that the so-called inferiority of women is part of a long historical process. "The worst curse that was laid upon woman," she says in *The Second Sex*, "was that she should be excluded from

. . . warlike forays. For it is not in giving life but in risking life
that man is raised above the animal; that is why superiority has
been accorded in humanity, not to the sex that brings forth, but to
that which kills" (p. 64).

In 1975 American feminist leader Betty Friedan conferred
with Beauvoir in Paris. As reported in the June 14, 1975, *Saturday
Review,* Friedan felt that the women's rights crusade in America
was on a plateau or perhaps even foundering; Beauvoir agreed
and stated that was also true in France. Friedan stated she thought
emphasis on the negative aspects of childbearing and motherhood
had hindered the movement; Beauvoir emphatically disagreed.
Housework took too much time, was nonsalaried, an exploitation
of women by men, and no woman should be permitted to stay
home and rear children. Friedan said she would never require all
women to work and put their children in child-care centers.
Beauvoir said that in an ideal society it would be necessary to prohibit home care for children because too many women would make
that choice if it were permitted. It was better in China, where all
women in a commune worked together to help darn the socks of all
the members. If women were not to be oppressed, the family and
the myth of the family had to be destroyed. It was not necessary
to have children. Friedan asked how the human race was to be
perpetuated and Beauvoir said there were already enough people
on earth. Friedan came home disappointed, finding Beauvoir sterile,
cold, and unable to identify with ordinary women.

In the epilogue of *Force of Circumstances,* published in
1963, Beauvoir is less the dominating five-year-old than we have
depicted her. She says that the one undoubted success in her life has
been her relationship with Sartre and that only once have they
gone to sleep at night without being in agreement with each other.
She prides herself on her financial independence but never meant
to say that a woman should be alone. She says she has not been led
by Sartre; she has followed joyfully down paths she chose to take.
However, she does not comment on two circumstances in her life
that must have been important to her as a woman—namely, (1)
Sartre's living with his mother while Beauvoir lived in a hotel
nearby, and (2) his adoption of a daughter.

Lytton Strachey. Biographer Lytton Strachey, author of

Eminent Victorians, was born in 1880 in Clapham Commons, England. A homosexual for thirteen stormy years, he shared an unusual ménage à trois with Dora Carrington, a bisexual, and Ralph Partridge, a heterosexual.

When Dora fell in love with Lytton, he was thirty-seven and twice her age. He was then an effusive, homely man with a shrill, unpleasant voice and was impoverished, not having fulfilled his early promise as a writer. He was quite incapable of having an erotic interest in her, and among members of the Bloomsbury set, who knew them both, her persistent pursuit of him was incomprehensible and much gossiped about. Some attributed her interest to a seeking after a father-figure. She was estranged from her parents because her dominating mother had reduced her good-natured father to a nonentity. As a child she had been closest to her three older brothers and had thought of herself as a boy.

She was casual about her bisexuality. Biographer Michael Holroyd, in his two-volume *Lytton Strachey* (1968), says, "it was perfectly natural for her to love several people, men and women, at the same time, and wish to enjoy sexual intercourse with all of them; though, as she was not strongly sexed, not very often" (p. 494). She was a vibrant, lovely girl with rosy cheeks, luminous blue eyes, a mop of blond hair, and a slim, boyish figure, and the Bloomsbury set adored her.

In 1917 she and Lytton set up housekeeping at Mill House, Tidbury, in a cottage purchased for them by some of the Bloomsbury group in order to give Lytton, who was ill, discouraged, and short of funds, a place to write. It was understood that Dora would be his companion and hostess, and she more than fulfilled the Bloomsbury group's expectations. She spoiled him with attention, bringing him tea, gardening, making jam, baking, turning the house into a charming country retreat. She handpainted the wallpaper, and drew nude pictures of Adam and Eve on the walls of his bedroom. She joked with and was good to his young male lovers, and was not jealous of them.

In less than a year they were joined by Ralph Partridge, a "macho," recently demobilized, young naval officer, who was a friend of one of Dora's brothers. Handsome, well-muscled, and sensuous, he seemed to Lytton a possible interesting sexual partner, but Ralph soon made it clear he was in love with Dora, not Lytton. She, however, did not reciprocate. Though she painted him in the nude, she had no apparent sexual interest in him. Lytton busied himself doing something about the young man's cultural illiteracy, and succeeded so well that Ralph soon became knowledgeable and articulate and became Lytton's secretary.

Eventually Dora and Ralph married. However, Dora saw no reason why she should not have other men, and other women, in her life. Ralph, who was faithful, was heartbroken when she had an affair with a close friend. Lytton tried, not always with success, to reconcile them when they had problems, but at no time did the ménage à trois break the bonds of friendship and affection that still bound them together. When Lytton's terminal illness with cancer worried all of them, Ralph grew weary of Dora's idiosyncratic ways. When he approached her, she fled from him; when he left her, she was miserable. Because neither Lytton nor Dora was capable of handling the mundane affairs of life whereas Ralph was clever about such matters, they were very dependent upon him. Even when he found another woman more to his liking, he loved Dora and Lytton so much he could not break his ties with them. The three suffered together during Lytton's terminal illness, and when he died, Dora, at the age of thirty-nine, shot herself.

Paul Tillich. Rollo May believes that theologian Paul Tillich needed so many women in his life because he was always seeking his mother, who died of cancer when he was seventeen. He always approached women, May says, with the same confidence with which he approached his mother—with the certainty that she would take him in her arms. He never was able to devote himself to any one woman.

Born in 1886 in Starzeddel, Germany, the firstborn son, with younger sisters, Paul may have had a love-hate relationship with his mother. After her death, he dreamed that his mother kept him dancing on a coin. She was enigmatic, reserved, and shy, not a woman who drew people to her.

There was no doubt of his uneasiness about his father, a Lutheran minister. Once he dreamed that his father was a snake. Another time, May says, he dreamed about climbing to the top of a tree and screaming when his father's arm reached for him and pulled him down. Interestingly, however, he was very close to his father during his younger years, and the two spent hours talking about philosophical matters.

Overtly, the Tillich family was an ordinary home with supportive parents and with a brilliant oldest son. However, they expected much from Paul, and all during his life he was plagued with depressions, which he called his "demons." He lived, May says, as if his emotions were always showing. He had the quality that great actors have, of making each person in his audience feel his attention was focused on the listener.

Describing the story of their marriage in *From Time to Time* (1973), Paul's widow, Hannah, states that there were three important loves in her life. While married to her first husband, Albert, who proposed to her three times before she accepted, she was, she says, a child-woman hiding her intellect. Albert was a loving man from a wealthy family and, she believes, might have been a great artist had she stayed with him, but she could not. It was Paul Tillich who awakened the erotic in her, whose body was like a "Gothic statue." He stimulated her imagination, as he did others', by pushing the image of God behind the concept of Heaven. Her third lover, Heinrich, read what she wrote, enjoyed her paintings, and made her aware of her own dignity.

Like Paul's father, Hannah's father was also a Lutheran minister who when drunk was querulous and forced his wife to have intercourse with him but when sober loved his children and adored his tiny wife. Her American-born mother played the piano and read Zola, Ibsen, Hamsun, and Tolstoy, and although she loved her husband she threatened to leave him, which distressed the children.

Hannah's first sex experiences, which she enjoyed, were with other girls, and when she became engaged to Albert, he was amazed at her passionate response and wanted to know how she had learned such sophisticated kissing. Amused by his naïveté, she did not tell him that girls kissed that way when they had sex. Although he painted her in the nude, he sedulously avoided any close physical contact with her because of his belief in her young innocence.

She met and was seduced by Paul Tillich, after her engagement to Albert. For Paul everything was power and force. His continuous seduction of women, she believes, was not a matter of individual attraction but was his tribute to womanhood, which was sacred to him. He had a strong feminine component and felt close to all women. She found having sex with him intensely exciting. Nevertheless, she went ahead and married Albert, since the wedding was planned and her parents were enthusiastic about the young artist from the well-to-do family. However, she decided that although she loved him she could not live the rest of her life with him because he was so unexciting sexually. When she became pregnant she left him.

She had already resumed her affair with Paul, and when she came to his filthy, untidy apartment she was amused, rather than dismayed, when another female—screaming, scratching, and hitting—had to be persuaded to leave in honor of the obviously pregnant visitor. Later she moved in with Paul's ex-brother-in-law, a Lutheran minister, who was living with a young social worker. Albert begged Hannah to come back to him and said he would not permit a divorce, but she refused. While she waited for her child to be born, Paul went on having other affairs.

After a long and hard labor, a baby boy was born, large and apparently healthy, although there was some worry because his eyes did not follow a candle. Soon after Paul wrote that he needed her, and not wishing to burden him with the baby, she placed it in a nursery near his apartment, where it sickened. Albert came and took it away, but it could not be saved. Paul was sympathetic. He told her a child born to his first wife—an older woman who betrayed him with his best friend, a fellow minister named Dox, while Paul was away at war—had died of pneumonia suffered because a clinic let it get too cold airing it on a balcony. Paul told Hannah that her child probably would not have been normal anyway, after having had so high a fever. Paul and Hannah's sister succeeded in convincing her that the child, who looked to her just like her detested mother-in-law, would have been abnormal had it lived, but Albert was so angry he gave her a divorce.

"Neither the deaths of my child and Paulus's child," she wrote later, in *From Time to Time* (1973), "nor our divorces and memories of our divorced spouses ever played any role in Paulus's

and my relationship" (p. 97). What did play a role was his behavior after she and Paul were married. Her family and their
friends came to the ceremony, and the officiating minister was the
husband of Paul's sister. Paul liked to believe that no one disliked
him and sought to be liked by everyone; Hannah enjoyed being
confronted by other people. He liked crowds and parties; she did
not.

One person she definitely did not like was Paul's friend,
Dox, who had seduced his first wife. At youth conferences Dox
presented a radical Lutheran theology, encouraged young people
to enjoy themselves sexually, and circulated descriptions of black
masses. On Paul and Hannah's wedding night, Dox arranged a
bachelor dinner for Paul and invited single women but not
Hannah. Paul said it was to be a sexual orgy. Hannah was stunned;
he had deflowered her, awakened her eroticism, and relieved her
of a twisted relationship with women, and now on her wedding
night was leaving her alone. She took her blanket and slept in the
maid's room. Paul came home late, but feeling virtuous. He had
been alone with a girl but had only talked to her, mostly about
Hannah and himself.

Hannah was very angry and might have left Paul had she
not soon met Heinrich, a dark, sensitive man who was a doctor of
philosophy and of law, a student of architecture, and a recent
enthusiast of psychoanalysis. Heinrich taught her about the occult,
which pleased Hannah, who often saw auras, and they eventually
were able to send each other telepathic messages when they were
not together.

She and Heinrich (who was married) had a physical need
for each other, but she would not have sex with him without Paul's
permission. Paul, who liked him also, was quite willing but asked
her not to tell him about their sex experiences. He never liked to
talk about sex and was angry when someone told him a dirty joke,
though he did turn to pornography in his old age.

She and Heinrich were scrupulous about not seeming to
have a physical attraction for each other in Paul's presence.
Heinrich tried to persuade Paul to confine himself to one extra
woman whom he especially liked to make them into a foursome,
but Paul preferred to have many women in his life and did so.

The ménage à trois lasted five years, during which time Heinrich had his own room in the Tillich apartment but was often away, as was Paul. The five years were happy ones. She had children and enjoyed them, as she had not enjoyed Albert's child. She repulsed the advances of Eve, a woman with whom she once had enjoyed sexual relationships.

Heinrich was unable to make love to her while he had a brief affair with another woman. After five years he asked Hannah to leave Paul, to devote herself entirely to him, but she had no intention of doing so. The impasse was ended when Paul accepted an invitation to become a professor of philosophy at the University of Frankfurt, and they moved without Heinrich.

Their relationship remained essentially the same through a long marriage, although there were no other ménages à trois. There were many women in his life, a few men in hers. They were quite close when he was old and ill and needed her.

Peripatetic Writers and Their Influence on Each Other

The unconventional and the sexually divergent walk in and out of each other's lives. They meet each other in Paris, in London, in New York. They publish each other's books, write about each other in their autobiographies, review each other's writings, attend each other's art exhibits. They are not socially isolated. Many had affiliations with those whom others called the Bloomsbury group, which was really two groups. The nucleus of the first was Virginia and Leonard Woolf. The second was formed by a larger and much less well defined set of English intellectuals who carried on the tradition after the first group stopped its informal meetings. Lytton Strachey and his brother and sister were closely associated with the first Bloomsbury group, were so much a symbol that members of the second group even imitated the peculiar Strachey way of talking, the high falsetto, irregular harsh rhythm. The ménages à trois did not exist in a social vacuum. Holroyd tells how a contemporary wit described the Bloomsbury groups as people who formed triangles and lived in squares. Those who were outsiders saw them as dilettantes, eccentrics, as wealthy men and women whose time could be put to better use.

Their powerful influence is traced by Elizabeth French Boyd, in *The Bloomsbury Heritage: Their Mothers and Their Aunts* (1976). The members of the Bloomsbury group, she says, made contributions in "journalism, politics, criticism, economics, philosophy, science, mathematics, even in painting and in promotion of the arts such as ballet and theatre" (p. 5).

There is no one among the English unconventional and the sexually divergent named in this chapter who was not a part of or did not owe something to the influence of the Bloomsbury groups. Lady Ottoline Morrell, who is in the survey sample as a woman "who had a strong influence on important men," is one of the youngest girls with brothers only, a tall, ugly and angular girl who looked like something out of Stonehenge. She was the most important hostess to the unconventional and sexually divergent of her day. At one time she was part of a triangle. Bertrand Russell was having an affair with her and with T. S. Eliot's wife during the same period of time. At Lady Ottoline's famous 500-acre estate at Garsington Place, hundreds of intellectuals from London and environs and from abroad were entertained, walking the wide lawns and admiring the ilex trees, peacocks, and statuary.

At Cambridge and at Oxford, young men formed literary clubs and made close friendships that lasted for a lifetime. Christopher Isherwood, W. H. Auden, Stephen Spender, and John Lehmann were thought of as four close and mutually supportive friends to whom others were drawn.

In New York City, a Swiss novelist and critic, Denis de Rougemont, found such a cultural center at 7 Middagh Street and said, of its occupants, according to Carson McCullers' biographer in *The Lonely Hunter* (1975), "All that was new in American music, in painting or choreography emanated from that house, the only center of thought and art that I found in any large city of the country" (p. 124).

Although his comment sounds like one of the impulsive impressions of travelers, there was some basis for his comment. The brownstone house belonged to George Davis, literary editor of *Harper's Bazaar*. Davis rented two rooms to one of the Three Hundred, the bisexual, brash, and independent Carson McCullers. A number of the other Three Hundred either lived there or visited there. Auden moved in and assumed the role of "matriarch" who made the rules and hired the help. Carson refused to have anything to do with housekeeping. Benjamin Britten and his friend, the operatic tenor Peter Pears, lived there, as did writer Christopher Isherwood. Hundreds of internationally known celebrities came to tea for an afternoon or stayed for a day, a week, or for years. It was probably here that the marriage in name only between W. H. Auden and Erica Mann was arranged so that she might obtain a visa to enter the United States. Anaïs Nin came to call one Sunday afternoon, and Carson was annoyed when her guest monopolized the attention of all the other guests and ignored her. Nin was irked with her hostess and, according to Carr, described her in her diary thus: "I saw a girl so tall and lanky I first thought it was a boy. Her hair was short, she wore a cyclist's cap, tennis shoes, pants. She came and pushed through the group like a bull with its head down . . . " (p. 129).

Sociologist Benjamin Zablocki, an authority on communes, says that they fail, not because they have money problems, but because of emotional problems, of conflict and confrontation between members. Within the ménages à trois the participants, when they become unhappy, do so because they reenact the conflicts their parents and grandparents experienced while living together in conventional settings. The setting is different; the jealousy, fear, boredom, anxiety, the illnesses, quarrels over rearing the children, the falling in and out of love are the same. Consciously, or unconsciously, they reenact the familiar family patterns. When three lesbians live together, for example, the first is the dominating "husband"; the second is the ailing, dependent, faithful "wife"; and the third is the sultry young "mistress."

Sexual divergency is not a modern phenomenon. Sappho was sexually divergent; Helen of Troy was a most unconventional woman. However, neither woman wrote thousands of pages of autobiography. Simone de Beauvoir did. So did Anaïs Nin.

Anaïs Nin, Jet-Set Intellectual

Anaïs Nin, heroine to many participants in the sexual revolution, was a member of the intellectual avant-garde and thus knew many of the Three Hundred and their friends. As a matter of principle, however, she is not communicative about the facts of her life and does not present biographical information sequentially. She respected the wishes of her husband and others of her family and of her friends who asked not to be described in her six published diaries, and they are only a small part of so far unpublished diaries kept in a bank vault.

Anaïs Nin's diaries flow with the force of her emotion. There are two major themes—her pleasure in being a mistress to creative men, and the sacredness of the inner journey. The trip to the moon, she states, is a trivial accomplishment compared with the journey to the core of the human heart. Moreover, she feels, the hero who is interested in politics and causes, but neglects his inner life, is outmoded; the real hero is the one who can find and cure his neurosis. She is impatient with people who waste time on causes. War comes not from the politicians, she thinks, but from the hearts of men. If each person helped every other person he or she met, violence and hatred would cease.

Women, she believes, have more access to the inner life since they are intuitive rather than logical, and so women bear the burden of preserving what is best and finest in the human spirit, nurturing men's creativity as well as their own. Women, she states, should enhance the beauty of their bodies as well as their minds and be proud of being women. When her marriage failed, she resolved never to be a wife but to always be a mistress. The peak experiences of her life have been sexual, the times when she has been closest to the truth hidden within her.

Her mother was the attractive and talented Rosa Culmell, daughter of the Dutch consul in Havana. At the age of twenty-nine, Rosa married an impoverished nineteen-year-old concert pianist, Joaquin Nin, who had attracted her attention while playing Beethoven's *Moonlight Sonata*. Always intensely maternal, Rosa had already reared her six younger brothers and sisters, who were left at home when their mother deserted the family.

Anaïs was born in Paris around 1903. The oldest child, she was followed by two boys. As a young girl she was so shy that visitors sometimes thought her retarded, and she would often find sanctuary beneath a round table with a crimson tablecloth that touched the floor. She read omnivorously and listened to the conversation of the intellectually sophisticated adults who came and went. The house near Paris reverberated with the sounds of music, and Anaïs adored her handsome father. To her he was almost a Leonardo da Vinci: a musician, composer, author of two books on the esthetics of art (which her mother typed), knowledgeable in medicine, architecture, and home decoration. He was also an amateur photographer and liked to take pictures of his daughter and youngest son in the nude.

When Anaïs was eleven her father deserted his family for a rich mistress. Rosa Nin took the children to New York. Her rich sisters bought them a brownstone, which she turned into a genteel boarding house, and tried to augment the family income by shopping in New York for wealthy Cuban relatives and friends. However, she was unable to run her financial affairs efficiently and was perpetually in debt. At fifteen Anaïs, who was then ready for high school, dropped out in order to help support the family and went to work as a model for artists or as a mannequin in dress shops.

She began making friends among artists and intellectuals, but this displeased her mother, especially when she wrote a passionate book about the life and work of D. H. Lawrence. During her twenties Anaïs began to travel, probably as a result of the marriage she does not discuss, and was sometimes in Paris, sometimes in New York. She seems to have been married at one point to a Parisian banker named Hugh Guiler, who later took the name Ion Hugo, became a film maker, and did the engravings for the first edition of her first published diary, which she (and probably he) hand printed. The cost of production was $400, and the Gotham Book Store in New York bought the entire first edition for only $100. New York writers, charmed by the young woman who defied publishers' rejections by publishing her own work, extolled her. Critics were less euphoric but accepting. She became a "writer's writer."

Anaïs had begun her compulsive diary writing when her father deserted the family, intending them as communications that he could read when she saw him again, but she continued writing compulsively for a lifetime. When she finally saw her father, she was by then living in Paris and was an extraordinarily beautiful young woman. However, the fervor of his appreciation of her physical beauty repelled her, and she began seeing a psychiatrist in New York to attempt to overcome her father fixations. When he tried to cure her by forbidding her to write her diaries, she refused and turned to Otto Rank for help. Rank enabled her to express her feelings about her father in a prose poem, *The House of Incest,* which became her second published book.

In her inward journey she found much to displease her with the persons closest to her. Her romantic relationship with her husband, Ion Hugo, ended when he could no longer understand her placing individual creativity above a wider concern for the contemporary social order. She felt she had to free herself of her mother, a possessive woman with explosive emotions, if she was to develop as a creative person.

Anaïs also found her father no longer a hero. Once his wealthy mistress called her for help in keeping him from committing suicide after he had refused her generous financial settlement in return for leaving her. The mistress was angered because he was unfaithful, because he gave her money to other women, and because he had seldom visited her when she was hospitalized with tuberculosis. After her weeping father told Anaïs he did not mind leaving his mistress but he could not bear to leave his fine car and his luxurious surroundings, she told the woman to treat her father like a spoiled child, and the mistress agreed. Anaïs grieved less for him than for her mother when they died. Both were a burden.

In addition, Anaïs was critical of her brother Joaquin, a music professor at the University of California at Berkeley, for being the son who pleased his mother, remained Catholic, and gave her the devotion and attention she craved. He proved, she said, that the only way to remain close to a parent was to become the desired ideal figure, to be the son who never loved anyone more than a mother. She found her brother Thorvald wore the same facial mask as did her mother. He cut himself off from the family, went to Australia, and talked only of money and practical affairs.

Even close friends came to displease her. Henry Miller was exceedingly important to her because it was she who discovered his

talent, arranged for the publication of his first book, *Tropic of
Cancer*, wrote its preface, and introduced him to the right people.
She was deeply disappointed, therefore, when she believed he was
turning from the inward journey to a concern for social issues. The
break in their friendship was never quite healed. Miller did not see
himself quite the same way, and described himself as a split personality with a superiority complex, an anarchist and nihilist who
liked asocial persons and misfits and was not interested in social
reforms.

For many years Anaïs was a popular lecturer on campuses
and before many women's groups. She had a dynamic personality
and a way with words that pleased her audiences. But despite her
popularity with the feminists, she always enjoyed the companionship of men. She recognized how much she was like her mother but
turned her maternal feelings to the mothering of the creative spirit
in the men she loved. She also had much of her mother's dominating
temperament. Otto Rank, who was particularly interested in the
creative personality, tried to use her as a lay therapist. She was not
successful in this role; she was too ready to be directive, to take an
active role in reorganizing the lives of the patients.

Directly or indirectly, Anaïs Nin influenced thousands of
men and women to seek meditation, sensitivity training, consciousness raising, and other techniques for stimulating awareness in
order to escape from the responsibilities of trying to remake a
society they find intolerable.

The Unmarried

Fifty-two of the Three Hundred never married. This remarkably heterogeneous group includes a Pope and two Catholic
priests, nine homosexuals, and fourteen of the forty-seven unconventional but heterosexual men and women. Compulsive commitment to a cause is given by their biographers as a reason for the
single status of Ralph Nader, Rachel Carson, Edward Heath, and
Dag Hammarskjöld. Others of the eminent who have not com-
mented on their motivations for not marrying include Harold Acton,

Cecil Beaton, Benjamin Britten, Greta Garbo, Uri Geller, and J. Edgar Hoover.

Some women do not marry although they have no animosity toward men or aversion to marriage. Phyllis Bentley, in *O Dreams, O Destination* (1962), speaks candidly and movingly of her spinsterhood. Her older brothers convinced her that she was homely and undesirable. When she was of marriageable age, there was a dearth of young men left in England since so many had been killed in World War II. She was thirty-seven before any man was able to make her believe that she was attractive to him. She recalls her daydreams of marriage that began at age eight and were eventually poured forth in her powerful stories of family life. Two other women writers among the unmarried also write warmly about families—Edna Ferber and Mazo de la Roche.

Some of the unmarried have live-in partners as a matter of principle, a practice that is increasing and no longer sensational in the Western world. Among the unmarried who dispensed with the sanction of church or state are Simone de Beauvoir, Lillian Hellman, Katharine Hepburn, Emma Goldman, and Jean-Paul Sartre. Single status is not necessarily permanent. Bernadette Devlin, who has an eight-year-old daughter born out of wedlock, recently married. Janis Joplin was planning to be married when she died. There may still be marriages among the unmarried eminent.

There are only six among the 317 who were the youngest child with three or more older siblings of the opposite sex: three men (John Lehmann, Robert Maugham, and Rudolph Nureyev) and three women (Phyllis Bentley, Lou Andreas-Salomé, and Mata Hari). The first four of the six never married: the last two derived no satisfaction from their marriages and lived as unconventional unmarried women most of their lives. The sexually adventurous life of Andreas-Salomé has already been described. Mata Hari deserted her husband and children to have an adventurous life as a dancer and spy.

Two other women who married lived most of their adult lives as single women: Daisy Bates and Lillie Langtry. Like Lou Andreas-Salomé and Mata Hari, they were close to their adolescent brothers during the years when boys are likely to conceal their anxieties about coping with their sexual maturation by boasting of conquests—real or imagined. It is this attitude that some women, both single and married, take toward their lovers and husbands.

A girl does not necessarily have to be the youngest child to be influenced as the only female in a large family. Daisy Bates had a brother younger than she with whom she roamed the country-side with complete freedom during her early half-orphaned years. In early adolescence she was taken into the household of wealthy friends of her deceased mother and traveled and studied with their five sons. Soon after her marriage she left her husband and son to become an amateur anthropologist and lived with the Australian aborigines.

Lillie Langtry, a minister's daughter reared on the Isle of Jersey, had six brothers. She was the fifth child. Her brothers put her through a rigorous training and influenced her to be even more rowdy and daring than they. She rode race horses bareback, ran nude on the beach when they dared her to do so, and joined them in acts of vandalism that harassed the community. She was closest to her brother, Reggie, who killed himself when she married. She drove her handsome, wealthy, devoted husband to drink and penury. She treated her lovers ruthlessly, including British King Edward VII, to whom she bore a daughter. Queen Alexandra was forced to pre-tend she did not know that Lillie was her husband's mistress. The women of the court could not express their feelings toward her openly until she committed a really unforgivable social blunder: she poured champagne down the King's neck at a formal dinner. That was beyond the pale, but is an understandable behavior in this woman who was still being her oldest brothers' incorrigible little sister.

Girls are more likely to compete with and be envious of their brothers because they do not have the freedom and the edu-cational opportunities brothers enjoy. Rosalind Franklin, brilliant young English physicist, had one older brother, two younger brothers close to her in age, and finally a sister eight years younger than she. Rosalind was intensely competitive with her brothers. She was quite unable to relate to her male colleagues in the laboratory, would not share data with them, and even lunged at them when they offended her. She prided herself on her stoicism and independence. During the war she accidentally knelt on a sewing needle and drove it deep into her knee joint; she walked several blocks, alone, to the doctor's office to have it removed. The doctor said that she had done the impossible in enduring so much pain. When she developed cancer she concealed her pain and kept working until a few weeks before her death. She was thirty-seven when she died, a bitter and disappointed woman.

Publisher John Lehmann, in two autobiographical volumes, attributes his lifelong feelings of inferiority to his relationship with his talented, aggressive, older sisters. Beatrix became an actress whose power and presence were so awesome that her mother fainted when John took her to a performance. Rosamond, at twenty-three, wrote *Dusty Answer,* a novel that won critical acclaim and became a best seller. John was not hostile toward or competitive with his sisters (in contrast to the reactions of girls with older brothers). He loved them, but they made him feel that girls were superior to boys. Consequently, he never had the courage to stop being a publisher and to try to become the creative writer he wanted to be.

Martin Green, in *Children of the Sun* (1976), tells how much John resembled his sister in his writing and says: "John could not compete with Rosamond, or find a creative mode in which he would not need to compete with her" (p. 291).

Lehmann's sisters loved him, babied him, taunted him, teased him. His mother babied him; his father, a writer for *Punch,* enjoyed his children only when they amused him. When he was little, John was left at home with his nurse while his parents took the girls to concerts and museums. Once, his sisters and the gardener's daughter staged a mock funeral with Rosamond, his favorite sister, as the corpse. The girls broke into hysterical laughter when he took them seriously and ran to tell his parents that Rosamond was dead; this was just one time out of many that he felt incredibly stupid.

Lehmann never married; women played no part in his social life. He was devoted to his mother, who doted on him and helped to subsidize his publications—including the early works of so many of his friends and contemporaries, such as Isherwood, Auden, Spender, Capote, and Vidal. For decades, according to Martin Green, he was largely responsible for forming both American and British tastes in literature; what he liked was accepted as good. He was rueful, but not resentful, when authors he discovered and published deserted him for other publishers.

The Sexually Divergent

It was not until the 1960s that English, French, and American autobiographies were published in which a number of living writers identified themselves as being homosexual.* Before then sexual divergency was presented in thinly disguised fiction, as in Marguerite Radclyffe-Hall's *Well of Loneliness* (1928). One factor influencing the changed climate of opinion was the 1957 report of the Wolfenden Commission in England which resulted in British law being changed so that private sexual activities between consenting adults were no longer the concern of the legal authorities. Another factor was publication of Alfred Kinsey's statistics showing the high frequency of homosexual acts at some period in the lives of American men.

In this survey, twenty-one of the Three Hundred were found to be sexually divergent. Those who have written autobiographies describing their sexual divergencies are Christopher Isherwood, Violetta Leduc, Maurice Sachs, Emlyn Williams, and Tennessee Williams. Those who have had biographies written about them are Lou Andreas-Salomé, W. H. Auden, Sir Roger Casement, Jean Cocteau, Colette, Jean Genet, Allen Ginsberg, Robert Maugham, Carson McCullers, Yukio Mishima, Marguerite Radclyffe-Hall, Vita Sackville-West and her husband Harold Nicolson, Lytton Strachey, Dorothy Thompson, and Evelyn Waugh.

Some authorities see sexual divergency as a genetic aberra-

---

* To our knowledge the first such disclosure was made by André Gide in *If It Die: An Autobiography*. It was first published in an edition of twelve copies in France in 1920. The French public edition appeared in 1924; the English translation was published in a Modern Library paperback in 1935. The book is very explicit about Gide's sexual orientation. There is a detailed description of his and Oscar Wilde's sexual activities with young boys in Algiers. The editor at Random House in a brief introductory paragraph makes the point that the book is more than just the frank confession of an "invert." The revealing autobiographies of Maurice Sachs and Roger Ackerley were both published posthumously. Sachs' book, *Le Sabbat,* was published in France in 1946. Ackerly died in 1967 at the age of seventy-one. His candid autobiography was first published in England in 1968.

tion, others as an endocrine disorder, a psychological condition, or as a mixture of these. Some see it as a normal variant of the more frequent heterosexual behavior, such as Kinsey, who viewed as normal any activity not harmful to others that produced an orgasm. Others see bisexuality as the best expression of the spontaneous affection members of the human race may once have had for each other in prehistoric days before it was conditioned by society to accept only the heterosexual expression as normal.

Researchers in different disciplines produce their own bits of evidence. Geneticists report that if one identical twin is homosexual, the other is more likely to be so than are fraternal same-sex twins. Endocrinologists report that homosexuals have low levels of the same sex hormones and higher levels of the opposite sex hormones. Clinicians have observed that homosexuals often dislike the parent of their own sex and are obsessively close to the parent of the opposite sex. Kinsey and others have noted that, in the absence of partners of the opposite sex, people will turn to members of their own sex for satisfaction; as evidence they point to surveys of homosexuality among prisoners, soldiers, cowboys, and boarding-school students. The noted psychiatrist Harry Stack Sullivan, for instance, whose career was hampered by intolerance of his sexual divergency, was reared in a neighborhood where his only playmate was a much older boy, with whom he developed a sexual relationship.

Whatever the true basis of homo- or bisexuality, we have found a remarkable similarity in the life stories of the twenty-one sexually divergent among the Three Hundred. For instance, we found that the male homosexual was closer to his mother and either disliked his father—or, his father was dead or often absent from home.* There is often a love-hate relationship between the boy and his mother; they find it hard to live together and hard to live apart. The mother is frequently unusually effeminate and coquettish. The

* Male homosexuals who grow up in a family where a father values maleness in a son may notice the effeminate qualities of a boy who is genetically or otherwise different and are hostile to him for clinging to his mother for love and protection; the boy thus develops a lifelong dependence or love-hate relationship with her; Tennessee Williams is an excellent example. The girl may reverse this pattern and be closer to the father or she may remain close to the mother and dislike men, seeing them as a threat to the mother, as did Violetta Leduc.

male homosexual often lives with his mother all her life, though not always harmoniously. We found that, like many other precocious boys who become eminent, male homosexuals are almost always nonathletic and exceptionally intelligent and are consequently rejected at school. These boys turn to bullies at school for protection and friendship, and in later years they often prefer the same type of young boy as a sexual partner. Female homosexuals were as girls often excessively "tomboyish," disdainful of "girlish activities," and become the "boy" the parents wished for. Often the sexually divergent come from well-to-do homes and are socially isolated from casual playmates, having less unsupervised coeducational play than less well off children frequently have.

Fourteen of the twenty-one sexually divergent say they were aware of homosexual feelings or were active homosexuals in early adolescence. No woman speaks of having sex play or intercourse with a girl or woman earlier than ten. Of the fourteen sexually divergent men, seven had male partners only. Four were married: Mishima, Nicolson, Waugh, and Emlyn Williams. Mishima married to please his mother and had two children, but only out of a sense of family duty. Harold Nicolson became homosexual after he was the father of two growing children. Evelyn Waugh and Emlyn Williams had brief episodes of being homosexual in college but were heterosexual after college, and married and had children. Robert Maugham was heterosexual in his youth but homosexual as an adult. Only two men, W. H. Auden and Maurice Sachs, say they had erotic feelings for girls or wanted very much to be a girl in early childhood.

Except for Marguerite Radclyffe-Hall, the only exclusively lesbian woman, the divergent women were bisexual. Colette had a daughter by the second of her three husbands. Dorothy Thompson had a son and three marriages, each lasting several years, and her affairs with women were brief. Vita Sackville-West, although she had two sons, was primarily homosexual. Lou Andreas-Salomé was married, but the marriage was not consummated, and although later she had many male lovers, she was primarily homosexual. Carson McCullers's one unhappy marriage ended when her homosexual husband killed himself.

Nine of the sexually divergent dressed oddly, in rather open defiance against being a typical boy or girl, although in today's climate of unisex dress, this no longer seems eccentric. One aim of unisex dress is to avoid stereotyping of sexual rules. Girls are expected to acquire the most admirable of what were thought of as male attributes; aggressiveness and freedom to be creative and self-sufficient. Boys are expected to become more generous, intuitive, and better able to express their emotions. The worst that can happen will be that a significant proportion of parents or surrogate parents (if parenting continues to be even more unpopular) will over-achieve their goals and produce brash, disruptive little Pippi Long-stockings or tearful, fearful, clinging little boys. On the other hand an over-concern about the nature of our neighbor's sexuality may inhibit the creative achievement of potential Michelangelos or Leonardo da Vincis among us.

We have already described the lives of four of the sexually divergent—Genet, Leduc, Mishima, and Tennessee Williams. Here we will consider W. H. Auden, Christopher Isherwood, Lytton Strachey (again), Maurice Sachs, Jean Cocteau, and Robert Maugham.

W. H. Auden. Poet Wystan Hugh Auden was born in 1907 in York, England, the youngest son of a sensitive and loving father, a physician, classicist, and antiquarian. His oldest brother, Bernard, became a farmer in Canada; John, the middle brother, became a geologist and mountaineer. Wystan was closest to his mother, a gentle woman, fond of music. He sang duets with her and was Isolde to her Tristan, although she was apparently unaware of the psychosexual implications. In *W. H. Auden: A Tribute,* edited by Stephen Spender, his brother John says, "Wystan was puzzled by the mystery of our parents, with their contrasted backgrounds and outlooks coming together in marriage, maintaining that each should have had different spouses" (p. 27). He adds: "Wystan never did escape from his mother, for right to the end he would continue, almost as her deputy, to say of any particular action, 'Mother would never have allowed that' " (p. 28).

When he was eight, Wystan went to boarding school. Although his pictures show him to be attractive, he regarded himself as fat, grubby, and awkward. A classmate remembers him as a cheerful, precocious, warmhearted boy who was the special "pet" of the headmaster's daughter. Although he had no aptitude for games, he made friends easily and excelled in music.

Later, at Gresham's School, he was given an open scholarship, skipped two forms, was thought lazy because he never seemed to study, and did a creditable job playing Kate in the *Taming of the Shrew*. He was otherworldly, juvenile, never self-conscious, wore corduroys during the age of the dandy, was friendly, and did not belong to any cliques. He also wrote poetry.

His father, on reading some of these poems, noted an erotic content. Dr. Auden was also bothered while watching his son and a Gresham classmate, home from school, playing an innocent game of diving into a pool with one boy straddling the other's shoulders. The doctor felt it necessary to make a gentle but embarrassing speech to the two of them about homosexuality, telling them confidentially that he had once had a close friendship with another boy but that it was possible to "go too far." He asked them if they had done so, but they assured him their friendship was platonic. Indeed, W. H. did not have his first homosexual affair until college. A classmate says, in the Spender book, "at this time it was fashionable, in my set, for undergraduates to regard their parents as brutal Philistines. Auden, on the other hand, much reverenced his father" (p. 44).

In *Forewords and Afterwords* (1973), a collection of essays and book reviews written mainly for the *New York Review of Books* and the *New Yorker*, W. H. Auden discussed a number of the sexually divergent and their works. He says that the love affair poet A. E. Housman describes in "When I Was One and Twenty" was an expression of unrequited love not for a young woman but for a fellow undergraduate at Oxford.

Housman was so overwhelmed with shame at what he considered an abnormal attraction, apparently, that he never permitted himself to fall in love again with anyone, male or female.

In an amusing essay on writer J. R. Ackerley's posthumous autobiography, *My Father and Myself*, published in 1964, in which Ackerley told how his life was affected by his homosexuality, W. H. Auden wrote, "Few, if any, homosexuals can honestly boast that their sex life has been happy, but Mr. Ackerley seems to have been exceptionally unfortunate" (p. 451). Ackerley's dilemma was that he liked to seduce heterosexual boys and men and wanted them to be faithful to him, a characteristic reminiscent of bisexual Violetta Leduc's persistent but unrewarded courtship of the homosexual Maurice Sachs and of artist Mary Cassatt's attempt to attract the misogynist, Degas.

W. H. had a faithful companion, a younger fellow poet, for over thirty years, but he knew how difficult it was to find the right homosexual partner and could observe the dilemma of less fortunate homosexuals with detachment and objectivity. "All sexual desire," he wrote, "presupposes that the loved one is in some way 'other' than the lover; the eternal and, probably, insoluble problem for the homosexual is finding a substitute for the natural differences, anatomical and psychic, between a man and a woman" (p. 451).

He saw this difference in his own father and mother, who were so unlike in temperament as well as in physique. His father was calm, analytical, scientific; his mother quiet and retiring. Even if the first passionate love between husbands and wives did not last, he realized, they could find unity and a common bond in rearing a family. Homosexuals, however, who could not have children, did not have that bond. The luckiest male homosexuals, he said, were those dissatisfied with their bodies who sought as partners a younger man or boy with the "ideal physique." If their needs were simple, they could avoid making emotional demands their partner could not meet. "Then, so long as they don't get into trouble with the police, those who like 'chicken' have relatively few problems; among thirteen- and fourteen-year-old boys there are a great many more Lolitas than the public suspects" (p. 451).

He saw no reason to be squeamish about paying for sexual favors in situations where one person enjoyed giving and the other enjoyed receiving. Ackerley, for instance, although he was a scholar from a well-to-do home, was fascinated with working-class partners, and on one occasion he bought a houseboat to make his impoverished young lover's daydreams come true. The real difficulty for persons from different classes, W. H. thought, was in maintaining a relationship, for when an intellectual and a nonintellectual working-class youth had no values in common it was usually the intellectual who first became bored.

John Auden saw his brother as a lonely man. In Spender's book he writes that, despite the fact that W. H. was famous, had many friends throughout America and Europe, and had long, satisfactory periods with congenial intellectual companions, "he was lonely, lacking as a result of his personal psychology, a family of his own, but remembering our own happy early years. Recently [just before his death] he wanted more and more to see his family, to be met at airports . . . amongst those things which will always remind us of him is the shy smile of recognition as he would come through the airport gates in his lopsided slippers" (pp. 29–30).

Still, what he lacked in intimacy by not having a wife and children, he may have gained in warmth for all humankind, which makes his poetry memorable. As he says in *Forewords and After-words,* "there is no perfect *form* of society; the best form can only be the form through which at any given historical moment or in any given geographical location, love for one's neighbor can express itself most freely, that is, it is a practical not an ideological matter" (p. 38).

Christopher Isherwood. One of W. H. Auden's closest friends and collaborators in writing projects was Christopher Isherwood, born in 1904 in High Lane, Cheshire, England. His mother, Kathleen, thirty-five when he was born, was an intensely feminine woman, who, he says, was still attractive and pink-cheeked in her late eighties. In her diaries, which she kept all her life, she recorded in detail her first son's precocity, his fragility, his affectionate and playful ways. For years they played "dressing up" together, and she let him wear her petticoats, jewels, furs, and even her "switch" made from her own hair. His father, Frank, a career military man who rose in the ranks, and who was often away from home, taught him to read by writing and illustrating a newspaper, *The Toy Drawer Times,* just for him. There was also a "nanny" and other servants who took care of the two children in their own wing of the house.

Christopher liked to look at his father's sturdy, muscular body and had erotic feelings when he saw him exercising in his shorts. Later, when he began to masturbate, however, he did not think of his father, but of someone who looked something like his mother who found him on a battlefield, naked and wounded. He liked having her look at his bleeding body, which never hurt him in his dreams.

At age eight he was sent away to St. Edmund's preparatory school. Here he felt strange, without an identity, miserable, not for his home, but for the self he had left behind. Though he tried to attach himself to big, rowdy boys he admired, they did not respond to him. When he became ill with what resembled rheumatic fever and had to be withdrawn from St. Edmund's, his mother worried about his being out of school. His father, however, was not sure Christopher should even be sent to a boarding school, although he continued to stay on. "The whole point of sending him to school," Christopher reported his father as saying, in *Kathleen and Frank* (1971), "was to flatten him out, so to speak, and to make him like other boys and, when all is said and done, I don't know that it is at all desirable or necessary, and I for one would much rather have him as he is" (p. 450).

His mother was aware of Christopher's defenselessness against other children—it had irritated her to watch a childhood playmate, a little girl, order him contemptuously about and see him obey her so meekly—yet when Christopher was eleven and his father was killed in battle, she and other relatives made much of him as the son of a hero and reminded him of his obligations to be as patriotic, brave, and dedicated to duty as his father was. Both he and his brother, Richard, reacted with resentment. Christopher rejected all that his father and mother stood for—imperialism, militarism, chauvinism—and for a time became a Marxist and later a pacifist, emigrating to the United States and working with the Society of Friends. Had his father lived, he writes, he probably would not have been able to understand him and "would have ended by disowning this Anti-Son" (p. 506). Christopher always felt jealous of his father, who came between him and his mother and, by dying, had "monopolized her emotions."

Although he and his mother still loved each other, serious conversations ended in both being hurt. She could never understand his political or philosophical beliefs. She could not accept his homosexuality, which she dismissed as a passing phase, and the Berlin bars where Christopher found working-class boys as sexual partners were beyond her comprehension. As he wrote in *Kathleen and Frank,* "How could she have been expected to understand why he got himself requested to leave Cambridge in 1925, why he then took a job as a secretary to a string quartet which had no prospects and paid only a pound a week, why he decided to become a medical student in 1928 but stopped studying after two terms? And how was she to explain to her friends why he had gone to Berlin?" (p. 487).

She had Richard to comfort her, and the younger son seems to have lived with her as long as she lived. She also took care of her own mother and of the boys' old nanny. When her husband died, time seemed to stop for her, and she resented every new idea and invention. Though it pleased her when Christopher's books began to be well reviewed, she still did not appreciate them.

Christopher found he could talk freely with his father's brother, Uncle Henry (though he had to conceal his disagreement with his uncle's enthusiasm for Mussolini), about his sexual divergency since they were both homosexuals, and "they giggled like age-mates over Henry's adventures with guardsmen and Christopher's encounters in the boy-bars of Berlin" (p. 492).

Lytton Strachey. We have already described the adult life of Lytton Strachey, but his childhood experiences are too typical of other sexually divergent to be omitted.

At the time of his birth in 1880 in Clapham Commons, he was the eleventh of thirteen children born to Sir Richard Strachey and the former Jane Maria Grant, daughter of Sir John Peter Grant. His mother was forty-three, his father sixty-nine. The Stracheys are one of the aristocratic families of England whom Galton studied. Data on the New World colony of Virginia, written by one of Lytton Strachey's ancestors, were used by Shakespeare in writing *The Tempest.* Sir Richard was a meteorologist and an administrator, quite important in British affairs in India. Lady Strachey was admired by Carlyle for her intelligence.

His mother saw Lytton's exceptional qualities before he was three. He intoned his own verse, though in incomprehensible language, liked to be absurd and amusing, and never stopped talking, characteristics he would have all his life. His mother dressed the "strange little creature" in petticoats because she thought knickerbockers absurd on such a frail, sickly boy.

Since he was never well, he was sent to a small private school. There he played the female parts in school productions. Later his mother sent him to an experimental laboratory school using the "natural" method of education because it was supposed to produce wholesome, healthy citizens, and Lytton was not healthy. However, there were no water closets and only cold showers. The headmaster screamed at them and predicted that sissy boys who showed physical weaknesses would end up blacking German boots. Lytton's health failed and he was sent to yet another school, where he was despondent and hostile and the other boys found him awkward and odd. Again he played the female roles in the school plays. He admired older, athletic boys, the kind most certain to despise him, and when they rejected him, he felt contempt for himself. He suffered intolerably.

Maurice Sachs. Born in Paris in 1906, Maurice Sachs seldom saw either of his parents until he was four, though he did not mind because he had the sole companionship of his loving English nurse, Suze. Suze, however, was scandalized when he wanted to urinate like a girl. He also refused to go to sleep until she promised he would wake up transformed into a little girl. His father, a lazy man who sponged off of rich women, bore the surname Etting-housen. When his father left his mother, Maurice took her name, Sachs, since they were rich, distinguished, scholarly freethinkers.

An excellent student, Maurice was sent to secondary school. However, he was expelled for homosexual activities, even though, he says in his autobiography, *Witches' Sabbath* (1964), fully half the student body and some of the male teachers often had sex with each other. At thirteen, this ended his formal schooling, although his family was not told why he was sent home.

While Maurice was away at school, his mother, the daughter of a wealthy industrialist, had exhausted her inheritance. She also exhausted the patience of her second husband, who felt cheated when he found he had not married a rich wife, and he left Maurice and his mother penniless. Wealthy relatives treated them contemptuously, and when his mother overdrew her account by 60,000 francs, the family would not help her return the money she had spent. Maurice helped her flee to London to escape arrest.

Maurice had determined to be a writer when he was thirteen

or so. After his mother went to London, one of the Sachs family friends, a man of wide learning who allowed Maurice to spend many hours reading in his library, took pity on Maurice and employed him as a secretary. However, Maurice was of little use, and quit to work as a waiter and do other odd jobs while he kept on reading and writing. The first really brilliant and famous Parisian writer Maurice met was Jean Cocteau, and Maurice papered his room with his photographs. He even prayed to his favorite portrait of Cocteau every day, getting down on his knees and seeking advice.

His first woman was a barmaid, who seduced him despite his reluctance, and though he managed to satisfy her it was without joy. By 1939, when he was age thirty-two, he had had sex with only four women but with countless boys. With boys, he said, he could always feel youthful, a partner in a childish complicity; he still wanted to be a child, not a man.

By then he was a successful writer. In 1939 he gave his autobiographical manuscript, *Witches' Sabbath,* to his publishers, leaving it to their discretion as to when it should be published. World War II intervened and publication was delayed, and he was last heard from in 1942, when he sent three pages to be added to the manuscript. He had tried to remake his soul; he wrote, but had not succeeded and so was leaving Paris, though he did not know where he was going. He would rid Paris, he said, of an unsavory character, of a self that horrified him, and go live somewhere in obscurity and be a man who did not disgust himself. What he seems to have done was go to Hamburg and work in a munitions factory. He was killed when the factory was bombed.

In *French Novelists of Today* (1967), Henri Peyre writes that Maurice Sachs "was an insolent scoundrel, a shameless *arriviste,* an exhibitionist, and a pretentious rival of Rousseau in his urge for confessions, but nevertheless an entertaining, a brilliant, and, at times, a pathetic writer" (p. 440).

Jean Cocteau. Born in a Parisian suburb in 1889, Jean Cocteau was the youngest of three children. His father abandoned his practice of law early in his career in order to be a Sunday painter, to go to the races, and to hobnob with the horsey set. He killed himself when Jean was ten, and if the family knew why, it never told. Jean was plagued with nightmares and dreamed that his father was not dead, that he was one of the unwelcome, noisy cockatoos that frequented the garden, and that his mother knew as well as he did that the cockatoo was his father, though she pretended not to.

Jean's mother was an immature, pretty, effusive woman who attended mass nearly every day and came from a distinguished and wealthy family. She doted on her frail, droll youngest son, laughed at him when he dressed up in girl's clothes, played with him for hours, and helped him to build an elaborate toy theater. On her husband's death she turned over running the house to a servant, Auguste, who in effect became the new head of the household and of whom Jean seems to have been jealous.

Jean and his mother had a love-hate relationship that lasted all her life. Once, when he was twelve and they were returning from a holiday, he asked her to hide a box of cigars intended for Auguste under her dress so she would not have to pay customs duties. Fearing one of Jean's tantrums if she refused, she did so. Then, as they were going through customs, he told an official about the box; she was made to disrobe, the cigars were found, and she was fined. Of course she was furious, and doctors were consulted about the possible ill health of her son. During this period he was freed from dreams about his father, the cockatoo, and began to dream that his mother was dead.

He was sent to several schools, all of which he hated. All the boys constantly masturbated, he said, and sadistic teachers delighted in calling on a boy when he was about to have an orgasm. "The classroom smelled of gas, chalk and sperm," says his biographer, Francis Steegmuller, in *Cocteau* (1970, p. 13). He was frequently expelled, and his mother constantly worried and fretted about him. "She was," he says, "an elderly little girl questioning an elderly little boy about his school, and urging him to behave. It is possible that my long childhood, which wears the mask of adulthood, comes to me from my mother, whom I resemble" (p. 22).

At school he sought out the magnetic and handsome bullies, and at fifteen was already well integrated into the sex role of the passive homosexual. He always wanted to be someone other than himself, not to make others be like him. Fretful of home restrictions, he ran away to Marseilles, where he lived for a year in an area of male and female brothels, working in an insect-infested restaurant, and being taken in by an old woman whose sympathy he gained by telling her about running away from a cruel family. Still, in later years he often spoke of its being his happiest year, the year he won his freedom. During this time his mother wept for him but acquiesced to his older brother's suggestion that they let him work out his problems himself. Finally, his bachelor uncle, a diplomat, found him and brought him home.

The love-hate relationship between Jean and his mother continued, and when he was eighteen she asked police, a magistrate, and even the mayor to help her control him. Later on, when he was famous, he usually lived with her, although he sometimes had his own quarters as well. She continued to nurse him through his frequent bouts with neurasthenia and the undiagnosed fevers that afflicted him, but he never stopped playing cruel pranks on his mother, though he seems not to have treated other people that way. Once, pretending to be someone else, he called her and told her that Jean was dead.

At twenty-three Jean was recognized as an extraordinarily gifted young poet and painter, the sensation of Paris, popular at poetry readings in the salons of the most celebrated hostesses. Ironically, his mother, as well as the Vicomtesse de Noailles, a brilliant aristocratic hostess, was very helpful in establishing his reputation. He met Harold Nicolson, wrote a poem about Nijinsky, and was thought irresistible by Diaghilev. Although he was an opium addict, he was a most versatile poet, novelist, playwright, and film maker for fifty-eight years, until his death in 1963 at the age of seventy-four.

Robin Maugham. The last of the sexually divergent we will describe, Robin Maugham, nephew of writer W. Somerset Maugham (himself sexually divergent), was born in 1916 in London. In *Escape from the Shadows* (1973) he tells of his bisexuality and of the course of events that resulted in his decision that he was primarily homosexual. In *Somerset and All the Maughams,* he tells more about his uncle and his sexual divergency than about himself, but in both books he repeats a story of a confrontation, at age three or four, with his father. No other of the sexually divergent hated his father so much as did Robin as a child and as a man.

His father was fifty when Robin was born, his mother in her

forties. Robin was the youngest child, with three older sisters—
old enough, in fact, that one sister had a son only four years younger
than he. One day Robin's father frightened his nurse and him by
coming to the nursery in what was obviously a dutiful attempt to be
friendly. When "the stranger" asked the terrified boy what he had
been doing that day, Robin was positive his father knew he had
picked his nose while walking with "Miss Crosspatch" and that she
had slapped him hard and that he had wept. His father thrust a
bar of chocolate in his hand and asked him how his lessons were
going. Incapable of making a reply, Robin ate the chocolate bar in
one embarrassed gulp. While his nurse stammered out a description
of Robin's prowess in arithmetic, Robin ended the distressful confrontation by vomiting on the floor.

Robin had his first experience with sexual desire when he
was only eight and observed a husky twelve-year-old boy, sweaty
and bare-legged, straddling a work horse. Robin nearly fainted with
the intensity of the strange feeling. "Alas," he wrote in *Escape from
the Shadows*, "I have known this feeling on many occasions since
that day. I had hoped the intensity of the pain would grow less as
I became older. It hasn't" (p. 2).

His next important sexual experience was with an eleven-
year-old girl, a grocer's daughter, with whom he had an idyllic love
affair for several weeks during summer vacation. They would lie
close together by a stream while he poured out his heart about how
much his father disliked him and how his mother loved him only
when he did nothing to annoy her. (He did not tell her that he had
an imaginary "other," a rude, naughty, masculine boy named
"Tommy" who did all the naughty things he dared not do.) The
romance ended when his father, discovering the girl had swung on
the garden gate and broken the hinges, thundered that her father
would have to pay for them, and Robin was forbidden to play with
her again. Later, there was another girl in his life, the sister of a
friend. Once her brother interrupted them when they were about
to have intercourse, an experience that embarrassed all three of
them.

Though a "walking dictionary," he hated school and disliked sports, except fencing. In fact, he hated Eaton so much that
for many years he would become nauseous when in its vicinity. At

Eaton he participated in homosexual relationships with other students and at Cambridge was also a homosexual.

The shadows from which he could never escape were those of his father and his uncle, neither of whom hesitated to demean and discourage Robin, though they hated each other. Once at Cambridge, when a play he had written was accepted for a short run by the Cambridge Amateur Dramatic Club, Uncle Somerset wrote him that he was only making himself ridiculous trying to write a full-length play and that it would only be booed. The play ran to packed houses and was well reviewed, but Somerset did not apologize or send congratulations. Even years later, when critics reviewed Robin's work and invariably mentioned his famous uncle, Somerset would be enraged and blamed his nephew.

Robin's most devastating encounter with his uncle occurred when he was eighteen, when he was permitted to visit him in Paris, something his parents had forbidden before then. Anxious to test his premise that Robin was homosexual, Somerset commissioned his male secretary and lover to seduce his nephew, but Robin was repulsed by the secretary's advances. He did, however, respond eagerly to another young man named Laurent and fell passionately in love with him, a fact he confided to his uncle. Somerset took vicious delight, for he was paying Laurent for each sexual encounter between them.

Appalled by the intensity of his attraction to Laurent, Robin wrote a letter and broke a secret engagement he had made with a charming girl named Gillian. At eighteen, he was to write later, he thought it was necessary to make a firm decision about his sexual identification, and had he known it was possible to be bisexual, his whole life might have been different. Robin was also very much involved in leftwing politics, which he felt might adversely affect his and her economic future. Gillian, surmising he might be having problems in sexual identification, was not surprised by his letter, and they remained life-long friends.

When Robin wrote his first novel, he gave his father an advance copy to read. His father was so outraged and disgusted that he proposed going immediately to the publisher to offer him 3,000 pounds to destroy the whole printing. Harold Nicolson, whom his father respected, rescued Robin by assuring his father that the novel was well written and would probably be well reviewed by the critics, which it was.

As a young adult, Robin lived on the fifth floor of his parents' home while he studied for his law examinations and spent his leisure time writing. He was closely monitored by his father, and once when he served his oldest sister a cocktail, his father was furious. The elder Maugham also did not like the looks of the young men who came to visit Robin, and once complained that one of them, drunk no doubt, had disturbed his sleep as he left the house. He was mollified when Robin assured him it was only Harold Nicolson who had stumbled on the stair. At only one period in his life was Robin able to escape his "shadows," and that was when he was on the front during World War I, which made the devastating experience more tolerable.

All four Maugham children loved their mother best, a bubbling, affectionate, laughing woman who believed her husband liked her parents better than her. The old man was jealous and resentful of the children's affection for her. When Robin was a frail and shy little boy with sisters so much older than he, his mother was a loving companion who warned him that his shyness and beauty would cause older boys to make physical advances to him, though he did not understand what she meant. They were not especially close until he was seventeen and could escort her to concerts and to the theater.

Robin understood his father better when he read the old man's 587-page autobiography. When he finished he left a small space in which to describe his family, and Robin, being the writer, was asked to help fill in the four lines or so reserved for this purpose. He described his sisters in three terse lines—Honor Earl, a well-known portrait painter; Diana Marr-Johnson, a novelist, playwright, and short-story writer; Kate Mary Bruce, also a novelist and playwright. Only one line was left to describe Robin and Somerset, and the son and father agreed on Robin's description as follows: "My son, Robin, writes novels, plays and stories." Only six words were left to describe the world-famous W. Somerset Maugham. Robin scrawled, in despair, "And so does my brother Willie." His father changed this to the colder sounding "I need not describe the works of my brother William Somerset Maugham." Indeed, in the entire book, Somerset received only three brief mentions by name.

Robin Maugham, who is properly Robert Cecil Romer Maugham, Second Viscount Maugham of Hartfield, has written much about the childhood rearing of his "Uncle Willie." Willie's father was solicitor to the British Embassy in Paris, a reticent, over-worked, but not unfeeling man. Willie, who was much younger than his older brothers who were away at school in England, was the close companion of his charming, lovable invalid mother. She died when Willie was eight; his father died two years later. Although the Maugham family had lived in a beautiful apartment in Paris, after the extravagant manner of the quite well-to-do, the four sons were left penniless. How Willie reacted to being given into the custody of a cold and rejecting uncle and to living in the austere atmosphere of an English rectory is immortalized in literature. Somerset Maugham used an unhappy marriage with a rather dreadful woman to excuse himself for his need for homosexual partners. His marriage was also useful to keep his public from learning about his sexual divergency. In his day the candor and honesty with which his nephew writes was not thinkable.

Robin Maugham's two books about himself and his uncle are of exceptional quality as literature. They are also valuable for their insight into the personal problems of those of the sexually divergent who have both literary talent and a deep understanding of the human psyche, perhaps a result of their difficulties in adjusting to rejection at home, at school, and in society.

Summary and Conclusions

The marital history of the Three Hundred eminent person-alities shows that 82 percent were married at some time in their lives: 44 percent were never divorced, 35 percent were divorced from one to five times, 3 percent were members of a ménage à trois. Eighteen percent were never married. The percentage of divorced subjects exceeds the percentage of divorced persons in any recent census from any Western nation. Can we assume that the process

of becoming the subject of biography is disruptive to family relationships, or that men and women who have strong intellectual and
physical drives also have strong sex drives?

The proportion of women among the Three Hundred is
double that of the Four Hundred but still only a third as many as
the men. When the eighty-one women in the current survey population are examined as a group we find that only seven have successfully combined marriage, children, and a career (two come from
England, three from the United States, one from Germany, and one
from Poland). Interestingly, none of the seven came from countries
where the most child care has been provided for working mothers—
the Scandinavian countries, the Soviet Union, and the People's
Republic of China.

The men and women in the survey sample did not differ in
the proportion of those who never marry; for both unmarried men
and women the percentage was 18 percent. However, more women
(45 percent) were divorced or separated compared to men (35
percent). A major difference is that more than half of the women
(58 percent) had no children, whereas almost all the married men
had children.

Among the parents of the Three Hundred, 68 percent were
never divorced, 8 percent were divorced, and 3 percent were never
married. Parents who stayed married were found to be no more
likely to produce eminent children who have only one marriage
than were divorced parents. Staying together in order to influence
the children to respect marital vows did not work in these families.

Among the total sample there were twenty-one who described themselves or are described by their biographers as being
sexually divergent: seven women and fourteen men. Eighteen of
the twenty-one (86 percent) had a close relationship with the
parent of the opposite sex. Nineteen (90 percent) had unsatisfactory,
often antagonistic, relationships with the parent of the same sex.
Fifteen (71 percent) had humiliating relationships with their peers,
were rejected because of odd dress or mannerisms, because of being
exceptionally precocious, and (boys only) because they were not
good athletes. Nine (43 percent) went to noncoeducational boarding school, where they had homosexual experiences. Nine (43 percent) liked wearing clothes of the opposite sex or preferred the

stereotyped activities appropriate to the opposite sex between the ages of three and ten.

Two thirds of the sexually divergent were only children or were the youngest child in the family. Such children are more likely to remain close to the mother after infancy.

The frequency with which the youngest boy with sisters, and the youngest girl with brothers, becomes sexually divergent, remains unmarried, or is unconventional in male-female relationships suggests that more attention should be paid to sibling relationships as they affect sexual identification.

Two thirds (fourteen of twenty-one) of the sexually divergent had mothers who were thirty-five years or older when the subject was born. This was in marked contrast to the sixteen percent of older mothers in the total survey population.

Whether these findings point to environment as the cause of sexual divergency cannot be determined until a valid way is found to evaluate the effect on both parents of rearing a child who shows tendencies toward sexual divergency. If no one were concerned about a particular child's sexual preferences, the homosexual child's environment would be markedly different. Some believe that bisexuality is the more natural form of sexuality and that these twenty-one were superior individuals who had to struggle with the prejudices and anxieties of those who did not understand them.

❧ 8 ❧

Political Personalities

*The end of the human race will ultimately be
that it will die of civilization.*

Ralph Waldo Emerson

Our sample of 317 persons was divided into four major groups
according to their achievements: 77 had achieved eminence in the
political arena; 92 were in literary fields; 75 in artistic fields; and
73 in other fields, including science, business, athletics, mysticism,
and religion. These four global areas of eminence are discussed
separately in this and the next three chapters.

Members of the four groups show marked differences in their
reactions to their parents, as their parents do to them. They also
differ in liking or disliking school, in the quality of their peer relationships, and in their reactions to their total social environments.
Because no one kind of home, school, or community could meet
these disparate needs, examining the differences may help us to discover more effective ways of meeting the needs of children who
differ so markedly in what they want from life. Most parents say
they do not believe in casting children into molds, but they may do
so more often than they realize.

When we decided to divide the Three Hundred into four

approximately equal categories it was easy to identify subjects who clearly belonged in the artistic and in the literary categories. Defining the political category was more difficult. Though clearly public officials and heads of state are political, we decided also to include subjects who made a career of any kind of political activity, whether democratic or authoritarian, conservative or radical, whether through nonviolent reform, armed struggle, or assassination.

We were aware that revolutionaries and reformers almost always come from families where the father is a liberal professional man or a liberal businessman. This was true of those who started the French Revolution, the American Revolution, and the Russian Revolution, and it was true of the leaders of the Free Speech Movement in Berkeley in 1964. We suspected, however, that there might be significant likenesses among other persons in the political category as to their childhood rearing. This supposition proved correct. Political personalities define themselves clearly. As children they are sober, honest, obedient, like school, are seldom delinquent, and get along well with others—the kind of boys and girls it is difficult not to become attached to. As a group, however, they learn early to organize, to manipulate, and to influence others. As political figures even their followers often resent their power and are suspicious of their motives. At what point and for what reason this metamorphosis takes place is not clear.

The seventy-seven persons in the political category include forty-two politicians and officials, twelve reformers, sixteen revolutionaries, two military leaders, and five spies and assassins. We have already described some of these political personalities in detail: Nancy Astor, Willy Brandt, Julian Bond, Abba Eban, Jimmy Carter, Indira Gandhi, Ho Chi Minh, Robert and Edward Kennedy, Henry Kissinger, Nadezhda Krupskaya, Malcolm X, George McGovern, Edmund Muskie, and Harold Nicolson. They and others are all involved in the political process, whether in preserving the status quo, in enhancing it, or in changing it through armed struggle.

The forty-two men and women designated as politicians and officials came from Argentina, Cuba, Czechoslovakia, England, Germany, India, Israel, Kenya, Nigeria, Pakistan, People's Republic of China, Spain, the United States, and the USSR. They represent many ideologies and types of government.

In this chapter and the next three we present the conclusions about the differences between the four large groups. This permits the perceptive reader to find in the life stories that follow not only the corroboration for the findings relating specifically to persons in a particular area of eminence but also evidence of other findings that apply to eminent persons in all areas of eminence, such as the nonurban birthplace, the love for learning in the home, the strong intellectual and physical drives in the whole family, and the motivating effect of being a poor relation. Each of the life stories illustrates several of these findings.

Statistically Significant Differences

There are a number of ways in which the persons in the political area of eminence differ significantly from the persons in the three other areas of eminence.

1. Women are underrepresented among the political persons. Although women make up 26 percent of the total sample, they constitute only 13 percent of the political group, half as many as would be expected if women were evenly distributed in the four areas.
2. Only children are underrepresented among the political persons (7 percent of the political, as opposed to 17 percent in the total sample).
3. Middle children (neither first- nor last-born) are overrepresented among the political (39 percent of the political, as opposed to 26 percent in the total sample).
4. Political persons have more intact marriages, that is, marriages not ending in divorce or separation (61 percent of the political, as opposed to 43 percent in the total sample).
5. The political persons excel in school performance, like school, are frequently honor students (31 percent) and, especially in the United States, are involved in debating, in school publications, and in school clubs. They are seldom rejected by peers.

6. Of the twenty-one sexually divergent men and women in the total sample, only two were political—Harold Nicolson and Roger Casement.

In the next few sections, we will describe American political personalities John Foster Dulles, Lyndon Johnson, J. William Fulbright, and reformer Norman Thomas. We will then discuss foreign political personalities, many of them revolutionaries: Jomo Kenyatta, Chou En-lai, Ché Guevara, Leonid Brezhnev, Nikolai Bukharin, Frantz Fanon, and Fidel Castro. We will then look at spies, assassins, and traitors, particularly Dietrich Bonhoeffer and Fritz Adler.

American Political Personalities

The least complicated households are those where there are no ideological conflicts between the generations, no differences in life-style, no economic crises, war, or revolution that impinge directly on the nuclear family. People in public office from such households like to keep things just as they are and often incur the displeasure of others who see a need for change. John Foster Dulles was one of them.

John Foster Dulles. In *John Foster Dulles: A Reappraisal* (1962), Richard Goold-Adams concludes: "A hundred and fifty years ago he would certainly have been regarded as a great man. His moral qualities, his toughness, his self-assurance, his energy, and his great intellectual capacity would have all constituted a complex of power and rectitude, which neither his friends nor his enemies could have denigrated. But in the modern world even these are not enough. Greatness requires at least some instinct for the feelings and aspirations of others, a humanity, a sensitivity which Dulles lacked" (pp. 302–303).

John's early life was singularly unclouded by trouble, either at home or at school. He was born in 1888, not at home in Watertown, New York, where his father, Allen Macy Dulles, was the Presbyterian minister, but in his grandfather's home in Washington, D.C. His birthplace is symbolic because it was his grandfather, not his father, who commanded his full respect and whom he was to emulate.

His mother, Edith Foster Dulles, could trace her ancestry back to Charlemagne, his father to a Scottish ancestor who emigrated in 1792 and became a prosperous merchant in Philadelphia. The paternal grandfather, who died when John was one year old, was a missionary; however, his maternal grandfather, John Watson Foster, Secretary of State under President Harrison, was the most important person in John's life during his childhood and early manhood.

John was not permitted to miss any religious activities at his father's church, went to Sunday school, church, and midweek prayer meeting. He read the Henty books and learned in school to admire Paul Revere and John Paul Jones. His father was more of an iconoclast than John ever became. Several of his congregation left his church and became Methodists when he said it was not necessary to believe in the virgin birth in order to become a Christian, and married couples when one or both had been divorced.

When John was graduated from high school, his grandfather provided funds for John's mother to take him and a sister to Switzerland for a year so they could learn French. When he returned, he was sixteen and old enough to go to Princeton, where he was a brilliant student. However, he was not a grind; he liked to bet, would take odds on almost anything, and spent hours playing whist and poker. At the end of his junior year he left classes early to go to the second Hague peace conference, where his grandfather, who was an advisor to the Chinese delegation, had arranged for him to be appointed a secretary to the delegation. After this experience, there was no doubt of John's ultimate ambition to go into politics, to the disappointment of his father, who wanted him to be a minister.

After graduating Phi Beta Kappa from Princeton, he was given a scholarship that enabled him to go to the Sorbonne to study philosophy for a year. His entire family joined him in Paris that summer, not an unusual event, since his mother had a small income that enabled them to spend summers in Europe, and in this way John had learned to speak Spanish and German as well as French.

After Paris he lived with his grandparents in Washington while going to law school at George Washington University. Although he completed the course work in two years, since he had not spent the required three years in residence, the university withheld his degree, a fact that hindered him in his career. Indeed, it was twenty-five years later when he was a distinguished statesman that the authorities finally gave him the degree.

He found it impossible to get a job with a law firm until his grandfather came to his rescue and introduced him to his old friend William N. Cromwell of the distinguished law firm of Sullivan and Cromwell. Cromwell liked the young man who could speak French, Spanish, and German. When John was only five years out of law school he had worked his way up to seventh place on the firm's letterhead.

On June 26, 1912, he married Janet Avery. His biographers Deane and David Heller, in *John Foster Dulles: Soldier for Peace* (1960), say it was "an extraordinarily happy marriage. Janet Dulles' devotion in forwarding his career became legendary" (p. 48). She traveled with him on journeys totaling over half a million miles, was known as the wife who was never left behind, and was always ready to leave for an international trip with only two hours notice. Although she won a national award from a women's magazine for "togetherness," she and her husband were necessarily somewhat remote from their three children, who did not share the parental interests.

Lyndon Johnson. Another conventionally reared boy in an intact family was Lyndon Baines Johnson, born in 1908 on a farm in the Pedernales Valley about sixteen miles from Fredericksburg, Gillespie County, Texas. When the ten-pound boy was born, his father, Sam Johnson, a state legislator, rode his horse to the home of his father, "Big Sam" Johnson, and together they galloped about the countryside spreading the news. Even on that first day, supposedly, there were high expectations for this firstborn; legend has it that the grandfather prophesied then that the boy would some day be a United States Senator.

According to Alfred Steinberg, in *Sam Johnson's Boy* (1968), the saying in the community was that "the Baines had the brains and the Johnsons had the guts" (p. 11). Indeed, mother and father were quite dissimilar in manner and character. The former Rebecca Baines was the daughter of a newspaper editor and politician from Fredericksburg whom Sam Johnson replaced in the legislature. Rebecca had come as a reporter to interview Sam, who was to succeed her ailing father, but was not impressed and thought him "cagey" and not very articulate. He, however, saw a striking and intelligent woman used to the ways of politicians and resolved at once to marry her. The marriage took place not long after the interview. She was twenty-six and he was twenty-seven.

Doris Kearns, in *Lyndon Johnson and the American Dream* (1976), believes that Lyndon was never quite sure whom he wanted to emulate—his mother, who valued culture and good manners, or his father, who was an ebullient, coarse, driving man among men. Rebecca wasted no time in trying to make a gentleman and a scholar out of their firstborn, and at four and a half he was reading quite well and was accepted as a first grader in the nearby country school. Since his mother had always held him in her lap when he read with her, his teacher found she had to do likewise or he would refuse to read. He was also given music and dramatic art lessons. However, as he grew older, he became less and less interested in schoolwork and became boisterous like his father, wanting to run and play with other boys. His mother, grieving over his lack of attention to his lessons, read his homework to him while he ate breakfast and followed him to the gate giving him instructions about the day's assignments.

Lyndon had an early introduction to politics. At eleven he was bouncing about in his father's Model T Ford accompanying him to political rallies as Sam Johnson—who was in office and sometimes out—campaigned for a seat in the legislature. Sam loved being in the state capital, though it interfered with his success as a farmer. In high school, which Lyndon entered early, he excelled in debating. At one point he was so confident that he and his partner would win the state debating championship that when they came in second he vomited from disappointment.

Impatient with his mother's anxieties over schoolwork, Lyndon decided not to go to college, and after graduation from secondary school he, along with some other boys, set out to see the world, leaving behind his three younger sisters and small brother.

He spent two years in California and the West waiting on tables, washing dishes, sometimes going hungry. Out of nostalgia or home-sickness he attended a political rally, and this may have helped him decide to come home, to the relief of his worried parents. Although the family's finances were at a low ebb, they were happy to hear he now wanted to go to college, and his mother called a friend, the president of the Southwest Texas State Teachers College, who promised to do what he could for him.

Lyndon became the president's secretary, and it was not long before he was a powerful man on campus. Anyone who wanted to see the president had to see Lyndon first, and the president jokingly said he was not sure which of them was president. Lyndon also made friends (and also some enemies) with other brash, aggressive boys who ran things on campus. He wrote editorials about getting along in the world by having a strong personality and by being an active member of campus or community groups and was active on the debating team.

After graduation he became debate coach in a Houston high school, and his debate team did so well that there was standing room only when the Houston team met challengers at home. It lost the state championship by only one vote. Because of his success as a debate coach, he was invited to go to Washington as an administrative aide to Congressman Richard Kleberg. In Washington he met Claudia Alta (Lady Bird) Taylor, another Texan, whose well-to-do father had given her a trip to the East as a graduation present. She now had a teacher's certificate and also a bachelor's degree in journalism. The story of his parents' romance was repeated: she thought him the most outspoken man she had ever met and was not impressed; he knew at once that she was the girl he wanted to marry. They were married six weeks later.

"One of the characteristics Lady Bird noticed in her husband," biographer Steinberg says, "was that he never opened a book or magazine. She began to mark passages she thought he should see, and she took to walking after him, attempting to read aloud to him, just as his mother had walked to the gate with him while instructing him on schoolwork" (p. 100).

J. William Fulbright. It is firstborn children who, by reason of the high rank they achieve or their being representative of a minority among the politicians, demand our attention when we search for political persons to use as examples. The middle born in general are less inclined to seek the limelight, are not so often the heads of state or controversial figures, and their personal lives as well as professional lives are less dramatic. We have already described middle borns Hubert Humphrey, Robert Kennedy, George McGovern, and Edmund Muskie. Others are Herbert Asquith, Eugene McCarthy, and Golda Meir. J. William Fulbright, the late U.S. Senator from Arkansas, is another.

The even tenor of William Fulbright's life is quite typical of the middle child, and his quiet, diplomatic manner enabled him to be repeatedly elected by a Southern constituency, even though he was a liberal and nonsegregationist. He was very much the product of his childhood environment, deeply influenced by his father's failure and sudden need to face economic realities and by his mother's values and love of learning. He was fortunate in receiving a scholarship that sent him abroad, a privilege he later was able to extend to many other students, and later in having a helpful wife.

Born in 1905 on a farm near Sumner, Missouri, he spent his boyhood in Fayetteville, Arkansas. There were six children in the family: Anna (the firstborn), Lucile, Jack, William (called Bill), and the twins, Roberta and Helen.

Jay Fulbright, the father, was the town banker, owned Coca-Cola franchises and several large tracts of land, was in the lumber business, and operated a small railroad to serve the lumber industry. When he would make an error in judgment in recommending an investment, he would compensate the loser, although he was under no legal obligation to do so. He met his wife, the former Roberta Waugh, when both studied for two years at the University of Missouri. "Miss Roberta" came from an aristocratic family of English descent whose members excused their improvidence by labeling those who worked hard and paid their debts as being "too concerned about money." However, she admired the fact that Jay Fulbright had inherited from his German ancestors, the Vulbrechts, just those qualities of working hard and paying his debts. They were pleased with each other.

The oldest son, Jack, was taller, stronger, and more athletic than Bill. However, perhaps the father demanded too much of his firstborn son, for they did not get along. Bill was both his mother's and his father's favorite son. Jack was admitted to Harvard, but Bill was pleased to stay home and go to the University of Arkansas, even though it was not fully accredited. Here he was the boy wonder—captain of the tennis team, star football player, member of every important club, a "B" student. He drove a fast car and liked girls, and the girls liked him.

When Bill was a sophomore, his father suddenly died, and he dropped out of college to try to help his mother make sense of the debacle. He was panic stricken, sure the family would soon be starving, and indeed his father's business partners did not let their sympathy for the widow keep them from trying to cheat her. However, Miss Roberta discovered their iniquities and turned the tables on them. In the process of exposing them she also cleaned out corruption in the county courthouse. She went on to become a humanitarian-reformer and the best known woman in northwestern Arkansas, taking over editorship of the family newspaper and making it an influence for good government.

At eighteen Bill was vice-president of a railroad and involved in the management of other businesses, but after a semester of being businessman, his mother urged him to go back to college. Life had more for Bill, she believed, than being a small-town banker. After graduation he went to Oxford as a Rhodes scholar, then spent a year roaming the Continent, where he met a young American anthropologist who took him on a dig. On Bill's return from Europe, his anthropologist friend called him to Washington, D.C., to help him straighten out his father's estate, since Bill was the only person he could trust.

In Washington he fell in love with the daughter of a wealthy cotton broker, Betty Williams, a gregarious, level-headed girl who nonetheless worried Miss Roberta, who doubted a rich man's daughter would fit into Fayetteville society, an opinion with which the Williams family agreed. However, the bride and bridegroom stayed in Washington, and Bill enrolled in law school at George Washington University, from which he graduated second in a class of 135. Later Miss Roberta was to remark that Bill had picked "the best of the litter," for it turned out that Betty Fulbright was a good campaigner who was well liked by her husband's country constituents. They had two daughters, Betsy and Roberta.

Reformers: The Example of Norman Thomas

Among the Four Hundred there were twenty reformers, including Jane Addams, Susan B. Anthony, Mahatma Gandhi, Martin Luther King, Jr., Albert Schweitzer, Margaret Sanger, and Bertrand Russell. They worked toward making many kinds of changes within the system: women's suffrage, birth control, peace, and so on.

However, the ratio of revolutionaries to reformers has reversed itself among the Three Hundred and the Four Hundred, for there are only five reformers among the Three Hundred— Rachel Carson, Danilo Dolci, Ralph Nader, Upton Sinclair, and Norman Thomas—compared with sixteen successful or unsuccessful revolutionaries. We have already described Carson and Nader. Here we will describe Norman Thomas.

In *Norman Thomas: Respectable Rebel* (1967), biographer Murray B. Seidler calls this political leader who never built a strong party nor ever won an election the "most successful failure" among political figures in the United States. During his years of leadership the Socialist Party platform provided the planks for the Democratic Party a decade later. He did the spade work for the New Deal, for social security, unemployment insurance, public works programs, and collective bargaining. He helped organize the American Civil Liberties Union and the Fellowship of Reconciliation. He had an intense hatred of war, injustice, and poverty.

Norman Thomas was born in 1884 in the Presbyterian manse in Marion, Ohio. His father, the Reverend Welling Evan Thomas, also the son of a Presbyterian minister, was a quiet, kindly man, well liked by his congregation and loved by his five children, of whom Norman was the oldest. He was quite happy to let his wife have the major voice in household matters and in the rearing of their children. He was quite orthodox and believed in Hell but had never met anyone he thought was going there. Norman's mother, Emma Mattoon Thomas, was an energetic and enthusiastic woman who could help her oldest son with his Latin while preparing dinner for the entire family. Until Emma was twelve she lived in North Carolina, where her father was president of a mission college for Negro students. If she had any biases, it was against the wealthy, whom she mistrusted. The only ambitions she had for her children were that they be healthy, well educated, and moral. When Norman, the Presbyterian minister, turned socialist, she took it in stride. Had he turned to card playing or drinking or been unfaithful to his wife or neglected his six children, she would have been heartbroken.

Except for being sick with respiratory infections during his first twelve years, Norman was the ideal child. Relatives said in his hearing that he probably would not make old bones. He read widely from his father's library; worked faithfully at his chores of milking the cow, raising chickens, and gardening; and sometimes washed dishes (but pulled down the blinds when he did so). In high school he was healthy and handsome and the tallest boy in the class. He played basketball, organized bobsled rides, once organized a science exhibit, and was president of his senior class. As an adult, his most outstanding quality was his eloquence, his quick repartee, his ability to think on his feet, his amazing ability to respond quickly and coherently to questions from the audience even while being heckled.

He wanted to go to Princeton, but the family could not afford it, and so he went to Bucknell instead, which was free to ministers' children. When he found Bucknell lacking academically, a wealthy uncle offered to pay his fees at Princeton. He took care of the rest of his expenses by tutoring other students and by working in a chair factory in the summer. He was graduated from Princeton *cum laude,* was Phi Beta Kappa, and class valedictorian.

His first job after graduation was in a Presbyterian settlement house, where his task was to keep youth gangs that frequented the institution from fighting and tearing up the place. Again his uncle intervened and took him as his companion on a leisurely trip around the world. When he returned, he was ready to forget his daydream of being a politician and enrolled at the Union Theological Seminary to prepare to become a Presbyterian minister. While still at the seminary he married the daughter of a wealthy banker, Violet Stewart, who was working as a volunteer in the church in which he was acting as assistant pastor. He found the seminary a stimulating place to be (as had Bonhoeffer and Tillich). One of his biographers, Bernard K. Johnpoll, in *Pacifist's Progress* (1970), characterized the seminary thus: "Union was a center of the Social Gospel movement. Its God was more ethical than super- natural. . . . Its basic aim was the creation of a heaven on earth by nonviolent economic and social revolution" (pp. 13–14).

His first regular position was as minister in an East Harlem Presbyterian church. He was also chairman of the American Parish Among Immigrants in New York. After seven years there, he became a Christian socialist, a consequence of his being forced to question the values of a capitalist society in which so many of his parishioners could not earn a decent living. He also developed a passionate and deeply personal hatred of war, which the Presbyterian church did not share. He joined and quickly became the spokesman for and leader of the American Socialist Party.

The sudden change in occupation and ideology was hard for his wife to accept, but she loved him very much and did not dispute his right to follow his conscience. Her wealthy father threatened to disinherit her but did not. Their six children grew up in a house full of interesting and important visitors. They also enjoyed the company of their father's younger brother, Evan, who had been in jail as a conscientious objector, had gone on a hunger strike in protest against prison conditions, and had been put in solitary con- finement. They were proud of their grandmother, who went directly to the Secretary of War and told him how things were in the federal prison. Although he told her he did not believe her—something no one had ever dared say to Minnie Mattoon Thomas before— Evan, despite a twenty-five-year sentence, was soon out of prison. Evan became a distinguished physician and a lifelong pacifist activist.

Like many insurgents and reformers, Norman Thomas was conventional in his behavior and manner. In *Norman Thomas: A Biography* (1964), Harry Fleischman quotes him as saying about his rearing: "The moral code was too narrow, for example, in its Sabbatarianism; it had both its blind spots and its overemphasis. Yet, even so, I challenge any Freudian to show that it led to as much nervous disorder, instability, or more unhappiness than the current laxity of standards. I am so old-fashioned as to be glad that I lived in a home, a time and an environment in which sin, yes and moral vices, were realities to be forgiven and cured but not condoned" (p. 31).

Foreign Political Personalities

We have tried to present the foreign political personalities, most of whom are revolutionaries, as we have presented the other eminent persons, as they themselves or their biographers describe them. These revolutionaries come from Africa, Latin America, China, and Russia and from much the same kind of upper-middle-class learning-centered homes as do the conservative and liberal political personalities. Foreign revolutionaries, like other politicians, are superior students, get along well with their peers, become involved while quite young in organizational activities, and as adults have helpful spouses and usually enjoy stable marital relationships. In their rearing and in their close interpersonal relationships they closely resemble other political figures.

Jomo Kenyatta. When as a small boy Jomo Kenyatta, now the aged president of Kenya, came to the Christian Mission School near Ngenda, Kenya, he was naked except for three wire bracelets and a cloth about his neck. He did not know how old he was because the Kikuyu have a superstition about numbers and counting and do not record things in years. He was, he thinks, born in 1897. The staff was dubious as to whether he would stay; herdboys who lost a goat sometimes came to stay for a few days because they were afraid to go home, or were simply curious. However, since the Presbyterian missionaries were eager to have new Kikuyu recruits, they accepted him and gave him a loin cloth. They also gave him a shirt, which he tried to put on with the buttons in back.

However, Kongo—his original tribal name—knew why he had come to the mission school. He had watched a missionary write a message on a paper which said something to another man. It was stronger magic than any practiced by his grandfather, an important medicine man, and Kongo knew that if there were a higher magic, he wanted to learn it. He had other reasons, also, for when his father died and his mother became the wife of her husband's brother, the uncle did not welcome the addition of two more sons since it meant they would have to be provided with goats to buy wives and for other rituals having to do with the boys' maturity. Then Kongo's mother died soon after the birth of a half-brother, and he was in the uncomfortable position of being a "poor relation." After Kongo had been at the mission school for a time, his uncle came to bluster and scold, but he knew and the missionaries knew that all his uncle really wanted was a gift of a blanket and some tobacco for relinquishing the burdensome Kongo to the missionaries.

His Scottish headmaster was a man of good character and was sympathetic by nature, but he ran the school in Spartan fashion, like a boarding school in Scotland. For infractions of the rules during their rest periods, the boys were sometimes made to stand on a table, and for fighting among themselves they might be whipped with a short rope. They slept on hard boards, rose at dawn, went to bed at dusk, had military drill, sang hymns, had prayers twice a day, and were taught much as the headmaster and the white teachers had been taught. They played football so that they might become manly and cooperative, vaulted horses and parallel bars to exorcise any possible devils within them, and learned to garden, sew, and wash dishes. They read simple versions of Old Testament stories in Kikuyu, and later read a new translation of St. Mark's gospel. Though he was baptized when other boys were baptized, he did not feel like a Christian, and he accepted his Christian name, Johnstone, with reluctance. Like other boys, however, Kongo often left school and went home, six miles away, and he accepted having age mates, who were to be close to him in later years. He was circumcised as he knelt naked with other boys his age in a stream, which ran red with blood as a tribesman flayed their foreskins with a sharpened stone.

Kongo was an observant, close-mouthed boy who took what he wanted from any situation in which he found himself. As he grew older, he went to other mission schools, where he learned some English, but wherever he went he performed the rituals he was forced to endure so he could get the education he desired. After secondary school it was necessary to go abroad if he were to go to college, and he was invited to attend Woodbrooke, a Quaker college in England.

At Woodbrooke a great fuss was made over the charming,

handsome, verbal African student. He wore pullovers and slacks and went for long walks in the country and enjoyed being treated as an equal. He accepted the Quaker ideas about racial equality and service to mankind, though he did not accept their ideas about pacifism. After Woodbrooke he went to London, where he met Paul Robeson and was influenced by W. E. B. Du Bois. He also met Communist Party members eager to recruit an intelligent young man from Africa. He also went to the USSR, as a tourist, he says, though he has never spoken freely about his travels there. He worked at the University of London translating textbooks into Kikuyu, earning barely enough to live on. However, he became a favorite student of the eminent anthropologist Bronislaw Malinowski, who was later to write the preface for his book *Facing Mount Kenya*. In this book Kenyatta maintained that individual interests must be downgraded in favor of group interests, as in the Kikuyu culture, because everything good came from the collective life of the community. He also spoke of the necessity for Africans to struggle for their freedom, to return to their tribal ways, till the soil, be self-sufficient, and face Mount Kenya in serenity.

After England, he returned to Kenya and became leader of a Christian-oriented group seeking to free Africa from colonialism. By this time so many Africans had been educated in missionary schools and had learned so many Old Testament stories that they identified themselves with the Israelites, and were looking for a Moses to lead them out of captivity. Although he had frequently been critical of the terrorist tactics of the Mau-Mau, he was imprisoned by the colonial government for six and a half years for aiding and abetting the Mau-Mau rebellion. After his release he was enthusiastically elected the first president of the Republic of Kenya, a "Moses" to his people.

Kenyatta has charisma and a powerful personality. His birthplace is a national shrine. The Kikuyu broadsheets have hailed him as the "Hero of Our Race," a "Saviour," and a "Great Elder." His picture is in every store window. As the first (and so far only) president of Kenya, he saw no reason to deny himself the luxuries he felt were his legitimate rewards for his years in prison and his elevation to the highest office in the land; he has received gifts from everywhere—from his own people, from resident Asians trying to curry favor, from businessmen wanting to trade with the government. When he rides abroad, motorcycle policemen precede his car with sirens shrieking and carloads of armed bodyguards follow him.

He is presently closer to the United States than to the Soviet Union, but his primary loyalties have always been to his age group among the Kikuyu with whom he was circumcised. He has ruled firmly, like a chief of tribal elders who is not to be disputed. Although the Kikuyu are only 20 percent of the population, most government posts are held by members of that tribe, a fact that brought criticism, especially by the Luo tribe. He has held power tenaciously, permitting only one political party, his own, to exist. When an opposition party headed by a former close young associate, a Luo, Oginga Odinga, gained favor and threatened Kenyatta's reelection, he declared it illegal, and Odinga was jailed as were some of his followers.

While working in England, he observed monogamy with the detached interest of a monogamist observing the tribal customs of the polygamist Kikuyu. He took an English wife, and a son by her, but told her when he married her that he had left behind a wife and two children in Kenya, to whom he must some day return. When he returned to Kenya to form the Christian-oriented organization to win freedom for his country, he married a third wife, whose death in childbirth with a second child grieved him sorely. At his presidential inauguration, his fourth wife, who bore him more children, was hostess to all his other wives and children. The modification of the polygamous tribal ways, however, pleased his people.

Chou En-lai. Chou En-lai said that he was an intellectual with a feudalistic background who came to communism not through early contact with peasants and workers but through reading and through contacts he made abroad.

Born in Huai-an in 1898 and an only child, he came from an extended Chinese family with considerable wealth. His mother, one of the four Wan daughters who married four Chou brothers, died when he was probably six. She was a kindly woman with a gentle temper and talented in art and literature, and Chou was always sentimental about her. His father, the poor relation of the family, was unemployed most of the time and took any kind of bureaucratic clerical job that would keep him in rice wine. Since his second uncle had no son of his own, the family decided that Chou should live with him, and after that Chou saw very little of his father. Later, in his old age, he asked his son, who had put him on a small pension, for more money, but Chou was not responsive.

At ten Chou moved into the home of his fourth uncle, a police commissioner, whom he came to regard as his father. In this household he formed a close attachment to one of his aunts, an illiterate woman with a peppery temper who ran her household in military fashion, with Chou as her second in command. Later he was as sentimental about her as he was about his mother.

His elementary school years were spent in a Protestant missionary school, where he learned less about Christian gospel than about Western culture—about Darwin, Mill, Rousseau, Robert Southey's pantocracy, Hawthorne's Brook Farm. However, to the distress of his elders, he failed an examination that would have prepared him to go to the United States to college. His uncles were also disappointed when he insisted on going to a modern secondary school, Nankai School of Tientsin, which was suspected of training students to be rebels.

The years he spent at the school were the happiest of his life. Since he had chosen the school against his uncle's will, he supported himself by being the principal's student assistant. His best subjects were social studies and languages; his poorest was science. The school encouraged students to specialize in the areas of their greatest competence. Chou wrote articles for the school paper and espoused free marriage and China's need for industrialization and warned of the impending war with Japan.

After graduation at age nineteen, feeling the need to see the world, he left for Tokyo, where he was met by a former school friend, Han, and his wife, both graduate students supported by the Chinese government. Since Chou was penniless, the Hans and four other Chinese foreign scholars pledged ten dollars a month to his keep while he prepared to take an entrance examination for Tokyo Teachers College. In the meantime there was news of riots and unrest in China and of major clashes with Japan in Manchuria. Four students supporting him returned home, and Chou moved in with the Hans, sleeping on the floor and helping with the household tasks. Finally, Chou's anxieties about what was happening at home became too great, and his friend's wife sold a ring to pay for his trip home.

No sooner had he arrived than he became involved in a student strike called because a student had been killed in an earlier demonstration. China had taken part in World War I, had emerged as a victor, but had been cheated, students felt, when rights to Manchuria had been transferred to Japan. Students had burned the house of the minister of communications and had beaten up the minister to Japan, who was home on leave. Embarking on his political career, Chou became active in the Tientsin Student League, was elected editor-in-chief of the league's paper, and organized strikes. He also attended Nankai University, a new school with an ultraliberal point of view. At that time Leo Tolstoy was his hero, but he was already beginning to read Marxist literature. In January 1920, Chou, then twenty-one, led a group of students to the governor's office to protest police brutality against student demonstrators. They were arrested and he was in jail until May. When he was released he quickly organized many more chapters of the student league. A teacher at the Nankai University and an attorney who had defended the jailed students gave him $500 to finance his further education in France. In France he became seriously involved in the international Communist movement.

A supportive knowledgeable wife who shares his beliefs is important to a politician, conservative or radical. Teng Ying-ch'ao is one of the most remarkable of the wives of politicians. Chou En-lai and his future wife met when they were secondary school students and were both involved in revolutionary activities. His biographer, Hsu Kai-Yu, in *Chou En-lai: China's Gray Eminence* (1968), describes their marriage as an exemplary one among the Chinese Communists. They had no differences in their goals and ideology. When they married, he had already laid the foundation for the Chinese Red Army; she had been director of the women's department of the Kwangtung Province and had already developed lasting friendships among the top women leaders. The supreme test of her endurance was on the Long March, when she was responsible for the special needs of the women and children. In addition to scarcity of food, the constant danger of attack, sandals with soles worn through, both Chou and his wife were often ill. She lost a child she had been carrying for six months and they never had another. But Chou maintained his iron discipline, and the most stouthearted survived to reach the Caves of Yenan. According to Hsu Kai-Yu:

> Still weak from the Long March, Teng Ying-ch'ao set about to fix up a cave for her husband whom she hardly saw for days at a stretch. . . . she used the locally made rice paper, and once it was pasted onto the latticed window frames, it didn't look too bad at all. She even thought of writing a poem or two on the paper to add a decorative touch. . . . With a borrowed table wiped spotlessly clean and a freshly laundered coverlet on the bed under a mosquito net, the place began to look livable, even luxurious, when she recalled the shelterless mud hovels in which she had spent many a night under the pouring rain on the grasslands of Northern Szechwan [pp. 124–125].

Ché Guevara. The parents of Ernesto (Ché) Guevara, like the parents of Chou En-lai and of most other famous revolutionaries, were aristocrats, with a long family history of wealth and influence. Ché was born in 1928 in Rosario, Argentina. His mother, Celia de la Serena, who could trace her ancestry back to the grandees of Spain, was born into a family of wealth and status. She, however, was a girl rebel of the post–World War I period, driving recklessly down boulevards closed to cars and among the first in her circle to have her hair bobbed. She became an unaffiliated political radical. Although the most eligible of bachelors wanted to marry her, she chose an impoverished rebel, one less aggressive than she. In *Ché Guevara: A Biography* (1969), Daniel James says: "Ernesto Guevara Lynch was practically a misfit; his background and education as an aristocrat made him scorn the bourgeois life, while at the same time the adventurous blood of his forefathers seemed to have thinned out in him. He was too easy-going, too *simpático*. Moreover, he had life too soft and had never known the goad of hardship or oppression" (p. 29). His Irish-Argentinian ancestors had been forced for political reasons to leave their country until a new regime was established and had sought their fortune in the California gold fields.

Ernesto failed to make competent use of his wife's inheritance and lost a small fortune in a maté plantation. Most of the time he was unemployed. Celia and Ernesto had only their revolutionary beliefs and their love for their children in common, and they frequently quarreled bitterly, often about money, although they liked to believe they did not value money. At one time a guest walked into the dining room and found them sitting at a table, each with a pistol in hand, threatening to kill the other or themselves. The house was chaotic, with books and papers strewn about. The five children, of whom Ché was the oldest, often had to prepare their own irregular meals. They and other children rode their bicycles through the house. The house was open to everyone they knew: wealthy friends, poor intellectuals, and tradesmen.

The Guevaras believed in giving their children freedom, and when Ché was eleven, he went hitchhiking for weeks with a younger brother. The father also felt his sons should have early experience with discomfort and danger, as he had not had, and so they worked for pay in the grape vineyards. Ché organized a gang of working-class boys from the streets and caddies from the golf course to fight boys from other upper middle class families like his own. He was very much the daredevil. When other children told him that eating chalk or sucking ink off the fingers was the same as taking poison, he deliberately ate a huge chunk of chalk and drank from a bottle of ink. He walked a high narrow fence where falling meant being impaled on sharp pointed sticks.

Ché seems not to have disliked his father, but he was closest to his volatile, rebellious, emotional mother, although she often annoyed him. One of the constant quarrels between the parents was over Ché's severe asthma attacks, which began at age two when his mother let him get chilled while swimming. His father blamed his mother for the son's illness. His mother accepted the blame and was tortured when he struggled for breath. The other four children were jealous of her solicitude for him and once ganged up on him and beat him. On another occasion he became severely ill after they doused his head in a bucket of cold water.

In part because his illness gave him time to read, he was a

precocious boy, and at thirteen he was reading Freud, Baudelaire, Dumas, Verlaine, and Mallarmé. He also read French as well as Spanish. Although he was a "loner" and more intellectual than his academic peers, he was not rejected by them. During his secondary school years he temporarily conquered his asthma with rigorous muscle-building exercises and by swimming and playing football. His continuing illness was a factor in his becoming a physician.

The whole pattern of his adult life was very much like that of his adolescence. He began anticipating his death very early. James quotes him as saying, "Fifteen years is an age when already a man knows what he is going to give his life for, and he has no fear of doing so when within his breast he naturally possesses an ideal which encourages him to immolate himself" (p. 45).

Finding the routine of a physician in private practice intolerable, he went hitchhiking about South America observing the poverty of the people and the inadequacies of their governments in helping. His first wife, Hilda Gadea Acosta, mother of his only child, tells how he worked with another physician for a time in a leprosarium. In *Ernesto: A Memoir of Ché Guevara* (1972), she writes, "Ernesto and Granados dealt with the patients without any qualms; they did not wear masks or gloves and they looked the patients in the face. The other doctors behaved differently, thus diminishing the human dignity of the patients" (pp. 14–15).

Ché's mother, who grew more revolutionary as she aged, was pleased with all his ventures. She had an uncanny ability to sense when he was nearing the end of a phase of his life, anticipating, for instance, when he and Fidel Castro were nearing the end of their close relationship. Celia Guevara died of cancer before a letter came from him addressed to his entire family. (He had been told she was dying.) The letter began: "Once more I feel under my heels the ribs of Rocinante" (James, 1969, p. 152).

Ché left Cuba mysteriously and showed up months later in New York, at the United Nations General Assembly, to denounce Yankee imperialism. From America he traveled on to Algeria, Mali, the Congo, Guinea, Ghana, Dahomey, and Egypt, then Ché disappeared again. He had left his wife, Hilda, and daughter in Guatemala and had taken another wife, Aleida March, in Cuba.

A woman named Tania, who turned out to be spying on him for East German and Soviet intelligence services, accompanied him to his death and hers in Bolivia.

Although Ché spoke of himself jokingly as a Don Quixote, being a well-read man he was no doubt aware that Cervantes, through his satirical presentation of his bumbling hero, was influential in hastening the demise of feudalism. Ché saw himself as one of the harbingers of the end of capitalism—a role to which his mother had dedicated him.

Leonid Brezhnev. A true working-class revolutionary, Leonid Ilyich Brezhnev, was born in 1906 in the eastern Ukrainian village of Kamenskoye, a one-industry steel town. When Leonid was a boy, the steel plant, which was owned by Germans, towered over the town, and at night the sky was lit by the flames from the furnaces. Top-level employees lived in a walled-off area, and supervisors had individual garden plots, but workers like the Brezhnevs lived in clay cottages on unpaved streets by the railroad tracks and had no running water or electricity. The Brezhnevs were well spoken of in Kamenskoye. The mother, Natalya, was a pretty girl who married at eighteen and had a great zest for living and a sense of humor. The father, Ilya, was a quiet, friendly man. Leonid, the firstborn, had a younger sister and a younger brother.

In an excellent biography, *Brezhnev: The Masks of Power* (1974), John Dornberg tells of an interview with a man who went to school with Leonid for eight years. The all-boys gymnasium was subsidized by the plant, but it was not a free school. Parents paid a stiff yearly tuition fee, equal to an ordinary steelworker's monthly wages. How the Brezhnevs paid the fees and how Leonid managed to pass the difficult entrance examination is not known, but in any case he was the only boy from a mill hand's family in the school. Leonid was a skinny, freckle-faced boy, hyperactive and inclined to be unruly, yet also silent and friendless. He was neither a poor nor an outstanding student. The work was difficult, the teachers often severe, and students had to master many subjects, including ancient, modern, and Russian history; Russian grammar and literature; Latin, German, and French; biology, chemistry, and physics; and mathematics, including algebra, geometry, and trigonometry.

When Leonid was eleven, the revolution started, the mill

closed, and food, clothing, and fuel became scarce. The students had no paper on which to write their lessons, and teachers, knowing their students were hungry, gave them hot water with sugar in it as a treat. For a time there was complete anarchy, and a hoodlum element took over. Unpopular teachers were shot in the public square by ex-pupils. Brezhnev did not participate in these acts, but instead joined a class on metallurgy given by an unemployed engineer in the abandoned steel mill.

When the period of anarchy was over and a Communist Youth Group was formed, Leonid had an advantage over other youths his age in that he was both a genuine worker's son and had been to a good school. He was given a four-year scholarship to the Technicum for Land Utilization and Reclamation in Kursk.

Brezhnev is described as being as eager as Kenyatta to have the luxuries and special privileges he did not have as a boy. He likes expensive Western clothing, nightclubs, good food, cars. He has a son, a metallurgical engineer, who has inherited his father's expensive tastes. His daughter, Galina, likewise dresses stylishly and is quite at ease and sophisticated in manner when she travels with her father. Still, as Dornberg writes, "Next to affairs of State and Party, Galina has been Brezhnev's greatest problem. Her penchant for men from the circus and her romantic escapades were the primary reason why her daughter Viktoria lived not with her but with Brezhnev" (p. 288).

Nikolai Bukharin. Like most revolutionaries, Nikolai Bukharin came from a liberal, professional family. He was born in 1888 in Moscow, the second son of two primary-school teachers. His mother was a sensible, affectionate woman, his father was a mathematician and a scholar, who shared with him his knowledge of natural history, encouraged his making a collection of birds and butterflies, and fostered the love of language and world literature that later made Nikolai known not only as one of the early Bolsheviks but also as a critic of literature and art. By age four and a half Nikolai was reading and writing quite well.

The father was unemployed for two years after he failed as a tax collector in poverty-stricken Bessarabia, but in later years did well as a czarist civil servant, rising to a rank that marked the family as upper middle class—embarrassment later to his revolutionary son.

In gymnasium and in college Nikolai became deeply involved in Bolshevik political activities, which his mother called his "crazy antics." At twenty-three he was like many another young radical, a wandering emigré in Europe, where he learned a number of new languages, including English, which he spoke very well.

More aware of world affairs than others who came to power after the Russian Revolution, he was highly critical of Stalin's terrorist tactics and maltreatment of the peasants. Consequently, he was arrested for treason, and following a public trial that was a travesty, was executed. His wife and son spent nearly twenty years in various prison camps. Freed by Khrushchev, they were able to get the criminal charges against Bukharin officially repudiated.

Frantz Fanon. Writer-revolutionary-psychiatrist Frantz Fanon was born in 1925, into a middle-class family in Martinique, an in-between child in a family of eight. Because he was the fourth boy and his mother preferred girls, she rejected him. In addition, Frantz was the darkest of her four boys, which may have reminded her of the prejudices of her family. They had resented her marriage to a man with a much darker complexion than she.

His mother's rejection hurt him. In *Black Skin, White Masks* (1968), he says that it was not uncommon to hear a mother in Martinique speak of one of her children as the "blackest." He saw himself as a man with an identity confusion and consequently as one who sought recognition from others all his life. He condemned racial discrimination in Algiers, where the Frenchmen did not like the Jews, the Jews did not like the Arabs, and the Arabs thought themselves superior to the Negroes.

Frantz's father worked as a government functionary, and although his salary was not high, his mother worked as a shopkeeper and thereby provided the extra income for luxuries such as meat on weekends and movies three times a year.

There was a strong love of learning in the Fanon family, and the children were fortunate to be among the 4 percent of the black children in Martinique who went to a Catholic black *lycée*.

Frantz was such a good student that he was able to obtain a university scholarship in any field of his choosing. Wanting to be of service to the poor, he first tried dentistry, but later took his degree in medicine and became a psychiatrist. However, he studied Marx as well as Freud and tried to synthesize their theories. Eventually he decided that colonialism could be destroyed only by armed struggle.

He was an embarrassment to his brothers and sisters, who were conventional in their politics and who became civil servants or married well-to-do husbands. He married Josie Dublé, a white woman from a socialist family background. The happy marriage and the birth of a son, Oliver, gave him the satisfactions he had not had in his own boyhood.

Leukemia cut his life short at the age of thirty-six. He was then deeply involved in the Algerian crisis and had just completed his major work, *Wretched of the Earth* (1968), which sold over half a million copies in the United States and which *Time* magazine called one of the five most important books of the decade.

Fidel Castro. The Cuban premier is one of the few among the Three Hundred who did not come from a home in which there was a love of learning. Born in 1927 on a 23,300-acre sugar plantation near Bíran in Oriente Province, Cuba, Fidel came from a family in which the father, Angel Castro, was an unschooled immigrant laborer from Spain who saw no reason why his children should not be content just to live in the paradise won by his shrewdness and hard labor, since no matter how many children he had, there was work and room for them on the ranch. He had two children by his first wife and seven by his second. Fidel's mother —a servant in a house where the mistress was ill—bore four illegitimate children, of whom Fidel was fourth. After the first wife's death, his parents married and had three more children.

When he was six, Fidel said he would burn the house down if he was not sent to school, although how he developed this intense desire for learning he has not disclosed. His father reluctantly sent him off to Santiago to live with his godparents and to be a day scholar at a nearby Jesuit school. The godparents were not kind to him, and fed him poorly and gave him little attention. However, his teachers were pleased with him, and when his parents saw he was serious about learning they sent him to the most prestigious

Catholic preparatory school in Havana. There he was popular with his peers, an outstanding athlete, and a good student, especially in the humanities, and in the graduation yearbook it was predicted he would be a lawyer. It was also observed that there was something of the actor in his makeup.

At the University of Havana he was soon in the center of the student radical movement. Indeed, the student movement was so alarming to professors that they stayed off campus and let assistants teach their classes. Despite his involvement in political dissent, Fidel kept up his grades and obtained his degree in law. After graduation he practiced for a couple of years, but earned little, since he preferred poor clients who had been wronged by the system.

While still at the university he married a girl whose father and brother were both important functionaries in the Batista administration, and they had a son, whom he loved very much. The marriage was a disaster for them both. Fidel was radical in his politics but not in his attitude toward marriage. After the unsuccessful attack on the Moncada Barracks in 1953, while he was incarcerated, his wife asked her brother for money, and his solution was to put her, illegally, on Batista's payroll. When the fraud was discovered, the resulting negative publicity shamed Fidel and made him willing to accept a divorce. When he rode triumphantly into Havana in 1959, his son, Fidelito, rode on the tank with his father. When the young Fidel became a student at the University of Havana, he used an assumed name so the other students would not treat him differently because of his father's position.

Angel Castro died before his son's successful revolution made it necessary for the family sugar plantation to be nationalized. Fidel's brothers Ramón and Raúl worked side by side with him, but his younger sister, Juana, and his mother sheltered anti-Castro forces on the ranch during the revolution. Juana is now an emigré in Miami.

Biographer Herbert Matthews and others believe that Communism was not the cause of the Cuban revolution but a result. Castro had expected that the United States would be glad to see Batista deposed and would be ready with help and normal trade relations, but when the United States turned against him in 1959 and 1960, he looked to the Soviet Union for help. Until then he was a humanist, not a Communist. In *Fidel Castro* (1969), Matthews says, "An oft-quoted remark of Castro's, published in the Havana *Revolución* on May 22, 1959, was that 'capitalism can kill man with hunger, while Communism kills man by destroying his freedom.' However, since 'humanism' was linked to liberal, democratic, non-Communist policies, it could not long survive the steady drift toward authoritarianism" (p. 161).

Spies, Assassins, and Traitors

There were no spies, assassins, would-be assassins, or traitors among the Four Hundred. Among the Three Hundred there are seven: Fritz Adler, Dietrich Bonhoeffer, Sir Roger Casement, Elie Cohen, Kurt Gerstein, Mata Hari, and Vidkun Quisling. Do they represent a rising tendency for individuals or small groups to try to effect change by violent means?

Elie Cohen, a Jewish boy from Alexandria, Egypt, who played "spy" as a child, was always a loner. Since he knew the Arabic language and the customs well, he became a successful Israeli spy until he was discovered and executed.

Kurt Gerstein of Münster, Germany, who despised his autocratic, powerful, pro-Nazi father, pretended to be a Nazi so he could infiltrate the Nazi concentration camps, sabotage them, and send out messages to the world about what was happening to the Jews. He did so quite successfully but was believed by the French authorities to be lying to save his skin and was thrown into a German prisoner-of-war camp, where he hanged himself.

In *Mata Hari* (1965), her biographer, S. Waagenaar, says she was not really a counterspy but boasted of being one because it was her way of life to boast and to deceive. Her father, Adam Zelle, called the Baron because he dressed and acted as if he were of the nobility, ran a successful hat shop in Leeuwarden, Holland. He dressed his little daughter, Margarete, as if she were a princess, and she would ride down the streets, extravagantly dressed, driving a beribboned cart drawn by two fine goats. When the Baron became bankrupt, she was well schooled in pretense and deceit. Later she left her husband and child and pretended to be a Javanese dancer. Still later she pretended to be a counterspy for the Germans.

Dietrich Bonhoeffer. When Dietrich Bonhoeffer and his twin sister, Sabine, were born in 1906 in Breslau, Germany, their father, Dr. Karl Bonhoeffer, was professor of psychiatry and neurology at the University of Breslau and director of the University Hospital for Nervous Diseases. In 1912 they moved to Berlin, where he became the leading psychiatrist and neurologist in the city.

Dr. Bonhoeffer was not too busy to keep a journal in which he recorded incidents that he felt were important in his children's lives and records of his interviews with them. They could always come to him when they were troubled and often did so. There are fewer records about Dietrich than about some of the other children because Dietrich had few problems and was a sturdy, boisterous, handsome boy who enjoyed his childhood, his friends, and his brothers and sisters, especially his twin, from whom he was inseparable during his early years.

The three younger children (the twins and the youngest child) lived upstairs where they could play noisily in their rooms, where the furniture was designed by their mother to fit their size and needs. Downstairs the three oldest boys had quarters of their own, with accommodations for their collections, animals, books, and experiments. The in-between children, Ursula and Christine, had a room of their own full of dolls and toys. Ursula was the sensible, motherly older sister; Christine was the resentful girl who wished she might have been a boy and always believed she could have been as talented as her brothers if girls were as free to study and work as were boys. Their mother was sympathetic, since she was an early woman suffragette and a community activist who helped to set up a home for aged women and to found a girls' school.

The Bonhoeffers were not pleased with German educational methods. Biographer E. Bethge says, in *Dietrich Bonhoeffer* (1970), "One of the family sayings was that Germans had their backs broken twice in the course of their lives; first at school, and then during their military service" (p. 7). The mother gave her eight children their first two years of schooling at home, making their lessons so enjoyable they believed they were playing. Dietrich Bonhoeffer once said the children had such shameless security that it may have made him less cognizant of the troubles less privileged children had to endure. Dietrich's mother was an efficient but kindly executive, but still could not have given so much time to her children had she not had a staff of five or more persons working in her home at all times.

The family had no serious troubles until Walter, the second son, a young man of tremendous promise, was killed two weeks after he marched off to fight in World War I. His mother was so grief stricken that she kept herself away from the family for almost a year. During this time Dietrich began to brood about the meaning of life, about religion, and about death. The Bonhoeffers were casual about religious observances—the father was an avowed agnostic, the mother a Moravian who expended her religious feelings in the social services—and although the children were confirmed, no one in the family attended church. However, at fourteen Dietrich had decided to become a Lutheran minister. His parents were somewhat disappointed and his brothers openly critical of this decision, telling him the church needed reforming. He replied that if it needed reforming, he would do it.

The sons became professional men and the daughters married lawyers. When Hitler came to power, Sabine and her Jewish husband left Germany and went to London. They begged Dietrich to join them there, but he refused because he felt there were already too few persons left who would speak out against the Nazis, and as a pastor and author of popular theological articles and books, he still had influence.

When the difficult decision was made to try to assassinate Hitler, Dietrich justified it by reasoning that it was evil not to try to stop evil. For some time it seemed as if the Gestapo had not found who had set the bomb that went off too soon to kill Hitler. Bonhoeffer felt so secure he became engaged to be married. That same day he was arrested. He was hanged at age thirty-nine on April 9, 1945, as were a brother and two brothers-in-law.

Afterwards, according to Bethge, his father replied to a letter of sympathy as follows: "I hear you know that we have been through a lot and lost two sons and two sons-in-law through the Gestapo. . . . But since we were all agreed on the need to act, and my sons were also fully aware of what they had to expect if the plot miscarried and had resolved if necessary to lay down their lives, we are sad, but also proud of their attitude, which has been consistent" (p. 836).

Fritz Adler. Born in 1879 in Vienna and raised in a home as child centered as was the Bonhoeffer home and also headed by a psychiatrist, Friedrich (Fritz) Adler developed an emotional intensity about injustice. From childhood, Fritz joined in his father's political activities, and eventually succeeded him as Secretary of the Austrian Social Democratic Party. When the psychiatrist told his son about the intolerable conditions in which working-class children lived, the boy wept, and was consoled only when he was told that as an adult he could work to change such situations. Fritz took his father very seriously, becoming an effective, active member of his father's party during secondary school and college. Dr. Adler advised his son to become a physicist and not to major in humanities, because he believed his son was becoming too intense and emotionally involved in his urgency to change the social system. In *Fritz: Story of a Political Assassin* (1972), R. Florence reports his father wrote his college son: "Why are you so bloody serious, so sad, so nervous, so gloomy? Why? A capable young man, capable of almost anything. . . . Why never a spark of humor or youth in you? Why are you so over-dedicated, like the head of a family with six children all yapping for food? If you would just commit some stupid silliness, I might be annoyed, but it would be comforting" (p. 29).

Fritz was a law-abiding citizen, husband, and father but was unable to tolerate the political situation in his country. Austria had declared war on Serbia. Many like himself protested the war and were hanged or imprisoned. Communication with the outside world was forbidden. To attract the attention of the rest of the world, Fritz assassinated the prime minister, Count Karl Stürgkh, then gave himself up to a policeman. His anguished father wanted him to plead insanity, but he refused, feeling that to do so would make his sacrifice useless.

Friedrich Adler was tried, found guilty, and sentenced to death. The Social Democrats were a strong political party and the public protest was so strong that the sentence was reduced to eighteen years in prison. His father was still alive when his son was freed by the new government after Austria's defeat in World War I. His excomrades welcomed him and made him the new chairman of the Austrian Social Democratic Party since his father was quite

ill. Life was not the same in the postwar world for Fritz Adler.
He would not accept the rising power of the Communist Party.
Stalin's tactics dismayed him. He went to Spain and could not
accept the tactics of the United Front. When the Second International refrained from taking a strong stand against Hitler when
he moved into Czechoslovakia, he resigned in protest. Disappointed
in Europe, he became an emigré in New York City, to which he had
been invited by the American Federation of Labor. In his old age
he lived with his daughter in Zurich. He spent his declining years
working on a biography of his father. Friedrich Adler and Dietrich
Bonhoeffer are two more examples of children tenderly reared in
socially conscious, humanistic homes that do not adequately prepare
them for the frustrations of having to live in a less than ideal
world.

Observations

Many circumstances important in the background of the
eminent are not different in the four major areas of eminence. These
include love of learning in the home and strong physical energy and
drive in the subjects, their parents, and their siblings. Other
similarities include having families who are poor relations or who
have dramatic financial ups and downs, being from an immigrant
family, being reared by both parents, and having similar patterns
of dominance within the home. Subjects do not differ in parental
marital history, closeness to mother or father, urban or rural birthplace, family religion, physical health, or early delinquency.

Artists, musicians, writers, and scientists often show a talent
in their field when they are quite young, but few parents predict
that their children are going to be politicians. It is only in retrospect
that one can see the development of political talent. These are the
children who are early organizers of group activities, get along well
with their peers, and are often inclined to be "bossy." When Hubert
Humphrey was three, for instance, his parents lost him in the crowd
when they took him with them to see a parade. He was found
enthusiastically leading the band as it followed him down the street.
Ordinarily, however, the politician waits until he is in secondary
school to be class president or to be a champion debater. The few

women politicians, who have to be exceptionally dedicated and able, are the most likely to evidence this organizing ability early. Three-year-old Shirley Chisholm bossed her cousins and her siblings. One may remember Indira Gandhi's thousand-member Monkey Brigade. Golda Meir, at age nine, organized a public meeting to raise funds for textbooks for needy children in her school.

As children they are described as being attractive, tall, well spoken, and popular. As adults they are described as being charismatic, imposing, strong featured, eloquent, persuasive. Whether establishment or radical, democratic or authoritarian, politicians share these qualities. Photographs in the biographies and autobiographies verify the subjects' physical attractiveness.

Politicians are more circumspect than are nonpoliticians in male-female relationships, since hints of scandal can be damaging to a political career, although nowadays there are more exposés of infidelities or indiscretions after an eminent politician is dead. Still, almost all elected male political figures are presented as being heterosexual and as being devoted to their families. Female political figures are more likely to be divorced or separated. Revolutionaries, reformers, and appointed officials, however, are as likely to be as conforming in their personal lives as are elected officials; indeed, the political radical may be quite conservative in his family relationships. An inclination to avoid intense emotional relationships with a series of partners seems to characterize most political figures, whether establishment or radical, democratic or authoritarian.

Family relationships are much the same in all countries regardless of the form of government. An exception is in the Third World, where the mission school often served as parental surrogate during the school years. The families where the mission school strongly influenced boys who were to become important political figures are those that produced Chou En-lai of China, Nnamdi Azikiwe of Nigeria, and Jomo Kenyatta and Oginga Odinga of Kenya. During the civil war in Angola in the early 1970s, the leaders of all three warring factions were trained in Protestant mission schools.

❧ 9 ❧

Literary Personalities

Let us dare to read, think, speak, and write.
John Adams

The ninety-two persons in the literary category include fifty-seven authors of fiction and drama, twelve writers of nonfiction, thirteen poets, and ten editors and publishers. Many are involved in more than one area: some poets write novels, some publishers are authors. We have already described some literary personalities in detail: Lou Andreas-Salomé, W. H. Auden, Colette, T. S. Eliot, Graham Greene, Christopher Isherwood, Doris Lessing, Malcolm Lowry, Flannery O'Connor, Anaïs Nin, Drew Pearson, Ezra Pound, Sylvia Plath, Marguerite Radclyffe-Hall, and Upton Sinclair. In this chapter we will describe others.

Statistically Significant Differences

1. Only children are overrepresented among the literary personalities: although they constitute only 17 percent of the total survey sample, they represent 26 percent of the literary figures.
2. Not surprisingly, the literary are overrepresented among those who were voracious readers in childhood—77 percent—com-

pared to 48 percent in the total sample. Despite their love of learning (or because of it), they are also overrepresented among those who disliked school, school teachers, and school curriculums—literary 52 percent; total sample 33 percent.

3. The literary are overrepresented among those who attempt or succeed in committing suicide: 11 percent, as opposed to 5 percent in the total sample.

4. Among those who extend family interests, the literary are underrepresented: only 27 percent as compared with 42 percent in the total sample.

5. Childhood homes of the literary are more apt to be described as being very unhappy—67 percent—than those of the whole sample (44 percent). For instance, literary personalities have more alcoholic parents (one or both) than do those in the total sample—11 percent versus 7 percent.

6. The literary are less likely to have one marriage not ending in divorce or separation (29 percent) compared with those in the total survey sample (43 percent). Moreover, more never marry (25 percent versus 19 percent) and more are divorced (42 percent versus 35 percent total).

7. Twenty of the twenty-one subjects who are identified as being sexually divergent, either by themselves or by their biographers, are literary personalities.

Writers resemble each other more closely than do politicians and are not easy to divide into categories. Poets, short story writers, publishers, novelists, and dramatists resemble each other in their life experiences and personal characteristics. Nor was the choice of which writers' life stories to present in this chapter easy to make. Two subjects, E. E. Cummings and Jessamyn West, were chosen because they come from comparatively happy homes which makes them exceptional among writers. Nikos Kazantzakis was chosen because of the many fields in which he excels and because he is the only one of the 317 born in Greece. Colette and all the others described were selected because of the voluminous amount of information provided by themselves and their biographers. We regret that space does not permit us to include sketches of such writers as Gerald Brenan, Andrei Codrescu, R. K. Narayan, Evelyn Waugh, and Emlyn Williams, each of whose autobiographies is provocative, informative, and well written. Once again perceptive readers will find illustrations of many specific findings in the following sketches.

The Early Life of the Writer: Jean-Paul Sartre as Example

There is no one among the Three Hundred who describes the early life of a writer as well as does Jean-Paul Sartre. *Les Mots* [*The Words*], his story of his first ten years of life, which he spent with his maternal grandparents, is a literary masterpiece, and is assumed to be the reason for his being awarded the Nobel Prize for literature. *The Words* describes circumstances common to the childhood homes of many of the Three Hundred, especially those that produced authors.

Awareness of Family Conflict. Like other writers-to-be, Sartre was acutely aware of the serious conflicts that created drama within his family. His grandfather, Charles Schweitzer, played the most important role in his intellectual and emotional development. The grandfather annoyed his own brothers at family gatherings by saying that his brother Augustus was the richest and his brother Louis (father of Albert Schweitzer) the most pious, but that he was the most intelligent. A writer and educator, owner of a fabulous library, founder of the Modern Language Institute of Paris, and a teacher of French to expatriate Germans, Schweitzer was an indulgent, playful man who tossed his grandson in his arms and let him nestle in his beard. When his two grown sons quarreled with him, he could shame them by playing happily with his grandson, the precocious half-orphan who was so loving and grateful. Sartre was his grandfather's lap-dog, his pet, the boy wonder to exhibit to his colleagues, the comfort of his old age, his insurance against death and senility. He did not plan for the boy's future, since he did not expect to live long enough to enjoy his fame or grieve for his failure. He loved him in the here and now.

Charles Schweitzer married when he was nearing middle age. Louise Guillemin Schweitzer, Sartre's grandmother, spent most of her days lying in a semidarkened room having headaches and regretting the loss of her virginity. To her husband's disgust, she read sensational stories and horror tales about a wife whose head was bashed on a headboard by a husband who was sex-crazed or about a bride found naked and gibbering on top of a tall chest in her bedroom the morning after her wedding day. Her own doctor had acquiesced when she asked him to inform her husband that the conjugal relationship made her ill and should be avoided, although Schweitzer had already managed, as Sartre says, to surprise her into bearing four children. She mistrusted her model grandson Jean-Paul, suspecting him of deviltry, calling his smiles smirks. When Sartre retaliated by being rude, he was hotly defended by his grandfather.

Sartre's mother, Anne-Marie, was married to an engineer and French naval officer who died shortly after Jean-Paul's birth. She returned to her parental home with a sickly infant who nearly had died while she nursed his father, but was received coolly; her mother said that her son-in-law had shirked his duty by dying when he was only thirty. Nevertheless, Sartre's grandmother was glad to turn over irksome household duties to her daughter.

Her parents refused to buy her new clothes or give her pocket money, and her father objected to her going out with her old friends, requiring her to be home by ten o'clock and waiting watch in hand to be sure she obeyed him. She soon resigned herself to being her son's big sister. There were three bedrooms—grandfather had one, grandmother had another, and "the children" were given the third. She often reminded him that they were not in their own home, that he must not be rude or noisy or do anything to make them more unwelcome than they were. The mother and son grew increasingly close as he grew older, and she told him her troubles. She also surreptitiously bought him comics and adventure stories and took him to the park and cinema or theater. Although Sartre's father's photograph hung above his mother's bed, she never told him anything about his father.

Sartre was an undersized, well-mannered boy with an adult vocabulary, but was considered so different that other children would not play with him although he would have gladly played a minor role in their games, such as playing dead or even playing the role of being tortured. His mother offered to ask other mothers to influence their sons to include him, but he forbade her to do so.

His mother's bachelor brother, Emil, who often was ordered

out of his father's house, was passionately devoted to Anne-Marie, although she disliked him; they frequently met in the park, where they discussed grandfather Schweitzer's faults. Emil died years later in a room cluttered with hundreds of old socks, shoes, and other drab reminders of a lonely life that had driven him mad. Her oldest brother, Georges, also quarreled with his father, but she seldom saw him, since he had his own wife and children. Grandfather Schweitzer did not especially care for his other grandchildren; he idolized only Jean-Paul.

The Schweitzers were not the only side of the family with conflicts. Dr. Sartre, Jean-Paul's other grandfather, on the day after their wedding, discovered that his wife's dowry could not be paid, that the father of the woman he thought was an heiress was in fact bankrupt. Although they went on to have four children, Dr. Sartre did not speak to his wife during their forty years of marriage.

Only-Child Fantasies. Children who are going to be writers are often only children and create fantasies to entertain themselves. Sartre learned to read when he was three by studying a storybook he had already memorized. At seven he was writing novels—long fantasies that combined his excellent knowledge of German and French classic literature with information gathered from comics and adventure stories that his mother bought him. His grandmother had predicted "brain fever" if he continued to read so many heavy adult books, and his mother had tried to save him from this supposed danger by surreptitiously buying him comics and exciting stories. The grandfather raged at his wife and daughter when he discovered the deception, but indulgently permitted the boy to continue reading the trash. In *Les Mots* (1964) Sartre writes, "Had he been my father, Charles Schweitzer would have burned the lot; being my grandfather, he chose regretful indulgence" (p. 76). Even today Sartre reads detective novels more readily than he does classical philosophers.

Dislike of School. Gifted children, especially those who become writers, dislike school and often manage to escape the conventional lockstep of education. When his grandfather sent Sartre to school, he had told the principal to expect a genius. However, the principal discovered that Sartre spelled poorly, and after a row

Sartre was withdrawn. He did not mind, since he liked being the lonely novelist much better. One summer his grandfather, who was a believer in democracy and public education, felt Sartre should, as a matter of principle, be sent to the village school, and once again he told the teacher to expect a genius. Since the grandfather was an author and a scholar from the city, the village teacher was impressed by his responsibility and always kept the boy within arm's reach, for which Sartre was grateful, since he was frightened by the other students.

On another occasion he was taken to a special school for gifted children. Here the mothers of all the boys would attend the classes, watching carefully to see what their sons did, then immediately take them home to prepare them for the next day's bitter competition. Since Jean-Paul excelled, he and his mother were given black looks by the other mothers, so she withdrew him after a tedious and unproductive semester. He had learned little and made no friends, although he felt that the other boys might have been friendly had they been permitted to play together. It was not until he was ten that he actually completed a year of school work and made friends.

The Poor Relation and the Father Who Does Not Provide. Being a poor relation and having a father who does not provide are seen as motivating factors in the homes of many literary personalities. Sartre says his fatherlessness was his good fortune; had his father lived, Jean-Paul probably would have gone to regular school much earlier than ten and would have been programmed to be an engineer like his father. He would not have had his long hours alone in his grandfather's library.

A psychiatrist once told Sartre that he had no superego. Had he had a father, Sartre believes, he would have developed one. Because he could not even love himself, he fled inward. If his father had left him property, his life would have been changed. No one told him "why the hell he had been born." He was no boy's master and no one belonged to him.

When his mother remarried when he was eleven, he still had no home of his own, although his engineer stepfather, a kindly man, dutifully accepted him. In *Les Mots*, Sartre says, "There is no good father, that's the rule. Don't lay the blame on men but on the bond of paternity, which is rotten. To beget children, nothing better; to *have* them, what iniquity. Had my father lived, he would have lain on me at full length and would have crushed me. As luck had it, he died young" (p. 19). Had his father lived, he would not have been free to make his own destiny or to change his mind freely about what he believed, or to do what he wanted to do. Because his father's death sent his mother back to her dominating parents and gave him his freedom, he was never to have the same reaction to life, he felt, as did those who had a father.

Writers who come from emotionally turbulent homes use their early experiences, often in a slightly disguised fashion, in their writing and because of these same childhood experiences also find interpersonal relationships difficult as adults. Sartre says emphatically that being an only child was essential to his becoming a writer. His brother-sister relationship to his mother predisposed him to have fantasies about a nonexistent little sister. At nine or ten he read a children's story about a little American boy and his sister, Biddy, whom he loved very much. Sartre longed all his life for a little sister just like Biddy and had fantasies about such a sister. He used the fantasy in three of his writings—in *The Flies, The Paths of Freedom,* and *Altona.* Later he wrote that it was the only family relationship that still moved him: "I have committed the grave mistake of often seeking in women the sister who never was: my suit was rejected and I had to pay the costs" (p. 55).

Sartre has not written about his personal life as an adult. His mother, after her second husband's death, came to live with him. Simone de Beauvoir still lives in a hotel nearby.

In 1955 he received a letter from an Algerian student, Arlette El-Kaim, who told him that she had been criticized for writing an essay praising his ideas. He met her and she became his secretary. In 1965 Sartre made her his adopted daughter. She helped him in his campaign against the Vietnam War and edited the summary of the conclusions reached by the Bertrand Russell Tribunal, of which Sartre was a member. Perhaps he has finally found a little sister.

Biographer Philip Thody, in *Sartre: A Biographical Introduction* (1971), says that a strong theme running through Sartre's work is that man's most fundamental need is to make sense of his own experience. Sartre himself says that he is precisely the same person at sixty that he was at five. As a very young child he was condemned to please, was afraid to cry, dared not laugh aloud or make a loud noise. He was a waif, a stray, a clown, a buffoon, a pampered poodle. He had no reason to be, no purpose.

He was used by his elders for their purposes. He enhanced his grandfather's egotism and vanity, gave his grandmother an excuse to be sulky, and gave his mother an excuse to be masochistic, to be proud of her humility and sacrifices. He was a badly spoiled child who had only the benevolent against whom to revolt. "A spoiled child isn't sad," Sartre says, "he's bored, like a king. Like a dog" (p. 93).

At five he went with his grandfather to the barbershop to have his curls cut off. He had been told he was beautiful and precious. He came home an ugly toad. His mother cried and locked herself in her room. The steel entered his nonexistent soul and gave him armor forever against disapproval and disappointment. By seven he had learned that nobody needed him but that he must learn to live for himself, to see that his own needs were met. At ten he was cynical and detached. Nothing could harm him anymore. Any failure could be put to use as an experiment in living. At ten he had faith in his ultimate survival. He learned to live a day at a time, or even a minute at a time. But he still suffered from boredom.

He grew into a cynical, detached adult who often found that he got what he had wished for at a time when he wanted something else much more. He concluded that man's destiny was absurd, that man alone could will nothing, that each individual existed only to confront others. He decided for himself what was right or wrong according to how well the resultant action would profit him. There was no other criterion. He saw himself as a whole man composed of all men, as good as all of them and no better than any. He reserved his right, as a man without a superego, to change his mind at will according to his feelings at the moment of decision.

He made a firm commitment, during the time of the Algerian war, to the positive use of violence. In his introduction to *The Wretched of the Earth* (1963) by Frantz Fanon, he speaks of the irrepressible violence going on in Algiers as "neither sound and fury

nor the resurrection of savage instinct nor even the effect of resentment: it is man recreating himself" (Fanon, p. 21). He continues,
"to shoot down a European is to kill two birds with one stone, to
destroy an oppressor and the man he oppresses at the same time:
there remains a dead man and a free man; the survivor" (p. 22).

The Dislike of School

Two other boys who had an intense dislike for school are
Hermann Hesse and Yevgeny Yevtushenko.

Hermann Hesse. Born in 1877 at Calw in the Black Forest
in Germany, Hermann Hesse disliked school intensely, much to the
dismay of his parents, who were ambitious for their only son. His
father, Johannes Hesse, was a missionary who was promoted to the
more prestigious task of publishing religious tracts and books for the
pietist sect to which he belonged. His wife, Marie Gundert Hesse,
also came from a missionary family.

When Hermann was six, according to his biographer,
B. Zeller, in *Portrait of Hesse* (1971), his mother wrote: "Humiliating though it would be, I am seriously thinking of putting
him in a corrective establishment, or in some other house. We are
too nervous, too weak, for him; our domestic life is not sufficiently
disciplined and orderly. All agree that he is gifted; he gazes at the
moon and the clouds, improvises at long stretches on the har-
monium, can draw very well with pencil or quill, sings well when he
wishes, and is never at a loss for a poem" (pp. 16–17).

At day school he met only one teacher he could love, and he
hated, derided, and feared the others. He was sent from one private
school to another. At fifteen he was given into the care of a friend
of the family, a faith healer, who attempted to exorcise the devil
in him. Hermann's response was to attempt suicide, and so his
frightened parents found a job for him doing gardening and caring
for retarded children. This work therapy was successful and he
began reading again—Cervantes, Dickens, Goethe, Ibsen, Sterne,
Zola, and his favorite, Korolenko. He went to work for a bookseller
and began to apply himself rigorously to his own education.

In 1899 his first publication appeared, a thin book of poems,
but it was not until 1927 that *Steppenwolf,* his first well-known
work, appeared. *Steppenwolf* expressed his negative views toward

wealth, technology, war, and nationalism and his belief in a time-less, indestructible world where some men and women, living close to nature and following the law of their conscience, preserved a faith in the essential goodness of humankind.

Yevgeny Yevtushenko. Another literary figure who had an intense dislike of school was Yevgeny Yevtushenko, who was born in 1933 in Zima Junction, near Lake Baikal in Siberia, where his grandparents lived. His greatgrandfather had been deported to Siberia long before the Russian Revolution for burning down his landlord's house. His children and grandchildren were revolu-tionaries. "Revolution was the religion of our family," Yevgeny writes, in *A Precocious Autobiography* (1963, p. 15).

His father taught him to read and write by the age of six, and by age eight he was devouring Dumas, Flaubert, Schiller, Balzac, Shakespeare, Jack London, Cervantes, Dante, Maupassant, Tolstoy, and Boccaccio, all of whom "made an indescribable salad in my head" (p. 20). During the war when the Germans were threatening Moscow, like many other Moscow children he was evacuated. He went back to his birthplace, Zima Junction, where he had two kindly uncles, both ordinary working men. It was here that he had his first direct experience with deprivation, which was compensated for by the kindliness of simple people and the pleasure of hearing folk tales and learning folk lore. One experience he never forgot came when he watched German prisoners being marched through the streets. Like other Russian children he had regarded the Germans as simply being mad beasts. The women onlookers shouted epithets at the German officers, who held their heads high and looked proud, and he had no pity for them. But when the common soldiers straggled by, the women stopped shouting. He wrote, "They saw the simple German soliders, thin, unshaven, covered with dirty bloodstained bandages, hobbling on crutches or leaning on the shoulders of their comrades. And the soldiers walked with their heads down. The street became dead silent" (p. 27).

When he returned to Moscow after the war, his parents were separated and his father had remarried. He could not cope with school and instead of studying wrote poems, which his mother destroyed. He was bored and inattentive, failed his school work, was regarded as a hoodlum, and was sent to a school for incor-rigible children. Expelled from that school, he was reluctantly accepted by his father as a laborer on a geological expedition, on condition he use an assumed name, since his father did not want to be humiliated by his behavior. He learned to work hard under primitive conditions, to eat any food, and to live with lice. Once again he was moved by the compassion of simple people, as fellow workers helped him with his blisters or carried his knapsack.

In 1956 his poem "Zima Junction" was published, which suddenly made him an important poet. Although the bureaucracy was critical of it, readers were enthusiastic and sent thousands of congratulatory messages. In the poem he praised the values of the simple men and women of the Soviet Union, the kind who lived in Zima Junction. He deplored the debasement of those ideals under Stalin.

The Youngest Child in a Socially Isolated Home: Colette

Colette is one of the five persons in our survey with the greatest amount of biographical material published about them. (Robert Kennedy, Lyndon Johnson, Anaïs Nin, and Simone de Beauvoir are the other four.) She once said that her family was very odd and that she had never met any other like it. She herself was the youngest child, was lonely, disliked school, and was sexually divergent. Indeed, she fits into today's scene better than she fit into the times in which she lived.

Born Sidonie Gabrielle Colette in the French village of Saint-Sauveur en Puisaye in 1873, she called herself simply Colette when she became an established author. She frequently remarked that there was no need for anyone to write a biography about her since she had already told everything there was to know. At various times in her life she returned by way of autobiographical writings to the idyllic walled garden of her childhood and wrote nostalgic descriptions of her mother's garden and her father's library.*

* In her old age, her third husband says that she used to crumble and eat dried flowers with the same kind of nostalgia. By these tactics the little French quail diverted attention from her nest, but one biographer, Margaret Crosland, went to her village, interviewed peasants with long memories of its most distinguished citizen's family, and examined old records. The story Margaret Crosland tells is much more plausible and interesting than are Colette's selective memories.

Colette's mother, Adèle-Eugénie-Sidonie Landoy, whom Colette calls "Sido" in her writings, was born in Paris in 1835. Sido was orphaned, and her brothers, who were journalists in Brussels, took her to live with them. The brothers led a bohemian life-style and had friends among the writers, actors, and artists of Brussels. Sido was not an attractive girl, and inherited her father's thick lips, but at eighteen she married, for wealth rather than love, a young man with a country estate in Saint-Sauveur. However, she disliked the country, the big house with its heavy furniture, the long dark halls, the chilly bedrooms, the husband who owned them. When he died, Sido, not yet thirty, was left with a homely small daughter, Juliette, and a handsome young son, Achille. She was also left her husband's estate.

According to French law, a widow could not marry until the evening of the day when the husband had been dead for nine months. At 8:30 on that evening Sido married Jules-Joseph Colette, who had come to the area a few years earlier as a tax collector. He was a one-legged man who had once been the captain of a Zouave regiment, a dashing, romantic figure who was nonetheless always defeated when he ran for local and district offices because he was a conservative in a liberal district. He collected rows of blank bound volumes, each dedicated to his wife, in which he planned to write books but never did. He wasted his wife's inheritance franc by franc.

His two stepchildren and her son, Leopold, born months after Sido's first husband's death, were sent away to boarding schools. Colette stayed home and went to the village schools, where she was rude to the teachers and made no friends. She read Balzac at age seven, and Zola at eight. Her father tried to censor her reading, but her mother did not, and Colette always managed to read what her father proscribed. For some reason, no biographer, including Margaret Crosland, who wrote *Colette: The Difficulty of Loving* (1973), comments on the strangeness of the mother's notions of what her eight-year-old daughter might enjoy reading. The Comte de Saint-Simon was an advocate of socialism and free love whose later followers became more involved in promoting the latter than the former. In her nostalgic *Earthly Paradise* (1966), Colette says, "The eighteen volumes of Saint-Simon were always at my mother's bedside at night. She found recurring pleasure in them and was surprised that when I was eight I could not share them all" (p. 15). The mother wondered when the child would be old enough to read some really interesting books. Was Colette trying to imply that her mother was reading the works of a Catholic saint or was Colette mocking the reader, giving a sly hint about her mother's true feelings about sexual freedom?

Paul Gauguin would have responded instantly to Colette's jibe, for his maternal grandmother, Flora Tristan Chazal, like Sido's mother, admired Saint-Simon. "For twenty years, Paul's grandfather grieved because his lovely young wife had left him to go about Europe preaching the doctrines of the Comte de Saint-Simon: socialism, sex equality, and free love of a noble sort. He obtained custody of his son through the courts. . . . [The court awarded the mother custody of the daughter who became Paul's mother, but her father had already kidnapped her.] When Chazal shot her, she was seriously injured and never fully recovered" (Goertzel and Goertzel, 1962, pp. 48–49). Chazal was sentenced to twenty-five years in prison. Almost every French citizen had a strong positive or strong negative reaction to the severity of his sentence. Sido must have been among them and opted for the wife.

There are other hints in Colette's sentimental writing about her parents which indicate her mother was not the otherworldly saint in the walled garden. Sido objected to Colette's second marriage, not because she minded the divorce, but because she did not approve of the institution of marriage. Why should any woman marry, she asked, unless she had to?

When her father had completely exhausted her mother's inheritance, Colette, who was now eighteen, and her parents and probably Leopold had to leave the estate and go to live with Sido's oldest son, Achille, who was a country doctor. Fortunately, the oldest daughter, the homely Juliette, had finally been married off when she was twenty-five. All Colette could find to do at her brother's home was read and help with the housework. However, her father did introduce her to a visiting Parisian, the dashing, ebullient Henri Gauthier-Villars, who was attracted to her. He was thirty-two and she was twenty. Colette married him to spare her brother the necessity of supporting her and to escape her home and to go to Paris.

Henri was the son of a well-to-do publisher and himself wrote and published under the pseudonym Willy, although he made himself seem more prolific than he actually was by devising plots for risqué novels and having them ghostwritten by lesser known writers. He added his bored and unhappy wife, who had not taken well to marriage, to his pool of ghost writers when he suggested she write a story about a schoolgirl facing growing up in a wicked world she did not quite understand. When he read her notebook, he realized that she had real talent and that her book would sell. *Claudine à l'Ecole,* published as a new novel by "Willy," quickly sold at least 50,000 copies. However, Colette was unimpressed, since she had not wanted to be a writer and did not want to write another book. Because they needed the money, her exasperated husband commanded her to write and locked her in her bedroom for three or four hours at a time.

Finally, after thirteen or fourteen years of quarreling, she left Willy. As a wife who left her husband, she had no right to share his income, though it came largely from her efforts. For a while she tried making a living as a mime, but after growing tired of being poor she started writing again. She was prolific and popular during most of her eighty-one years. H. Peyre, in *French Novelists of Today* (1967), says that Colette is much overrated, but that she "possessed the classical art of omission." He says of her: "She could chisel swift, sensuous sentences admirably, convey the color of an adolescent girl's eyes or the earthy fragrance of rain-soaked gardens, the lusciousness of pears or peaches melting in the mouth" (p. 276).

Peyre also notes Colette's dislike of men. Most of her male characters were aging roués, and her only tenderness was for brainless young gigolos.

She was not happy with her first or second husband. The only friends of Willy that she liked were homosexual males who had no designs on her or him. Although they had a daughter when she was forty, Henri, her second husband, said he divorced her because he was weary of her tales of adultery and incest. Her third husband was a man much younger than Colette; she always called him "my dear friend." He admired her talent, was faithful and tender to her when she was an old woman almost immobilized by arthritis, and wrote two biographies about her.

Women in Colette's novels, however, are wise, tender, amusing, clever, foolish, and very real. She writes of the lesbian experience with the delicacy of an artist who portrays in pastels the romance of two fragrant rosebuds moved to ecstasy by the warmth of a gentle west wind. In *The Pure and the Impure* she speaks of her "hermaphroditism" as a positive quality in a writer. It added a sensuous quality and made her more responsive to her environment. R. D. Cottrell says, in his comments in *Colette* (1974) that she "moved briefly and temporarily in lesbian circles is . . . indisputable" (p. 40). During the interval between her marriages to Willy and to her second husband, she and a woman friend turned a vaudeville audience into a rioting mob. She and her friend, Madame de Morny, the former Marquise de Belboeuf, who had also left her husband, were miming a drama, *Rêve d'Egypte*. The ex-husband was fuming in the audience because his coat of arms was printed on the program. When "Missy," as Madame de Morny was called by her friends, dressed as a male but obviously feminine, gave Colette a long and passionate kiss as part of the performance, the audience rioted, threw objects at the performers and beat each other with umbrellas.

Colette continued to have problems with her mother. Once when her brother Leopold (who was her mother's favorite but never hers) stayed with Colette, Sido wrote her to make certain that Leo—even though he was forty-four years old—practiced at the piano daily. Henri de Jouvenal, Colette's second husband, of whom her mother approved, asked Sido to visit, but she replied she could not come to Paris because a cactus she cherished might blossom while she was gone. Neither Colette nor her mother showed affection for young children. It seems possible that much of Colette's euphoric writing about her mother is a childish plea for the love and close companionship she never had from her. When Colette was a child, Sido told her she looked like a boy even when she was sewing. Sido's rejection of her daughter's boyish appearance and Colette's closeness to her father may be causally related to her bisexuality.

E. E. Cummings

The poet Edward Estlin Cummings (who signed himself e. e. cummings) is one of only a dozen or so among the Three Hundred who came from homes they describe as being ideal and in which family relationships were exceptionally close. In these respects he is unlike most of the literary figures. However, in two other respects he resembles them. First, his parents were humanitarian and idealistic, as are the parents of so many of the literary, which means that when their children first find themselves under the control of people who are unjust or cruel, they are overwhelmed by frustration. Estlin might not have survived his first such experience—imprisonment at age twenty-three in France—had not his father persisted in finding where he was and seeing that he was freed. Second, Estlin illustrates the observation that happily married parents are no more likely than are parents who are divorced to produce happily married sons and daughters.

E. E. Cummings was born in 1894 in Cambridge, Massachusetts, the first of two children. His father was a Unitarian minister and his mother, Rebecca Haswell Clarke, was descended from Unitarian ancestors. The father and mother were devoted to each other. In one poem about her, he wrote that if there are any heavens, his mother will have one all to herself, a heaven of "Blackred" roses, and that her husband will be standing near, then he will bow and the whole garden will bow. Estlin was also devoted to her. He once said, "Never have I encountered anyone so joyous, anyone healthier in body and mind, anyone so quite incapable of remembering a wrong, or anyone so completely and unaffectedly generous" (Norman, 1972, p. 17).

The Cummings lived in a three-story, rambling colonial house, and Estlin had his own tree house with a real glass window and a small stove. The Cummings house was a neighborhood center where Estlin and his sister, Elizabeth, six years younger than he, had a swing, sandpile, and playground equipment. The Cummings raised children, not lawns, and Reverend Edward Cummings never minded the noises the children made if they were happy noises. He was six foot two, a handsome man, a *summa cum laude* Harvard graduate, a first-rate sailor, a woodsman, an amateur carpenter and architect, and a preacher who told his congregation that the Kingdom of Heaven was no spiritual roof garden but something inside them.

Rebecca's brother, George Clarke, a bachelor lawyer with a gift for joyous living, lived with the Cummings and was Estlin's favorite adult after his father and mother. There was an aunt, Jane Cummings, and a courtesy aunt who was a friend of Rebecca's. The aunts had a jolly way of reminding Estlin to keep his knickerbockers buckled. Instead of nagging him about a knickerbocker leg dangling about an ankle, each took an option on one of his legs for her own and would shout to the owner, "There goes your leg" (p. 22).

During the evenings by the fireside the children read and were read to, always from the classics such as *Robinson Crusoe, Pickwick Papers,* and *Lorna Doone* (Estlin's feminine ideal). His grandmother and aunts gathered about to play the piano and sing, his mother copied her favorite poems in her scrapbook, his father painted. This idyll continued through Estlin's school years, which were pleasant and productive and in which he was fortunate to have teachers who were in love with their subjects. At Harvard he met men who were to be life-long friends, such as John Dos Passos. He was an editor of the *Monthly,* was graduated in 1915 *magna cum laude,* and delivered the commencement address. He received his M.A. from Harvard Graduate School of Arts and Sciences a year later.

It was not until 1917, when he joined the American-sponsored volunteer Norton-Harjes Ambulance Corps and sailed for France, that his world went sour and his parents suffered their first intense anguish about a son who had never given them any trouble. His motivations for becoming a volunteer were mixed. It was obvious to him that the United States would soon go to war, and he preferred to be a volunteer working as a civilian to being drafted. Also he wanted to be where the action was and to be useful to the injured and the dying. He regretted the war, was dubious about the horror tales told about the Germans, and thought

Tolstoy might possibly be right about the immorality of all wars. Being an ambulance driver appealed to his love for adventure.

He became close to another volunteer, a twenty-year-old student from Columbia University, Walter Slater Brown, who was to be a life-long friend. No sooner were they in France than they began to express their disillusionment in letters home. Brown was especially critical, and in one letter told how French troops made poison-gas attacks on the Germans, then knifed the living survivors. He reported that someone told him about a priest, no less, who had boasted of joining the troops and of having finished off eighteen Germans, proving it by pulling eighteen ears out of his pocket. Estlin's letters were not as incriminating as Brown's, but they were not exactly tactful, considering that he knew his letters would be read by French censors. Estlin complained of the lack of organization, red tape, delays, and mismanagement, how the corps were idle for weeks even when urgently needed, how there were more drivers than ambulances. Predictably, Brown and Estlin were arrested, convicted of being dangerous to French security, and told they could not go home until the war was over. Sent to an internment camp, Estlin first wrote cheerful letters, stating that he was still learning, having an educational experience, and would be free soon. But after a few weeks of confinement, filth, and inadequate diet, he changed the tone of his communications, and then there were no more letters.

Dr. Cummings tried frantically to free his son. The recruiter for the volunteer ambulance corps was indifferent, at one point not even informing him for six weeks that it was a different Cummings who had drowned when a ship was torpedoed. Estlin's father wrote a long, pleading letter to President Wilson, but it had no effect. The American embassy in France was equally ineffective. Finally, Secretary of State Lansing persuaded the French to release Estlin, and Senator Henry Cabot Lodge later did the same for Brown. Estlin had a skin rash and was emaciated; Brown had scurvy.

Dr. Cummings was furious for years over these indignities to his son and suggested his son write up his story. In 1920 he did so, in poetic prose, in *The Enormous Room*. His father wrote the foreword, describing his son's physical condition when he was released. Dr. Cummings was always certain of his son's importance as a writer and said he would be remembered not for his own work but for being the father of e. e. cummings.

Cummings used his revulsion against war as the basis for what is probably his best literary work. When the parental home, like that of E. E. Cummings, is ideal or altruistic, the writer is more likely to write about impersonal matters, about characters who are influenced by social forces.

Stuart Cloete

In his amusing autobiography, *A Victorian Son* (1973), novelist Stuart Cloete tells how his mother tried to turn him into a homosexual when she found that her last child was a son, not the girl she had wanted. Born in Paris in 1897, Stuart was the fifth of five sons. His mother was thirty-seven when he was born, his father forty-seven, and his next oldest brother was already twelve.

His mother did not expect to have another child. She dressed him up in girl's clothes and tried to forget that he was a boy. However, since he had older brothers he was aware of his masculinity, and resented her trying to turn him into a little girl. One time, for instance, when he was dressed in an imported English frock and lace-trimmed drawers, they stopped to see a dairy farm, and Stuart deliberately rolled in a mound of fresh cow dung. As he grew into manhood, his mother embarrassed him by treating him in public as if he were her young lover. As a child, Stuart loved and admired his handsome and aggressive father, but lost respect for him as he grew older. His father was a flamboyant business promoter, who was often away from home working on deals that frequently fell through; he also handled his rich wife's dowry unsuccessfully. As a result, his father and mother quarreled bitterly about money, and Stuart was always insecure about being suddenly poverty stricken.

At boarding school in England he was bullied, starved, incarcerated, and taught nothing by poorly trained teachers. Other boys called Stuart "Froggy" because he was born in France. He hated Sandhurst also. Seduced by a maid when he was scarcely pubescent, he came to believe, after being wounded in World War I, that the only things worthwhile in life were making love and making war. He liked risking his life and stated, "I have always done what I have been afraid of doing" (p. 302). The war left him with weak lungs, however, and he turned to writing tales of man's need to assert his virility through courage and violence.

Although he had an exceptionally happy marriage, it seems that he spent much of his life trying to prove to his mother that he was her little *boy* and not her little *girl*.

Ring Lardner, Jr.

Author of *The Lardners: My Family Remembered* (1976), Ring Lardner, Jr., was one of the Hollywood Ten blacklisted for Communist association during the 1950s. Himself a writer, he tried all his life to avoid taking on any literary enterprise that would invite comparison with his famous humorist-writer father or to give any publisher the appearance of trading on his father's reputation. He was repeatedly mistaken for his father by casual acquaintances who assumed that he was the author of the *New Yorker* short stories they had read in their high school anthologies. He felt comfortable writing a novel but avoided writing short stories. It was not until his old age, after having weighed the advantages and disadvantages of bearing his father's name, that he declared for a balance on the plus side.

During his youth he and his three brothers were supervised by a neurotic and dominating nurse who required them to have a bowel movement each day at a certain hour and inspected their feces to determine what they should eat during the day. When they did not eat all the food on their plates, she threw tantrums and beat her head on the floor. She fed them so strictly on her version of healthy food that later, when he was briefly incarcerated during the McCarthy era for refusing to be an informant, he found prison fare quite palatable. Her neuroticism was exacerbated by her unrequited love for the boys' father.

The mildly alcoholic father, Ring Lardner, and gregarious mother, Ellis, who acted as his literary agent, were unaware of their sons' trials during their long absences. They had the money and the leisure to enjoy life in the company of the F. Scott Fitzgeralds, Ernest Hemingways, and the like. Ring Lardner, Sr., died at age forty-eight, but his death did not change their life-style. One son was later killed in Spain while fighting with the Abraham Lincoln Brigade. Columnist Heywood Broun could not remember that the father ever said a word about politics, economics, or world affairs, but, as Ring, Jr., quotes Broun, "Under an insulation of isolation and indifference Ring boiled with a passion against smugness and hypocrisy and the hard heart of the world" (p. 280). The remaining sons became writers, although none with the reputation of their father.

Cissy Patterson

Newspaper publisher Eleanor Medill (Cissy) Patterson was born in Chicago in 1881. Her mother was Eleanor Medill, daughter of Joseph Medill, owner and publisher of the *Chicago Daily Tribune,* and she married *Tribune* employee Joseph Patterson, who later became editor. Cissy's mother was a greedy, ill-mannered, loud-voiced woman who drove her competent, easy-going husband to drink. Cissy disliked her mother, and soon found out that the easiest way to annoy her was to "make up" to her father. Still, she was a poor little rich girl, neglected by both parents, and was brought up by the servants. She read risqué books given her by her mother's sister, with whom her mother had a life-long feud. Cissy grew up envious of and competitive with her brother, Joseph, and her cousin, Robert Rutherford McCormick. She tried to climb a church tower in her neighborhood but was dragged down by an irate janitor. Sent to a girls' finishing school in Connecticut, she fell ill of tachycardia and had fainting spells. She quickly recovered in a sanitorium in Tennessee, but refused to leave, and stayed on until it was too late to go back to school.

Suddenly she was a beautiful young woman, ready and eager to be a debutante. She made a disastrous marriage to Count Joseph Gizycka, who insulted her on her wedding day; the custody suit later and her kidnapping of her daughter was a front-page scandal. Her second husband, Cal Carrington, was a real cowboy on a working ranch; she also had many lovers because she equated monogamy with monotony. She made dramatic exits and entrances and wore strange costumes, but friends called her a shy person in fancy dress. As publisher she ran a great empire in a ruthless fashion, destroying friendships, then grieving that she had done so. When her former employee Drew Pearson divorced her daughter, the neurotic Countess Gizycka, she was friendly with him. But when he disagreed with her and said so in print, she became a bitter enemy.

Illness and Creativity: Jessamyn West

Born in 1907 in the hardscrabble, rocky hills of Jennings County, Indiana, novelist Jessamyn West was the first of the two girls and two boys born to Eldo and Grace Milhous West. Her father, a handsome schoolteacher, decided to move to Whittier, California, to join relatives in a group starting a Quaker Church community there. The Wests took along only one piece of furniture: a bookcase that had come down in the family.

Jessamyn's father had a fondness for words, especially for dictionaries and encyclopedias, and her mother also played with words, often coining new ones. Her father was inclined to be shy and melancholic. Her mother was an untidy, overweight, merry woman, a superlative cook, who took in the aged and ill. She was a permissive mother who trusted her children to look after themselves even on long hikes through rattlesnake country. Although beds often went unmade and the house was cluttered, the family members were comfortable with each other. However, Jessamyn sometimes felt that children with parents who were so much in love with each other were practically half-orphans, and she was ashamed of her mother's appearance. For years she felt sorry her mother was not more like her grandmother, who kept a tidy house and was properly interested in the social issues of the day. When Jessamyn cleaned the house, as she often did, she took all the furniture out of each room, which irked her parents, although they let her do as she pleased. Once her father teased her as she was lowering a desk out of an upper story window by yelling, "Drop it!" She did.

Both parents liked the outdoors and spent many nights away from home, camping out under the redwood trees in their own homemade version of a recreational vehicle. Mrs. West also abhorred large social gatherings. The parents went camping instead of attending Jessamyn's college graduation exercises, which hurt her feelings.

It was not until Jessamyn was married, living away from home with her husband, and had almost completed her doctoral degree in English that the family had its first experience with near tragedy. The doctors at the college infirmary had been indifferent to Jessamyn's complaining of excessive fatigue, but when she visited her parents, her mother took her at once to the family doctor. Within three days she was in the terminal ward of a tuberculosis sanitarium. Her husband had to return to his teaching job and left her in her mother's care, but visited her whenever he could.

Every other day for two years Jessamyn's mother, who was determined her daughter would live, made an eighty-mile round trip to see her in the terminal ward, bringing the vitality of the outside world with her. One day, for instance, she brought zinnias, roses, a frosted root beer, a box of chocolate peppermints, a box of Cracker Jack, a pencil sharpener, ten new books, two blotters, purple grapes, and a hyacinth bed jacket. At the end of the second year the doctors told Mrs. West to take Jessamyn home and let her die among her loved ones. Brisk and matter of fact, she told her daughter that if she really believed Jessamyn was going to die, she would put the electric heater in the bath water and encourage her to hasten her death.

When Jessamyn was too ill and discouraged to read, listen to the radio, or play with her kitten, her mother, who had almost total recall for her childhood, talked to her hours on end about Jessamyn's great-grandparents, about Jennings County, about the peculiar dialect of the Hoosiers, about her own life as Grace Milhous back on the farm in Indiana. In the pre–Civil War days, Quaker solidarity had been destroyed by differences over the abolition movement. George Fox and William Penn had repudiated the hireling ministry, instead instituting silent meetings; they were also pacifist, civil libertarian, and against ideas of racial superiority. However, the members of the Midwest meeting that Jessamyn's great-grandparents had attended questioned the abolition movement, believing slaves were possessions and that it was not right to rob slaveowners. They wanted to be more like other Protestants and have a minister, singing, and ritual. The Quakers thus divided into two major groups, the silent-meeting Friends and the Quaker Church group. Jessamyn West and her cousin, Richard Nixon, were among those whose ancestors belonged to the latter and left the Midwest to start a community in California in what is now Whittier. (Richard Nixon's father was Jessamyn's favorite First Day School teacher.) "The Meeting Grace [her mother] attended was silent," Jessamyn wrote, in *The Woman Said Yes* (1976), "unlike the California Meeting I knew, which was brisk and noisy, with a hired preacher whose sermons were as pulpit-thumping as anything a Baptist or Methodist could deliver" (p. 55). One result of the evangelical enthusiasm was the fading away of the historical testimonies on peace and racial equality, themes Jessamyn used in her first book, *Friendly Persuasion.*

For months on end Jessamyn lived in the world of her great-grandparents, the Milhous family of Indiana. She learned the Hoosier dialect from her word-loving mother, to say "work-brickle" instead of "industrious," and "feeling dauncey" instead of "feeling not up to par." She became so well acquainted with her great-grandfather's house that she could have found her way about it in the dark. When at last she was able to hold a clipboard and pencil she began to write short stories about the world of her great-grandparents. Her husband persuaded her to submit them for publication, and they were accepted. The short stories became the nucleus of *Friendly Persuasion,* which was so successful that Hollywood bought the movie rights.

Her publisher asked her to come to New York. Although she was then well enough to live with her husband, Jessamyn was fearful; she would miss her rest periods, she felt, and might become ill again. But her mother scolded her: " 'You are already dead,' Grace told me, 'living as you do. Afraid to take a deep breath, or laugh till you cry, or cry till you run out of tears.' . . . 'I think you are starting another kind of sickness if you don't go to New York for two months. . . . worse than the other. . . . in the mind, not the body' " (p. 76).

Jessamyn went to New York, and enjoyed it. She met other

writers and began to feel like a writer herself. She did not get sick. When she saw her mother on the way home, she was her old non-coddling self: "Well," she said bruskly, "I see that you are still alive" (p. 77).

Conclusion

Among the Three Hundred 26 percent of the subjects were sickly children. A fourth of the Four Hundred also had health problems. In many homes a devastating illness or injury gave the young man or woman the necessary period of aloneness during which to use latent literary talent. Although there are fewer stories like that of Jessamyn West among the Three Hundred than there were among the Four Hundred, evidence of medical progress in conquering tuberculosis and other diseases, and although a great many of the sickly children among the Three Hundred were not seriously ill, still their parents used their frequent colds or their fragility to keep them at home, where they could teach them themselves. A great many of the sickly children became healthy, indefatigable adults.

Members of the Three Hundred have strong physical drive as well as talent and intellectual drive. They do not necessarily limit themselves to working in one major area. Some subjects, for example, who are classified as literary have made other significant contributions. Having one goal and only one goal is not a prerequisite for eminence. Fifty-eight of the Three Hundred accomplished high achievements in more than one field of eminence. One of these, Jean Cocteau, has already been described; Paul Robeson is another. Two others are Nikos Kazantzakis and André Malraux.

There is a similarity in the latter two's work lives, though not in their personal lives. Kazantzakis, born in 1885 in Crete, was a novelist, poet, dramatist, philosopher, travel writer, and lecturer who received the Nobel Prize for literature. He was also minister of public welfare during a crucial period in modern Greece, when he was responsible for the care of 150,000 Greek refugees. In addition, he served as director of UNESCO's Department of Translations of the Classics. He wrote over thirty books. One of his poems, *The Odysseus,* has 333,333 lines. When John Lehmann published the translation of his novel, *Zorba the Greek,* it was called one of the truly great novels of this century. He traveled to many countries lecturing in the interests of world peace and international cooperation. Both France and England asked him to study the cultural status of their countries.

His father was an irritable and sometimes savage man, a wealthy landowner, merchant, and army officer, who wanted more from his firstborn and only son than the boy could accomplish. In his early years, he disappointed his father because he hated school, although he was thrashed unmercifully by sadistic teachers. He thought of his college days at the University of Athens as a waste of time. Fortunately, he had a wise and good maternal grandfather after whom he modeled his life. His mother was also a sweet though timid woman, and he had two younger sisters whom he loved dearly. After receiving a law degree he studied art and literature for four years.

Whereas Nikos Kazantzakis was hopeful for the human race, André Malraux found humankind an absurdity. His *Man's Fate,* like *Zorba the Greek,* was widely translated and called a germinal book. André's father was a promoter of "ephemeral companies," as his son characterized them, one who lived by his wits but whose wits often failed him. [The paternal grandfather was an impulsive man. When he saw a boy mishandling an ax, he took it from him to demonstrate how it should be used, split his own skull and died.] Malraux's mother left his father and went into a grocery business with her mother. André was a constant reader, and at seventeen he quit school forever and began buying and selling rare books to earn a living. He had, however, inherited a streak of paternal impulsiveness and while on his honeymoon he and a friend tried to smuggle out quantities of archeological art objects from Angkor Wat to sell in France. They were apprehended, and their case became a national scandal in France, albeit a somewhat romantic and amusing one to everyone but themselves. The intelligentsia of France pled for clemency, and the two were sentenced to a year in prison and given probation. An enterprising publisher gave Malraux a generous advance to write a book he was certain would sell well because of the publicity, and he was proved right. André's career was accelerated, and he soon became a well-known author. Later he served in the de Gaulle government as minister of culture and was responsible for the safety of the Mona Lisa when it was on loan in the United States.

The literary personalities were often lonely, unhappy, and difficult, both as children and as adults. As children they reacted sensitively to sounds, smells, colors, tastes, and the feel of things. Indeed, as small children most were intensely responsive to the emotional climate in their homes and were often acute observers of the family dramas being played out before their eyes.

As mentioned, they were often physically ill or handicapped. They also were homely, and their photographs as children and as adults are less attractive than those of politicians, athletes, and performers.

Daydreams were especially important to embryonic writers, and the girls particularly created for themselves elaborate fantasy worlds peopled by characters quite real to them. All were early, constant readers of the classics, hungry devourers of the printed page and had less need of constant companionship with peers than did other children. They were often endured rather than enjoyed and were seldom thought of as boys or girls who would be the well-known person in the family. Sometimes they seemed to act deliberately in ways that encouraged others to ignore or dislike them. Many were rejected by parents, siblings, teachers and playmates. They were peaceable children unless pushed too far into doing things such as studying arithmetic or playing competitive games that kept them from reading and writing. They were happiest when there was a good family library, when their reading was uncensored and when there was someone who would read what they wrote and took their work seriously or who would talk with them about books and ideas. As adults they did not necessarily feel they had to be close to other writers, but there were times when they needed and sought a congenial group of friends whose conversation they enjoyed. They were impatient with organizations, were seldom political activists, and were often unhappy in their personal relationships.

ꙮ 10 ꙮ

Artistic Personalities

Art is man's expression of joy in labor.
                                        William Morris

The seventy-five persons in the artistic category include painters, sculptors, actors and actresses, dancers, musical composers and performers, and film directors. Many of the subjects had achievements in more than one of these fields. Among the artistic personalities already described in some detail are Beniamino Bufano, Jean Cocteau, Helen Hayes, Janis Joplin, Oskar Kokoschka, Käthe Kollwitz, and Henry Moore.

Statistically Significant Differences

1. A larger proportion of the artistic personalities (71 percent) have supportive brothers and sisters than do others in the survey population (53 percent).
2. The artistic have a much lower level of regular schooling than do others in the total sample. For example, 41 percent of the artistic had an eighth-grade education or less, compared with only 26 percent of the total sample. And only 22 percent of the

281

artistic went to college, compared to 51 percent in the total sample.

3. The artistic are underrepresented among those who were all-around good students: 23 percent compared with 39 percent in the total sample. The artistic are twice as likely to show a pattern of "mixed" performance in school subjects: 23 percent compared with 11 percent in the total sample.

4. The artistic are much more likely to have special schooling: 66 percent, compared with 20 percent in the total sample. Forty-one artistic personalities attended art, music, drama, or dancing school, while only eleven did so from all the other categories of eminence.

5. The artistic are half as likely to be omnivorous readers (23 percent) compared with the total sample (48 percent).

6. The artistic are overrepresented among the precocious: 43 percent compared with 34 percent in the total sample.

7. The artistic are overrepresented among first- and second-generation immigrants: 29 percent compared with 18 percent in the total sample.

The artistic personalities described in this chapter were chosen from among those for whom the most biographical information is available. Some show the greater degree of amity in families where several members are talented. The musician Varèse and the actor Olivier represent families where the father is rejecting but where the mother is not overpossessive and does not cling to the son in lieu of a close relationship to the father. Varèse's mother could not cope; Olivier's mother had an impish sense of humor and was not overpossessive. Varèse and Olivier illustrate the finding that it takes not only a rejecting father but also an overpossessive mother to produce sexual divergency in a son. Augustus John, who recalls the complicated adult histories of all those who participate in a ménage à trois, is included because few among the Three Hundred illustrate so many of the findings: the troubled middle-class home; the early defiance of conventional education; the athletic prowess that gave him status among his peers; the rejection of the father; the closeness to the sister that seems to be responsible, in part, for his inability to have a close commitment to any other woman and his resultant unconventionality; and his role as the famous father who inhibited the careers of his sons.

Families in Which There Is Little Conflict

Warmly cohesive families who share the same talent are those of Calder, Renoir, and Wyeth. We will describe them here.

Alexander Calder. Alexander Calder was the third notable sculptor in his family. His grandfather, Alexander Milne Calder, born in Scotland, is best known for his figure of William Penn which tops the dome of Philadelphia's city hall. Alexander's father, A. Sterling Calder, was a National Academician and one of the outstanding sculptors of his generation. In *Calder* (1971), Alexander's biographer says, "Despite the vast differences between their sculptures, the elder Calder seems always to have been tolerant, even sympathetic to his son's experiments, and their relationship remained close and affectionate" (p. 16).

Alexander grew up very familiar with his parents' studio. His mother was a painter, and she and his father often used the unusually handsome child as a model. *The Bear Cub,* a figure of Alexander as a sturdy five-year-old boy, is one of his father's best-known pieces. However, neither he nor his older sister showed any interest in art as children, and when Alexander went to college he majored in engineering. After graduation he worked as an engineer for four years, but he did not like the mathematical aspects of engineering, and returned to the family tradition of working in the field of art. He was earning only $75 a month, doing illustrations for *Police Gazette,* when he began making amusing toys with bits of wood and metal. Some were sold, but no one took them seriously as art.

At age twenty-eight he went to Paris and while there entertained Joan Miró and other artists he met with his "circus," a collection of mechanical toys. They were enthusiastically recognized as genuine abstract art, and an exhibition was arranged. The critics were delighted with the work of the American who had so amusingly combined his knowledge of engineering and his natural artistic bent.

On the way home he met Louise James, a grandniece of

William and Henry James, and their shipboard romance culminated in marriage. Calder made her wedding ring, and this experience was so satisfying that he began making jewelry, which later became museum pieces.

Calder always worked at his art as if he were still a boy playing with his father's tools. An emotionally uncomplicated person, he had close relationships with his wife, parents, sister, and two daughters.

The Renoirs. Like Alexander Calder, the children of Auguste Renoir were also intimately familiar with the family studio. The Renoirs had been skilled artisans for generations. Auguste Renoir, who began his life as an artisan, was a famous artist long before his son, Jean, the film maker, was born. Jean is also his father's affectionate and skillful biographer. Jean Renoir's great-grandfather was a cobbler whose children were all skilled artisans or married artisans. His grandfather was a tailor, and his shop was in the family's living room. The four sons slept in the attic, but they were a close, warm family, supportive of each other, and their mother kept a tidy house. The four sons and the daughter wore their Sunday best every day of the week. Auguste Renoir remembered the family flat, no bigger than a pocket handkerchief, with nostalgia. It was old, but elegant. The stairs were stone, the bannisters were wrought iron lace. The sons were all apprenticed to skilled trades and Lisa, the radical-feminist daughter, after some hesitancy, renounced her principles and consented to marry an engraver rather than follow the utopian socialists Saint-Simon and Fourier.

When Auguste completed his grade-school education, he was apprenticed to the owner of a porcelain works and began painting flowers around the edges of plates. Soon he varied the routine by drawing historical figures and copying the old masters in the center of the plates, which pleased his employer. Lisa, who could never endure seeing anyone exploited, told Auguste's employer that her young, timid brother should not be doing a man's work for a boy's pay. Auguste was embarrassed, but Lisa won her demands for him.

Auguste was a recognized Impressionist, and well remembered by the many women he had loved, when at age forty he married a lovely eighteen-year-old seamstress. He became a devoted husband to his young wife and a maudlin, overanxious father to his three sons. He gathered his family about him closely, as his father had done, and from his attic studio was acutely cognizant of all that went on in the rooms below. He was delighted when his wife nursed the babies and liked to see them close to their mother, kneading her breast with their chubby hands. Babies were little animals, he said, and needed body contact. All bottle babies, he was certain, would be nobodies or criminals. When their first son was born, he and his wife would come home during theater intermissions to make sure the baby was happy with his nurse, but when Jean was born, in 1894, they stopped going out altogether and stayed home with him until he was old enough to go places with them. He boarded up windows the children might fall through, sandpapered the sharp corners of the mantelpiece so that no small boy would be hurt, and painted bright pictures of flowers on the walls of their nursery. He was reluctant to send them to school because he believed children should be children of nature until they were ten.

In *Renoir, My Father* (1962), Jean says, "What strikes me most when I go back to the time when I first began to be really conscious of the world about me is the certainty I have retained of [Auguste] Renoir's unfaltering strength. Everything he did seemed to me to be ineluctable" (p. 323).

Andrew Wyeth. When N. C. Wyeth and Howard Pyle established their studio at Chadds Ford, Pennsylvania, and also founded the Brandywine River Museum, they set the stage for rearing two more generations of Wyeth artists, Andrew Wyeth and his son, James. As James says in *Current Biography*, "We are all artists in our family, except the dog."

N. C. Wyeth, a noted illustrator of children's books and an art teacher, had five children—the artists, Henrietta, Carolyn, and Andrew; Nathaniel, an engineer; and Ann, a musician and composer. His wife, the former Carolyn Bockius, was a city girl who found living in the country a challenging but sometimes lonely experience. She came from an academic family of considerable distinction, as did her husband. The Wyeths had come to Cam-

bridge, Massachusetts, before the American Revolution and generations of Wyeths had attended Harvard. Moving to Chadds Ford
was a major change in their lives.

Andrew, the youngest son, was rather frail and was never
sent to school, but instead was tutored by a local resident. The boy
was happy at home and grew into a muscular man who could box,
fence, and fly airplanes. He entered a picture in an adult art show
at fifteen and had his first one man show at twenty.

N.C. Wyeth liked to have his family near him. When his
daughter married artist Peter Hurd, he bought them an abandoned
schoolhouse near his home, and after several years of using it as a
studio they added a wing and moved in. In 1940 it became the
home of Andrew and his bride, eighteen-year-old Betsy James, who
at first found the closeness of the family rather overwhelming. They
had two sons—Nicholas in 1943 and James in 1946—and the
schoolhouse was used again later as a studio by Andrew and
James.

James was also a sickly child, and after completing sixth
grade he, too, chose to stay home to try being an artist and be
tutored in his school lessons. When he began his daily routine in
his father's studio, his Aunt Carolyn taught him to draw cubes and
spheres. His father was laconic and made few suggestions, but they
were always helpful and encouraging.

Paul Robeson. In the Calder, Renoir, and Wyeth families
it is clear that the parents enjoyed having their children at home
with them and that the children profited by the companionship of
their talented parents during their formative years. Other than the
inevitable illnesses, accidents, and deaths in the family, there were
no accounts of intense domestic traumas in these art-centered
homes.

Not every eminent artist comes from a family where talents
are shared, but some may have sympathetic, proud parents who
recognize their children's special abilities and are eager to help
them make the most of them. Paul Robeson is a case in point. The
youngest of five children, Paul was born in Princeton, New Jersey,
where his father was a Presbyterian minister and his mother a
schoolteacher before her marriage. All but one of the five children

were college graduates. The Robeson family experience also encouraged dissent. To be able to dissent as a matter of conscience was a part of the family tradition. Paul's mother came from a Quaker family. His father quarreled with the Presbyterian hierarchy and started a church of his own. His mother lost her eyesight and died tragically of burns, but his father never spared himself in helping his son to excel in many areas—as an All-American football star, Rhodes scholar, and a stage, film, and operatic star. Paul Robeson achieved in more areas of eminence than did anyone else in the Three Hundred.

In some households, eminent artistic personalities emerged not because of parental encouragement but despite its absence. For instance, even when Leonard Bernstein was doing well, his father objected to his interest in music. Lenny reacted by being a frail, severely handicapped asthmatic child, always in terror of the aggressive neighborhood boys. He was never in good health until an aunt stored her piano at his home and he had the use of it. Arthur Rubinstein was another musician who emerged despite conflict.

Arthur Rubinstein. Neither of Arthur's parents was musical, and their lack of love for music was a barrier between him and them. Although they recognized that he was a prodigy and were proud of him, they were unable to really appreciate or evaluate his remarkable performance or to rejoice in his professional development. He was also estranged from them because they sent him away from Lodz, Poland, to live in Berlin when he was ten years old. In his autobiography, *My Young Years* (1973), a richly written and very personal document, he says that his mother had little understanding of anything he stood for:

> I knew she was a perfect wife and mother in her own way; the rest of the family worshipped her like a saint. With my father, it was a different thing; he was unmusical, too, but he tried, he inquired—and he was a fine philosopher; a little Talmudic, perhaps, but with an open mind for new ideas. He was a failure in business, because he was too honest, and too indifferent toward money. What I liked best about him was his universality. . . . I suppose that the main reason for the estrangement

from my family lay in the fact that my parents sent me
to live among strangers, who made a strong impact on
my mind and my character at an age when I was most
vulnerable [pp. 71–72].

Born in 1886 in Lodz, the youngest of seven children,
Arthur was an unwanted child. His mother would have terminated
the pregnancy had not her sister persuaded her not to. His next
oldest brother was seven years older than he, and his oldest sister
was soon to be married. His musical talents showed early. When
he was three and a half, he screamed and slapped his sister's hands
when she played a wrong note on the piano, and he could play any
melody that he heard. At age four, when he was taken to be
evaluated by Professor Joseph Joachim in Berlin, he hummed the
second theme of Schubert's *Unfinished Symphony*, played it with
the right harmonies, and transposed the tune into another tonality.
The professor kissed him, gave him chocolate, and said he would
probably be a great musician some day; however, he advised
Arthur's parents not to start his training until he was older. At six
the child played for charity concerts in his home town. At ten
Arthur was brought again to the Berlin professor, who kept his
promise to direct his musical education but made his mother agree
she would not exploit the boy's unusual talent until he was a mature
musician. Another professor was appointed to direct his musical
career, but the man terrified Arthur. If Arthur was unprepared for
a lesson, the old man's beard would slowly rise to a horizontal position as he drew his lower lip and bit it with rage.

A tutor, who was probably the most important person in
Arthur's intellectual development, was found for Arthur, but he
soon stopped trying to give him regular lessons. Since Arthur had
no interest in mathematics, his teacher agreed that not knowing
geometry would not prejudice his future as a musician. Instead,
they read Plato, Aristotle, Goethe, Heine, Kleist, Balzac, Maupassant, Dostoevsky, Gogol, and Tolstoy. When Arthur was eleven, his
tutor was treating him as if he were adult and listened to his ideas
and opinions.

Laurence Olivier. There was conflict in the Olivier home
but not about the son's choice of occupation. Rather, father and

son had a severe personality clash. Laurence (Larry) Olivier was born in 1907 in Dorking, England, the third and youngest child of Gerald Kerr Olivier, a rector of the Church of England and of his gypsylike mother, the former Agnes Crookenden. The firstborn was Larry's sister, Sybille, and the second was his brother, Richard, two and one half years older than he. His father had wanted to be an opera star and was once offered training by a famous tenor, but he had had to refuse because his mother, mindful of the six generations of clergymen in the family, threatened to disinherit him. However, he defeated his mother's plans for him and defeated himself while doing so. Although he was an excellent orator, he was a failure as a clergyman. He seldom stayed at a church, which was always in a working-class area of London, for more than a year since he insisted on a ceremonious high church Episcopal service and probably preached sermons his parishioners could not understand.

As a small boy, Larry imitated his father, copied his gestures and manner of delivery and at four dictated sermons and played at preaching. When Larry showed early and remarkable talent for the stage, his father, mindful of his own wasted talents, encouraged him, built him a toy theater when he was little, took him to the theater when he was older, and sent him to the Central School of Speech Training and Dramatic Arts when he was seventeen. Although he appreciated his son's talents and helped him plan his career, he could not stand being in his company. The Reverend Olivier was dour and autocratic; Larry was a showoff, prankster, and wit, able to turn his father into a raging volcano.

At school he was aloof and superior, respected for his acting ability, but not popular. He was not poor in sports, but he was unable to be the cricketer his six-foot father had once been. At age ten he impressed Ellen Terry with his acting ability. At age fourteen he played Katherine in *The Taming of the Shrew* at Stratford-on-Avon and had national notices. People were either devoted to Larry or could not stand him at all. When he had the center of the stage, he was happy; when he was unnoticed, he acted the clown.

It was to his mother that he was always close. Not only did he look like her, dark and gypsylike, but he had the same mis-

chievous sense of fun and both were mimics. John Cottrell, in
Laurence Olivier (1975), reports that his sister says, "Father didn't
like Larry, and Larry was terrified of him. Mummy was just everything. She was the most enchanting person. Hair so long she could
sit on it. She absolutely made our childhood. Always saw the funny
side of everything. She adored Larry. He was hers. He always
amused her very much" (p. 16).

Larry's mother died of a brain tumor at age forty-eight when
he was twelve. After his first two marriages failed and he was embarking on his third, to Joan Plowright, according to Cottrell,
"Years later, when talking about the terrible sense of loss he felt
after his mother's death, Olivier said that he had been 'looking for
her ever since. Perhaps with Joanie I have found her again'" (p.
310).

Edgard Varèse. A composer who really disliked his father
was Edgard Varèse. Born in Paris in 1883 to an exceptionally cruel
and dominating father and a pitiful mother who could not cope,
Edgard was the oldest son, and as such was expected to be an important businessman like his wealthy father. Soon after his birth he
was given to a maternal great aunt and uncle who lived in Villars.
The important male figure in his life was his grandfather, a peasant
and a homespun Socrates who had a little vineyard in Villars, made
his own wine, and was a good cook. In later years Edgard told his
wife that she and his grandfather were the only two persons he ever
truly loved.

When Edgard was ready for secondary school, he moved
back into his parents' home in Turin, where the father had business
interests. In Turin he heard concerts, met musicians, and began to
compose, making distorted sounds on the piano and on his mando-
lin recalling the sounds in nature and the C sharp of a train
whistle. His father, who expected Edgard to take over the family
business interests, was outraged at the discordant sounds and at his
son's serious interest in music and he put a black shroud on the
family's grand piano and hid the key.

His mother was not able to help him nor did she encourage
him in any way. As Fernand Ouellette, in *Edgard Varèse* (1968),
says, "As a mother she was too much crushed, too much humiliated
by her husband to display the normal warmth and tenderness all

children expect" (p. 10). Her having given him away as an infant did nothing to make the relationship closer. Shortly before she died, at age thirty-one, she begged him to try to protect the younger children in the family from the husband she called a "murderer."

Edgard's wife reports that he remembered himself as a belligerent, aggressive boy who liked to fight other boys on the streets. When his father slapped his stepmother, who was good to his brothers and sisters, Edgard beat his father soundly and left home. Although Edgard was only seventeen, a Turin music teacher, who had recognized his talents and had given him free tuition, and the local Catholic bishop had a shouting match with his father to get his legal permission to let Edgard go to Paris to study music; the bishop played a trump card by threatening to enlist the help of his good friend the Cardinal. Varèse went to Paris, where for a time he was half-starved and slept in the street, until a cousin found him a job as a librarian and he entered music school. When his father came to Paris and offered to turn over his business to him if he would come home, Edgard refused to be reconciled.

Henry Miller describes his reaction to Varèse's music, in *Air-Conditioned Nightmare,* saying that when he first heard it he was stunned; his emotions rose to such a crescendo that he felt as if he had been given a sock in the jaw. Indeed, Ouellette speculates that only Varèse's deep affection for his grandfather kept his music from expressing an utter hatred, which would have made it intolerable. "How deep that hatred might have gone," he writes. "This aggression manifests itself, it seems to me, even in Varèse's way of shattering or attacking a sound" (p. 11).

Augustus John. Artist Augustus John is the most unconventional of the forty-seven unconventional persons among the Three Hundred, having been involved in at least three ménages à trois and having had sexual relationships with hundreds of women. To the Londoners of his day he was also the stereotype of the artist, the eccentric, handsome roué in a beret, and the Bloomsbury set adored him.

He was born in 1878 in Tenby, Wales, the third of four children. His mother, a competent amateur artist and musician, died at thirty-five of rheumatic gout and exhaustion, when Augustus John was six and a half. His melancholy father, a lawyer, moved his four children to a dark, gloomy house in Tenby, because he and Augusta were happy in Tenby in their younger days. To the children the house was a tomb. Their father disciplined them sternly. He was a town eccentric because he was so conservative. His collars were the stiffest, his manners forbiddingly correct, and the only recreation he permitted himself was to attend church. He had few clients, and he disciplined his children severely.

All of the children were shy and, like their father, given to depression. The two girls developed a sign language of touching and grimacing because their father did not like to hear children's voices; even at the table their unappetizing meals were eaten in silence. However, their schooling was not neglected, and they had tutors and governesses. Augustus was a wild, fearless boy who dived, swam, climbed trees, and rode horseback without regard for his safety. Sent to a secondary school, he was so unruly that he was boxed on the ear and had poor hearing the rest of his life. Still when his father saw that he had artistic talent, he found him an art teacher in Tenby and later sent him to the Slade art school in London when he was sixteen.

He was a mediocre student until, during a summer holiday, he cut a huge gash in his head in a diving accident as a result of which his head was shaved. When he returned to school, he wore a velvet smoking cap to hide his scar and shaved head and he had grown a red beard, and suddenly he was seen as being extraordinarily handsome. During his convalescence his personality had changed; the little boy who played at being a Red Indian, and the young man who dressed like a gypsy, established his reputation for talent and eccentricity at seventeen. His sketches were so bold and original in design that other students picked up his discards and treasured them. His teachers at Slade were convinced that he would be one of their outstanding graduates.

He married Ida Nettleship, a talented scholarship student at Slade whom many other men wanted to marry. According to biographer Michael Holroyd, in *Augustus John* (1975), "Ida was a very sexually attractive girl, with slanted Oriental eyes, a sensuous mouth, dark curly hair, and a dark complexion. There seemed to be some wild, untamed quality about her . . ." (p. 75). The daughter of an anxious mother who worked as a seamstress for important women, such as Ellen Terry and the wife of Oscar Wilde, and an alcoholic artist father, Ida was accustomed to meeting unconventional and talented people. Ida's mother was horrified when she met the untidy, bearded, impoverished Augustus, but could do nothing to stop the marriage. For a time they lived on his almost nonexistent income, but by the time the first of six children came along his work was selling better. Augustus was exhilarated at becoming a father and loved babies, although older children annoyed him. Ida, although she became the mother of five, found mothering difficult.

Later Augustus fell madly in love with Dorelia McNeill, a quiet, unassuming, sympathetic and very beautiful young woman who worked as a typist, went to art classes in the evening, and lived on the fringes of the exciting artistic world. Augustus wrote her passionate letters and begged her to be his mistress, but she refused. He introduced her to Ida, who thought her charming, and to his sister, Gwen, who was also enchanted with her, and the two went on a month-long walking tour of England and the Continent, sleeping in hayracks and by the roadside. Gwen, who was quite unconventional, saw no reason why Dorelia and Ida and Augustus should not live under one roof. Augustus told Ida he could not live without Dorelia, who in turn wanted to live with him, but she also liked Ida. Ida, who felt happy in Dorelia's company, since she had the gift of serenity that Ida did not, realized no one woman could satisfy Augustus' sexual needs, though two women might do so. Finally, Gwen convinced Dorelia to do what Ida urged her to do: join in a ménage à trois. Dorelia consented, and brought order and serenity to the disorganized household. (Augustus always believed Gwen was a better artist than he, and the two often exhibited their work together, though Augustus was much more successful financially. In later years, Dorelia and Ida agreed that neither of them meant as much to Augustus as did Gwen.)

Before the ménage was established, Augustus had fled to Antwerp to escape his domestic problems, and afterward he continued to wander. In his absence the two women grew extraordinarily close, looking after the house and children together, making clothes for each other, and playing chess in the evenings. Because the house was cold, when Augustus was away, they slept together to keep warm; when he was home Ida often felt guilty when she was in bed with Augustus knowing Dorelia was lying alone nearby.

There was such intense criticism about the arrangement from the community and from relatives that in 1905 they accepted Ida's suggestion that they go to Paris, where the two women and the children could live together while Augustus, who was hard to be with on a day-to-day basis, would live in a studio nearby and spend part of his time in London.

In Paris Ida had a fourth son, "another beastly boy," as she put it, named Edwin after his maternal grandfather. However, she was happy in the new setting and, feeling more like a mistress than a wife, spent money freely and hired two girls to help in the house. Dorelia, who was able to be happy anywhere, coped with every practical difficulty. Augustus was often in his studio, but was helpless and fearful, terrorized by his own growing children. When he struck his two eldest sons, he was reminded of his own father and was ashamed.

He fell in love with his most attractive model, Alick Schepeler, who lived with a friend, Frieda Bloch, and enthusiastically told Ida and Dorelia he planned to set up another ménage à trois with these two women and that eventually they would all live together. But when they angrily rejected the idea, accusing him of trying to establish a small city with his women, he was simply bewildered. The affair with Alick was soon over, but Dorelia had begun posing for other artists to earn a living and it was not long before she, Ida, and Augustus were all living in separate establishments.

Ida died shortly after the birth of her fifth child. For several years, Dorelia refused to resume her relationship with Augustus. He was ill and lonely for her, and responded by kidnapping his three oldest children from his mother-in-law. Finally they did begin sharing a life together again, but by then she was indifferent to the other women in his life. While she and her children lived in Alderney-by-the-Sea, most of the week he lived in London, where he was an established, successful artist, who fascinated all the women he encountered. In London he had continuous affairs with models and art students (he felt that he could not paint a woman well unless he knew her sexually) and others he happened to meet. He was no easier to live with in his sixties than in his twenties, but late in life he fathered his last son by another woman. He and Dorelia had no children at home anymore and sought custody of the boy, but were permitted to have him only during summer holidays.

Dorelia, who simply let life happen to her, continued to love him, and had a faithful suitor who in turn loved her. She never quarreled with Augustus about his affairs, though she could be very angry when he was late for lunch. In their old age they were happy with each other and were seen as "Darby and Joan" by their contemporaries.

The sons and daughters of Augustus John were happy as growing children and were rebellious or unhappy as adults. The youngest of Ida's sons killed himself. They suffered, Holroyd says, from living with a god, a powerful and charismatic man, and were permanently cast as demigods.

Observations

There is less conflict within a family when a child chooses what is regarded as the family occupation or profession. There are families who paint, families who sculpt, families who act, families who are musical. As we have seen, among them are the families of Calder, Renoir, and Wyeth. The Picasso home resembles these three rather closely. Other artistic families include those of Charles Aznavour, Sir John Barbirolli, Charles Ives, Georgia O'Keeffe, Edith Piaf, John Sloan, the Soyer twins, and Maurice Utrillo. Among the Three Hundred the myth of the lonely, temperamental artist starving alone in a garret is not upheld.

Another myth that is not supported is that of the dominating stage-mother who turns her children into premature adults by pushing them into a career they do not enjoy. Stage mothers and stage fathers are well regarded by most of the child performers—at least those who became eminent. (Others, who disappointed their ambitious mothers, may well have other reactions.) Those who appreciate their stage mothers include Fred Astaire, Aznavour, Margot Fonteyn, Helen Hayes, and Pola Negri. Beatrice Lillie resented her mother's preference for her sister, but not her early training and experience. Judy Garland and her mother were not congenial largely because her mother and the studio introduced her to drugs when she was a young adolescent, giving her drugs to make her alert and responsive in the morning and other drugs to make her sleep at night.

Actors, actresses, and directors seem to come from the more troubled homes. One of the most unhappy children, who was also an unhappy adult, was Marilyn Monroe. The film directors, several of whom were immigrants, also had problems in their childhood homes. Frank Capra has already been described. Ingmar Bergman, who was estranged from his Lutheran minister father, was introduced to film making by an uncle who gave him a camera and by his mother and sister who were his admiring audience. Actresses Greta Garbo and Ingrid Bergman had traumatic experiences as children, as did dancer Katherine Dunham. It seems that those who create fantasy, whether in literature or art, are more likely to be complex and unhappy persons.

A few fathers feel that a son's becoming a dancer or an artist casts doubts on the son's masculinity, or they fear the son may be unsuccessful. As we have seen, Bernstein's father thought his child would turn out to be a bum if he became a musician. Varèse's father put a black shroud on the family piano. Benny Bufano's father tore up his son's sketches and beat him when he persisted in his artistic interests. Juan Gris's father refused to provide for training in fine arts and reluctantly sent him to a school in Madrid that trained industrial artists. With his sister's help, Gris ran away to Paris. Rudolph Nureyev's father, a teacher in the Red Army, had three daughters before he had the son he longed for so much, and when the son did little at home or in school but dance about and beg to be trained as a ballet dancer, the father was outraged. However, such cases, though dramatic, are in the minority. For the most part we found the artists and performers lived in a world of their own making and were more or less content with themselves and their surroundings.

❧ 11 ❧

The Others

There is nothing permanent but change.
                                            Heraclitus

Unlike the political, literary, and artistic, the seventy-three "other" subjects in the Three Hundred are a disparate lot, having in common only the fact that they do not fit any of the previous categories. They include scientists, educators, physicians, philosophers, religious leaders, psychiatrists, psychoanalysts, mystics, psychics, labor leaders, business people, athletes, adventurers, and people who achieved eminence by being close to persons of eminence.

Because this category includes such a disparate group, any differences between the various subgroups tend to cancel each other out. The scientists and the psychotherapists, for instance, have a very high level of formal education, whereas the athletes and the psychics have little schooling. We found no statistically significant differences between the seventy-three others as a category and the data on the 317 persons in the total survey sample. However, there is a tendency for the others, as compared with the total sample, to dislike teachers (38 percent versus 32 percent), to be bored with the curriculum (54 percent versus 47 percent), and not to be voracious readers (38 percent versus 48 percent).

Scientists

Scientists, most of whom are not subjects of book length biographies, have been studied by McClelland and others (1958), Roe (1953), Torrance (1961), Knapp and Goodrich (1952), Brandewein (1955), and others. They describe the young male scientist as being responsible and independent, as having only a few close friends and not wanting more, as showing very little rebellion and often taking much pleasure in the father-son relationship. He also values his mother as a homemaker but is inclined to be aloof from her because she does not understand his work, and he takes little interest in girls until he is in college, when he tends to marry the first girl with whom he "goes steady." Physical scientists are intensely masculine and see no need to flex biceps or have affairs to prove their masculinity; they resolve their Oedipal conflicts early and ordinarily have no problems in their psychosexual relationships. They believe problems are to be solved with reason and logic, not by blows and are typically able to express indignation only when they think another scientist has violated scientific ethics. Scientists both young and old value endurance, stoicism, dignity, and self-control.

Scientists themselves are largely responsible for the lack of biographies about them. They do not lend themselves easily to being subjects, since they resent any invasion of their privacy, are embarrassed by anything approaching an emotional display, and are disinclined to be introspective. Their idea of a proper biography is the entry under their names in *Who's Who* or similar publications.

The scientists among the Three Hundred are Niels Bohr, Rosalind Franklin, Karl von Frisch, George Gamow, Otto Hahn, Julian Huxley, Frédéric Joliot-Curie, Alfred Kinsey, Ernest Lawrence, Louis Leakey, Margaret Mead, and Stanislaw Ulam. Two, Mead and Franklin, are women, a higher proportion than is found among Nobel Prize winners or those listed in *Men and Women of Science*. Outstanding women scientists are not ignored by publishers, who are eager to publish books about women, but there are very few of them. We will discuss in detail Bohr, Kinsey, Leakey, and Frisch.

Niels Bohr. Biographer Ruth Moore, an outstanding science writer, says in *Niels Bohr* (1966), "It is not given to many men to change the course of the world. Niels Bohr, though, once altered the course of history. The age of the atom came into being largely through his scientific work and influence, and few men have had a more directive effect on the lives of their fellow men and the earth" (p. 1). It was he who first applied the quantum theory successfully to the problem of atomic structure and helped scientists in the United States make the atomic bomb at Los Alamos. After the war, he advocated an open world of scientific ideas and the international control of atomic weapons.

Niels was born in 1885 in Copenhagen, where his father was professor of physiology at the University of Copenhagen. Christian Bohr was not only a noted scientist but also a vigorous man who helped make soccer Denmark's national sport and who introduced classes at the university for female students. One of his students, Ellen Adler, became his wife.

The Bohrs were an exceptionally happy couple and enjoyed being parents. The first child was a daughter, Niels was the second, and two years later Harald was born. Harald and Niels were inseparable. Harald, who was the most brilliant and verbal and who later became a mathematician, liked to tease, but Niels, even when urged to take turns teasing, could not.

The children were cherished by their parents and grandparents. The father took them on expeditions, to soccer games, to see the fishwives scaling fish at the wharf, to go boating and skiing. He had memorized many of Goethe's poems and recited them when they went on hikes. At bedtime he read aloud from Shakespeare and Dickens. When his friends from the university came to visit, the children were permitted to sit and listen. Niels's mother, who came from a wealthy family, was accustomed to entertaining. There were foreign visitors in the home and artists, writers, and musicians as well as scholars and scientists. An aunt who had a positive effect on Niels's life was Hanna Adler, a charismatic spinster and educator who founded a coeducational school. She took her nephews to museums and during walks in the fields filled them with nature lore and encouraged them to talk about anything on their minds.

Though fascinated with words and communication, Niels was not easily able to communicate in either writing or speech. He was a poor lecturer, who was likely to stop to ponder, leaving his audience wondering, then resume talking without sharing what he was mulling over. He had no techniques for trying to impress and was shy, honest, deliberate and thoughtful. He began to publish early, and at twenty-one he added to the basic knowledge of surface tension.

His marriage to Margrethe Norlund was, Moore says, "the beginning of an almost idyllic love that never wavered for the remainder of their lives" (p. 27). An alive, warm, gentle woman, Margrethe was clever in mathematics and understood her husband's work. All of his early papers and correspondence are in her handwriting. Like Niels's own parents, they enjoyed being parents and had five sons, whom they reared much as he had been reared.

In 1921 Bohr received the Nobel Prize for his work in determining the structure of the atom. In 1957 he received the first Atoms For Peace award.

Alfred C. Kinsey. The man whose research on sexual behavior of the human male and female was so controversial a quarter century ago was born in Hoboken, New Jersey, in 1894. Despite the subject matter of his research, his personal life could not have been more exemplary, and his life is typical of the scientist except for his rejection of his family. Most scientists are close to their fathers; he was not. His father, a self-made man, was head of the department of manual arts at the Stevens Institute of Technology, where he had begun as a teen-aged shopboy. When he advanced in status, he moved his family from working-class Hoboken to middle-class East Orange. A member of the Methodist church, he was so intent on strict observance of the Sabbath that he would not let his children ride to church on Sunday, not even with the minister.

In *Kinsey: A Biography* (1971), Cornelia V. Christenson, his secretary, says, "Kinsey's mother, Sarah Ann Charles, a carpenter's daughter, had only four years of schooling. This minimal education betrayed itself only in her letter writing, not in her manner of speaking, Clara Kinsey, her daughter-in-law, recalls. Clara calls her mother-in-law 'the sweetest person I have ever known.' With this disposition it is no wonder that she submitted readily to the domination of her disciplinarian husband" (pp. 14– 15). Christenson is one more biographer who supports our observation that mothers who have dominating and unreasonable husbands often turn into women who cannot cope. Alfred was never close to his parents nor to his younger brother and sister.

As a high school and college student Alfred was aloof, shy, a perfectionist. He did not seek people out but was friendly when approached, and he was well liked because he was good looking, always smiling, and was an accomplished pianist. His father would not permit him to date in high school and he had little time or money to spend on girls in college, although he did have a few romances. He had presence and personal charm and was an outstanding student. At the end of his sophomore year in college he changed his major from mechanical engineering to biology. Even though his father refused to continue paying for his college expenses, he stuck to his decision and was helped by scholarships and by the widow of the school board chairman of East Orange High School.

When he was thirty and had his doctorate and was an assistant professor of biology at Indiana University, he found the perfect wife. Christenson reports he wrote a friend describing Clara Bracken McMillen thus: "Did I tell you that I am to be married early in June?. . . The girl is a graduate student in Chemistry at Indiana University. She is a very brilliant scholar; is one of the best athletes in the place. She knows the birds better than I do, knows the flowers and trees, etc., is a capable hiker and camper, a champion swimmer. We are to spend the major part of June hiking in the wildest country in the White Mountains" (p. 46).

His anticipation of a happy married life was more than fulfilled. Clara Kinsey had collected butterflies since girlhood, and as a chemistry student she could understand his work as a biologist. When he began his collection of a million gall flies and began to study their habits and physical characteristics, she was one of his most able assistants, especially when they traveled about the world looking for rare specimens. Kinsey's research on gall flies occupied him for years, and he published frequently. When they were newly married she had intended to continue her graduate work, but they had four children in rather rapid succession, so Clara abandoned her career. They bought a home and enjoyed music, gardening, and friends while he climbed the academic ladder.

Asked to teach a class in marriage counseling, which was very popular, he became aware of the lack of scientific information on human sexual behavior and so began his work in this area. In *Dr. Kinsey and the Institute for Sex Research* (1972), Wardell B. Pomeroy, an associate who worked with him for many years, emphasizes that Alfred's curiosity about the sex lives of others was constructive, never prurient. He was a warm but rigid, dominating, patriarchal figure who expected to be obeyed. He never quite conquered the effects of his strict Methodist upbringing. Indeed, he felt so handicapped in establishing a rapport with his interviewees because he neither smoked nor drank that he deliberately studied how to do both, and although he could not conquer his aversion to tobacco he was able to learn to tolerate rum, and in fact made a study of the various types of rum and rum recipes.

Louis S. B. Leakey. In *Making of a Scientist* (1953), Anne Roe says that anthropologists more often than physical scientists have problems in interpersonal relationships. Certainly this was true of Louis Seymour Bazett Leakey.

He was born a premature baby in 1903 at the Church Missionary Society's station at Kabete, Kenya, ten miles from Nairobi, which at that time was a cluster of shacks near the railroad. His mother, an amiable, patient woman, was thirty-five when Louis was born. His father was a missionary. He had two older sisters, and his brother Douglas was born five years later.

Since he had no European playmates, except his siblings, his parents encouraged him to make friends with African boys, and he learned to walk, talk, and play like a Kikuyu. He was initiated into the tribe and given the name Wakaruigi. He built his own house as a part of the Kikuyu ritual and lived in it. In the evening he listened to folk singers and tellers of folk tales.

Although he had been well prepared academically by his father, by intermittent tutors, and by his own reading, he was not prepared for the company of his peers when he went to school in England. They laughed at his distinctive walk and ridiculed his Kikuyu background. He was unpopular, had no close friends, and was put in the lowest form because he knew no Greek. Later, when he sought to enter Cambridge, the university observed he lacked a modern foreign language. He insisted on his rights, pointing out that Kikuyu *was* a modern language, and when he was asked to supply a statement from someone who could attest to his knowledge of the language, he submitted a sworn statement by a Kikuyu chief who signed the document with a thumb print.

Cambridge did not take to him. Though he was good looking and aggressive, he dressed oddly, was ordered off the tennis court for wearing tennis shorts, and was thought unbalanced and impetuous. During his second year he received a severe head blow on the rugby field, and thereafter had severe headaches and epileptic seizures and had to take medication for the rest of his life. When his physician ordered a year of outdoor living and a rest from his studies, he cannily persuaded the directors of the British Museum of Natural History to let him join a fossil-hunting expedition to Tanganyika. Since the head of the expedition had never been in Africa, the twenty-two-year-old student made all the arrangements. After this trip, he was committed to the new science of paleoanthropology and became one of its most controversial and important practitioners.

He married a fellow anthropologist, who worked with him for many years. She was a loving and helpful wife, respected by his friends and parents, and they had two children. In his middle years, however, he divorced her and married a much younger woman. To his scientific friends and especially to his parents, the second marriage was hard to accept, but she was also a helpful and loving wife, and bore him three more children.

Karl von Frisch. Making collections is to a scientist what debating is to a politician. The youngest of four boys, Karl von Frisch, was born in 1886 in Vienna, where his father was a practicing urologist, university teacher, and scientist. His maternal grandfather, three uncles, and two brothers were also university professors. His mother was a lovely woman who used her gifts of mind and heart to give joy to others. Until secondary school, Karl was educated at home, where his father taught him how to use the microscope and his mother indulged his making collections.

In his autobiography, *A Biologist Remembers* (1967), he says that he remembers far more about his animals than about school, and indeed his observations on some of the animals were published while he was still in secondary school. He had his own zoo, which he began with frogs and newts and to which, during his secondary school days, he added nine different species of mammals, sixteen species of birds, twenty-six cold-blooded terrestrial vertebrates, twenty-seven fish, and forty-five species of nonvertebrates. His mother never complained about his zoo; his father took him across the city to see a man who taught him how to build an aquarium for tropical fish. Though his parents supported this interest, when he decided to become a zoologist, his father explained that he might make more money as a physician, but he respected his son's decision.

When he was thirty, he married Margarethe Mohr, a nurse. His first words to her had been, "Can you draw?" and indeed she drew very well. She illustrated a small book he published, *Six Lectures on Bacteriology for Nurses*. On their honeymoon he kept her busy washing out the little dishes he used in training bees to recognize certain scents. All his life he had a pet parrot, and his wife allowed him to let it feed from his plate.

As a zoologist he had made epoch-making discoveries on the language, behavior, and senses of the honey bee and equally fascinating work on fish. In his meticulously indexed small autobiography, there are references to minnows, earthworms, parakeets, cows, dolphins, chimpanzees, lice, bats, and other creatures. There are also hundreds of references to bees, to their internal clock, their language, their tailwagging dance, their phylogenetic development.

Karl and Margarethe had four children. His only son, Otto, is a zoologist, of whom he says, "What he brought into the house in the way of birds and other animals far exceeded anything I myself had dared to inflict on my long-suffering family" (p. 172).

Other Professional People

Among other professional people there are several religious and philosophical leaders, and a number of them have already been described: Booth, Buber, Khan, Krishnamurti, Pope Paul VI, Teilhard, and Watts. Teachers and doctors do not appear often in recent biographies, a reflection, perhaps, of widespread dissatisfaction with public schools and with medical services. There are only two educators among the Three Hundred. One is Mary McLeod Bethune, who started a college for black students. The other is A. S. Neill, who began Summerhill as the ultimate rebellion against a father who loved to teach yet disliked children. Exposés of the medical profession are more popular than are biographies of the kind that rewarded popular doctors among the Four Hundred, including the Mayos, the Menningers, or Wilfred Grenfell, who rode the ice floes to reach his patients. Among the Three Hundred there is only one practicing medical doctor, Christiaan Barnard, the genial South African surgeon who performed the first human heart transplant.

Among the Three Hundred there are five psychiatrists or psychoanalists: Hélène Deutsch, Erik Erikson, Carl Jung, Jules Masserman, and Wilhelm Reich. Jung and Reich are the most controversial because of their struggles to reconcile the occult with the scientific.

We will now consider three well known psychotherapists who had similar associations during their formative years in Vienna and whose marked differences in the theories of human development they created seem to emerge directly from traumatic childhood experiences. Carl G. Jung, who was contemptuous of his clergyman father, created a new religion superior to that of his father, based on the myths and superstitions in which his mother and her family believed so strongly. Wilhelm Reich caused the death of his father and mother by telling his father about his mother's infidelity. His biographers believe that his theory about the efficacy of the orgasm in the cure of cancer and other illnesses and in dispelling attack from creatures from outer space is related to his guilt feelings about the death of his parents. If an orgasm in itself is so all-important, the infidelity of his mother should not have been regarded so seriously by the father whom he hated and feared. Consequently, he could absolve himself from responsibility for their deaths. Erik Homburger Erikson, who could not identify himself

satisfactorily to his classmates as either Gentile or Jew, German or
Dane, eventually became eminent when he made the identity
crisis a central theme in his theory of human development.

Carl Jung. Born in 1875 in Kesswil, a small town on Lake
Constance in Switzerland, Carl Jung was the son of a Lutheran
minister who was often in poor health, who lost his savings in poor
investments, and who moved the family often from one small
country church to another. He was unhappily married and was
regarded with contempt by his wife and son. When Carl was nine
a sister was born, but he was very jealous of her and never accepted
her either as a child or as an adult.

The Jungs were deeply influenced by the superstitions of the
country folk whom they served. In *C. G. Jung: The Haunted
Prophet* (1976), biographer P. J. Stern says of his mother's relatives: "her numerous family seemed to consist mostly of bizarre
characters, tottering on the edge of madness. Trances, visions,
hallucinations, and prophetic mutterings were, so to speak, the
daily diet of the Preiswerks" (p. 36). When he was six he was
frightened by the sudden feeling that his mother had two personalities. Her Number One personality was that of a housewife, an
ordinary, chatty, cozy person with whom he felt close. Her Number Two personality, which frightened him, was that of a witch.
As Jung says in *Memories, Dreams, Reflections* (1963), "That
personality was unexpectedly powerful: a somber, imposing figure
possessed of unassailable authority—and no bones about it. I was
sure that she consisted of two personalities, one innocuous and human, the other uncanny. . . . She would then speak as if talking
to herself, but what she said was aimed at me and usually struck
to the core of my being, so that I was stunned into silence" (pp.
48–49).

Carl was a precocious child, and his father taught him to
read Latin well when he was six. As a student in the village school,
he was disliked by the teachers and by his peers, upon whom he
often played tricks. Although he knew what he was doing, he felt
he could not help himself and blamed his classmates for "making"
him behave that way.

His childhood was complicated by a neurosis that developed
after a boy at school shoved him and he was hit on the head and

was almost unconscious. After that episode he had epilepticlike seizures whenever he tried to study. This illness gave him a six-month reprieve from school, which he spent happily at home reading. He regressed to preschool days and drew battle scenes, daydreamed, and worried about hellfire and damnation and his relationship with God. However, when he overheard his father saying his son had been diagnosed as an incurable epileptic, he cured himself by deliberately reading, having a seizure, and reading again until the seizures stopped and he could go back to school. After that experience he became a compulsive student and excelled in his schoolwork. (Stern says that, as a therapist, he was hard on his neurotic patients because he had cured himself of a severe neurosis and felt they should too.)

His life was troubled by dreams from early boyhood. He dreamed of a great column of flesh, like the penis of a giant, sitting on a throne. He dreamed that detached heads floated from his mother's bedroom. He dreamed that God sat high on a throne over the cathedral in the town square and defecated on the new roof and demolished it, and that God confided in him that he existed outside the church, not in it. This experience was to mould his life, and thereafter he felt he alone knew God.

Carl was so careless of his person that he had narrowly escaped death by accident several times, and one time, when he was twelve, he stood up in a gondola and began to row it. The father of a boy who was with him was furious, and humiliated Carl with a dressing down. He found solace for his hurt feelings by becoming suddenly aware that he was two persons. "One of them," he wrote, "was the schoolboy who could not grasp algebra and was far from sure of himself; the other . . . was an old man who lived in the eighteenth century" (pp. 33–34).

Jung lived with two personalities all during his life. He was a conforming student at school, but he shared with his mother a belief that it was a poltergeist who split the living room table and left a broken knife on the bread basket. He studied the required courses at school but studied spiritualism on his own. He read seven volumes of Emanuel Swedenborg and made friends with a young man who had a large library about the occult.

His fidelity to his Number Two personality began to influence his work and studies. He chose to do his doctoral thesis on a young cousin of his, Helene Preiswerk, a medium who spoke in tongues. In his thesis he did not acknowledge the personal relationship, called her "S.W.," and identified her as a girl "with a poor inheritance." While he was still studying her, the medium was discovered to be a fraud, concealing objects in her garments instead of materializing them "out of nowhere," but Carl dismissed the fraud lightly. He called her a hysteric, "as were most mediums," who had been pressured too much and was expected to produce phenomena when she was not able to do so, and turned therefore, quite naturally, to deception. Her spirit guide was Samuel Preiswerk, their mutual ministerial grandfather who sometimes flirted in a vulgar fashion with the women at the seances. In his thesis he noted that she, too, had a Number One and Number Two personality.

When Carl was twenty-seven and had completed medical school, he married a twenty-year-old heiress to whom he had been attracted when she was an adolescent. Her mother, who had once been in love with his father, approved the match. Emma was a serious, shy girl who had wanted to go to college but had not been permitted to do so, and she worshipped the charismatic older man, becoming not only his wife but also his follower and student. They had five children.

Carl became world famous as a scientifically oriented psychiatrist. He introduced the terms *introvert* and *extrovert* into the language and did extensive research on the word-association test and extended its usage. In 1911 he broke with Freud and the psychoanalytic movement and began work on his own theory of personality, which he called Analytical Psychology.

Although he saw patients, he had very little contact with other people, not even with his wife and children. On the estate on which they lived he had his own separate cottage where he could be alone. He was overwhelmed by visions of a world drenched in blood, and he feared madness would overwhelm him as it had already overwhelmed his friend Friedrich Nietzsche and his cousin the medium, Helene Preiswerk. Yet he deliberately let himself descend into madness, or near madness, so that he might discover the process of recovery. At this time his constant dream companion was an old man, Philemon, who had bull's horns and the wings of a kingfisher, and they talked endlessly together. There was also a woman in his dreams, young and beautiful, a talented psychopath. He disciplined his dreams until they turned into abstract designs he called *mandalas*. Out of this six years of self-analysis came new terms and concepts, that of the collective unconscious, the archetypes, the shadow, the *anima,* the *animus,* the *persona.* He steeped himself in myths and became close to Gnosticism, the doctrine of early Christian sects, which placed inquiry and intuition above truth and faith and followers of which were supposedly able to transcend matter. Only a select few could attain this state of being and were the man-God.

He emerged from this six years with a tremendous confidence in his new powers and beliefs. Although he had been critical of other psychiatrists who charged exorbitant fees, he forgave himself for doing so because he had a rich wife to whom he would feel inferior if he did not earn a good income. His patients were almost all wealthy women, many of whom were American.

He became an autocrat in his own house. His children dared not speak at the table, and he was often rude to his mother. He relegated his wife to the role of "earth mother," persuaded a wealthy, unhappy patient, Toni Woolf, to be his mistress, and invited her to dinner each Sunday despite the objections of his wife and children. Both women were disturbed by the relationship, since they had been close friends, and one of his assistants saw them together in joint sessions in which they analyzed each other. He and his assistant convinced both women that his wife was fated to play the role of the earth mother and that Toni Wolff was fated to be the Hetaera, a cultivated female concubine in Greek mythology. After several years of devotion, Toni insisted he divorce Emma and marry her, but he refused to do so; she then had another emotional breakdown, more serious than before. Despite the stormy years of their marriage, Emma and he were close in their old age when she became the dominant personality and was still the strong earth mother he had trained her to be.

Women were not his only admirers. In *Jung and the Story of Our Time* (1975), Laurens van der Post, an English-South African writer who was his close friend, says "I have, I believe, known many of those the world considered great, but Carl Gustav Jung is almost the only one of whose greatness I am certain" (p. 3). No one who writes about him dismisses his two personalities as unimportant, although they differ in the interpretation of them. In *C. G. Jung and Hermann Hesse: A Record of Two Friendships* (1966), Miguel Serrano, a Chilean writer and diplomat, speaks of him thus: "If Jung was a man of science capable of expressing his discoveries in the ordinary language of men, he was also a strange being who narrated improbable experiences in a language that was at odds with that of official science. He gave new terms to those mysteries which emanate from the eternal tradition of man" (p. 112).

The complexities of Carl Jung reflected his childhood. As he told van der Post about his six-year period of near madness:

> He found himself turning to the child in himself as if instinct too were exhorting him to become like the child again. . . . He went back . . . to his eleventh year, when he had had a passion for playing with blocks . . . and began to gather stones on the lake shore by his house at Küsnacht and build miniature villages with them. . . . Even so, in order not to lose all identity he had to remind himself over and over again of such realities as that his name was Carl Gustav Jung and that he was a doctor of medicine, a psychiatrist of growing reputation, a man of standing in the everyday world [pp. 155–156].

Torn between the occult and the scientific all of his life, Jung tells in *Memories, Dreams, Reflections* how in a single day his doorbell rang without cause, his daughter saw a ghostly figure flitting about the rooms, and his son drew a picture which Jung saw as a spirit message to him. He believed in the lore of the ancient astrologers and the Chinese game of chance, I Ching. He was resentful when a physician would not let him die when he was ill in 1944 and recalled him from an afterlife he found entrancing. When his wife died, he was comforted by hearing sounds of distant music and dancing, which meant to him that she was being welcomed warmly into her afterlife.

Jung was apolitical, but his devotion to the ancient folk

heroes led him to regard Hitler, and later, Mussolini, as modern folk heroes who could make Europe strong. He mistrusted democracy and preferred a strong oligarchy. Hitler was a revival of the god, Woden, who, he believed, was an important element in the German collective unconscious. He rejoiced in the Hitler Youth, who turned away from the state religion, worshiped nature, and roamed the countryside. During the peak of his disillusionment with Freud, who deplored his preoccupation with the occult, Jung said that Jews, having no homeland, could not make seminal contributions to human thought. Five years after Hitler took power, Jung was disillusioned and in his later years had a number of Jewish disciples and friends to whom he was devoted.

The Reichs. Peter Reich is the son of Wilhelm Reich and his third wife, the former Ilse Ollendorff. The only child of this marriage, Peter was born in 1944 in Forest Hills, Long Island. Wilhelm was born in Dobrzynica in the Galicia area of the Austro-Hungarian Empire in 1897, where his father was a well-to-do farmer. His father was such a domineering, ill-tempered man that the easiest way to insult Wilhelm and his brother was to tell them that they resembled him. It is not known why Wilhelm felt obliged to tell his father that his mother was having an affair with her son's tutor, but in any event she killed herself after being confronted by her husband. In turn, Wilhelm's father tried to arrange his own suicide to look like an accident so that his sons could collect his life insurance. He overturned his canoe and was exposed to icy water, but he did not drown or freeze. Three years later he died of tuberculosis. Wilhelm had reason to feel he had caused the death of both of his parents.

He was, in late adulthood, a very complex personality advising sexual freedom but denying himself that freedom. He had three marriages and three divorces but was not known to be promiscuous. Indeed, he told his wife that he feared his followers would use his orgone theory as an excuse for sex without love and commitment. He was himself a very modest man and even bathed in his undershorts. He believed that a man's sexual drives were over at age forty-five.

His career had an auspicious beginning. When he was twenty, the orphaned Wilhelm came directly to Vienna after his discharge as a German soldier in World War I. He had enjoyed his war experiences, and he never returned to his childhood home. He became a medical student and decided to take up psychiatry, and within a year was made a member of the Vienna Psychoanalytic Society. Even while still a medical student he was sent patients by Sigmund Freud. In 1927 he sought analysis with Freud but was not accepted. Like Jung he felt he had lost his father figure, and he spent several months in a Swiss sanitarium with a diagnosis of hypomania. He joined the Communist Party and set up a Socialist Society for Sex Consultation and Sexological Research. In 1924 he was expelled from both the Communist Party and the International Psychoanalytical Association. It was after these bitter rejections that he evolved theories about health and sex which were mystical rather than scientific and had to be accepted on faith.

In 1938 he came to the United States. He began treating patients for cancer, emotional problems, and other diseases with his "orgone boxes"—coffinlike wooden boxes that were not medicated or wired for any kind of electric treatment. In 1949 the Wilhelm Reich Foundation was incorporated as a nonprofit research foundation and educational corporation in the state of Maine, and in 1950 the family moved to Maine permanently. In 1954 the U.S. Food and Drug Administration got an injunction against their use. Refusing to obey the injunction, he was arrested, tried, found guilty, and sentenced to two years in prison. In prison he was found to be paranoid and transferred to another federal prison for psychiatric treatment, though the psychiatrists there declared him sane and competent. He died in the prison hospital of a heart attack.

Wilhelm was a dynamic, charismatic man with a lucrative practice that supported a center with a staff. He was deeply committed to his orgone theory and left funds to support a foundation to carry on his work after his death. After twenty years he still has a small, devoted following, and orgone boxes are still being used by Reichian therapists. His orgone theory postulates that psychoneurotics are unable to discharge energy effectively during orgasm and dam up their energy in what he calls "sexual stasis." In *Wilhelm Reich* (1971), biographer C. Rycroft says, "His conviction was, if I understand him rightly, that life could be freer and more untrammeled than civilized societies allow it to be, and that if man could live by his instincts and not in submission to his character armor not only would life be freer and richer than it is but also many moral problems and indeed many physical illnesses including cancer would never occur" (p. 33). Among the biographies of Wilhelm Reich are one written by his son Peter, *A Book of Dreams,* and another by Peter's mother, Ilse Ollendorff Reich, *Wilhelm Reich: A Personal Biography.* We will draw from both accounts.

Ilse's Story. Ilse describes her husband's delight with their son as an infant, and recalls that in 1948 he bought Peter a Hopalong Cassidy outfit, complete with two guns in holsters. Both parents tried not to pressure Peter, not to use him for their own purposes, or as an extension of their own egos. They tried to protect him from harm. They loved him and each other. Ilse continued to work as her husband's research assistant and after they moved to Maine she played the triple role of professional woman, wife, and mother.

Ilse says that during his most trying years Wilhelm's most satisfying relationship was with Peter. When his work in the laboratory was over for the day, he would fire two shots from a rifle to signal Peter he was free, and Peter would race happily to the observatory. They listened to the radio, watched television, and took walks together. Wilhelm (who had a lifelong fascination with the military) taught Peter how to handle a rifle.

In 1952, shortly after he recovered from his first heart attack, Wilhelm became seriously disturbed about what he saw as a "deadly orgone energy" (DOR), which he ascribed to an attack from outer space. He constructed a "Cloudbuster"—an arrangement of pipes on a turntable that could be manipulated in any direction, with the pipes connected by cables to the ground or to flowing water. It was designed to neutralize orgone energy and to ward off the effect of an attack. He sought to escape the danger by never sleeping two nights in the same place, and sent the bewildered Peter and his mother to live in the village. When he ventured to return to the laboratory, he had several serious blackouts. Some of his assistants left, unable to follow his thinking. He was able to use his Cloudbuster apparently to end a drought, for which many of his rural neighbors were grateful. Then he started to use the machine and a "space gun" to repulse spaceships he thought were threatening to land nearby, and he began to believe that he alone had the key to the survival of life on Earth. In the "Oranur Experiment," radium needles were used in the "space gun," and everyone in the laboratory, including Ilse, was immediately affected with radiation sickness, which caused nausea, conjunctivitis, and general malaise.

By the time Peter was twelve his parents' relationship had started to deteriorate. Ilse was increasingly fearful about what her husband was doing, and he made irrational accusations about her supposed infidelities. When the FDA cracked down on the orgone box in 1954, she left him. He responded by directing his fury at the outside world against her, calling her a murderer who belonged to those who tried to destroy life whenever it tried to function in a healthy way.

Wilhelm came to believe that President Eisenhower and officials at a nearby Air Force base were his admirers and protectors, and even completely redecorated his home in anticipation of the President's visit which, of course, never came. He installed a complete dining-room, placed comfortable chairs in front of the fireplace, bought new glassware and silverware. None of it ever was used, since Reich never again was to stay at the observatory except for brief vacations. When Peter went to see his father that summer, he told his mother he did not want to visit him again. Ilse wrote: "I think one has to recognize, as painful as the admission may be, that Reich's logic had carried him on and on, so far out into space that at some point he began, sometimes, to lose contact with reality. He was able to pull himself back again and again, but the continued pressure forced him to seek escape into the outer regions, into a more benevolent world" (p. 128). She also said that Reich had no sense of humor; he could not poke fun at himself.

When Ilse planned to take Peter with her to Europe in 1956, Wilhelm tried to influence him not to go because he felt that Peter was in danger from deadly poison in the air. Although Peter still half trusted his father, he was ambivalent and chose to go with his mother. However, he did pay his father a brief visit, and while there became a terrified witness as FDA agents destroyed accumulators, journals, bulletins, and pamphlets because his father had refused to stop using the orgone box.

Reich's appeal from the FDA injunction was denied. On

March 12, 1957, Reich entered the federal prison at Danbury,
Connecticut. He was there only ten days. During a psychiatric
examination he was diagnosed as paranoid. The sympathetic psychiatrist—who told Ilse he respected Reich very much as a man who
in his younger years had made notable contributions to psychiatry—
suggested that he be sent to Lewisburg, a federal penitentiary with
psychiatric treatment facilities. There Reich refused to submit to
psychiatric treatment. Although the psychiatrists agreed with the
Danbury diagnosis, they decided to declare him legally sane, since
they did not see any gain in keeping this once famous man in
custody. Ilse says, "they felt that a man of Reich's standing should
not be made to suffer from the label of legal insanity" (p. 151).

At age fifteen Peter visited his father twice in prison and
was one of three persons Wilhelm chose as a correspondent. He
wrote to Peter about the superiority of the EA (a spaceship powered
by DOR) over the Sputnik. He died in prison on November 3,
1957, of a heart attack.

Peter's Story. When he was in the third grade, his father
made him a member of the Cosmic Engineering Corps (CORE),
which dealt with cosmic phenomena, outer space, spaceships,
weather conditions, droughts, and rainmaking. It was for real, not
playing, and Peter was serious about his commitment. When he was
in the fifth grade he tried to tell another boy about how a machine
of his father's could make rain, and the boy laughed at him. Peter
was hurt and began to be wary of talking about his father's work
to others.

When his father died, Peter was utterly lost and unhappy.
During his adolescent years, he tried to keep his belly soft and
relaxed, as his father had taught him. Sometimes he screamed as he
rode alone in a car. Perhaps his father was right; other people had
seen spacecraft and believed in them. Even when he was twenty-
two he was still not entirely sure that a flying saucer might not
come and take him away.

Ten years after Wilhelm Reich's death, the only persons
residing at Orgonon were Tom Romm, an elderly Maine native, and
his wife. Peter found Old Tom, who was working where the
Cloudbuster once had stood. Tom joked about the time tourists
fiddled with the Cloudbuster five days in a row and precipitated

seven days of rainfall. The Cloudbuster was gone, crated up in the barn. Tom was tearing down the platform on which the Cloudbuster once had stood because he feared the Tuesday-Thursday museum visitors might hurt themselves clambering about on it. Peter climbed up to the platform and began handing down pieces of rotten wood to Tom. They worked in an easy rhythm. The sun was hot. Peter wiped the sweat from his face. As they worked, Peter looked toward the horizon. The sun was going down in a blaze of shimmering light. Peter had a frightening illusion, that of seeing beyond the horizon into a fearful unknown. This was the platform where for years he had stood to watch for the coming of the enemy that would carry him away, somewhere far beyond that same horizon. He closed his eyes and felt the old fears again. He opened them; the sun had set and there was nothing to fear. Grass would soon grow where the Cloudbuster had once stood.

Erik Erikson. If Erik Homburger Erikson, born in suburban Frankfurt, Germany, in 1902, had not had an identity crisis of his own, he might not be the authority on the identity crisis. His Danish parents separated before his birth. When he was three, his mother married his pediatrician, a Jewish physician named Theodore Homburger, who adopted him. The home was pleasant and upper middle class; his mother was a cultured woman who read the Danish classics, was fond of art, and had many artists as friends.

Child psychiatrist and biographer Robert Coles says that Erik disliked school and found its formalism and rigidities repellent. The German students made prejudicial comments about Jews, and the Jewish students called him a goy who lived in a Jewish home. He felt he had no identity and was neither German, Jewish, nor Danish. He decided not to go to college but to become an artist, and after graduation from gymnasium and wandering through Europe for a year, he attended an art school. He exhibited his woodcuts and etchings and at twenty-five was considering becoming licensed as an art teacher when a friend, Peter Blos, asked him to join him at a school in Vienna for children of American and British mothers undergoing psychoanalysis with Anna and Sigmund Freud.

At the school he learned to encourage the children to work with their hands as well as their heads, to have their own ideas and to express their preferences, and to take responsibilities in the functioning of the school. He married Joan Serson, a Canadian-American woman who had come to teach English, and they had a baby. The clinically oriented mothers of their pupils approved of the teacher who brought her thriving baby to school in a laundry basket, nursed it, and let the students help with its care. Erikson published several articles on his work at the school, completed training as a Montessori teacher, and in 1933 finished his analytical training and was made a full member of the Vienna Psycho-analytic Society.

With Hitler in power in Germany, Dollfuss in Austria, and Mussolini in Italy, they left Europe and went to the United States, where he became Boston's first child analyst. He was accepted at Harvard where he expected to work toward a doctoral degree, but though he was very successful as a clinician, Erikson was too impatient to endure the classroom, and he left to study Indian children. He was a popular professor at Harvard, but he had no academic degrees.

Joan Erikson participated fully in everything her husband did and edited everything he wrote, including *Identity: Youth and Crisis, Childhood and Society,* and *Gandhi's Truth.* When their third child was born, it was the first room-in baby in Boston.

He has been singularly fortunate in his marriage, as has his wife. Their oldest son, Kai T. Erikson, won the MacIver award of the American Sociological Association in 1957 for his research published in *Wayward Puritans: A Study in the Sociology of Deviance.*

Mystics and Psychics

The attention being paid to mystics and psychics is part of the contemporary surge of interest in the paranormal—in faith healing, extrasensory perception, telepathy, reincarnation, witchcraft, I Ching, extraterrestrial life, demonology, spiritualism, psychic energy, and so on.

The psychics in our sample are Edgar Cayce, Joseph De Louise, Jeane Dixon, M. B. Dykshoorn, Arthur Ford, Eileen Garrett, Uri Geller, Peter Hurkos, Sybil Leek, and Paramahansa Yogananda. As a group they come from the lower classes, although Dixon came from a well-to-do family. Only one, Ford, a minister, had more than a secondary school education. There was little evidence of any love of learning in the childhood homes. They were not voracious readers and they did not like school. Cayce's father and uncle, however, were both country school teachers and were not pleased with Cayce's progress until he slept on his textbooks and knew all the answers as if by magic.

The psychics in our sample were not delinquent. They observed conventional moralities, were often religious, and were more likely to be conservative than liberal or radical. If the special ability comes, as it seems to, like lightning that strikes without regard for whom it strikes, it would choose persons who represent the greater number of us, the working people. There is also a tendency for special abilities to run in families. Many generations of women in Leek's family have been witches. The grandfather of De Louise was a psychic. For most of the psychics in our sample, the child who had strange powers was frightened and the parents were puzzled and dismayed.

We have chosen to present two psychics who have offered themselves as subjects for scientific experimentation—Uri Geller and Peter Hurkos—and also Edgar Cayce, who has the most biographical material published about him. Uri Geller's performance was subjected to controlled experimentation at Stanford Research Institute in Menlo Park, California, and at the University of London; the results of the latter experiments were published in the distinguished journal *Nature*.

Uri Geller. In his autobiography, *Uri Geller: My Story* (1975), Uri tells of a strange happening in a garden when he was three or four. It started with a high-pitched ringing in his ears, then all noises stopped and the trees did not wave in the wind. He looked up at the sky and saw a silvery mass of light, which he thought might be the sun, coming toward him. "This was not the sun, and I knew it," he says. "The light was too close to me. The color was brilliant. I felt as if I had been knocked over backward. There was a sharp pain in my forehead. Then I was knocked out. I lost consciousness completely. I don't know how long I lay there, but when I woke I rushed home and told my mother. She was angry and worried" (p. 96). She scolded him for making up a story.

Uri was born in 1946 in Tel Aviv two years before the founding of Israel, to which his father and mother had come as refugees from Hungary. His father was an Israeli soldier and was affectionate to the boy. His mother, whom he also loved, worked as a seamstress. Later his parents were estranged and separated. His mother remembers, as he does not, how he always knew whether or not she had won at cards and how much. He would say things she had planned to say. He detested school so much that his watch supposedly sympathized with him and kept moving its hands rapidly. Even after he told his mother about the watch and she took it to a jeweler, it still raced, but only at school. The other children and the teacher laughed at him when he called them to observe his watch hands race, and so he gave up wearing the watch. When a classmate's watch stopped, he supposedly told its hands to move, and they obeyed him.

When he ate soup at home, his spoon bent and spilled hot soup into his lap. His mother was annoyed and ashamed of him when these things happened in a restaurant because her friends thought he was clumsy. At school he learned to conceal his "difference" until a secondary school teacher became interested in his special abilities and encouraged him. He decided to use his abilities commercially; with a friend's help he began to give demonstrations and his career was underway.

Peter Hurkos. Pieter Cornelis van der Hurk (who calls himself Peter Hurkos in the United States) was born in 1911 in Dortrecht, Holland, where his father was a house painter who wanted to be an opera singer. At birth he weighed only four and a half pounds, and he was sickly and blind until six months because the amniotic membrane or caul wrapped around his head at birth had injured his eyes. He screamed night and day from the pain of the eye drops that removed the remnants of the caul, which was thought by the Dutch to ensure that the baby would have second sight.

As a child he was moody and would run away to the woods for three or four days when he was crossed or teased. He was not fond of being with people, was a poor student, and once threw an ink pot at a teacher and was expelled from school. He ran away from home at fourteen, but because he looked eighteen, was six feet tall, and had broad shoulders he found work as a cook's helper on a ship. On one of his leaves he married a beautiful Dutch girl, Bea van der Berg, who won him away from the sea. They had two children, and Pieter settled down to work with his father as a house painter.

One day in 1941 he fell off a ladder and suffered a brain concussion and severe neurological damage that since then has left him unable to remember numbers, even his own phone number. He began to have a distorted sense of time, and for weeks he did not even know his family by sight, though he could recognize them by the sound of their voices. The world was a uniform grey, and he was terrified when unbidden thoughts flashed into his mind. When he touched a water pitcher, he heard sounds, walls talked to him, and he covered his head with a pillow to keep out the noises.

When the doctors and nurses said they did not believe him when he told them there was something wrong inside his head, he was angered and began telling them things about themselves. He told one doctor that he had a mistress by whom he had a child and was fearful his wife would learn about his second family. When another patient wandered into his room Pieter felt a sudden panic because he knew the man would be dead in a few days, and he was. He had a vision of his son in a burning room and begged his wife to go home and look after the child; in a few days the child was rescued from a burning bedroom by city firemen.

Eventually, he began to use his unwanted ability to be of service to others, especially to find dead bodies or lost articles. His gift was no pleasure to him. It came sporadically, not always accurately, and often inappropriately. In social situations he antagonized men and women by suddenly blurting out facts they would rather have left unknown. When asked by the police to find a dead body, he could often tell irrelevant details about the person's past life but was not always able to locate the body or person, though sometimes he succeeded.

These flashes of knowledge became such a burden and so embarrassing that he submitted himself to scientific study in hopes he might be rid of them. The terms "psychic" and ESP had no meaning to him and he was impatient with those who used them because he did not understand them; all he wanted was to be rid of the affliction. Too unsophisticated to offer himself as a subject to a research center of a university interested in psychics, instead he subjected himself in the United States to investigation by organizations of enthusiastic believers in psychic powers; they were resistant to his pleas to be freed from what he considered an intolerable affliction. He went back to Holland disappointed.

Reporter Norma Lee Browning, at first cynical about the man she was told to interview, was won over by his apparent honesty and problems and consented to write his biography, *The Psychic World of Peter Hurkos* (1970). After her experience with him she is inclined to believe that there may be persons who have these kinds of reactions after a brain injury. "Is it possible," she asks, "that the remembering and forgetting—the blacking-out of some memory areas and the supernormal subconscious recall in others—was in Peter's case caused by physiological brain damage, a concussion?" (p. 280).

Pieter has no such reservations, and tells everyone he is the way he is because he fell on his head. He believes he died and came back to life with an unwelcome second personality that shares his head with him.

Edgar Cayce. Born in 1877 on a farm near Hopkinsville, Kentucky, Edgar Cayce had not one but many imaginary playmates. As Thomas Sugrue reports in *There Is a River: The Story of Edgar Cayce* (1970), "They were nice little boys and girls, and he had wondered for a long time why other people didn't see them; but one day he found out that they didn't like other people to see them. His father came to ask to whom he was speaking, and when he turned around to point out his playmates, they were gone. They came back after his father left. But his mother could see them sometimes, and it made him happy" (p. 35). They grew as he grew.

When he was seven he went to school, where he was often scolded for daydreaming. Although his father, a farmer who was sometimes his public school teacher, beat him for his strange ways and inattention, his mother, whose own father also had second sight, always believed in Edgar's strange responses. His Uncle Lucian, also his teacher at times, punished him severely for getting the answers to his schoolwork wrong. In desperation he slept on his textbooks and astounded his teachers and upset his father by being able to answer any question about the material in the books, even able to spell all the words in the spelling book. However, this ability soon left him.

At age fifteen he was hit on the base of the spine by a ball, and whereas ordinarily he was a conforming boy he now began acting queerly in class—giggling, making faces, and throwing spitballs—and outside of class doing such things as rolling on the ground, laughing unnaturally, standing in the middle of the road and blocking traffic, throwing things at his sisters, and making faces at his father. When his father put him to bed, Edgar suddenly became serious; asked that a poultice of corn meal, onions, and herbs be placed on his head; and when he awakened later he was well again and could remember nothing that had happened since the ball hit him.

Labor Leaders

Although the labor union is a powerful force in Western culture, there are only two labor leaders among the Three Hundred, Jimmy Hoffa and Cesar Chavez. They have sometimes been in sharp opposition to each other.

Jimmy Hoffa. The former Teamsters Union president was imprisoned for conspiracy and fraud and after his release disappeared and is presumed to have been murdered. His rise to the top, however, is a Horatio Alger story of a half-orphaned boy who made good. He was born in 1913 in the southern Indiana mining town of Brazil, where his father operated a steam-powered oil-drilling rig and worked for one employer all his life. The Hoffas were of Pennsylvania Dutch, German, and Irish descent, and there were coal miners, blacksmiths, and farmers among their ancestry.

Jimmy's mother took in washings to augment the family income, and he helped her by picking up the laundry and delivering it. When he was seven his father died, leaving four children, of whom Jimmy was the second. His mother opened a restaurant and enlarged her laundry facilities, and the children helped. When they made poor grades at school, they were punished by being given castor oil. The girls were straight "A" students, but though Jimmy excelled in gym he disliked school. He was bashful with girls.

At age fourteen he left school, thinking he should do more to help his mother, and his first job was as a stock boy in a dry goods store. After the stock market crash of 1929, he worked in a grocery warehouse and, as he put it in *The Trials of Jimmy Hoffa* (1970), began to be conscious of the "plight of the small guy functioning at the low end of the economic totem" (p. 42).

Cesar Chavez. The president of the United Farm Workers (UFW) and advocate of nonviolent social change was born the second of six children on a large farm in North Gila Valley, Arizona, in 1927. Cesar Chavez laughs at people who tell him to "go back where you came from" (meaning Mexico), for his paternal grandfather was a homesteader in the valley three years before Arizona became a state. His grandfather had fifteen children, and so Cesar grew up in a community where almost everyone was related. They lived well in a community where they were its "first" citizens. His father was the storekeeper and postmaster on his grandfather's land, and he continued to give credit to his customers even when they could not pay. Because of the duststorms and the Great Depression of the thirties, the family had to leave their ancestral home and become migrant farm workers in California.

Cesar attributes the unusual love and understanding in the Chavez home to the fact that he was the child of older parents. His father and mother were thirty-eight and thirty-two, respectively, when they married. The children delighted them. His mother was an impulsive and friendly woman, quick to speak and act, and was always kissing and hugging them. Cesar gives her credit for instilling him with the courage to keep his belief in nonviolence. He said she never met a stranger nor made an enemy. Though illiterate, she had an endless stock of sayings and often reminded him of the Golden Rule, that he should always turn the other cheek, that it took two to make a fight, that if he used his eyes and his tongue and his mind he would be able to get out of trouble without fighting. (Not that he always remembered; once when his cousin swung his cat by the tail, Cesar chased the boy away with a shotgun, which the cousin did not know was unloaded.) Later, when he read the writings of Gandhi and St. Francis, it was like hearing his mother all over again.

His mother never let her children borrow from each other

but said that everything should be freely shared. The UFW staff and the Chavez family operate in the same fashion, living as simply as possible; sharing food, shelter, and other necessities; organizing cooperative nursery schools and medical services; helping each other build homes and gardens. Cesar has tried to live by the ideals of Gandhi and Martin Luther King, Jr., and on the few occasions when his followers have used violence he has been disapproving.

Jacques Levy, who has written the most informative book about Cesar Chavez as a personality, tape-recorded his conversations while riding with him as he went about attending to his union duties, and the 500-page *Cesar Chavez: Autobiography of La Causa* (1975) is written in Cesar's own idiomatic speech. Levy quotes him as saying, "if we make democracy work, I'm convinced that's by far the best system. And it will work if people want it to. But to make it work for the poor, we have to work at it full time. And we have to be willing to just give up everything and risk it all" (p. 538).

Business People

There are few biographies of important business men and women. Is it because the subjects prefer not to be publicized, because biographers do not understand how big business operates (just as they do not understand the work of most scientists), or are there other reasons? Howard Hughes made and lost and made millions again in various business enterprises, but it is Hughes the eccentric recluse who attracts the biographer and the reader. Jellinek-Mercédès is written about by his son, who quite obviously wants to defend his father, who was wrongly accused of being a traitor to his country.

Coco Chanel, Helena Rubinstein, and Elizabeth Arden are among the few women who have made fortunes as entrepreneurs, but the beauty business is a glamourous one and women are attracted to biographies of women. Moreover, each of these three was a poor girl who made it big and the reader can easily identify with her, which is not true of the heads of vast conglomerates.

Only the biographies of RCA executive David Sarnoff attempt to explain the complexity of achievement within the great corporation. The most personal of these, *David Sarnoff: A Biography* (1966), was written by his nephew E. Lyons, after Sarnoff died.

Athletes and Explorers

The athletes in the survey are Muhammad Ali, Lou Gehrig, Stanley Koufax, Mickey Mantle, Willie Mays, James Naismith, Joe Namath, Edson Pelé, and Babe Ruth. Athletic talent, like musical or artistic talent, reveals itself early. Muhammad Ali, for instance, was a sturdy, well-coordinated infant. Joe Namath, although he was very much a mother's boy, had four older brothers who recognized their small brother's special abilities and began training him early. Babe Ruth's talents were recognized by a teacher in the boys' correctional institution to which his parents sent him. Athletes' fathers are often also athletically inclined. Pelé's father was a soccer player. The fathers of Willie Mays and Mickey Mantle were semiprofessional baseball players. The athletes in this sample came from working-class homes, disliked school, and were almost always poor students. Ali is unique in that he improvises poetry.

James Naismith, although he is classified here as an athlete, could also be classified as a teacher. Born in Grand Calumet Island, Canada, in 1861, he was orphaned when his father, who worked in the lumber mills, and his mother both died of typhoid. His college fees were paid by fundamentalist Protestant relatives after he promised to become a minister, but he disappointed them by becoming a YMCA secretary instead. In college he had taken a course on using physical recreation in reforming delinquents, and he tried to use the techniques he had been taught with a group of unruly young men who frequented his YMCA (an idea that infuriated his relatives, who thought he was rewarding delinquency). However, the boys laughed at him when he taught them leapfrog and prisoner's base and injured each other when they played indoor lacrosse, and so he invented basketball. The fame quickly became popular in Canada and soon spread to the United States.

The explorers in our sample are Sir Francis Chichester, Thor Heyerdahl, and Eric Shipton. All came from middle-class homes in which the children read books and had a wide choice of life experiences. Thor Heyerdahl's parents lived in Larvik, Norway, a little coastal town at the entrance to Oslo Fjord, where Thor's father owned a brewery. There was money in the family, and Thor's mother felt she was superior to her neighbors because she was better educated and had artistic leanings. The villagers in turn felt superior to her because both she and her husband had previous marriages and children from those unions. The only child from his parents' second marriage, Thor was given every educational advantage, but he disliked school. Thor was close to his mother, who thought none of the village children were suitable companions for him. Mother and son liked to be left alone and were content to be at home reading and drawing.

At seven Thor drew scenes of South Sea islands and pictured himself being there, and all during his childhood he was drawn toward the sun. After he had done graduate work in zoology and ethnology, he left Norway and for two years lived on a South Sea island and studied the natives. His young wife accompanied him and their son was born there; however, his first marriage ended in divorce, and he later remarried.

Persons Close to Persons of Eminence

There are persons close to men of eminence whose lives add new dimensions to or present the woman's point of view on the political and social scene. Among them are excellent biographies or autobiographies of the wives of famous men: Ruth Dayan, Lady Bird Johnson, Nadezhda Krupskaya, Anne Morrow Lindbergh, and Jacqueline Kennedy Onassis. Several made contributions uniquely their own. Some anticipated the new life-styles of the seventies: Lou Andreas-Salomé, Nancy Cunard, Zelda Fitzgerald, Lillie Langtry, Frieda Lawrence, Lady Ottoline Morrell. Anna-Marie Rasmussen was the conventional housemaid who married the rich young man who disappointed her by wanting to live the simple life; she helps the reader to understand the Rockefellers. Mary de Rachewiltz was the daughter of Ezra Pound. Rose Fitzgerald Kennedy had three famous sons.

There are also sons of famous men and women who rebelled

against being compared with their ancestors: Michael Chaplin, Jan Myrdal, and Peter Reich.

The Underrepresented: Twins and the Adopted

We are aware that many segments of the population are underrepresented in biography—the children who suffer from inadequate nutrition, who come from homes where learning is not valued, or from communities that do not provide libraries and schools. Two other groups who may *not* suffer any of these deficiencies—who indeed may be well fed and expensively educated—are also markedly underrepresented as subjects of biography. These are twins and the adopted. Since a primary aim of this survey is to encourage the flow of able and creative persons into the international talent pool, we should look at how twins and the adopted have been reared to see why they seem to have been condemned to mediocrity.

Twins: Moses and Raphael Soyer. Twins are rarely the subject of biography. Among the Four Hundred, Diego Rivera had a twin brother who died at one and a half years of age. Thornton Wilder also had a twin, who died at birth. Among the Three Hundred there is one set of twins both of whom are in the sample, Moses and Raphael Soyer. Meyer Weisgal had a sister who lived until she was a young adult; Dietrich Bonhoeffer had a sister who lived longer than he and is one of his biographers.

It is generally accepted that twin births occur approximately once in every eighty births, although there are national and racial variations. Twins are a favorite subject of study by geneticists, but we are not aware of any studies of eminence among twins, and clearly they are underrepresented among the eminent.

Twins, especially the second of a pair, are exposed to a greater number of birth injuries, but once that factor is eliminated they are no more likely to be mentally deficient than are other children. Nevertheless, they often come to kindergarten or first grade with verbal and social handicaps. They develop ways of communicating with each other very early which are nonverbal. Sometimes they improvise a twin-language. They depend on each other for friendship, which hinders their interacting with other children.

They are a mild sensation wherever they go, which may satisfy their achievement needs.

As they grow older, they are expected to have the same experience, which hinders their employment, delays mating, and limits their choice of many other activities. Probably the most significant deprivation to twins is the lack of stimulating communication with adults. Since twins learn early to amuse each other, it is easy to ignore them.

If the scarcity of twins were limited to the Four Hundred or Three Hundred, there would be little reason to be concerned, but the count is sparse through the ages. The Bach twins, Johann Ambrosius and Johann Christian, were musicians. The Stanley twins, F. E. and F. O., gave the world the Stanley Steamer. Robert Brode, physicist, and Wallace Brode, chemist, are twins. So are the personal advice columnists Abigail van Buren and Ann Landers. Former New York mayor John Lindsey has a twin brother who is a lawyer. The Swiss Piccard twins are probably better known than any other set of twins who lived into the twentieth century, but we found no biography of them.

Eleanor McGovern, wife of Senator George McGovern, in her autobiography, *Uphill: A Personal Story* (1974), illustrates most of the observations made by those who study the social life of twins. Eleanor cannot remember when she learned she and her sister Ila were twins. As toddlers they talked together in a gibberish only they understood. They were dressed alike. When her twin was not present, Eleanor was intensely shy. She was puzzled when people asked how the twins related to each other. She had no concept of quarreling with her twin. Neither of them, she says, became whole, self-confident personalities until they went through a painful period of living apart when they were young adults.

After high school they were accepted at Dakota Wesleyan University and given secretarial jobs, but after their first year there was no more money from home and they had to separate. Eleanor went to work as a legal secretary. Ila started nursing school in Rochester, Minnesota. Both were acutely miserable without the twin. Eleanor describes her reaction to the separation thus: "I was nearly ill from self-consciousness; and both of us suffered from a numbing, dead-end inadequacy we had never felt before. Our self-confidence had been as a pair, and the cleaving of our twinship left us only half human beings with the other half to be rebuilt" (p. 60).

The Soyer twins, Moses and Raphael, are the only pair of twins in the total sample of 730 persons surveyed in *Cradles of Eminence* and in this volume. They were born in 1899 in Borisoglebsk, a muddy, ugly, provincial town southeast of Moscow. Abraham Soyer, the father, was the Hebrew teacher to the Jewish children of the town and was also a writer of short stories, children's stories, and novelettes after the style of Chekhov.

Moses and Raphael were fraternal, not identical twins, and were their parents' first born. In his memoir, *Self-Revealment* (1969), Raphael writes, "My father was fond of telling what happened when my twin, Moses and I were born. I was sickly and had to be taken to a doctor some miles away. It was frankly hoped that I would not come back since there was another child. I could consider this a rejection and an abandonment of me. Against all laws of Freudianism, I do not" (p. 12).

Their mother was only eighteen or nineteen when they were born and looked like a Renoir painting in those happier days. Both twins remember how lovely she once looked as she sat working with bright wool yarns, embroidering the Jewish fairy-tale designs her husband drew for her on linen tablecloths. Abraham, who was facile with a drawing pen, had a fondness for artistic expression and decorated the walls with postcards and cheap prints of Raphael, Rembrandt, and Michelangelo.

The Soyer family lost its prestige and its security in a single day. An impulsive sort, Abraham had already lost his wife's dowry through speculation, and he had opened his home to students who wanted a safe place in which to write revolutionary tracts. Told by a friendly neighbor that the secret police were almost at his door, he burned the incriminating literature; nevertheless he was told to leave Russia. He sold his possessions and took refuge with relatives in Philadelphia.

Moses and Raphael had been doing very well as first-year cadets in the gymnasia, had read every Russian novel in their father's library, and knew some German and French. In Philadelphia, however, the five older Soyer children were placed in first grade because they knew no English. The intellectually sophisticated twins were humiliated; to be in a class with babies was unthinkable. When they could manage to escape the classroom, they did so, and explored Philadelphia together.

After eight months of agonizing search, their father found a poorly paying job in a Yeshiva in New York, where he was employed to teach resistant boys to read and write Hebrew. It was not a job to his liking, but he could find no other. He rented an apartment that was so small his wife, Bela, said the rooms looked like closets, but nevertheless the eight moved in.

For Bela the sudden move had been catastrophic, and she was never happy in exile. She had long, silent, weeping jags and would sing over and over a Russian folk song about a maiden who wept that she was ever born and who wished she had been drowned as an infant. When her children complained, she told them when they were older they would understand why she needed to sing that song. Still, she was not cross or cruel and fulfilled her duties to her family to the best of her ability. For many years she was hospitalized for mental illness.

Raphael, the younger twin, was no happier out of school than in school. He was unable to accept himself and placed no value on his existence. He stopped trying to perfect his English, withdrew almost entirely from social contacts (even running to his room when the doorbell rang), and took long solitary walks.

His father tried to cure him with sarcasm ("The iceman is coming, why don't you hide under the kitchen table?"), but the technique did not work. It was his aggressive and positive twin, Moses, who led him out of his depression by bringing home guests who were intellectual and artistic, young men Raphael enjoyed and to whom he could relate.

The twins were as unlike in temperament as adults as they were in childhood—Moses was happily gregarious and outgoing, Raphael was content with a few close friends—but they were alike in political stance and in being respected as social realists in the art world. Both twins stayed good friends because they decided in their student years to be two separate individuals. As Raphael wrote in *Self-Revealment,* "Moses and I became increasingly and painfully aware of the special problems of being twins who had the same interests and attitudes, which tended to make our paintings look alike. When the time arrived, on Moses' initiative, we decided to go to different art schools" (p. 57). Yet David Soyer, writing in 1970, said that when his father and his twin both lived in New York they talked to each other by telephone every day and sometimes twice a day.

The Adopted: David Leitch. Another source of useful talent not being adequately used is adopted persons who do not know who their biological parents were. The only adopted contemporary public personalities of whom we are aware are the television master-of-ceremonies Art Linkletter and the playwright Edward Albee. Neither of these men has a book-length biography about him. Neither of them knows who his biological parents were. Among the Three Hundred there were two who were adopted by their stepfathers: former president Gerald Ford and Erik H. Erikson. There were no adopted persons among the Four Hundred who did not know the identity of their biological parents. When Jack London did discover who his father was from other children in school, he suffered a severe identity crisis.

Among the Three Hundred there is only one subject, David Leitch, a journalist who does not know the identity of his biological parents and uses his autobiography, *God Stand Up for Bastards* (1973), to ask his father and mother to please make themselves known to him. He raises questions that social workers raise in writing about adopted children with whom they have worked. In the interests of confidentiality the records are sealed. It would be difficult to arrange adoptions otherwise; the adoptive parents want to be certain that the child for whom they are assuming full responsibility will not be taken from them and will come to accept them fully as parents. The biological parents do not want the child to show up on their doorstep begging for sanctuary when it is going through some unresolved adolescent crisis. The third party in the triangle, the child, is not consulted. Adults who were adopted children are almost never studied.

Adoptive children usually move upward in social status when they are adopted. Someone is certain to make them conscious of their obligation to be grateful to the adoptive parents who, in turn, are uneasy with the mystery of nature versus nurture. A biological parent knows what the unpleasant traits in the family are likely to be; the adoptive parent is on the alert for signs of hereditary weaknesses. When a child bites, fights, cheats, snatches, stays out late, or is caught having sex play with a neighbor's child, the adoptive parents may panic, and the adopted child, even if nothing is said, feels the anxiety. If it erupts into a family quarrel during the adolescent years and "bad blood" is mentioned by a distracted parent, there are two common reactions—acquiescence that leads to passivity, and anger or rebellion that leads to delinquency.

Leitch gives us an insider's description of how it is to be an adopted child. In 1937, eight days after he was born, an advertisement was placed in the London *Daily Express* offering a newborn baby for adoption. Prospective adoptive parents were to come to the Russel Hotel in Bloomsbury for a private viewing of the infant. The man and woman who brought the infant to be inspected called themselves Truda and Paul Griffith. Both were in their twenties. She was a talkative, pretty blonde; he sat grimly in a corner and said nothing. David prefers to think that this man was not his father. The questions Truda asked were largely about financial status. A family was chosen, and the baby was given over.

In his adoptive father's will David Leitch was given three letters written by his mother, trying to make excuses for not coming to see the "dear little fellow in his new booties." Leitch says, "Truda's few hundred words evoked a sense of total comprehension and sympathy I had never previously experienced. . . . Before reading Truda's letters I had not known with absolute certainty, precisely how someone else was feeling at a given moment, and I have never had the same experience since" (pp. 16–17). She was trying her inadequate best to behave decently and was not pulling it off. She wrote as he did when he was trying to break off relations with a woman. "It was clearly only a matter of time," he wrote, "before she packed her grip and headed for the hills" (p. 17). She had promised to come to see him every month after giving him to his new parents.

When he was an undergraduate he tried to find his parents, but succeeded only in finding their names in a marriage registry. His father gave his occupation as an advertising agent. However, David had long considered himself illegitimate and was not able to drop that concept of himself.

His adoptive parents were not happy together, and he was not happy with them. Adopting a child may have been an attempt to shore up a disintegrating marriage, but they remained dull, silent, and apart. Even when they were not fighting, they had the air of people who wished they were someplace else. Even their quarrels were low-keyed. They were honest people, but with limited internal resources and were fearful and unimaginative; they disliked American soldiers, Jews, spivs, and men wearing bright colored ties.

As a young journalist, David Leitch often excused himself for his personal problems by saying he was adopted and did not know what his potentialities were for good or bad. He used his autobiography as a means of advertising his need not to be close to his parents but to know who they were and what kind of people they were. We sent a letter to him in care of his publishers inquiring whether he ever did find his parents; it was returned "no known address."

Knowing very little about the natural parent is said to inhibit the adopted child and its adoptive parents. Subjects of biography take calculated risks; they are the unreasonable adventurers, the idiosyncratic and the eccentric. Adopted children, however, seem to settle for being safe, secure, and commonplace and so are grossly underrepresented.

❧ 12 ❧

Reflections on the Eminent Personality

> *Neither the life of an individual nor the history*
> *of a society can be understood without*
> *understanding both. Yet men do not usually*
> *define the troubles they endure in terms of*
> *historical change and institutional contradiction.*
> *Seldom aware of the intricate connection*
> *between the patterns of their own lives and the*
> *course of world history, ordinary men do not*
> *usually know what this connection means for the*
> *kinds of men they are becoming and for the*
> *kinds of historymaking in which they might take*
> *part. They do not possess the quality of mind*
> *essential to grasp the interplay of man and*
> *society, of biography and history, of self and*
> *world.*
>
> C. Wright Mills

The link between history and biography has always been one of the most elusive aspects in our understanding of the human condition.

The varieties of personalities confronting the varieties of social and historical change have long provided material for poets, playwrights, and storytellers. But only in the last two hundred years, with the growth of the social and psychological sciences, have people tried to *systematically* interpret the relationship between the individual and society.

The usual tendency in social science is to specialize in some limited dimension of either personality or society, although the greatest thinkers have been aware of this limitation and tried to overcome it. Freud devoted his life to probing the depths of the psyche, yet ended his career with speculations about the nature of civilization. Marx devised complex models of the economic structure he believed determined the course of human societies, yet he began his career with speculations about the nature of individuals and their alienation from society. Yet neither of these seminal thinkers, nor the myriad social psychologists who have emerged since, have offered a satisfactory theory of the interaction of the individual with society.

Social psychology, in particular, has limited its perspective by focusing on the ways in which typical individuals adjust to social structures. Groups of college freshmen, or other typical populations, are given questionnaires or run through small-group laboratories, and something is learned of how these ordinary people react to predictable situations. Even the newer and less systematic approaches within this field have made something of a fetish out of studying everyday life in its most banal settings and manifestations. However, the study of important historical situations and of the people who shape them is left to journalists, biographers, and historians.

The present study is unusual in that it tries to apply systematic research techniques to a population of historically *unique* individuals, people who have had a greater than average impact on the society around them. The people we have studied are, of course, not only products of their societies and times but also products of their families, of parents who carried their own burdens and attempted their own creative responses to the world around them. Unlike the "ordinary men" Mills was so eager to awaken, our subjects were acutely aware of this impact. Through their politics, their

writing, their art, and other activities they brought their personalities to bear upon the world. And by means of the very biographies that provided us with our data, their lives became part of
the popular culture of our society.

Our findings can be divided into three areas. The first concerns the family backgrounds in which the eminent personalities
were formed. While no one type of home can be shown to be
necessary for the achievement of eminence, there are certain fea-
tures which occur frequently and which might be of interest to
parents who are concerned with helping children to maximize their
potentials. The second area concerns the personal lives of the eminent, most particularly their intimate lives, as adults. This area is
given great emphasis in the biographies; indeed, a major function
of biography seems to be to reveal the intimate lives of the eminent.
The third area is their public achievement, the work that brought
them fame and that constitutes their impact on society.

While these three areas can be distinguished logically,
perhaps our most striking finding is the extent to which they are
merged. A surprisingly large number of our subjects are famous
precisely because of their skill in exposing their feelings and personal
behaviors. This is especially true of the artists and writers, who
constitute such a large proportion of the sample. Yet, to a surprising
degree it is also true of the politicians, many of whom achieved
fame as insurgents confronting the world with their personal
visions. On the other hand, scientists, businessmen, adventurers,
and others whose achievements are less personal are unlikely to be
subjects of biography.

This finding reflects the concerns of the American public in
the late 1960s and 1970s. It is a tendency that existed when we
wrote *Cradles of Eminence* in the early 1960s, but not to such an
overwhelming extent. In some ways, it presents a disturbing picture
of the condition of our society. We seem to be turning inward, to be
preoccupied with our sex lives, our feelings, our relationships. We
turn to writers and artists in order to immerse ourselves in their
feelings, to politicians in the hope that they can somehow provide
moral guidance or at least hold us together. Rather than putting
our personal troubles aside in order to deal with public issues, we

contribute by bringing our personal issues to the attention of society. This is perhaps more in keeping with a declining than with an ascending civilization.

Observations

The eminent man or woman is likely to be the firstborn or only child in a middle-class family where the father is a businessman or professional man and the mother is a housewife. In these families there are rows of books on the shelves, and parental expectations are high for all the children. The to-be-eminent child, his or her grandparents, parents, aunts, uncles, sisters, and brothers are likely to be verbal, inquiring, critical, argumentative, energetic, and experimental. The family has well-defined, strongly held values. The child who will become eminent resembles the rest of the family but is "more so," and may have manners and habits that make the parents anxious or critical. Sisters and brothers, especially if they are making acceptable, conventional use of their own talents, find it easier to be close to the sibling who dares to do what they wish they might have done. Siblings are often helpful and give encouragement and sometimes financial aid. These families usually share the same abilities and approximate goals—one child in a family does not become an actor and another a physicist. Despite differences in the family, frequent financial crises, and dissension, the family home remains the ultimate haven to the eminent in times of personal crisis.

Children who become eminent love learning but dislike school and schoolteachers who try to confine them to a curriculum not designed for individual needs. They respond well to being tutored or to being left alone, and they like to go to special schools such as those that train actors, dancers, musicians, and artists. They like performing in school plays, writing for school magazines, editing the yearbook, being on the debate team, experimenting in the laboratory, collecting and classifying specimens. They dislike rote learning and repetition and reading the book every other student is required to read. The boys are often disinclined or unable to participate in competitive sports; many have especially poor peer relationships in secondary school. Both girls and boys are frequently socially isolated as adolescents and learn to take rejection and to adjust to being loners.

The eminent may be neurotic but seldom psychotic. When emotional illness does occur, it takes the form of severe depression, during which periods they may attempt suicide or be too incapacitated to function. Their childhood delinquencies are minor. Depression comes rather frequently to those who are tenderly reared in permissive homes where they are taught to reject injustice, discrimination, violence, cruelty, and indifference to the rights of others. When they later have to cope with these problems themselves, they may become depressed or suicidal.

There are a number of handicaps with which the eminent may cope as children: economic insecurity in the home, being orphaned or half-orphaned, having a rejecting or overcritical parent, being a poor relation, being an undersized boy or an oversized girl, being fat or clumsy or otherwise unattractive, having poor eyesight or a speech impediment or recurrent asthma, being sexually divergent, being discriminated against because of race or religion or nationality. As a result, perhaps, they are more self-directed, less motivated in wanting to please than are their peers or siblings. They need and manage to find periods of isolation when they have freedom to think, to read, to write, to experiment, to paint, to play an instrument, or to explore the countryside. Sometimes this freedom can be obtained only by real or feigned illnesses; a sympathetic parent may respond to the child's need to have long, free periods of concentrated effort.

Generalizations about the eminent may be misleading since, as adults, they often become highly achieving because they resist being stereotyped. They treasure their uniqueness and find it hard to be conforming, in dress, behavior, and other ways. Even as adults they retain a naïveté that comes from being open, like a child, to new experiences. They continue to react strongly to stimuli—sexual, esthetic, emotional, intellectual. However, they are not easy to live with, and their close friends have to be patient with their idiosyncratic behavior. They are also much more likely to be divorced or to remain single than are other adults, and they are likely to be inadequate as parents.

Some generalizations may be made about the four categories of eminent personalities—political, literary, artistic, and other. Politicians were handsome, charming, tactful. They used the school as a workshop, were elected to offices, formed clubs, and even became active members of national or international political organizations. Children of conservatives had the most idyllic homes, which is not always an advantage. Among the politicians surveyed in the Three Hundred and the Four Hundred, the most idyllic homes were those of John Foster Dulles and Thomas E. Dewey. Both are described by their biographers as being handicapped in their political careers by an emotional barrier between them and the common people. They could not understand or accept political opposition from those who did not share their acceptance of the existing social order which had been so good to Dulles and Dewey. Children of liberal parents, though they may become reformers or revolutionaries, usually maintain their family ties since parents and children agree on goals if not on the means to achieve them. The liberal homes are more troubled because the parents themselves are more open to change, experience financial stress, are immigrants, or are socially isolated in the community by the father's being a political liberal or an agnostic in the conservative community in which the children are reared. The children of liberals are more likely to become agents of change and consequently are also more likely to become subjects of biography than are the children of the contented conservators of the status quo.

Novelists, dramatists, actors, stage and film directors, all those who traffic in fantasy, remember their homes as having tragic elements, of which they made effective use in their creative productions. Even those who created fantasies of the pleasures of others had and have more problems in their own interpersonal relationships at home and at school, as children and as adults. Writers use those with whom they have had traumatic, emotional relationships; artists use those they observe, as Whistler did when he used his mother, a creative writer and artist, as an unsentimental study in black and white. Both can be callous in the use of other human beings, although artists are less critical than writers of other people. Even when they are in a situation where they may be emotionally affected, they are observant of that which is unique in a human body or in the landscape. The work of graphic artists and sculptors does not require an immediate audience, and so they are able to work alone. They are reluctant to share an intimate, personal creative experience with those who may find their work displeasing, and so they enjoy being appreciated by other artists and are delighted when a critic praises them or a patron discovers them. They are casual, somewhat shy, and quite earthy in their interpersonal relationships. They have physical relationships with partners whom others might consider absurdly inappropriate because of differences in age or interests, and prefer to stay with that partner although they may not think it necessary to be faithful. They are hospitable and enjoy good food and pleasant surroundings.

The scientists are often born to young parents and live in circumstances where they are free to roam outdoors, to collect specimens, to experiment. They are comfortable with their parents, who are ordinarily happy in their relationship to each other, and so they grow up oblivious to the emotional problems of adults. Consequently, scientists are embarrassed by displays of strong emotion and avoid such situations in their own lives. Scientists abhor large social groups where there is idle conversation, gossip, and flirtation. They dislike confrontation but may become very heated over differences among themselves about research, or by a political situation that threatens their freedom of inquiry or communication. They are affectionate husbands and fathers but neglect their families when their work absorbs them.

The Four Hundred and the Three Hundred

The resemblance between the Four Hundred, who achieved eminence as defined by our criteria prior to 1962, and the Three Hundred, who did so since 1962, is remarkably close when the total samples are compared with respect to geographical distribution, love of learning in the childhood homes, strong dislike of school, personal attributes of the parents and the offspring, sibling supportiveness, social class, traumatic vicissitudes in the fathers' careers, and the need of subjects to compensate for physical and environmental handicaps.

There are differences between the Four Hundred and the

Three Hundred in their fields of eminence, although literary, political and artistic personalities dominate both populations. There are more women, more revolutionaries, and more Third World personalities in the Three Hundred and fewer reformers and explorers. There are differences in alcoholism, in mental illness, in dominating mothers, in reaction to the death of a sibling, in the incidence of identified sexual divergency, and of marriage and divorce.

For instance, fourteen of the twenty-three children of alcoholics among the Four Hundred became humorists or performers. There were famous names among them: George Bernard Shaw, Irwin S. Cobb, Stephen Leacock, Charlie Chaplin. However, although there were two alcoholic mothers and eleven alcoholic fathers among the parents of the Three Hundred, none produced a humorist; rather they became writers, politicians, or reformers, and one actor (Marlon Brando). Our 1962 observation that the convivial, pleasure-seeking alcoholic has children who express the same attribute in a more creative fashion was not repeated here. Neither of the two humorists among the Three Hundred, P. G. Wodehouse and James Thurber, had alcoholic fathers. We have the biographies of more suicides than there were in the Four Hundred and also of more people suffering from severe depression. Have we lost the ability to laugh at ourselves, and why?

Among the Four Hundred fully one fourth of the mothers were described as being dominating mothers of such famous men as Pablo Casals, Douglas MacArthur, Franklin D. Roosevelt, and Frank Lloyd Wright. Among the Three Hundred only 7 percent are so described, and instead there are many more rejecting and deserting mothers. The strong reaction against "momism" in the 1930s and 1940s is reflected in the newer biographies in which mothers who once made a career of making a son famous began instead to have careers of their own. The child psychologist Urie Bronfenbrenner speaks to this point. "There was a time when some American families suffered from what was called 'momism'. We know from clinical experience that a child brought up by his mother and only his mother, twenty-four hours a day, is likely to be a sick child with a sick mother" (Bronfenbrenner, 1977, p. 43). He believes, however, that the pendulum has swung too far in the opposite direction. He thinks every young child should be close most of its time to at least one adult who is "crazy" about it. The child should have some day care, some mothering, some fathering, and even some experience with people who are cool toward it.

Bronfenbrenner believes we have made our children feel useless because we never let them do anything much more important than taking out the garbage; they are given little experience in being responsible for other human beings. He suggests that the notion of caring for others be introduced into the school curriculum in the elementary school and that children be permitted to be helpful to old people and also to children younger than they. He deplores the do-your-own-thing ethic that ignores the needs of others—the old, the ill, the minorities. Children estranged from adults are easily drawn into a destructive peer culture.

In many ways Bronfenbrenner supports the findings of our survey. Writing in *Psychology Today* (May 1977) on the erosion of the American family, he notes the importance for children of close companionship during the early years, of homes where a love of learning is passed on to the next generation, of children being needed by their parents, of closeness with siblings, of children's experiencing a "little coolness" in order to be inoculated against despair when they are disappointed and frustrated. Children and adults, he believes, need to be more familiar with each other's worlds.

Factual Findings and
Statistically Significant Differences

Only one fourth (24 percent) of the eminent personalities come from large cities. An additional few (4 percent) come from suburban areas. More than half (56 percent) come from villages, towns, or small- or medium-sized cities. The remainder (16 percent) come from farms. Regardless of birthplace, subjects of biography are usually living in metropolitan areas when they become eminent.

A love of learning, often accompanied by a strong intellectual and physical drive, characterizes almost all (90 percent) of the parents of the eminent. Grandparents and siblings of the eminent often share the same qualities. When the children are very young, parents read to them, sing to them, talk to them. While still young they are taken to zoos, museums, concerts, and theaters. The family often has a large library. Half of the eminent are early voracious readers.

Six out of every ten fathers had a moderately or highly successful career. The remaining four out of ten fathers were either very unsuccessful or experienced dramatic ups and downs in their careers. Those fathers who experienced "ups and downs" had what might be called a Micawber complex. The latter were usually middle-class fathers who were naïve, hopeful, experimental, spontaneous, ebullient, eccentric—all qualities associated with creativity—but who did not fulfill themselves and so their families suffered. Unsuccessful fathers usually suffered from factors beyond their control, such as sickness, job dislocation, forced emigration, and economic depression. The children in these families did not ordinarily suffer from lack of basic necessities, but they did have severe anxieties about their futures, motivating them to succeed.

Nineteen percent of the eminent personalities were first- or second-generation immigrants. The immigrant father often found it difficult to do as well, economically, as he did in his country of origin. Among the Three Hundred in the United States, first- and second-generation immigrants far outnumbered those whose ancestors came to this country before or soon after the American Revolution (44 percent versus 6 percent).

While most (64 percent) of the subjects were reared by both parents, more than a third (36 percent) were not. Of the latter, half were reared by the mother only, the other half were passed around from one relative to another, were cared for by the father only, or found a permanent home with another relative. Only three subjects spent a major part of their childhood in an institution.

The emotional climate in a home is difficult to assess. More of the subjects or their biographers (44 percent) described the parental home as unhappy than as happy (29 percent). The remaining subjects (27 percent) were neither enthusiastic nor critical of their childhood homes and had affection for their parents although they found fault with them. Even those from happy homes, with rare exceptions, found something to criticize about their rearing.

Older mothers, thirty-five years or older when the child was born, account for 16 percent of all the survey sample. Only one subject was born to a mother under eighteen.

Sometimes grandfathers (6 percent) and grandmothers (7 percent) were the major influence in the child's rearing. When a father died, the maternal grandfather often played the role of surrogate father when his widowed daughter came home with her child or children.

When parents were divorced (8 percent), the maternal grandmother often became the surrogate mother. Parents who stayed married were no more likely than were divorced parents to produce eminent children who themselves had only one marriage.

Half of the eminent (53 percent) had good relationships with their siblings. A firstborn among the eminent might become the surrogate father; when parents could not cope, the firstborn often gained in maturity by doing so. The older brothers of girls who became eminent gave them financial assistance in order to help them further their own talents. Siblings of the eminent were close to each other because they frequently had the same skills, talents, and attitudes. Parents quite often got more satisfaction, as do teachers, from boys and girls who were less creative and nonconforming than the to-be-eminent.

Sexual identification seemed to be difficult for girls who had several brothers only and for boys who had several sisters only. They might become sexually divergent or markedly antagonistic to and exploitive of the opposite sex, or might never marry. The sibling relationship is largely unexplored in studies of child development. Within the Three Hundred, we have found, the manner in which siblings related in a given family was sometimes indicative of how the eminent would react in a marital relationship.

As mentioned, half of the Three Hundred were early, eager readers. A few were reading by the time they were three; many others read well at four. When they went to school, their reading habits were well formed and they continued to educate themselves by reading voraciously and were resentful of interruptions in their self-initiated activities by classroom routines. Consequently, school played a secondary role in developing their talents.

Sixty percent of the Three Hundred disliked school, 30 percent spoke favorably of their school years, and the others either did not express a clear like or dislike of school or never went to school at all. Tutors, governesses, and parents who served as teachers were well accepted.

Rejection by their classmates made school intolerable for those boys (16 percent) who were bullied and rejected, usually because they were nonathletic and scholarly and therefore were dubbed effeminate by other boys. Scholarly girls disliked school less than did the boys. Thirty percent of both boys and girls were aloof and withdrawn at school and felt they did not fit in. Of those who liked school (39 percent), most became politicians or scientists. Writers were especially unhappy in school.

Half of the sample had a high school education or less, including some who never went to school at all. The other half had more than a high school education, ranging from those who had a semester of college to those who had graduate degrees. Scientists were likely to have graduate degrees. Athletes and psychics had the least formal education. The overall count is: 8th grade or less (including no school), 15 percent; some high school, 11 percent; high school graduate, 23 percent; some college, 9 percent; college graduate, 19 percent; some graduate work, 4 percent; graduate degree, 19 percent. While they were in the classroom, they did well even though they were not always happy. Twenty percent were honor students. Only eight percent failed.

As mentioned, the eminent come predominantly (80 percent) from middle-class business and professional homes. In some of these families the parents were barely scraping along, in some they were comfortable but could not afford luxuries, in some they were well-to-do and could afford vacation trips and could provide a college education. Fifteen percent of the eminent come from homes in which the parents lived on inherited wealth or investments, or held top-level executive or diplomatic positions. Very few of the eminent (6 percent) knew what it was like to be hungry or to lack money to pay the rent.

Fewer than half (42 percent) became eminent by extending

a family interest or the parental profession. Among those who did were some of the happiest, closest families, especially those who were artists, musicians, or actors.

More fathers (18 percent) are seen as rejecting than are mothers (12 percent). One fourth of the Three Hundred (24 percent) were not close to either parent. Another fourth (24 percent) were close to both parents. One third (35 percent) said they felt closer to their mothers; 17 percent were closer to their fathers.

When a parent died, the child received more attention from the surviving parent, especially if it was the mother. Widow's sons are high in any listing of the eminent. More fathers (18 percent) died before the to-be-eminent child was twenty-one; 10 percent of the mothers died before the child reached its majority.

Those among the Three Hundred who had serious mental illness (9 percent), those who committed suicide (2 percent) and those who attempted suicide (3 percent) were almost all manic depressives. One was alcoholic; only two were delusional. It would seem that manic-depression is the one kind of mental illness which permits an individual to become productive enough to be the subject of biography.

In almost half of the instances where there was a suicide, a suicide attempt, or mental illness among the Three Hundred, the subject was reared after the fashion now recommended by most authorities on child rearing. That is, he or she was raised in a child-centered home by congenial, well-functioning, highly literate parents who enjoyed parenthood. They enriched the child's life and provided the best schooling they could afford. They were permissive but often overanxious and overexpectant, although they knew they should not be. The parents were also highly moral, though not religious fundamentalists, and brought up the child to be responsive to the needs and rights of others. An appreciable number of talented, sensitive young people reared in this kind of home, when faced with circumstances in the larger world of school or work where past rules guiding their behavior were no longer applicable, become frustrated and too depressed to function and even suicidal.

Among the Three Hundred the proportion of men and women who did not marry was the same, 18 percent. However, more women (45 percent) were divorced than were men (35 percent). A striking difference is that the majority of the women (58 percent) had no children, while almost all of the married men had children. Only seven of the eighty-one women were able to combine marriage, children, and a career.

Fifteen percent of the Three Hundred were described as being unconventional in life-style according to the mores of their time. These forty-seven individuals had an influence on contemporary society beyond their number. They include five of the twelve persons who have the largest amount of biographical material published about them: Simone de Beauvoir, Colette, Carl Jung, Anaïs Nin, and Ezra Pound. There are three women among these twelve and each had her own unconventional life-style. Others among the unconventional had considerable biographical material but were not among the "top" twelve.

Among the Three Hundred there were seven women and fourteen men who described themselves or were described by their biographers as being sexually divergent. Two thirds of these sexually divergent were only children or were the youngest child in the family. Of these twenty-one persons, almost all (nineteen) had unsatisfactory, often antagonistic, relationships to the parent of the same sex, and almost all (eighteen) had a close relationship with the parent of the opposite sex. Two thirds (fourteen) were born to mothers who were thirty-five years old or older when the subject was born. This is more than four times as great as the 16 percent of older mothers in the total survey population.

Of the 306 subjects for whom birth order could be determined, fifty-one (16 percent) were only children, ninety-two (30 percent) were firstborn, eighty-one (26 percent) were middle children, and eighty-two (27 percent) were youngest. As in other studies of excellence, the only and firstborn combined are overrepresented.

The statistically significant ($p < .05$) differences between the experiences of people who achieved eminence in each of four categories were given at the beginning of Chapters 8 through 11, but we will briefly summarize them here.

Persons who became eminent political figures had as children positive reactions to the classroom, to their teachers, and to the curriculum. They were often honor students, they enjoyed debating, and they often wrote for or edited the school paper. Only children seldom become politicians; in-between children frequently do. Eminent political figures seldom attempted or committed suicide, had fewer divorces, often had only one marriage, and were conventional in life-style.

Literary figures were most likely to have been only children, least likely to be in-between children. Future writers did not relate as well to their siblings as did future politicians, artists, and others. Homes that produced literary figures were often unhappy; parents quarrelled, siblings squabbled, there were financial troubles, and the parents were more likely to be alcoholic. The literary figures were also much more likely to grow up to be homosexuals. Future writers were bored with the school curriculum and disliked their teachers. However, they enjoyed being published in the school paper and read voraciously. They were more likely than were other eminent persons to attempt or commit suicide. They were notably unconventional in their life-styles and were the most likely to have several marriages.

The artistic figures had the lowest level of formal education, but they had special schooling. Their homes ranked highest in having siblings who were congenial and supportive of each other. They were not voracious readers.

The only ways in which the entire category of others differed significantly from the three more homogeneous categories are that they showed the most dislike for school and were the most bored with the secondary school curriculum.

Among the underrepresented in the total sample surveyed are the twins and the adopted. There was one full set of twins and only two were one of a pair of twins. There was only one adopted person. Also underrepresented are the military, practicing physicians, and scientists.

Biographical Notes

Not all of the 317 subjects can be described in one volume. The biographical notes are included to enable the reader to identify each of the subjects. We have included the area of eminence, the year and place of birth, the birth order, the father's occupation, and the mother's occupation if other than housewife.

The books named are those that are required to justify inclusion in the sample (two books for American born and one for foreign born since 1962; Americans who had one book before 1962 and one since are also included). Some books are listed because they were exceptionally informative. This does not mean that there are not other books that were also useful and used. While doing the study we examined an estimated 3,000 volumes.

The individuals we chose to write about in detail were those whose lives emphasized a given finding, such as the significance of birth order or the love for learning in the home. They are not necessarily the most eminent of the 317 subjects. Autobiographies, more often than biographies, give information about childhood. Biographers who are close relatives are good informants.

Once the sample was established, we felt free to use any source from which to collect information. The books in this section were all found, as were many others not listed, in the Menlo Park Public Library. Asterisks preceding certain books indicate that they are especially informative about the childhood experience as it seems to affect the adult life.

Acton, Harold. Writer. Born 1904, of British-American parents in Florence, Italy. 1st of 2. Father inherited wealth.

    Acton, H., *Memoirs of an Aesthete,* 1971.

Adler, Friedrich W. Assassin, secretary of the Social Democratic Party. Born 1879, Vienna. 1st of 3. Father a physician.

    Florence, R., *Fritz: Story of a Political Assassin,* 1972.

Agee, James Rufus. Novelist and screenwriter. Born 1909, Knoxville, Tennessee. 1st of 2. Father a businessman.

    *Agee, J., *Letters of James Agee to Father Flye,* 1962. (There is no one satisfactory biography of the half-orphaned, gifted, precocious, self-destructive youth, but this volume is the most helpful.)

    Moreau, G. *The Restless Journey of James Agee,* 1977.

Agnew, Spiro T. Vice-President of United States. Born 1918, Baltimore, Maryland. Only of father, 3rd of 3 of mother. Father a restaurateur.

    Lucas, J., *Agnew: Profile in Conflict,* 1970.

    Witcover, J., *White Knight: The Rise of Spiro Agnew,* 1972.

Ali, Muhammad. Boxing champion. Born 1942, Louisville, Kentucky. 1st of 2. Father a sign painter; mother a houseworker.

    *Schulberg, B. W., *Loser and Still Champion,* 1972.

    Torres, J., *Sting Like a Bee,* 1971.

Alliluyeva, Svetlana. Daughter of Joseph Stalin. Born Moscow, 1925. 3rd of 3 of father, 2nd of 2 of mother. Father was dictator of Soviet Union.

    Alliluyeva, S., *Only One Year,* 1969.

    *Payne, R., *The Rise and Fall of Stalin,* 1965. (A better account than the daughter's of the mother's suicide.)

Andreas-Salomé, Lou. Psychoanalyst, writer. Born 1861, Saint Petersburg, Russia. 6th of 6. Father a government official.

    Binion, R., *Frau Lou: Nietzsche's Wayward Disciple,* 1968.

    Peters, H. F., *My Sister, My Spouse,* 1962. (Story of an extremely neurotic adolescent who became a therapist.)

Angelou, Maya. Actress, editor, composer, entertainer. Born 1928,

Saint Louis, Missouri. 1st of 2. Father a dietician and a doorman; mother a card dealer, realtor, and nurse.

* Angelou, M., *I Know Why the Caged Bird Sings,* 1969. (Forthright, well-written story of raped, neglected, gifted child from a broken, disadvantaged home.)

Angelou, M., *Singin' and Swingin' and Gettin' Merry Like Christmas,* 1976.

Arden, Elizabeth. Cosmetics businesswoman. Born 1878, Woodbridge, Ontario, Canada. 5th of 5. Father a farmer.

Lewis, A., *Miss Elizabeth Arden: An Unretouched Portrait,* 1972.

Asquith, Herbert Henry. British Prime Minister. Born 1852, Morley, Yorkshire, England. Middle of 5. Father a minor employee in wool trade; grandfather a manufacturer.

* Jenkins, R., *Asquith: Portrait of a Man and an Era,* 1964. (Scholarly presentation of rearing and education of a widow's son.)

Astaire, Fred. Dancer. Born 1899, Omaha, Nebraska. 2nd of 2. Father a brewery worker; mother a business manager for her children.

Green, S., *Starring Fred Astaire,* 1973.

Thompson, H., *Fred Astaire,* 1970. (Exceptionally well-adjusted adult who had an exceptionally happy childhood despite being a child performer.)

Astor, Nancy. 1st woman in British House of Commons. Born 1879, Danville, Virginia. 7th of 11. Father a labor contractor.

Collis, M., *Nancy Astor,* 1960.

* Sykes, C., *Nancy: The Life of Lady Astor,* 1972.

Auden, W. H. Poet. Born 1907, York, Yorkshire, England. 3rd of 3. Father a physician.

Auden, W. H., *Forewords and Afterwords,* 1973.

Spender, S. (Compiler), *W. H. Auden: A Tribute,* 1975.

Ayub Khan, Mohommad. President of Pakistan. Born 1907, Rehena, India (now in Pakistan). 5th of 9. Father a major in Hodson's Horse, a cavalry regiment.

Ayub Khan, M., *Mohommad Ayub Khan,* 1967.

Azikiwe, Nnamdi. President of Nigeria. Born 1904, Zungeru,
    Nigeria. 1st of 3. Father a defense department civil
    servant.
    Azikiwe, N., *My Odyssey: An Autobiography,* 1970. (Re-
    ports on trials of living in a polygamous, quarrel-
    some household.)
Aznavour, Charles. Entertainer, song writer. Born 1924, Paris. 2nd
    of 2. Father an Armenian restaurateur; mother a
    seamstress.
    Aznavour, C., *Aznavour by Aznavour: An Autobiography,*
    1972. (A happy, cohesive, warm second-generation
    family; parents emigrated from Armenia to France.)
Babel, Isaac. Writer of novellas. Born 1894, Odessa, Russia. 1st of
    2. Father a businessman.
    * Babel, N., *The Lonely Years,* 1964. (Daughter well in-
    formed about the early parental history and effect
    on Babel of his dominating father.)
Bagnold, Enid. Playwright. Born 1889, Rochester, Chatham, En-
    gland. 1st of 2. Father a commander in the Royal
    Engineers.
    Bagnold, E., *Autobiography,* 1964. (Cheerful, unconven-
    tional story of a woman who combined a career,
    having children, and a happy marriage; lost her
    virginity to Frank Harris without appreciable trauma
    or guilt.)
Baldwin, James. Author, playwright. Born 1924, Harlem, New
    York City. 1st of 9. Stepfather a preacher.
    Baldwin, J., *Notes of a Native Son,* 1955.
    * Ecknan, F. M., *Curious Passage of James Baldwin,* 1966.
    (Exceptionally gifted boy born into disadvantaged
    home.)
Barbirolli, Sir John. Orchestra conductor. Born 1899, London. 1st
    of 2. Father a music teacher; mother a waitress be-
    fore marriage.
    * Reid, C., *John Barbirolli,* 1971. (Happy extended Italian-
    French family shares love for music.)
Barnard, Christiaan. Heart surgeon. Born 1923, Beaufort West,
    South Africa. 2nd of 4. Father a minister.

Barnard, C., and Pepper, C. B., *One Life,* 1969. (Moving portrait of altruistic father who served as pastor of a black church.)

Bates, Daisy. Political reformer, self-styled anthropologist. Born 1873, Ashbury House, Ireland. 4th of 4. Father landed gentry.

Salter, E., *Daisy Bates,* 1972. (Innocuous tale of an unconventional, poorly educated woman who left her husband and son to be of service to Australian aborigines.)

Beaton, Cecil. Photographer. Born 1904, London. 1st of 4. Father a timber merchant.

Beaton, C., *The Years Between,* 1965.

Beauvoir, Simone de. Author. Born 1908, Paris. 1st of 2. Father a lawyer.

* Beauvoir, S. de, *A Very Easy Death,* 1966. (Devastating description of the antagonism between her mother and father.)

* Beauvoir, S. de, *All Said and Done,* 1974.

* Cottrell, R. D., *Simone de Beauvoir,* 1974. (Scholarly study.)

* Leighton, J. S., *Simone de Beauvoir on Women,* 1975. (Excellent biography of a complicated personality; clarifies her reasons for rejecting the traditional female role.)

Beaverbrook, William. Newspaper magnate. Born Maple, Ontario, Canada, 1879. 5th of 5. Father a minister.

* Taylor, A. J. P., *Beaverbrook,* 1972. (Severely rejected youngest son is never accepted by his parents or siblings.)

Bentley, Phyllis. Novelist. Born 1894, West Riding, Yorkshire, England. 4th of 4. Father a textile manufacturer.

* Bentley, P., *O Dreams, O Destination,* 1962. (Accomplished novelist writes about her unhappy childhood with humor and compassion for those who nearly destroyed her.)

Bergman, Ingmar. Film maker. Born 1918, Uppsala, Sweden. 2nd of 3. Father a clergyman.

* Bjorkman, M., and Bjorkman, S., *Bergman on Bergman*,
    1973. (Grandmother made his early life tolerable.)
  Wood, R., *Ingmar Bergman*, 1969.
Bergman, Ingrid. Actress. Born 1915, Stockholm. Only child.
    Father a frustrated artist, camera shop operator.
  Quirk, L. J., *Ingrid Bergman*, 1970.
Bernstein, Leonard. Musician. Born 1918, Lawrence, Massachusetts.
    1st of 3. Father owner of hair-supplies company.
  Ewen, D., *Leonard Bernstein*, 1961.
  Gruen, J., *The Private World of Leonard Bernstein*, 1968.
Bethune, Mary McLeod. Political reformer, civil libertarian. Born
    1875, farm near Marysville, South Carolina. 13th
    of 17. Father a farmer.
  Holt, R., *Mary McLeod Bethune: A Biography*, 1964.
  Sterne, E. G., *Mary McLeod Bethune*, 1957.
Bohr, Niels. Physicist, philosopher. Born 1885, Copenhagen. 2nd of
    3. Father a professor of physiology.
  * Moore, R. E., *Niels Bohr: The Man, His Science, and the
    World They Changed*, 1966. (Competent book about
    a competent father and two sons, all scientists; well-
    integrated family.)
Bond, Julian. Georgia legislator. Born 1940, Nashville, Tennessee.
    1st of 3. Father a college president; mother a teacher,
    librarian.
  Metcalf, G. R., *Up from Within*, 1971.
  Neary, J., *Julian Bond, Black Rebel*, 1971.
  * Williams, R. M., *The Bonds: An American Family*, 1971.
    (Richly documented study of an unusual family.)
Bonhoeffer, Dietrich. Theologian, would-be assassin. Born 1906,
    Breslau, Germany. 6th of 8. Father a professor of
    neurology and psychiatry.
  * Bethge, E., *Dietrich Bonhoeffer: Man of Vision, Man of
    Courage*, 1970.
  Leibholtz-Bonhoeffer, S., *The Bonhoeffers: Portrait of a
    Family*, 1971. (Twin sister tells the tragic story of
    her brother and three others in family executed for
    abortive attempt to assassinate Hitler.)
Booth, Evangeline. Salvation Army leader. Born 1865, London.

7th of 7. Parents were founders of the Salvation
Army.

Levine, S. A., *Evangeline Booth: Daughter of Salvation,*
1970.

Brando, Marlon. Actor. Born 1924, Omaha, Nebraska. 3rd of 3.
Father a salesman.

Morella, J., and Epstein, E. Z., *Brando: An Unauthorized
Biography,* 1973.

Thomas, B., *Marlon: Portrait of the Rebel as an Artist,*
1974.

Brandt, Willy. Chancellor of West Germany. Born 1913, Lubeck,
Germany. Only child. Father unknown; mother
clerk in co-op store.

Binder, D., *The Other German: Willy Brandt's Life and
Times,* 1975.

Brandt, W., *My Road to Berlin,* 1960.

Brecht, Bertolt. Poet, playwright. Born 1898, Augsburg, Germany.
2nd of 2. Father a paper-mill manager.

Demetz, P. (Ed.), *Brecht,* 1962.

Hill, C., *Bertolt Brecht,* 1975.

Brenan, Gerald. Writer. Born 1897, Malta. 1st of 2. Father a sub-
altern in an Irish regiment and businessman.

* Brenan, G., *A Life of One's Own: An Autobiography,*
1963.

* Brenan, G., *A Personal Record,* 1975. (Two erudite,
highly readable, intensely personal volumes needed
for understanding the Bloomsbury era.)

Breton, André. Writer. Born 1896, Tinchebray, France. Only child.
Father a small businessman.

Balakian, A., *André Breton: Magus of Surrealism,* 1971.

Brezhnev, Leonid I. Secretary of Communist Party, USSR. Born
1906, Kamenskoye, Ukraine, Russia. 1st of 3. Father
a steelworker.

* Dornberg, J., *Brezhnev: The Masks of Power,* 1974.
(Good description of a classroom in early revolutionary Russia.)

Britten, Benjamin. Composer. Born 1913, Lowestoft, Suffolk, England. 1st of 3. Father a dental surgeon.

Howard, P., *The Operas of Benjamin Britten*, 1969.
White, E. W., *Benjamin Britten: His Life and Operas*, 1970.
Buber, Martin. Philosopher. Born 1878, Vienna. Only child. Father
    a farm manager; grandfather a scholar.
    Hodes, A., *Martin Buber: An Intimate Portrait*, 1971.
Bufano, Beniamino (Benny). Sculptor. Born 1898, San Fele, Italy.
    1st of 14. Father made paper flowers.
    Brown, S., and Wilkening, H., *Bufano: An Intimate Bi-
        ography*, 1972.
    Falk, R., *Bufano*, 1975. (Study of an impossible generation
        gap between immigrant father and talented first-
        born son.)
Bukharin, Nikolai I. Revolutionary, executed. Born 1888, Moscow.
    2nd of 3. Father a mathematician, tax inspector;
    mother a school teacher.
    * Cohen, S. F., *Bukharin and the Bolshevik Revolution: A
        Political Biography*, 1973.
Calder, Alexander. Sculptor, creator of mobiles. Born 1898, Lawn-
    ton, Pennsylvania. 2nd of 2. Father a sculptor;
    mother a painter.
    Arnason, H., *Calder*, 1971.
    Calder, A., *An Autobiography with Pictures*, 1966.
Capra, Frank. Movie director, producer. Born 1897, near Palermo,
    Sicily. 8th of 9. Father a farmer; mother olive plant
    worker.
    * Capra, F., *Frank Capra: The Name above the Title: An
        Autobiography*, 1971. (Persistent love of learning in
        a boy from a disadvantaged, rejecting family.)
Carson, Rachel L. Author, conservationist, zoologist. Born 1907
    near Springdale, Pennsylvania. 3rd of 3. Father a
    farmer; mother a teacher.
    * Brooks, P., *House of Life: Rachel Carson at Work*, 1972.
    * Sterling, P., *Sea and Earth*, 1970.
Carter, Jimmy. President of the United States. Born 1924, Sparks,
    Georgia. 1st of 4. Father a farmer and businessman;
    mother a nurse.
    Kucharsky, D., *The Man from Plains: The Mind and Spirit
        of Jimmy Carter*, 1976.
    * Wheeler, L., *Jimmy Who? An Examination of Presidential*

Candidate Jimmy Carter: The Man, His Career, His Stand on the Issues, 1976.

Cary, Joyce. Novelist. Born 1888, Londonderry, Ireland. 1st of 7. Father an engineer.

> Foster, M., *Joyce Cary: A Biography,* 1968.

Casement, Sir Roger. Diplomat, executed. Born 1864, Sandycove, near Dublin. 4th of 4. Father a gentleman of leisure.

> * Inglis, B., *Roger Casement: A Ghost in England's Haunted House,* 1973.

Cassatt, Mary. Artist, follower of Degas. Born 1845, Allegheny, Pennsylvania. 5th of 7. Father a stockbroker.

> Bullard, E., *Mary Cassatt,* 1972.
>
> Sweet, F. A., *Miss Mary Cassatt,* 1966.

Castro, Fidel. Revolutionary, Cuban Premier. Born 1927, on sugar plantation near Bíran in Cuba. 5th of 7 of father; 3rd of 5 of mother. Father a farmer; mother a cook.

> Lockwood, L., *Castro's Cuba, Cuba's Fidel,* 1967.
>
> Mankiewicz, F., *With Fidel: A Portrait of Castro and Cuba,* 1975.
>
> Matthews, H. L., *Fidel Castro,* 1969.

Cayce, Edgar. Hypnotist, healer. Born 1877, Hopkinsville, Kentucky. 1st of 3. Father a farmer and schoolteacher.

> Cayce, E., *The Outer Limits of Edgar Cayce's Power,* 1971.
>
> Stearn, J., *A Prophet in His Own Country: The Story of Young Edgar Cayce,* 1974.
>
> Sugrue, T., *There Is a River: The Story of Edgar Cayce,* 1970.

Céline, Louis-Ferdinand. Writer. Born 1894, Courbeuoie, near Paris. Only child. Father an insurance salesman; mother a lace shop owner.

> McCarthy, P., *Céline,* 1976.

Chanel, Coco. Businesswoman, perfume manufacturer. Born 1883, Saumur, France. 1st of 6. Father a tradesman; mother a tradeswoman.

> Ganante, P., *Mademoiselle Chanel,* 1973.

Chaplin, Michael. Son of Charlie Chaplin; actor and writer. Born 1946, Beverly Hills, California. (British citizen.) 1st of 8 of mother; 3rd of 10 of father. Father a movie actor and producer.

* Chaplin, M., *I Couldn't Smoke the Grass on My Father's Lawn*, 1966. (Young man in rebellion against being the son of a famous father.)
Chavez, Cesar. President of United Farm Workers. Born 1927, North Gila Valley, Arizona. 2nd of 6. Father a storekeeper.
    Taylor, R. B., *Chavez and the Farm Workers*, 1975.
   * Levy, J., *Cesar Chavez: Autobiography of La Causa*, 1975. (In-depth interviews recorded in colloquial language.)
Chichester, Sir Francis. Solo sailor. Born 1901, Shirwell, North Devon, England. 2nd of 4. Father an Anglican rector.
    Chichester, F., *The Lonely Sea and the Sky*, 1964.
    Leslie, A., *Francis Chichester*, 1975.
Chisholm, Shirley S. U.S. Congresswoman. Born 1924, Brooklyn, New York. 1st of 5. Father a factory worker; mother a seamstress.
    Brownmiller, S., *Shirley Chisholm*, 1970.
    Haskins, J., *Shirley Chisholm*, 1975.
Chou En-lai. Premier of People's Republic of China. Born 1898, Huai-an, China. Only child of mother; 1st of 3 of father. Father an unsuccessful clerical worker.
   * Hsu Kai-Yu, *Chou En-lai: China's Gray Eminence*, 1968. (Excellent contribution to an understanding of the extended Chinese family structure.)
Cloete, Stuart. Novelist. Born 1897, Paris. 5th of 5. Father a financier.
    Cloete, S., *A Victorian Son*, 1973. (Mother tried, he says, to make a homosexual out of him—and failed.)
Cocteau, Jean. Poet, novelist, dramatist. Born 1891, Maisons-Lafitte, near Paris. 3rd of 3. Father a Parisian lawyer.
    Cocteau, J., *Journals of Cocteau*, 1957.
   * Steegmuller, F., *Cocteau*, 1970. (Talented, delinquent youth who was famous poet at sixteen.)
Codrescu, Andrei. Poet. Born 1946, Sibiu, Rumania. Only child. Father a government official; mother a photographer.
   * Codrescu, A., *Life and Times of an Involuntary Genius*,

1975. (Highly verbal young poet tells of living through politically turbulent times with extraordinary relatives.)

Cohen, Elie. Spy, executed. Born 1924, Alexandria, Egypt. 2nd of 8. Father operated a tie shop.

Aldouby, Z., and Bollinger, J., *The Shattered Silence*, 1971.

Ben-Dau, *Spy from Israel*, 1969.

Coleman, Ronald. Actor. Born 1906, Ealing, near London. 3rd of 5. Father a silk merchant.

Coleman, J., *Ronald Coleman: A Very Private Person*, 1975. (Daughter's affectionate account of an admirable man.)

Colette. Novelist. Born 1873, St. Sauveur-en-Puisaye, Burgundy, France. 4th of 4. Father a retired captain of Zouave infantry.

Colette, *Earthly Paradise*, 1966.

* Cottrell, R. D., *Colette*, 1974.

* Crosland, M., *Colette: The Difficulty of Loving*, 1973. (Author's interviews of persons close to the family reveal differences from Colette's descriptions of her childhood.)

Cookson, Catherine. Novelist. Born 1906, Tyne Dock, Northumberland, England. Only child. Father unknown.

* Cookson, K., *Our Kate*, 1971. (Warmly related story of illegitimate, sickly, peer-rejected girl from a disadvantaged family.)

Cummings, E. E. Poet. Born 1894, Cambridge, Massachusetts. 1st of 2. Father a minister.

* Cummings, E. E. *The Magic Maker*, 1972. (A pleasant narrative of an exceptionally happy home.)

Dupee, F. W. (Ed.), *Selected Letters of E. E. Cummings*, 1969.

Cunard, Nancy. Journalist, political reformer. Born 1896, Nevell Holt, estate near London. Only child. Father owner of Cunard Lines.

Fielding, D., *Those Remarkable Cunards: Emerald and Nancy*, 1968. (Story of three generations of unconventional women.)

Davis, Angela. Revolutionary. Born 1944, Birmingham, Alabama.

1st of 5. Father a teacher, gas station operator;
mother a teacher.

Davis, A., *Angela Davis: An Autobiography,* 1974.

* Nadelson, R., *Who Is Angela Davis? The Biography of a
Revolutionary,* 1972. (Written by school and college
classmate.)

Dayan, Moshe. Israeli general, foreign minister. Born 1915,
Degania, Palestine. 1st of 3. Father a farmer; mother
a teacher.

Dayan, M., *The Story of My Life,* 1976.

Teveth, S., *Moshe Dayan: The Soldier, the Man, the
Legend,* 1973.

Dayan, Ruth. Divorced wife of Moshe Dayan. Born 1917, Haifa,
Palestine. Only child. Father a scholar, author;
mother a chemist.

Dayan, R., and Dudman, H., *And Perhaps . . . The Story
of Ruth Dayan,* 1973.

De La Roche, Mazo. Novelist. Born 1885, Brian, Ontario, Canada.
Only child. Father a shopkeeper.

Hambleton, R., *Mazo De La Roche of Jalna,* 1966.

De Louise, Joseph. Psychic. Born 1927, Gibellina, Sicily. 2nd of 3.
Father a farmer; mother a caterer.

De Louise, J., and Valentine, T., *Psychic Mission,* 1971.

Deutsch, Hélène. Psychiatrist. Born 1884, Prizemyśl, Poland. 4th of
4. Father a lawyer.

* Deutsch, H., *Confrontation with Myself,* 1973. (In-depth
story of a troubled adolescent.)

Devlin, Bernadette. Revolutionary. Born 1948, Cookstown, County
Tyrone, Ireland. 3rd of 6. Father a carpenter.

Devlin, B., *The Price of My Soul,* 1969.

Dietrich, Marlene. Actress. Born 1904, Weimar, Sax-Weimar,
Germany. 2nd of 2. Father a soldier.

Frewin, L., *Dietrich: The Story of a Star,* 1967.

Dinesen, Isak. Novelist. Born 1885, Rung Stedlund estate, Denmark. 2nd of 4. Father a writer, inherited wealth.

* Lasson, F., *The Life and Destiny of Isak Dinesen,* 1970.

Hannah, D., *"Isak Dinesen" and Karen Blixen: The Mask
and the Reality,* 1971.

Dixon, Jeane. Psychic. Born 1918, Washington, D.C. 5th of 5.
Father a businessman.
* Denis, B., *Jeane Dixon, the Witness*, 1976. (Intensive in-
terviews with many persons intimately involved in
her life.)
Dixon, J., and Noorbergen, R., *Jeane Dixon: My Life and
Prophecies*, 1969.
Dolci, Danilo. Pacifist reformer, writer. Born 1924, Sesana, near
Trieste, Italy. 1st of 2. Father a railroad station
operator.
* McNeish, J., *Fire Under the Ashes: The Life of Danilo
Dolci*, 1966. (Careful analysis of a complex
personality.)
Dubček, Alexander. Secretary of Communist Party of Czechoslo-
vakia, writer. Born 1921, Uhrovec, Slovakia. 2nd of
2. Father a carpenter.
Shawcross, W., *Dubček*, 1970.
Du Bois, W. E. B. Socialist reformer, writer. Born 1868, Great
Barrington, Massachusetts. Only child. Father a
barber; mother a domestic.
Du Bois, W. E. B., *Autobiography of W. E. B. Du Bois*,
1968.
Du Bois, S. G., *His Day Is Marching On*, 1971.
Dulles, John Foster. U.S. Secretary of State. Born 1888, Washing-
ton, D.C. 1st of 5. Father a minister.
Goold-Adams, R. J. M. *John Foster Dulles: A Reappraisal*,
1962.
Heller, D., and Heller, D., *John Foster Dulles: Soldier for
Peace*, 1960.
* Hoopes, T., *The Devil and John Foster Dulles*, 1973.
Dunham, Katherine. Choreographer, anthropologist. Born 1919,
Glen Ellen, Illinois. 2nd of 2 of father; 7th of 7 of
mother. Father a cleaning shop operator.
Dunham, K., *A Touch of Innocence*, 1959.
Dunham, K., *Island Possessed*, 1969.
Duvalier, François. President for life, Haiti. Born 1907, Port-au-
Prince, Haiti. Only child. Father a school teacher;
mother a bakery shop clerk.

Diederich, B., *Papa Doc: The Truth about Haiti Today,*
    1969.
Dykshoorn, M. B. Clairvoyant. Born 1920, s'Gravenzande, Holland.
    Only child. Father a canal-boat flower salesman.
Dykshoorn, M. B., and Felton, R. H., *My Passport Says
    Clairvoyant,* 1974.
Dylan, Bob. Composer, performer. Born 1941, Duluth, Minnesota.
    1st of 2. Father an appliance store operator.
    Grey, M., *Song and Dance Man,* 1972.
  * Thompson, T., *Positively Main Street: An Unorthodox
    View of Bob Dylan,* 1971.
Eban, Abba S. Israeli diplomat. Born 1915, Cape Town, South
    Africa. 2nd of 4. Father a businessman.
    St. John, R., *Eban,* 1970.
Ehrenburg, Ilya G. Novelist. Born 1891, Kiev, Russia. 1st of 3.
    Father a brewer.
  * Ehrenburg, I., *People and Life, 1891–1921,* 1962. (Rich
    details about a young revolutionary's early years.)
    Ehrenburg, I., *The Post-War Years, 1945–1954,* 1967.
Eichmann, Adolf. Nazi leader, executed. Born 1906, Solingen,
    Germany. 1st of 5. Father an accountant.
    Arendt, H., *Eichmann in Jerusalem,* 1963.
Eliot, T. S. Poet, critic, playwright. Born 1888, Saint Louis, Mis-
    souri. 6th of 6. Father a brick manufacturer.
    Kirk, R., *Eliot and His Age,* 1971.
    Matthews, T. S., *Great Tom,* 1973.
    Sencourt, R., *T. S. Eliot: A Memoir,* 1973.
Epstein, Jacob. Sculptor. Born 1880, New York City. 3rd of 3.
    Father a businessman.
    Buckle, R., *Jacob Epstein, Sculptor,* 1963.
    Epstein, J., *Epstein: An Autobiography,* 1975.
Erikson, Erik Homburger. Psychotherapist, author. Born 1902,
    Frankfurt, Germany. Only child. Stepfather a
    physician.
  * Coles, R., *Erik H. Erikson: The Growth of His Work,*
    1970. (Comprehensive and perceptive analysis.)
    Evans, R., *Dialogue with Erikson,* 1967.
    Roazen, P., *Erik H. Erikson: The Power and Limits of a
    Vision,* 1976.

Fanon, Frantz. Revolutionary. Born 1925, Martinique. Middle of 8.
Father a minor government official; mother a
shopkeeper.
Geismar, P., *Fanon*, 1974.
Gendzier, I., *Frantz Fanon*, 1973.
Ferber, Edna. Novelist. Born 1885, Kalamazoo, Michigan. 2nd of
2. Father a department store owner; mother a
saleswoman.
Ferber, E., *A Kind of Magic*, 1963.
Ferber, E., *A Peculiar Treasure*, 1973 (revised).
Fitzgerald, Zelda. Wife of novelist F. Scott Fitzgerald. Born 1900,
Montgomery, Alabama. 6th of 6. Father a lawyer.
Mayfield, S., *Exiles from Paradise*, 1971.
Milford, N., *Zelda: A Biography*, 1970.
Fonda, Henry. Actor. Born 1905, Grand Island, Nebraska. 1st of 3.
Father a printer.
Fonda, Jane. Actress, political activist. Born 1936, New York City.
1st of 3 of father; 2nd of 3 of mother. Father an
actor.
Fonda, Peter. Actor. Born 1939, Brentwood, California. 2nd of 3
of father; 3rd of 3 of mother. Father an actor.
* Brough, J., *The Fabulous Fondas*, 1973. (Excellently or-
ganized; makes relationships clear.)
Kiernan, T., *Jane: An Intimate Biography*, 1973.
Springer, J. S., *The Fondas: The Films and Success of
Henry, Jane, and Peter Fonda*, 1970.
Fonteyn, Margot. Dancer. Born 1919, Reigate, Surrey, England.
2nd of 2. Father an engineer.
Fonteyn, M., *Margot Fonteyn: An Autobiography*, 1976.
Ford, Arthur A. Psychic. Born 1897, Titusville, Florida. 4th of 4.
Father a steamboat captain; mother a realtor.
Ford, A., *The Life Beyond Death*, 1971.
Spraggett, A., and Rauscher, W. V., *Arthur Ford: The Man
Who Talked with the Dead*, 1973.
Ford, Gerald R. President of the United States. Born 1913, Omaha,
Nebraska. 1st of 4 of mother. Father a wool mer-
chant; adoptive father a paint store owner.
Hersey, J. R., *The President*, 1975.

* terHorst, J. F., *Gerald Ford and the Future of the Presidency*, 1974.

Vestal, B., *Jerry Ford Up Close: An Investigative Biography*, 1974.

Forester, C. S. Novelist. Born 1899, of British parents in Cairo, Egypt. 5th of 5. Father a diplomat.

Parkinson, C. S., *The Life and Times of Horatio Hornblower*, 1970.

Frankfurter, Felix. U.S. Supreme Court Justice. Born 1882, Vienna. Birth order unknown. Father a salesman.

Baker, L., *Felix Frankfurter*, 1969.

Lash, J. P., *From the Diaries of Felix Frankfurter*, 1975.

Mendelson, W. (Ed.), *Felix Frankfurter: A Tribute*, 1964. (Inadequate description of siblings; no description of mother.)

Franklin, Rosalind. Physicist. Born 1920, London. Middle of 5. Father a financier and businessman.

Sayre, A., *Rosalind Franklin and DNA*, 1975.

Watson, J., *The Double Helix*, 1969. (Clear characterization of Franklin as coworker.)

Frisch, Karl von. Biologist. Born 1886, Vienna. 4th of 4. Father a professor of surgery.

Frisch, K. von, *A Biologist Remembers*, 1967.

Fulbright, J. William. U.S. Senator. Born 1905, Sumner, Missouri. Middle of 6. Father a wealthy entrepreneur.

Coffin, T., *Senator Fulbright: Portrait of a Public Philosopher*, 1966.

Johnson, H. B., *Fulbright, the Dissenter*, 1968.

Fuller, R. Buckminster. Architect, inventor. Born 1895, Milton, Massachusetts. 2nd of 3. Father an importer.

* Fuller, R. B., *Ideas and Integrities: A Spontaneous Autobiographical Disclosure*, 1969. (Original, provocative.)

* Kenner, H., *Bucky: A Guided Tour of Buckminster Fuller*, 1973. (Breezy, objective, informative.)

* Rosen, S., *Wizard of the Dome: R. Buckminster Fuller, Designer for the Future*, 1969. (Tooth-and-claw attitude of rich uncle turns thirteen-year-old against avarice.)

Gamow, George. Physicist, cosmologist. Born 1904, Odessa, Russia. Only child. Father a teacher.

Gamow, G., *My World Line: An Informal Autobiography*, 1970.

Gandhi, Indira Nehru. Prime Minister of India. Born 1917, Allahabad, India. Only child. Father Prime Minister of India.

* Mohan, A., *Indira Gandhi: A Personal and Political Biography*, 1967. (Relationship to father and mother told meaningfully.)

Garbo, Greta. Actress. Born 1905, Stockholm. 3rd of 3. Father a laborer.

Bainbridge, J., *Garbo: The Famous Biography*, 1971.

Zierold, N. J., *Garbo*, 1969.

Garland, Judy. Actress, suicide. Born 1922, Grand Rapids, Michigan. 3rd of 3. Father a movie theater operator; mother a piano player.

Deans, M., *Weep No More, My Lady*, 1972.

*Edwards, A. *Judy Garland: A Mortgaged Life*, 1975. (Moving story of emotionally unstable girl.)

Garrett, Eileen J. L. Psychic. Born 1893, Meath County, Ireland. Only child. Parents were servants; stepparents well-to-do farmers.

Garrett, E. J., *Many Voices: The Autobiography of a Medium*, 1968.

Gehrig, Lou. Baseball player. Born 1903, New York City. Only child. Parents were janitor and cook in a college fraternity house.

* Gehrig, E., *My Luke and I*, 1976. (Excellent characterization of a resourceful mother by her daughter-in-law.)

Graham, F., *Lou Gehrig: A Quiet Hero*, 1942.

Geller, Uri. Psychic. Born 1946, Tel Aviv. Only child. Father a store owner; mother a seamstress.

* Geller, U., *Uri Geller: My Story*, 1975. (An unassuming account of his strange experiences.)

Genet, Jean. Poet, criminal. Born 1910, Paris. Parents unknown.
Sartre, J.-P., *Saint Genet: Actor and Martyr,* 1963.
* Thody, P., *Jean Genet,* 1968.
Gerstein, Kurt. Political reformer, spy, anti-Nazi. Born 1905,
Münster, Germany. 6th of 7. Father a magistrate.
* Friedlander, S., *Kurt Gerstein: The Ambiguity of Good,*
1969. (Sensitive story by a Jew about Nazi concen-
tration camp employee who commits suicide when
French doubt his having been a saboteur.)
Joffroy, P., *A Spy for God: The Ordeal of Kurt Gerstein,*
1971.
Ginsberg, Allen. Poet. Born 1926, Newark, New Jersey. 2nd of 2.
Father a teacher and poet.
* Ball, G. (Ed.), *Allen Verbatim,* 1974.
Kramer, J., *Ginsberg in America,* 1969.
Giraudoux, Jean. Playwright, novelist. Born 1882, Bellac Limousin,
France. 2nd of 2. Father a town official.
La Maitre, G., *Jean Giraudoux: The Writer and His Work,*
1971.
Goldman, Emma. Anarchist leader. Born 1869, Kovno, Lithuania.
1st of 3 of father; 3rd of 5 of mother. Father an inn-
keeper; mother a domestic.
* Drinnon, R., *Rebel in Paradise,* 1971. (Scholarly, well
presented.)
Graham, Martha. Choreographer. Born 1894(?), Allegheny, Penn-
sylvania. 1st of 3. Father a physician.
Armitage, M., *Martha Graham,* 1966.
McDonaugh, D., *Martha Graham: A Biography,* 1973.
Gramsci, Antonio. Revolutionary. Born 1891, Ales, Sardinia, Italy.
3rd of 3. Father a city registrar; mother a landlady,
seamstress.
Fiori, G., *Antonio Gramsci: Life of a Revolutionary,* 1971.
Greene, Graham. Novelist, short story writer. Born 1904, Berk-
hampstead, Hertfordshire, England. 4th of 6. Father
a teacher.
Devitis, H. A., *Graham Greene,* 1964.
Greene, G., *A Sort of Life,* 1971.

Gris, Juan. Artist. Born 1887, Madrid. 13th of 14. Father a businessman.

Kahnweiler, D. H., *Gris: His Life and Work,* 1967.

Guevara, Ernesto (Ché). Revolutionary. Born 1928, Rosario, Argentina. 1st of 4. Father a planter.

* Gadea, H., *Ernesto: A Memoir of Ché Guevara,* 1972. (An objective book by his first wife.)

James, D., *Ché Guevara: A Biography,* 1969.

Sinclair, A., *Ché Guevara,* 1970.

Hahn, Otto. Physical chemist. Born 1879, Frankfurt, Germany. 3rd of 3 of father; 4th of 4 of mother. Father a glazier.

* Hahn, O. *My Life: The Autobiography of a Scientist,* 1970. (Excellent example of the rearing of a scientist.)

Hammarskjöld, Dag. Secretary-General of the United Nations. Born 1905, Upland, Sweden. 5th of 5. Father a Swedish Prime Minister.

Hammarskjöld, D., *Markings,* 1964.

Lash, J. P., *Dag Hammarskjöld,* 1961.

Hari, Mata. Spy, executed. Born 1876, Leeuwarden, Holland. 1st of 4. Father a hat store owner.

Waagenaar, S., *Mata Hari,* 1965.

Hayes, Helen. Actress. Born 1900, Washington, D.C. Only child. Father a wholesale meat firm owner; mother an actress.

Hayes, H., and Funke, L., *A Gift of Joy,* 1965.

Hayes, H., and Dody, S., *On Reflection: An Autobiography,* 1968.

Heath, Edward. Prime Minister of Great Britain. Born 1916, Kent, England. 1st of 2. Father a carpenter and builder; mother a lady's maid.

Laing, M. I. *Edward Heath, Prime Minister,* 1973.

Hellman, Lillian. Author. Born 1905, New Orleans. Only child. Father a businessman.

Hellman, L., *Scoundrel Time,* 1976.

Hellman, L., *An Unfinished Woman: A Memoir,* 1969.

Hellman, L., *Pentimento: A Book of Portraits,* 1973.

Hepburn, Katharine. Actress. Born 1909, Hartford, Connecticut. 1st of 5. Father a urologist.

Dickens, H., *Hepburn*, 1971.

Higham, C., *Kate*, 1975.

Kanin, G., *Tracy and Hepburn: An Intimate Memoir*, 1971.

Hesse, Hermann. Novelist, poet. Born 1877, Calw, Germany. Middle of 8. Father a minister.

Boulby, M., *Hermann Hesse: His Mind and His Art*, 1967.

* Zeller, B., *Portrait of Hesse*, 1971.

Ziolkowski, T. (Ed.). *Autobiographical Writing*, 1972.

Heyerdahl, Thor. Sailor on scientific mission. Born 1914, Larvik, Norway. 5th of 5. Father a brewery owner.

Heyerdahl, T., *Kon-Tiki*, 1950.

Heyerdahl, T., *Fatu-Hiva: Back to Nature*, 1974.

Heyerdahl, T., *The Ra Expeditions*, 1971.

Ho Chi Minh. President of Vietnam. Born 1890(?), Kimlien, Annam (Vietnam). 3rd of 3. Father a farmer, court official.

Cameron, J., *Here Is Your Enemy*, 1966.

Halberstam, D., *Ho*, 1971.

Hoffa, James R. President of Teamsters Union. Born 1913, Brazil, Indiana. 2nd of 4. Father an oil-drilling rig operator.

Hoffa, J. R., *The Trials of Jimmy Hoffa*, 1970.

Sheridan, W., *The Fall and Rise of Jimmy Hoffa*, 1972.

Hoffer, Eric. Author, philosopher, longshoreman. Born 1902, New York City. Only child. Father a cabinet maker.

Hoffer, E., *An American Odyssey*, 1968.

Koerner, J. D., *Hoffer's America*, 1973.

Hoover, J. Edgar. Director of FBI. Born 1895, Washington, D.C. 4th of 4. Father a minor official in U.S. Geodetic Survey.

* Demaris, O., *The Director*, 1975. (Thoughtful, well written.)

De Toledano, R., *J. Edgar Hoover: The Man and His Times*, 1973.

Hughes, Howard R. Industrialist, movie producer. Born 1905, Houston, Texas. Only child. Father inventor of oil drilling bit.

Gerber, A. B., *Bashful Billionaire: The Story of Howard Hughes,* 1967.
Kistler, R., *I Caught Flies for Howard Hughes,* 1976. (Written by disgruntled former long-time employee.)
Humphrey, Hubert H. Vice-President of the United States, U.S. Senator. Born 1911, Wallace, South Dakota. 2nd of 4. Father a pharmacist.
*Humphrey, H. H., *The Education of a Public Man: My Life and Politics,* 1976.
* Ryskind, A. H., *Hubert: An Unauthorized Biography of the Vice President,* 1968.
Hurkos, Peter. Psychic. Born 1911, Dortrecht, Holland. 2nd of 3. Father a house painter, amateur artist.
Browning, N. L., *The Psychic World of Peter Hurkos,* 1970. (The author writes as a sceptic who is impressed.)
Hussein. King of Jordan. Born 1935, Raghdan Palace, Amman. Only child of mother. Father was King of Jordan.
Snow, P. J., *Hussein: A Biography,* 1972.
Huxley, Julian. Biologist. Born 1887, London. 1st of 5 of father; 1st of 4 of mother. Father an essayist, magazine editor; mother director of girls' school.
* Huxley, J., *Memories,* 1970.
Isherwood, Christopher. Author. Born 1904, High Lane, Disley, Cheshire, England. 1st of 2. Father a military officer.
Isherwood, C., *Christopher and His Kind, 1929–1939,* 1977. (Discusses interpersonal relationships among homosexuals.)
* Isherwood, C., *Kathleen and Frank,* 1971. (Exceptionally valuable document on sexual divergence.)
Ives, Charles E. Composer. Born 1874, Danbury, Connecticut. 1st of 2. Father a band master, music teacher.
Perlis, V., *Charles Ives Remembered: An Oral History,* 1974.
Rossiter, F. R., *Charles Ives and His America,* 1975.
Jellinek-Mercédès, Emil. Industrialist. Born 1853, Leipzig, Germany. 2nd of 3. Father an orientalist, philosopher.

Jellinek-Mercédès, G., *My Father, Mr. Mercédès,* 1966.
(Story of a son interested in engines, not degrees.)

John, Augustus E. Artist. Born 1878, Tenby, Wales. 3rd of 4. Father
a lawyer.

* Holroyd, M., *Augustus John: A Biography,* 1975. (A shy
boy who becomes a "sex object" because of a change
of costume that resulted from a blow on the head.)

Johnson, Lady Bird. Wife of President Lyndon Johnson. Born 1912,
Karnack, Texas. 3rd of 3. Father a wealthy farmer,
merchant.

Carpenter, L., *Ruffles and Flourishes,* 1970.

* Montgomery, R., *Mrs. L.B.J.,* 1964.

Johnson, Lyndon Baines. President of the United States. Born 1908,
Gillespie County, Texas. 1st of 5. Father a farmer,
state legislator; mother taught elocution.

* Harwood, R., *Lyndon,* 1973.

Johnson, S., *My Brother Lyndon,* 1970. (Naïve but
meaningful.)

* Kearns, D., *Lyndon Johnson and the American Dream,*
1976. (Author believes he vacillates, tries to like both
parents who are quite different.)

* Steinberg, A., *Sam Johnson's Boy: A Close-up of the
President from Texas,* 1968. (About the early years
when his mother tutored him relentlessly.)

Joliot-Curie, Frédéric. Physicist. Born 1900, Paris. 6th of 6. Father
a wealthy manufacturer.

Biquard, P., *Frédéric Joliot-Curie: The Man and His
Theories,* 1966.

Jolson, Al. Actor, singer. Born 1888, Srednik, Russia. 4th of 4.
Father a rabbi.

Freedland, M., *Jolson,* 1972.

Sieben, P., *The Immortal Jolson: His Life and Times,*
1962.

Joplin, Janis. Singer. Born 1943, Port Arthur, Texas. 3rd of 3.
Father an oil refinery supervisor; mother a secretary.

Dalton, D., *Janis,* 1971.

Friedman, M., *Buried Alive: The Biography of Janis Joplin,*
1973. (A daughter who was very close to her father.)

Jung, Carl Gustav. Psychotherapist, philosopher. Born 1875, Kes-
swil, Switzerland. 1st of 2. Father a Lutheran pastor.
* Jung, C. G., *Memories, Dreams, Reflections,* 1963. (The
most definitive statement on his childhood.)
* Stern, P. J., C. G. *Jung: The Haunted Prophet,* 1976.
* Van der Post, L., *Jung and the Story of Our Time,* 1975.
(Jung as mystic and as family man.)
Kaufman, George S. Playwright. Born 1899 in Pittsburgh, Penn-
sylvania. 3rd of 4. Father a manufacturer.
Meredith, S., *George S. Kaufman and His Friends,* 1974.
Teichmann, H., *George S. Kaufman: An Intimate Portrait,*
1972.
Kazantzakis, Nikos. Politician, philosopher. Born 1885, Candia,
Crete. 1st of 4. Father an army officer, merchant.
Kazantzakis, H., *Nikos Kazantzakis: A Biography Based on
His Letters,* 1968.
Kefauver, Estes. U.S. Senator. Born 1903, Madisonville, Tennessee.
2nd of 4 (oldest brother died). Father in farm imple-
ment business.
Gorman, J. B., *Kefauver: A Political Biography,* 1971.
Swados, H., *Standing Up for the People: The Life and
Work of Estes Kefauver,* 1972.
Kennedy, Edward M. U.S. Senator. Born 1932, Boston. 9th of 9.
Father a financier, ambassador to Great Britain.
Kennedy, Robert F. U.S. Attorney General, assassinated. Born
1925, Boston. 7th of 9. Father a financier, ambas-
sador to Great Britain.
Kennedy, Rose F. Mother of E. M. and R. F. Kennedy, as well as
President J. F. Kennedy. Born 1890, Boston. 1st of 6.
Father a mayor of Boston.
Cameron, G., *Rose: A Biography of Rose Fitzgerald Ken-
nedy,* 1971.
* Clinch, N. G., *The Kennedy Neurosis,* 1972. (Describes
the compulsive drive for power and recognition.)
David, L., *Ethel: The Story of Mrs. Robert F. Kennedy,*
1971. (Shows sharp contrast between the rearing
of RFK and of his wife Ethel and a certain few
but important likenesses.)

* Schoor, G., *Young Robert Kennedy*, 1969. (Details of his schooling.)
* Walen, R. J., *The Founding Father*, 1964. (Strong on family values.)

Kenyatta, Jomo. President of Kenya. Born 1893(?) on Mount Kenya. 1st of 2 of father; 1st of 3 of mother. Father a tribesman.
* Murray-Brown, J., *Kenyatta*, 1973. (Excellent description of jungle boy in mission school.)

Khan, Aly S. Playboy, diplomat, deity. Born 1911, of Italian mother and Egyptian father in Turin, Italy. 1st of mother. Father a ruler and deity.
Slater, L., *Aly: A Biography*, 1965. (Illegitimate son experiences series of severe alienations and culture shock.)

Kinsey, Alfred C. Biologist of sexual behavior. Born 1894, Hoboken, New Jersey. 1st of 3. Father a manual arts teacher.
* Christenson, C. V., *Kinsey: A Biography*, 1971. (A female employee describes her employer.)
* Pomeroy, W. B., *Dr. Kinsey and the Institute for Sex Research*, 1972. (A male colleague tells about his "proper" boss and restrictive father.)

Kissinger, Henry A. U.S. Secretary of State. Born 1923, Fürth, Germany. 1st of 2. Father a teacher in Germany, clerk in United States.
Kalb, M., and Kalb, B., *Kissinger*, 1974.
Landau, D., *Kissinger: The Uses of Power*, 1972.
Stoessinger, J. G., *Henry Kissinger: The Anguish of Power*, 1976.

Kokoschka, Oskar. Pacifist painter. Born 1886, Pachlarn, Austro-Hungary. 1st of 3. Father a bookkeeper after losing own business.
* Hodin, J. P., *Oskar Kokoschka: The Artist and His Times—A Biographical Study*, 1966.
Kokoschka, O., *My Life*, 1974.

Kollwitz, Käthe. Artist, peace activist. Born 1867, Koenigsberg, East Prussia. 5th of 5. Father a stone mason, carpenter.
Bittner, H., *Käthe Kollwitz*, 1959.

Klein, M. C., *Käthe Kollwitz: Life in Art,* 1972. (Describes children taught in private school supervised by grandfather.)

Nagel, O., *Käthe Kollwitz,* 1972. (Close, socially conscious extended family.)

Korda, Alexander. Movie producer, director. Born 1893 near Turkeve, Hungary. 1st of 3. Father a soldier, estate overseer.

Kulik, K., *Alexander Korda: The Man Who Could Work Miracles,* 1975.

Koufax, Stanley. Baseball player. Born 1935, Brooklyn, New York. 1st of 2. Grandfather a plumber, mother an accountant.

Hano, A., *Sandy Koufax: Strikeout King,* 1964.

Koufax, S., and Koufax, L., *Koufax,* 1966.

Krishnamurti. Philosopher, writer, lecturer. Born 1896, Madanapalle, southern India. 8th of 11. Father a British administrator.

Fouere, R., *Krishnamurti: The Man and His Teaching,* 1964.

Lutyens, J., *Krishnamurti: The Years of Awakening,* 1975.

Krupskaya, Nadezhda. Wife of V.I. Lenin. Born 1869, Warsaw, Poland. Only child. Father a lawyer before the Russian Revolution, administrator after; mother a writer.

McNeal, R. H., *Bride of the Revolution: Krupskaya and Lenin,* 1972.

Langtry, Lillie. Actress. Born in 1853 on isle of Jersey, England. 5th of 6. Father an Anglican clergyman.

Brough, J., *The Prince and the Lily,* 1975. (Describes intense reaction to social rejection in adolescence.)

Gerson, N. B., *Because I Loved Him: The Life and Loves of Lillie Langtry,* 1971. (Describes how an only girl reared among brothers finds the female role difficult.)

Lardner, Ring, Jr. Author. Born 1915, Niles, Michigan. 4th of 4. Father an author.

Geismar, M. D., *Ring Lardner and the Portrait of a Family,* 1972.

Lardner, R., Jr., *The Lardners: My Family Remembered,*
    1976. (Describes how four sons make similar adjust-
    ment to home environment.)
Lawrence, Ernest Orlando. Physicist. Born 1901, Canton, South
    Dakota. 1st of 2. Father state superintendent of
    schools; mother a teacher.
    * Childs, H., *An American Genius: The Life of Ernest
        Orlando Lawrence,* 1968. (Describes intense love for
        learning, close family.)
    Davis, N. P., *Lawrence and Oppenheimer,* 1968.
Lawrence, Frieda von Richtofen. Wife of novelist D. H. Lawrence.
    Born 1879, Metz, Germany. 2nd of 3. Father an
    army engineer.
    Green, M. B., *The von Richtofen Sisters: The Triumphant
        and the Tragic Modes of Love,* 1974.
    Lucas, R., *Frieda Lawrence: The Story of Frieda von
        Richtofen and D. H. Lawrence,* 1973.
Leakey, Louis S. B. Paleoanthropologist. Born 1903, of English
    parents in Kabete, Kenya. 3rd of 4. Father a
    missionary.
    * Cole, S. M., *Leakey's Luck: The Life of Louis Seymour
        Bazett Leakey, 1903–1972,* 1975. (Describes how
        missionary's son, reared as a native boy, is rejected
        in English public school.)
    Leakey, L. S. B., *By the Evidence: Memoirs, 1932–1951,*
        1974.
Leduc, Violetta. Novelist. Born 1907, Arras, France. Only child.
    Father dead; mother an interior decorator.
    Leduc, V., *La Bâtarde,* 1965. (Contains lengthy introduc-
        tion by Simone de Beauvoir. Describes, in powerful
        personal idiom, an illegitimate girl's lesbian experi-
        ences in boarding school.)
Leek, Sybil. Psychic. Born date unknown, Staffordshire, England.
    Only child. Father a Shakespearean actor.
    Leek, S., *Diary of a Witch,* 1968. (Poorly told; too much
        left unexplained about family members.)
    Leek, S., *My Life in Astrology,* 1972.
Lehmann, John. Author, publisher. Born 1907, London. 4th of 4.
    Father a magazine writer.

* Lehmann, J., *In My Own Time: Memoirs of a Literary Life*, 1969. (A literary classic. Describes a little boy overwhelmed by three older sisters.)

Leitch, David. Journalist. Born 1937, Nottingham, England. Only child. Foster father a business executive.

Leitch, D., *God Stand Up for Bastards*, 1973.

Lessing, Doris May. Novelist, critic. Born 1919, of English parents in Kermanshah, Persia. 2nd of 2. Father a bank manager, rancher.

* Lessing, D. M., *A Small Personal Voice: Essays, Reviews, Interviews*, 1974. (Her characterizations of her parents are unexcelled among the 317 eminent personalities.)

Lillie, Beatrice. Actress. Born 1898, Toronto, Canada. 2nd of 2. Father a clerical worker; mother a concert singer.

Lillie, B., *Every Other Inch a Lady*, 1972. (Inadequate presentation; tries too hard to be amusing.)

Lindbergh, Anne Morrow. Writer, wife of aviator Charles Lindbergh. Born 1907, Englewood, New Jersey. 2nd of 4. Father a financier, ambassador to Mexico; mother an acting president of Smith College.

Lindbergh, A., *Bring Me a Unicorn, 1922–1928*, 1972.

Lindbergh, A., *The Hour of Gold, 1929–1932*, 1973.

Lipchitz, Jacques. Sculptor. Born 1891, Druskienki, Lithuania. 3rd of 3. Father a prosperous building contractor.

Lipchitz, J., *My Life in Sculpture*, 1972. (Interesting but inadequate; too much not told.)

Lipchitz, J., *Jacques Lipchitz: Sketches in Bronze*, 1969.

Lodge, Henry Cabot. Diplomat. Born 1902, Nohant, Massachusetts. 2nd of 3. Father a poet and also his father's secretary, inherited wealth.

Hatch, A., *The Lodges of Massachusetts*, 1973.

Miller, W. J., *Henry Cabot Lodge: A Biography*, 1967.

Lowry, Malcolm. Novelist, suicide. Born 1909, Merseyside, Cheshire, England. 4th of 4. Father a cotton broker.

Day, D., *Malcolm Lowry: A Biography*, 1973.

Luce, Henry R. Publisher. Born 1898, of American parents in Tengchow, China. 1st of 4. Father a Presbyterian missionary.

Kobler, J., *Luce: His Time, Life, and Fortune,* 1968.

Swanberg, W. A., *Luce and His Empire,* 1972.

Maclaine, Shirley. Actress. Born 1934, Richmond, Virginia. 1st of 3. Father a high school principal.

Maclaine, S., *You Can Get There from Here,* 1975.

Maclaine, S., *Don't Fall Off the Mountain,* 1970.

Malcolm X (Little). Revolutionary, assassinated. Born 1925, Omaha, Nebraska. 7th of 9 of father; 4th of 5 of mother. Father a preacher, also organizer of Marcus Garvey back-to-Africa movement.

Clarke, J. H., *Malcolm X: The Man and His Times,* 1969.

Goldman, P. L., *The Death and Life of Malcolm X,* 1973.

Malraux, André. Novelist, Minister of Culture of France. Born 1901, Bondy, near Paris. 1st of 3 of father; only child of mother. Father a businessman.

* Malraux, A., *Antimemoirs,* 1967. (A very personal document.)

* Payne, P. S. R., *A Portrait of André Malraux,* 1970. (A scholarly work, detailed and well written.)

Mantle, Mickey. Baseball player. Born 1931, Spavinow, Oklahoma. 1st of 5. Father a semipro baseball player.

Devaney, J. B., *Baseball Life of Mickey Mantle,* 1970.

May, J., *Mickey Mantle Slugs It Out,* 1972.

Masserman, Jules H. Psychiatrist, author. Born 1905, Chudnor, Russia. 1st of 2. Father a tailor.

Masserman, J. H., *A Psychiatric Odyssey,* 1970.

Maugham, Robert. Novelist. Born 1916, London. 4th of 4. Father a barrister.

* Maugham, R., *Escape from the Shadows,* 1973. (Dramatically moving account of the rearing of a homosexual; high literary quality.)

Mayakovsky, Vladimir V. Poet, suicide. Born 1893, Forest of Bagdadi, Russia. 3rd of 3. Father a forester.

Mayakovsky, V. V., *Mayakovsky,* 1965.

Woroszylski, W., *The Life of Mayakovsky,* 1971.

Mays, Willie. Baseball player. Born 1931, Fairfield, Alabama. Only child of father; 1st of 11 of mother. Father a semipro baseball player.

Einstein, C., *Willie Mays: Coast to Coast Giant*, 1963.

May, J., *Willie Mays: Most Valuable Player*, 1972.

McCarthy, Eugene. U.S. Senator. Born 1916, Watkins, Minnesota.
3rd of 4. Father a cattle buyer.

Eisele, A., *Almost to the Presidency: A Biography of Two American Politicians*, 1972.

Herzog, A., *McCarthy for President*, 1969.

McCullers, Carson. Novelist. Born 1917, Columbus, Georgia. 1st
of 3. Father a watch repairman.

* Carr, V. S., *The Lonely Hunter: A Biography of Carson McCullers*, 1975.

* Evans, O. W., *The Ballad of Carson McCullers*, 1966.

McGovern, George, U.S. Senator. Born 1922, Avon, South Dakota.
2nd of 4. Father a minister.

Anson, R. S., *McGovern: A Biography*, 1972.

* McGovern, E. S., *Uphill: A Personal Story*, 1974.

Mead, Margaret. Anthropologist. Born 1901, Philadelphia. 1st of
4. Father a professor of economics; mother an
encyclopedia writer.

* Mead, M. *Blackberry Winter: A Memoir*, 1972. (Study
of an aggressive first-born girl.)

Mead, M., and Baldwin, J., *A Rap on Race*, 1971.

Meir, Golda. Prime Minister of Israel. Born 1898, Kiev, Russia.
2nd of 3. Father a cabinetmaker; mother a grocer.

* Agress, E., *Golda: A Portrait of a Prime Minister*, 1970.

Mann, P., *Golda: The Life of Israel's Prime Minister*, 1971.

Meir, G. M., *My Life*, 1975.

Meynell, Francis. Editor, author. Born 1891, London. 7th of 7.
Father an editor; mother an editor and poet.

* Meynell, F., *My Lives*, 1971. (Exceptionally sensitive story
of unusually supportive parents.)

Miller, Henry. Novelist, essayist, critic. Born 1891, New York City.
Only child. Father a tailor.

* Gordon, H., *The Mind and Art of Henry Miller*, 1967.

Widmer, K., *Henry Miller*, 1963.

Miró, Joan. Artist. Born 1893, Montroig, Spain. 2nd of 4. Father
a goldsmith, watchmaker, farmer.

Diehl, G., *Miró*, 1974.

Lassaigne, J., *Miró: A Biographical and Critical Study,*
  1972.
Mishima, Yukio. Novelist, revolutionary, executed. Born 1925,
  Tokyo. 1st of 3. Father a government clerk, in-
  herited wealth.
  Nathan, J., *Mishima,* 1974.
  Scott-Stokes, H., *The Life and Death of Yukio Mishima,*
    1974.
Mitford, Nancy. Novelist. Born 1904, London. 1st of 7. Father
  inherited wealth.
  Acton, H., *Nancy Mitford: A Memoir,* 1975.
Modotti, Tina. Photographer, revolutionary. Born 1896, Undine,
  Italy. 2nd of 6. Father an actor, musician.
  Constantine, M., *Tina Modotti: A Fragile Life,* 1975.
Mondrian, Piet. Artist. Born 1872, near Amersfoort, Holland. 1st
  of 5. Father a teacher.
  Elgar, F., *Mondrian,* 1968.
  Wijsenbeek, L., *Piet Mondrian,* 1968.
Monroe, Marilyn. Actress, suicide. Born 1926, Los Angeles. 3rd of
  3 of mother. Father unknown; mother a clerical
  worker.
  Giles, F. L., *Norma Jean,* 1969.
  Hoyt, E. P., *Marilyn: the Tragic Venus,* 1965.
  Monroe, M., *My Story,* 1974.
Moore, Henry. Sculptor. Born 1898, Castleford, Yorkshire, England.
  6th of 7. Father a miner.
  Hall, D., *Henry Moore: The Life and Work of a Great
    Sculptor,* 1966.
  Read, H., *Henry Moore: A Study of His Life and Work,*
    1966.
  Sylvester, D., *Henry Moore,* 1968.
Moraes, Dom F. Poet. Born 1940, Bombay. Only child. Father a
  pathologist and editor; mother a physician.
  Moraes, D. F., *My Son's Father: A Poet's Autobiography,*
    1968. (Describes father's admirable response to wife's
    mental illness.)
Morrell, Lady Ottoline. Unconventional woman. Born 1873, near
  London. 5th of 5. Father inherited wealth.

Darroch, S. J., *Ottoline: The Life of Lady Ottoline Morrell,* 1975.
* Morrell, O., *Memoirs* (2 vols.), 1974.
Moses, Anna May Robertson (Grandma). Artist. Born 1860 on farm in Washington County, New York. 1st of 10. Father a flax grower.
Kallir, O., *Grandma Moses,* 1973.
Moses, A. M., *Grandma Moses: My Life's History,* 1952.
Mosley, Sir Oswald. Conservative Member of Parliament. Born 1896, London. 1st of 3. Father inherited wealth.
Skidelsky, R., *Oswald Mosley,* 1975.
Muni, Paul. Actor. Born 1895, Lemburg, Austria. 3rd of 3. Father an actor; mother an actress.
Druxman, M. B., *Paul Muni: His Life and His Films,* 1974.
* Lawrence, J., *Actor: The Life and Times of Paul Muni,* 1974.
Muskie, Edmund S. U.S. Senator. Born 1914, Rumford, Maine. 2nd of 6. Father a tailor; mother a domestic worker.
* Lippman, T., Jr., and Hansen, D. C., *Muskie,* 1971.
* Nevin, D., *Muskie of Maine,* 1972.
Myrdal, Jan. Novelist, essayist. Born 1927, Stockholm. 1st of 3. Father an economist, diplomat; mother a sociologist, diplomat.
* Myrdal, J., *Confessions of a Disloyal European,* 1968. (Includes description of school experiences of a highly gifted child.)
Nabokov, Vladimir. Novelist. Born 1889, Saint Petersburg, Russia. 1st of 5. Father a jurist.
Dembo, L. S., *Nabokov: The Man and His Work,* 1967.
Field, A., *Nabokov: His Life in Art,* 1967.
Nader, Ralph. Consumer advocate. Born 1934, Winstead, Connecticut. 4th of 4. Father a restaurateur.
Buckhorn, R. F., *Nader: The People's Lawyer,* 1972.
* McCarry, C., *Citizen Nader,* 1972. (Describes how son extends parental values.)
Naismith, James. Inventor of basketball. Born 1861, Grand Calumet Island, Ontario, Canada. 3rd of 4. Father a farmer.
Webb, B. L., *The Basketball Man: James Naismith,* 1973.

Namath, Joe Willie. Football player. Born 1943, Beaver Falls, Pennsylvania. 4th of 4. Father a steel mill worker.

    Fox, L., *Broadway Joe and His Super Jets,* 1969.

    Namath, J. W., *I Can't Wait Until Tomorrow,* 1969.

    Sziknoki, R. N., *Namath, My Son Joe,* 1975.

Narayan, R. K. Novelist. Born 1906, Chennaptna, India. Middle of 6. Father a secondary school principal.

    Narayan, R. K., *My Days,* 1974.

Negri, Pola. Actress. Born 1889, Lipno, Poland. Only child. Father a tin master, revolutionary (killed).

    Negri, P., *Memoirs of a Star,* 1970.

Neill, Alexander S. Headmaster of Summerhill School. Born 1883, Forfar, Scotland. 3rd of 8. Father a teacher.

    Hemmings, R., *Children's Freedom: A. S. Neill and the Evolution of the Summerhill Idea,* 1973.

    Neill, A. S. *Neill, Neill, Orange Peel: An Autobiography of the Headmaster of Summerhill School,* 1972.

Nicolson, Harold. Diplomat. Born 1886, of English parents in Tehran, Iran. 1st of 4. Father a chargé d'affaires in British embassy.

    Nicolson, N. (Ed.), *Diaries and Letters of Harold Nicolson* (3 vols.), 1966.

Nin, Anaïs. Diarist, novelist. Born 1903, Neuilly, near Paris. 1st of 3. Father a pianist, composer; mother kept boarding house in New York.

    Evans, O. W., *Anaïs Nin,* 1968. (Adequate appraisal of the subject.)

    Nin, A., *The Diary of Anaïs Nin, 1931–1934,* 1966. (There are also five additional volumes for 1934–1966.)

    Miller, H., *Letters to Anaïs Nin,* 1965.

Northcliffe, Alfred. Newspaper magnate. Born 1865, Sunnybank, near Dublin. 1st of 11. Father a barrister.

    Ferris, P., *The House of Northcliffe,* 1972.

Nureyev, Rudolph. Dancer. Born 1938, Irkutsk, Mongolia, USSR. 4th of 4. Father a teacher.

    * Nureyev, R., *Nureyev: An Autobiography with Pictures,* 1962.

    Percival, J., *Nureyev: Aspects of the Dancer,* 1975.

O'Connor, Flannery. Writer. Born 1925, Savannah, Georgia. Only
child. Father's occupation unknown.
> Feeley, K., *Flannery O'Connor: Voice of the Peacock*, 1972.
> Hendin, J., *The World of Flannery O'Connor*, 1970.

O'Connor, Frank. Novelist. Born 1903, Cork, Ireland. Only child.
Father a drummer; mother a bookbinder.
> O'Donovan, M., *My Father's Son*, 1968.
> * O'Donovan, M., *An Only Child*, 1961. (Describes rivalry
> of alcoholic father and son for affections of the
> mother.)

Odinga, Oginga. Leader of Uhuru movement. Born 1911(?),
Nyamira Kango, Kenya. 1st of 5 of mother. Father
a tribesman.
> * Odinga, O., *Not Yet Uhuru: The Autobiography of
> Oginga Odinga*, 1967. (Excellent description of mis-
> sion schools.)

O'Faolain, Sean. Novelist. Born 1900, Cork, Ireland. 3rd of 3.
Father in constabulary; mother a lodging house
operator.
> * O'Faolain, S., *Vive Moi!*, 1964.
> Doyle, P. A., *Sean O'Faolain*, 1968.

O'Hara, John. Novelist. Born 1905, Pottsville, Pennsylvania. 1st of
8. Father a physician.
> * Bruccoli, M. J., *The O'Hara Concern: A Biography of
> John O'Hara*, 1975. (Cogent presentation of delin-
> quent and driven adolescent.)
> Grebstein, S. N., *John O'Hara*, 1966. (Good chronology of
> peripatetic writer.)

O'Keeffe, Georgia. Artist. Born 1887, Sun Prairie, Wisconsin. 2nd
of 7. Father a farmer.
> Amon Carter Museum of Western Art, *Georgia O'Keeffe*,
> 1966.
> O'Keeffe, G., *Georgia O'Keeffe*, 1976. (Describes pleasant,
> artistic family.)

Olivier, Laurence K. Actor. Born 1907, Dorking, near London.
3rd of 3. Father an Anglican clergyman.
> Cottrell, J., *Laurence Olivier*, 1975.
> Gourlay, L., *Olivier*, 1974.

Onassis, Jacqueline Kennedy. Widow of President John F. Kennedy. Born 1929, Southampton, New York. 1st of 2 of father; 1st of 4 of mother. Father a stockbroker.

Gallagher, M. B., *My Life with Jacqueline Kennedy*, 1969.

Thayer, M., *Jacqueline Kennedy: The White House Years*, 1971.

Patterson, Eleanor Medill (Cissy). Publisher. Born 1881, Chicago. 2nd of 2. Father *Chicago Tribune* editor.

Healy, P. F., *Cissy: The Biography of Eleanor M. "Cissy" Patterson*, 1966. (Describes a girl who was jealous of her brother and male cousin.)

Hoge, A. A., *Cissy Patterson*, 1966.

Paul VI. Head of Roman Catholic Church. Born 1897, Concesio, Italy. 4th of 4(?). Father a farmer.

Hatch, A., *Pope Paul VI*, 1966.

Pearson, Drew. Journalist. Born 1897, Evanston, Illinois. 1st of 4. Father a college professor, chautauqua organizer.

Klurfeld, H., *Behind the Lines: The World of Drew Pearson*, 1968.

Pilat, O. R. *Drew Pearson: An Unauthorized Biography*, 1973. (Describes an aggressive, useful, oldest child.)

Pelé, Edson. Soccer player. Born 1940, Três Coracões, Brazil. 1st of 4. Father a soccer player, postal employee.

Kowet, D., *Pelé*, 1976.

Piaf, Edith. Singer. Born 1915, Paris. 1 of 17 of father (all illegitimate); 1st of mother. Father an acrobat; mother a singer.

Berteaut, S., *Piaf*, 1972.

Plath, Sylvia. Poet, suicide. Born 1932, Boston. 1st of 2. Father a college professor; mother a business school instructor.

   * Butscher, E., *Sylvia Plath: Method and Madness*, 1976. (Interesting, detailed, serious study, but did not interview people closest to subject; confuses Unitarianism with Protestant fundamentalism.)

   * Plath, S., *Letters Home: Correspondence, 1950–1963*, 1975. (Sensitively edited by A. S. Plath.)

Steiner, N. H., *A Closer Look at Ariel: A Memory of Sylvia Plath*, 1972. (Introduction by George Slade.)

Pollock, Jackson. Artist. Born 1912, on sheep ranch in Cody,
Wyoming. 5th of 5. Father and mother ranchers.

> Friedman, B. H. *Jackson Pollock: Energy Made Visible*,
> 1972.
>
> O'Connor, F. V., *Jackson Pollock*, 1967.

Porter, Cole. Composer. Born 1891, Peru, Indiana. Only child.
Father a pharmacist.

> Eells, G., *The Life That Late He Led: A Biography of Cole
> Porter*, 1967. (Describes extremely mother-domin-
> ated and rejected child.)
>
> Kimball, R. (Compiler), *Cole: A Biographical Essay by
> Brendan Gill*, 1971.

Pound, Ezra L. Poet. Born 1885, Hailey, Idaho. Only child. Father
manager of land office.

> * Kenner, H., *The Pound Era*, 1971.
>
> * Rachewiltz, M. de, *Discretions*, 1971.
>
> * Reck, M., *Ezra Pound: A Close-up*, 1967. (Well
> organized.)

Priestley, John Boynton. Novelist. Born 1894, Bradford, West
Riding, England. Only child. Father a teacher.

> Cooper, S. J., *J. B. Priestley: Portrait of an Author*, 1970.

Pritchett, Victor Sawdon. Novelist. Born 1900, Ipswich, East
Suffolk, England. 1st of 4. Father a shopwalker,
stationer, needlework manufacturer; mother a
saleswoman.

> * Pritchett, V. S., *A Cab at the Door: A Memoir*, 1968.
> (Valuable contribution to understanding the family.)
>
> Pritchett, V. S., *Midnight Oil*, 1972.

Quinn, Anthony. Actor. Born 1915, of Irish father and Mexican
mother in Chihuahua, Mexico. Only child. Father a
camera man, revolutionary; mother a house maid.

> Quinn, A., *The Original Sin: A Self-Portrait*, 1972.

Quisling, Vidkun. Norwegian politician, Nazi collaborator, executed. Born 1887, Fryesdal, Norway. 1st of 4.
Father a pastor.

> Hayes, P. M., *Quisling: The Career and Political Ideas of
> Vidkun Quisling, 1887–1945*, 1972. (Childhood
> experiences effectively described; many interviews.)

Rachewiltz, Mary de. Daughter of poet Ezra Pound. Born 1925,
        of expatriate American parents in Bressanone, Italy.
        Only child. Father a poet; mother a concert violinist.
    * Rachewiltz, M. de, *Discretions,* 1971. (Poetic, insightful
        story of relationship between illegitimate daughter
        and famous father she seldom saw.)
Radclyffe-Hall, Marguerite. Novelist. Born 1880, Westcliff, near
        Bournemouth, England. Only child. Father inherited
        wealth, poet.
    Dickson, L., *Radclyffe-Hall at the Well of Loneliness: A
        Sapphic Chronicle,* 1975.
Rasmussen, Anna-Marie. Married Steven Clark Rockefeller. Born
        1938, Borya Island, Norway. 1st of 2. Father a
        country store owner.
    Rasmussen, A.-M. *There Was Once a Time,* 1975.
Reagan, Ronald. Governor of California, actor. Born 1911, Tam-
        pico, Illinois. 2nd of 2. Father a shoe salesman;
        mother a saleswoman.
    Boyarsky, B., *The Rise of Ronald Reagan,* 1968.
    Brown, E. G., *Reagan: The Political Chameleon,* 1976.
Reich, Peter. Son of psychotherapist Wilhelm Reich. Born 1944,
        New York City. 3rd of father; 1st of mother. Father
        a psychiatrist; mother a medical researcher.
Reich, Wilhelm. Psychotherapist, author. Born 1897, Dobrzynica,
        Austria. 1st of 2. Father a wealthy farmer.
    Greenfield, J., *Wilhelm Reich vs. the USA,* 1974.
    * Reich, I. O., *Wilhelm Reich: A Personal Biography,* 1969.
    * Reich, P., *A Book of Dreams,* 1973. (A difficult story well
        told; unusual circumstances.)
    * Rycroft, C., *Wilhelm Reich,* 1971.
Renault, Louis. Industrialist. Born 1887, Paris. 4th of 6. Father a
        wealthy businessman.
    Rhodes, A., *Louis Renault: A Biography,* 1969.
Renoir, Auguste. Artist. Born 1841, Limoges, France. 2nd of 5.
        Father a tailor.
Renoir, Jean. Film director. Born 1894, Paris. 2nd of 3. Father an
        artist.
    Bazin, A., *Jean Renoir,* 1973.

Bosman, A., *Pierre-Auguste Renoir,* 1962.

* Renoir, J., *Renoir, My Father,* 1962. (Unusually well written.)

Richtofen, Manfred von. Aviator. Born 1892, Breslau, Germany. 2nd of 4. Father a soldier.

Burrows, W. E., *Richtofen: A True History of the Red Baron,* 1969.

Richtofen, M. von., *The Red Baron,* 1969.

Riou, Roger. Priest, political reformer. Born 1909, Le Havre, France. 3rd of father; only child of mother. Father a cook; mother a maid.

* Riou, R., *The Island of My Life: From Petty Crime to Priestly Mission,* 1975. (Excellent story of rehabilitation of a delinquent.)

Robeson, Paul. Singer, actor. Born 1898, Princeton, New Jersey. 5th of 5. Father a minister; mother a school teacher.

Gilliam, D. B., *Paul Robeson: All American,* 1976.

Hamilton, V., *Paul Robeson: The Life and Times of a Free Black Man,* 1974.

Robinson, Edward G. Actor. Born 1893, Bucharest, Romania. 5th of 6. Father a building contractor, businessman.

Robinson, E. G., with Spigelgas, L., *All My Yesterdays,* 1973.

Roethke, Theodore. Poet. Born 1908, Saginaw, Michigan. 1st of 2. Father a florist.

Malkoff, K., *Theodore Roethke: An Introduction to His Poetry,* 1966.

* Seager, A., *The Glass House: The Life of Theodore Roethke,* 1968. (Sympathetic story of recurrent mental illness.)

Rubinstein, Arthur. Pianist. Born 1886, Lodz, Poland. 7th of 7. Father an accountant after own business failed.

* Rubinstein, A., *My Young Years,* 1973. (Describes amusing yet often lonely years of musical prodigy sent to live in lodgings.)

Rubinstein, Helena. Businesswoman, cosmetics manufacturer. Born 1870, Krakow, Poland. 1st of 8. Father a merchant.

O'Higgins, P., *Madame: An Intimate Biography of Helena Rubinstein*, 1971.

Ruth, George Herman (Babe). Baseball player. Born 1895, Baltimore, Maryland. 1st of 8. Father a saloon keeper; mother worked with father.

Creamer, R. W., *Babe: The Legend Comes to Life—A Look at the Life and Times of George Herman Ruth*, 1974. (Describes delinquent, severely rejected boy.)

Ruth, C. M., *The Babe and I*, 1959.

Sachs, Maurice. Writer, executed by Nazis as spy. Born 1906, Paris. Only child. Father lived off wealthy women.

* Sachs, M., *Witches' Sabbath*, 1964. (Brilliant, cynical autobiography of a homosexual.)

Sackville-West, Vita. Novelist. Born 1882, Knole estate, England. Only child. Father a country gentleman.

Nicolson, N., *Portrait of a Marriage*, 1973. (Excellent study of lesbian mother, inadequate study of homosexual father, by their oldest son.)

Saint-Exupéry, Antoine de. Author, aviator. Born 1900, Lyons, France. 3rd of 5. Father an insurance inspector.

Cate, C., *Antoine de Saint-Exupéry*, 1970.

* Saint-Exupéry, A., *Airman's Odyssey*, 1942. (Describes doubly rejected son.)

Sarnoff, David. Chairman of RCA. Born 1891, Uzlian, Russia. 1st of 5. Father a housepainter, paperhanger.

* Lyons, E., *David Sarnoff: A Biography*, 1966.

Tebbel, J. W., *David Sarnoff: Putting Electrons to Work*, 1963.

Sartre, Jean-Paul. Philosopher, author. Born 1905, Paris. Only child. Father a naval officer (died 1907).

Beauvoir, S. de. *The Prime of Life*, 1962.

* Sartre, J.-P. *Les Mots*, 1964. (Describes the first ten years of an immensely hurt boy; a literary classic.)

* Thody, P., *Sartre: A Biographical Introduction*, 1971.

Schoenberg, Arnold. Composer. Born 1874, Vienna. One of several children. Father a shoe shop owner.

Reich, W., *Schoenberg: A Critical Biography*, 1971.

Selassie, Haile. Emperor of Ethiopia. Born 1892, Ejarsa Gora,
Ethiopia. Only child of mother. Father a politician,
soldier.

> Mosley, L. *Haile Selassie: The Conquering Lion*, 1964.

Shankar, Ravi. Musician, composer. Born 1920, Benares, India.
4th of 4. Father a statesman, scholar.

> Shankar, R., *My Music, My Life*, 1968. (Introduction by
> Y. Menuhin.)

Shipton, Eric Earle. Mountaineer, diplomat. Born 1907, Ceylon. 2nd
of 2. Father a tea planter (died 1909).

> Shipton, E. E., *That Untravelled World: An Autobiography*,
> 1969.

Simenon, Georges. Novelist. Born 1903, Liège, France. 1st of 2.
Father a railroad clerk; mother a saleswoman.

> * Simenon, G., *Letter to My Mother*, 1976. (Bitterly honest
> appraisal of a mother and, incidentally, a father by a
> son who disliked her as much as she disliked him.)
> * Simenon, G., *When I Was Old: Simenon on Simenon*,
> 1971.

Sinatra, Frank. Singer, actor. Born 1915, Hoboken, New Jersey.
Only child. Father a bartender, boilermaker; mother
a ward worker.

> Shaw, A., *Sinatra: Twentieth-Century Romantic*, 1968.
> Wilson, E., *Sinatra: An Unauthorized Biography*, 1976.

Sinclair, Upton B. Novelist, social reformer. Born 1878, Baltimore,
Maryland. Only child. Father a whiskey and straw
hat salesman.

> Harris, L. A., *Upton Sinclair: American Rebel*, 1975.
> Sinclair, U. B., *The Autobiography of Upton Sinclair*, 1962.
> Yoder, J. A., *Upton Sinclair*, 1975.

Singer, Isaac Bashevis. Writer. Born 1904, Radzymin, Russia. 4th
of 4. Father a rabbi.

> Buchen, I. H., *Isaac Bashevis Singer and the Eternal Past*,
> 1968.
> * Singer, I. B., *In My Father's Court*, 1969. (A literary
> classic; unforgettable tale of a failure-prone father
> and his devoted wife.)

Sloan, John. Artist. Born 1871, Lock Haven, Pennsylvania. 1st of
    3. Father a cabinetmaker.
    Goodrich, L., *John Sloan, 1871–1951,* 1952.
    St. John, B., *John Sloan,* 1971.
Solzhenitsyn, Alesandr. Novelist. Born 1918, Kislovodsk, USSR.
    Only child. Father a student, soldier; mother a
    stenographer.
    * Reshetovskaia, N. A., *Sanya: My Life with Alesandr
    Solzhenitsyn,* 1975. (The author, a secondary school
    classmate, remarried Solzhenitsyn's first wife when
    she thought him dead; gives the best account of his
    early years.)
    Solzhenitsyn, A., *Solzhenitsyn: A Pictorial Autobiography,*
    1974.
Soyer, Moses. Artist. Born 1899, Borisoglebsk, Russia. 1st of 6
    (twin). Father a teacher, writer.
Soyer, Raphael. Artist. Born 1899, Borisoglebsk, Russia. 2nd of 6
    (twin). Father a teacher, writer.
    Soyer, R., *Moses Soyer,* 1970.
    * Soyer, R., *Self-Revealment: A Memoir,* 1969. (Writes as
    well as, or better than, he paints; insightful.)
Steichen, Edward. Photographer. Born 1879, Luxembourg. 1st of
    2. Father a miner; mother a milliner.
    Steichen, E., *A Life in Photography,* 1963.
    Steichen, P., *My Connemara,* 1969.
Steinbeck, John. Novelist. Born 1902, Salinas, California. 3rd of 4.
    Father a county treasurer, flour mill manager;
    mother a teacher.
    O'Connor, R., *John Steinbeck,* 1970.
    Steinbeck, E., and Wallsten, R. (Eds.), *Steinbeck: A Life
    in Letters,* 1975.
    Valjean, N., *John Steinbeck, the Errant Knight: An Intimate
    Biography of His California Years,* 1975.
Strachey, Lytton. Biographer. Born 1880, Clapham Commons,
    England. 11th of 13. Father a meteorologist.
    * Holroyd, M., *Lytton Strachey: A Critical Biography,*
    1968. (A monumental two-volume work; necessary
    reading for understanding the Bloomsbury group
    and its influence.)

Sukarno. President of Indonesia. Born 1901, Surabaja, Java. 2nd
    of 2. Father a teacher; mother a temple maiden
    (scrubwoman).
    Legge, J. D., *Sukarno: A Political Biography*, 1972.
    Sukarno (as told to C. Adams), *Sukarno: An Autobiography*, 1965.
Suyin, Han. Author, physician. Born 1917, Peking. 2nd of 4.
    Father a scholar, engineer.
    Suyin, H., *A Many Splendored Thing*, 1952.
    Suyin, H., *A Mortal Flower*, 1966.
    Suyin, H., *The Crippled Tree*, 1965.
Taylor, Elizabeth. Actress. Born 1932, of American parents in
    London. 2nd of 2. Father an art dealer; mother an
    actress.
    Sheppard, D., *Elizabeth: The Life of Elizabeth Taylor*,
    1974.
    Waterbury, R., *Elizabeth Taylor*, 1964.
Teilhard de Chardin. Theologian, paleontologist, philosopher. Born
    1881, House of Sarcenat, Orcines, France. 1st of 7.
    Father a scholar, inherited wealth.
    Cuénot, C., *Teilhard de Chardin: A Biographical Study*,
    1965.
Thomas, Norman. Socialist politician. Born 1884, Marion, Ohio.
    1st of 6. Father a Presbyterian minister.
    * Fleischman, H., *Norman Thomas: A Biography*, 1964.
    Johnpoll, B. K., *Pacifist's Progress: Norman Thomas and
    the Decline of American Socialism*, 1970.
    Seidler, M. B., *Norman Thomas: Respectable Rebel*, 1967.
Thompson, Dorothy. Journalist. Born 1894, Lancaster, New York.
    1st of 3. Father a Methodist minister; mother a
    church organist.
    * Sanders, M. K., *Dorothy Thompson: A Legend in Her
    Time*, 1963.
    Sheean, V., *Dorothy and Red*, 1963.
Thurber, James. Humorist. Born 1894, Columbus, Ohio. 2nd of 2.
    Father secretary of Ohio Republican Executive
    Committee.
    Bernstein, B., *Thurber: A Biography*, 1975.

Morsberger, R. E., *James Thurber,* 1964.

Tobias, R. C., *The Art of James Thurber,* 1969.

Tillich, Paul. Theologian, educator. Born 1886, Starzeddel, Prussia. 1st of 3. Father a Lutheran minister.

May, R., *Paulus: Reminiscences of a Friendship,* 1973.

Tillich, H., *From Time to Time,* 1973.

Tillich, H., *From Place to Place: Travels with Paul Tillich and Without Paul Tillich,* 1976.

Trudeau, Pierre Elliott. Prime Minister of Canada. Born 1919, Montreal. 1st of 3. Father owner of gas stations.

Newman, P. C., *A Nation Divided: Canada and the Coming of Pierre Trudeau,* 1969.

Stewart, W., *Trudeau in Power,* 1971.

Ulam, Stanislaw M. Mathematician. Born 1909, in Lwów, Poland. 1st of 3. Father a lawyer.

Ulam, S. M., *Adventures of a Mathematician,* 1976.

Ustinov, Peter. Actor. Born 1921, London. Only child. Father a distinguished journalist; mother an artist.

* Ustinov, N. B., *Klop and the Ustinov Family,* 1973. (Perceptive work by talented artist married to talented journalist and mother of famous actor and producer; foreword by her son.)

Utrillo, Maurice. Artist. Born 1883, Paris. Only child. Father unknown; mother an artist.

De Polnay, P., *Enfant Terrible: The Life and World of Maurice Utrillo,* 1969.

Varèse, Edgard. Composer. Born 1883, Paris. 1st of 5. Father a businessman.

Ouellette, F., *Edgard Varèse,* 1968.

* Varèse, L. M., *Varèse: A Looking Glass Diary,* 1972. (Describes intensely troubled childhood.)

Vining, Elizabeth Grey. Author. Born 1902, Philadelphia. 2nd of 2. Father an X-ray equipment manufacturer.

* Vining, E. G., *Quiet Pilgrimage,* 1970. (Describes how three women in one household struggle to use their talents.)

Vining, E. G., *Windows for the Crown Prince,* 1952.

Von Stroheim, Eric. Actor, director. Born 1885, Vienna. 1st of 2. Father a military officer.

Curtiss, T. Q., *Von Stroheim*, 1971.

Finler, J. W., *Stroheim*, 1968.

Wallace, George. Governor of Alabama. Born 1919, Clio, Alabama. 1st of 4. Father a farmer; mother director of bureau of disease prevention.

* Frady, M., *Wallace*, 1968. (Objective, detailed, well done.)

Wallace, G., Jr., *The Wallaces of Alabama: My Family*, 1975.

Warren, Earl. Chief Justice, U.S. Supreme Court. Born 1891, Los Angeles. 2nd of 2. Father a train repairman, landlord.

Katcher, L., *Earl Warren: A Political Biography*, 1967.

Weaver, J. D., *Warren: The Man, the Court, the Era*, 1967.

Waters, Ethel. Singer, actress. Born 1900, Chester, Pennsylvania. 1st of 2 of mother. Father did not acknowledge her; mother a domestic.

Waters, E., *To Me It's Wonderful*, 1972.

Waters, E., *His Eye Is on the Sparrow: An Autobiography*, 1951.

Watts, Alan. Writer, lecturer. Born 1915, Chislehurst, Kent, England. Only child. Father a wholesale tire salesman.

Stuart, D., *Alan Watts*, 1976.

* Watts, A., *In My Own Way: An Autobiography, 1915–1965*, 1972. (Describes a childhood rich in sensual experiences, but resentment of parents' absorption in each other.)

Waugh, Evelyn. Novelist. Born 1903, Hamstead, near London. 2nd of 2. Father director of publishing firm.

* Sykes, C., *Evelyn Waugh: A Biography*, 1975.

Waugh, A., *My Brother Evelyn and Other Portraits*, 1967.

* Waugh, E., *The Early Years*, 1964.

Weisgal, Meyer Wold. Politician, Weitzman Institute founder. Born 1894, Kikl, Poland. 4th of 11 of father; 5th of 6 of mother. Father a cantor.

* Weisgal, M. W., *Meyer Weisgal . . . So Far*, 1971.

Welk, Lawrence. Conductor. Born 1903, Strasburg, North Dakota. 6th of 8. Father a farmer.

Welk, L., *Ah-One, Ah-Two: Life with My Musical Family*, 1974.

Welk, L., *Wunnerful, Wunnerful! The Autobiography of Lawrence Welk*, 1971.

West, Jessamyn. Novelist. Born 1907, Jennings County, Indiana. 1st of 4. Father a farmer, businessman.

* West, J., *To See the Dream*, 1957. (Well-told story of affectionate family whose members sometimes failed to understand each other.)

* West, J., *Hide and Seek: A Continuing Journey*, 1973. (Insightfully describes two families.)

West, J., *The Woman Said Yes: Encounters with Life and Death—Memoirs*, 1976.

White, T. H. Novelist. Born 1906, of English parents in Bombay. Only child. Father a district police superintendent.

* Warner, S. T., *T. H. White: A Biography*, 1968. (Talented writer tells of another talented writer's rearing.)

Williams, Emlyn. Playwright, actor, director. Born 1905, Rhewl Fawr, North Wales. 1st of 3. Father a stoker, grocer, innkeeper, miner.

* Williams, E., *George: An Early Autobiography*, 1962.

* Williams, E., *Emlyn: An Early Autobiography, 1927–1935*, 1974. (Both valuable resource material; powerfully, entertainingly describe how a boy from a disadvantaged home and community made good use of his talents.)

Williams, Tennessee. Playwright. Born 1911, Columbus, Missouri. 2nd of 3. Father a shoe salesman.

Maxwell, G., *Tennessee Williams and Friends*, 1965.

* Williams, T., *Memoirs*, 1975. (Unforgettable, candid book by a man of literary talent; tells of his sexual divergency.)

Wodehouse, P. G. Humorist. Born 1881, Guilford, Surrey, England. 3rd of 4. Father in diplomatic service in Hong Kong.

Jasen, D. A., *P. G. Wodehouse: Portrait of a Master*, 1974.

Wind, H. W., *The World of P. G. Wodehouse*, 1971.

Wood, Grant. Artist. Born 1892, Anamosa, Iowa. 2nd of 4. Father
a farmer.
Brown, H. F., *Grant Wood and Marvin Cone: Artists of an
Era,* 1972.
Garwood, D., *Artist in Iowa,* 1944.
Woolf, Leonard. Publisher, autobiographer. Born 1880, London.
3rd of 9. Father a barrister.
* Woolf, L. S., *Growing: An Autobiography of the Years
1904–1911,* 1961.
* Woolf, L. S., *Sowing: An Autobiography of the Years
1880–1904,* 1960.
Wyeth, Andrew. Artist. Born 1917, Chadds Ford, Pennsylvania.
5th of 5. Father an artist.
Logsdon, G., *Wyeth People: A Portrait of Andrew Wyeth
as He Is Seen by His Friends and Neighbors,* 1971.
McClanathan, R., *The Brandywine Heritage: Howard Pyle,
N. C. Wyeth, Andrew Wyeth, James Wyeth,* 1971.
Wyeth, N. C., *The Wyeths: The Letters of N. C. Wyeth,
1901–1945,* 1971.
Yevtushenko, Yevgeny. Poet. Born 1933, Zima Junction, Siberia.
1st of 5 of father; only of mother. Father a geologist;
mother a geologist, entertainer.
* Yevtushenko, Y. *A Precocious Autobiography,* 1963.
(Honest, powerful, well written.)
Yogananda, Paramahansa. Mystic. Born 1893, Gorakhpur, India.
4th of 8. Father a corporation vice-president.
Yogananda, P., *Autobiography of a Yogi,* 1969.
Zhukov, George K. Soviet general. Born 1896, Strelkovka, Kaluga
Province, Russia. 2nd of 3. Father a cobbler; mother
a freight hauler.
Chaney, O. P., *Zhukov,* 1971.
Zhukov, G. K., *The Memoirs of Marshall Zhukov,* 1971.
Zorach, William. Sculptor. Born 1887, Euberick, Lithuania. 7th
of 10. Father a peddler.
Zorach, W., *Art Is My Life: The Autobiography of William
Zorach,* 1967.

References

ACTON, H. *Memoirs of an Aesthete, 1939–1969.* New York: Viking Press, 1971.

ACTON, H. *Nancy Mitford: A Memoir.* New York: Harper & Row, 1975.

AGEE, J. *Letters of James Agee to Father Flye.* New York: Braziller, 1962.

AGRESS, E. *Golda: A Portrait of a Prime Minister.* New York: Sabra Books, 1970.

ALDOUBY, Z., and BOLLINGER, J. *The Shattered Silence.* New York: Coward, McCann & Geoghegan, 1971.

ALLILUYEVA, S. *Twenty Letters to a Friend.* New York: Harper & Row, 1967.

ALLILUYEVA, S. *Only One Year.* New York: Harper & Row, 1969.

ALVAREZ, A. *The Savage God: A Study of Suicide.* New York: Random House, 1972.

Amon Carter Museum. *Georgia O'Keeffe.* Fort Worth, Texas: Amon Carter Museum, 1966.

ANGELOU, M. *I Know Why the Caged Bird Sings.* New York: Random House, 1969.

ANGELOU, M. *Gather Together in My Name.* New York: Random House, 1974.

ANGELOU, M. *Singin' and Swingin' and Gettin' Merry Like Christmas.* New York: Random House, 1976.

ANSON, R. S. *McGovern: A Biography.* New York: Holt, Rinehart and Winston, 1972.

ARENDT, H. *Eichmann in Jerusalem.* New York: Macmillan, 1963.

ARMITAGE, M. *Martha Graham.* Brooklyn, N.Y.: Dance Horizons, 1966.

ARNASON, H. *Calder.* New York: Viking Press, 1971.

ASHMAN, C. R. *Kissinger: The Adventures of Superkraut.* New York: Lyle Stuart, 1974.

ASQUITH, C. *Diaries, 1915–1918.* New York: Knopf, 1968.

AUDEN, W. H. *Forewords and Afterwords.* New York: Random House, 1973.

AYUB KHAN, M. *Mohommad Ayub Khan.* New York: Oxford University Press, 1967.

AZIKIWE, N. *My Odyssey: An Autobiography.* New York: Praeger, 1970.

AZNAVOUR, C. *Aznavour by Aznavour: An Autobiography.* Chicago: Cowles, 1972.

BABEL, N. *The Lonely Years.* New York: Noonday Press, 1964.

BAGNOLD, E. *Autobiography.* Boston: Little, Brown, 1964.

BAINBRIDGE, J. *Garbo: The Famous Biography.* New York: Holt, Rinehart and Winston, 1971.

BAKER, L. *Felix Frankfurter.* New York: Coward, McCann & Geoghegan, 1969.

BALAKIAN, A. *André Breton.* New York: Oxford University Press, 1971.

BALDWIN, J. *Notes of a Native Son.* New York: Dial Press, 1955.

BALDWIN, J. *Nobody Knows My Name.* New York: Dial Press, 1961.

BALL, G. (Ed.). *Allen Verbatim.* New York: McGraw-Hill, 1974.

BARNARD, C., and PEPPER, C. B. *One Life.* New York: Macmillan, 1969.

BAYLEY, N. "Comparison of Mental and Motor Test Scores for Ages 1–15 Months by Sex, Birth Order, Race, Geographic Location, and Education of Parents." *Child Development,* 1965, *36,* 379–411.

BAZIN, A. *Jean Renoir.* New York: Simon & Schuster, 1973.

BEATON, C. *Photobiography.* New York: Doubleday, 1951.

BEATON, C. *The Years Between.* New York: Holt, Rinehart and Winston, 1965.

BEAUVOIR, S. DE. *The Prime of Life.* New York: World, 1962.

BEAUVOIR, S. DE. *A Very Easy Death.* New York: Putnam's, 1966.

BEAUVOIR, S. DE. *The Second Sex.* New York: Modern Library, 1968. (Originally published 1949.)

BEAUVOIR, S. DE. *All Said and Done.* New York: Putnam's, 1974.

BEN-DAU. *Spy from Israel.* Hartford, Conn.: Prayer Book, 1969.

BENTLEY, P. *O Dreams, O Destination.* New York: Macmillan, 1962.

BERNSTEIN, B. *Thurber: A Biography.* New York: Dodd, Mead, 1975.

BERTEAUT, S. *Piaf.* New York: Harper & Row, 1972.

BETHGE, E. *Dietrich Bonhoeffer: Man of Vision, Man of Courage.* New York: Harper & Row, 1970.

BINDER, D. *The Other German: Willy Brandt's Life and Times.* New York: New Republic, 1975.

BINION, R. *Frau Lou: Nietzsche's Wayward Disciple.* Princeton, N.J.: Princeton University Press, 1968.

BIQUARD, P. *Frédéric Joliot-Curie: The Man and His Theories.* New York: Eriksson, 1966.

BITTNER, H. *Käthe Kollwitz.* New York: Yoseloff, 1959.

BJORKEGREN, H. *Alesandr Solzhenitsyn: A Biography.* New York: Third Press, 1972.

BJORKMAN, M., and BJORKMAN, S. *Bergman on Bergman.* New York: Simon & Schuster, 1973.

BOSANQUET, M. *The Life and Death of Dietrich Bonhoeffer.* New York: Harper & Row, 1968.

BOSMAN, A. *Pierre-Auguste Renoir.* New York: Barnes & Noble, 1962.

BOULBY, M. *Hermann Hesse: His Mind and His Art.* Ithaca, N.Y.: Cornell University Press, 1967.

BOYARSKY, B. *The Rise of Ronald Reagan.* New York: Random House, 1968.

BOYD, E. E. *The Bloomsbury Heritage: Their Mothers and Their Aunts.* New York: Taplinger, 1976.

BRANDEWEIN, P. F. *The Gifted Student as Future Scientist.* New York: Harcourt Brace Jovanovich, 1955.

BRANDT, W. *My Road to Berlin.* New York: Doubleday, 1960.

BRENAN, G. *A Life of One's Own: An Autobiography.* New York: Farrar, Straus & Giroux, 1963.

BRENAN, G. *A Personal Record.* New York: Knopf, 1975.

BRONFENBRENNER, U. "The Erosion of the American Family." *Psychology Today,* 1977, *10* (12).

BROOKS, P. *House of Life: Rachel Carson at Work.* Boston: Houghton Mifflin, 1972.

BROUGH, J. *The Fabulous Fondas.* New York: McKay, 1973.

BROUGH, J. *The Prince and the Lily.* New York: Coward, McCann & Geoghegan, 1975.

BROWN, E. G. *Reagan: The Political Chameleon.* New York: Praeger, 1976.

BROWN, H. F. *Grant Wood and Marvin Cone: Artists of an Era.* Ames: Iowa State University Press, 1972.

BROWN, S., and WILKENING, H. *Bufano: An Intimate Biography.* Berkeley, Calif.: Howell-North, 1972.

BROWNING, N. L. *The Psychic World of Peter Hurkos.* New York: Doubleday, 1970.

BROWNMILLER, S. *Shirley Chisholm.* New York: Doubleday, 1970.

BRUCCOLI, M. J. *The O'Hara Concern: A Biography of John O'Hara.* New York: Random House, 1975.

BUCHEN, I. H. *Isaac Bashevis Singer and the Eternal Past.* New York: New York University Press, 1968.

BUCKHORN, R. F. *Nader: The People's Lawyer.* Englewood Cliffs, N.J.: Prentice-Hall, 1972.

BUCKLE, R. *Jacob Epstein, Sculptor.* New York: World, 1963.

BULLARD, E. *Mary Cassatt.* New York: Watson, 1972.

BURKHART, W. B. *Women in Prison.* New York: Doubleday, 1973.

BURROWS, W. E. *Richtofen: A True History of the Red Baron.* New York: Harcourt Brace Jovanovich, 1969.

BUTSCHER, E. *Sylvia Plath: Method and Madness.* New York: Seabury, 1976.

CALDER, A. *An Autobiography with Pictures.* New York: Pantheon, 1966.

CAMERON, G. *Rose: A Biography of Rose Fitzgerald Kennedy.* New York: Putnam's, 1971.

CAMERON, J. *Here Is Your Enemy*. New York: Holt, Rinehart and Winston, 1966.

CAPRA, F. *Frank Capra: The Name Above the Title: An Autobiography*. New York: Macmillan, 1971.

CARPENTER, L. *Ruffles and Flourishes*. New York: Doubleday, 1970.

CARR, V. S. *The Lonely Hunter: A Biography of Carson McCullers*. New York: Doubleday, 1975.

CATE, C. *Antoine de Saint-Exupéry*. New York: Putnam's, 1970.

CAYCE, E. *The Outer Limits of Edgar Cayce's Power*. New York: Harper & Row, 1971.

CHANEY, O. P. *Zhukov*. Norman: University of Oklahoma Press, 1971.

CHAPLIN, C., JR. *My Father, Charlie Chaplin*. New York: Random House, 1960.

CHAPLIN, M. *I Couldn't Smoke the Grass on My Father's Lawn*. New York: Putnam's, 1966.

CHICHESTER, F. *The Lonely Sea and the Sky*. New York: Coward, McCann & Geoghegan, 1964.

CHILDS, H. *An American Genius: The Life of Ernest Orlando Lawrence*. New York: Dutton, 1968.

CHRISTENSON, C. V. *Kinsey: A Biography*. Bloomington: Indiana University Press, 1971.

CLARKE, J. H. *Malcolm X: The Man and His Times*. New York: Macmillan, 1969.

CLINCH, N. G. *The Kennedy Neurosis*. New York: Grosset & Dunlap, 1972.

CLOETE, S. *A Victorian Son*. New York: Stein & Day, 1973.

COCTEAU, J. *Journals of Cocteau*. New York: Museum Publishers, 1957.

CODRESCU, A. *Life and Times of an Involuntary Genius*. New York: Braziller, 1975.

COFFIN, T. *Senator Fulbright: Portrait of a Public Philosopher*. New York: Dutton, 1966.

COHEN, S. F. *Bukharin and the Bolshevik Revolution: A Political Biography*. New York: Knopf, 1973.

COLE, S. M. *Leakey's Luck: The Life of Louis Seymour Bazett Leakey, 1903–1972*. New York: Harcourt Brace Jovanovich, 1975.

COLEMAN, J. *Ronald Coleman*. New York: Morrow, 1975.

COLEMAN, J. C. *Abnormal Psychology and Modern Life* (5th ed.) Glenview, Ill.: Scott, Foresman, 1976.

COLES, R. *Erik H. Erikson: The Growth of His Work.* Boston: Little, Brown, 1970.

COLETTE, S. (R. Phelps, Ed.). *Earthly Paradise: An Autobiography Drawn from Her Lifetime Writings.* New York: Farrar, Straus & Giroux, 1966.

COLETTE, S. *The Pure and the Impure.* New York: Farrar, Straus & Giroux, 1967.

COLETTE, S. *Evening Star.* Indianapolis, Ind.: Bobbs-Merrill, 1973.

COLETTE, S. *Looking Backwards.* Bloomington: Indiana University Press, 1975.

COLLIER, P., and HOROWITZ, D. *The Rockefellers: An American Dynasty.* New York: Holt, Rinehart and Winston, 1976.

COLLIS, M. *Nancy Astor.* New York: Dutton, 1960.

CONSTANTINE, M. *Tina Modotti: A Fragile Life.* New York: Paddington Press, 1975.

COOKSON, K. *Our Kate.* Indianapolis, Ind.: Bobbs-Merrill, 1971.

COOPER, S. J. *J. B. Priestley: Portrait of an Author.* New York: Harper & Row, 1970.

COTTRELL, J. *Muhammad Ali.* New York: Funk & Wagnalls, 1967.

COTTRELL, J. *Laurence Olivier.* Englewood Cliffs, N.J.: Prentice-Hall, 1975.

COTTRELL, R. D. *Colette.* New York: Ungar, 1974a.

COTTRELL, R. D. *Simone de Beauvoir.* New York: Ungar, 1974b.

CREAMER, R. W. *Babe: The Legend Comes to Life—A Look at the Life and Times of George Herman Ruth.* New York: Simon & Schuster, 1974.

CROSLAND, M. *Colette: The Difficulty of Loving.* Indianapolis, Ind.: Bobbs-Merrill, 1973.

CUÉNOT, C. *Teilhard de Chardin: A Biographical Study.* New York: Helicon Press, 1965.

CUMMINGS, E. E. *The Magic Maker.* Indianapolis, Ind.: Bobbs-Merrill, 1972.

CURTISS, T. Q. *Von Stroheim.* New York: Farrar, Straus & Giroux, 1971.

DALTON, D. *Janis.* New York: Simon & Schuster, 1971.

DARROCH, S. J. *Ottoline: The Life of Lady Ottoline Morrell.* New York: Coward, McCann & Geoghegan, 1975.

DAVID, L. *Ethel: The Story of Mrs. Robert F. Kennedy.* New York: World, 1971.

DAVIS, A. *Angela Davis: An Autobiography.* New York: Random House, 1974.

DAVIS, N. P. *Lawrence and Oppenheimer.* New York: Simon & Schuster, 1968.

DAY, D. *Malcolm Lowry: A Biography.* New York: Oxford University Press, 1973.

DAYAN, M. *Moshe Dayan: The Story of My Life.* New York: Morrow, 1976.

DAYAN, R., and DUDMAN, H. *And Perhaps . . . The Story of Ruth Dayan.* New York: Harcourt Brace Jovanovich, 1973.

DEANS, M. *Weep No More, My Lady.* New York: Hawthorn Books, 1972.

DELACEY, P. R. "A Cross Cultural Study of Classificatory Ability in Australia." *Journal of Cross Cultural Psychology,* 1970, *1,* 293–304.

DE LOUISE, J., and VALENTINE, T. *Psychic Mission.* Chicago: Regnery, 1971.

DEMARIS, O. *The Director.* New York: Harper & Row, 1975.

DEMBO, L. S. *Nabokov: The Man and His Work.* Madison: University of Wisconsin Press, 1967.

DEMETZ, P. (Ed.). *Brecht.* Englewood Cliffs, N.J.: Prentice-Hall, 1962.

DENIS, B. *Jeane Dixon, the Witness.* New York: Doubleday, 1976.

DE POLNAY, P. *Enfant Terrible: The Life and World of Maurice Utrillo.* New York: Morrow, 1969.

DE TOLEDANO, R. *J. Edgar Hoover: The Man and His Times.* New York: Manor Books, 1973.

DEUTSCH, H. *Confrontation with Myself.* New York: Norton, 1973.

DEVANEY, J. B. *Baseball Life of Mickey Mantle.* Englewood Cliffs, N.J.: School Book Service, 1970.

DEVITIS, H. A. *Graham Greene.* Boston: Twayne, 1964.

DEVLIN, B. *The Price of My Soul.* New York: Knopf, 1969.

DICKENS, H. *Hepburn.* New York: Citadel, 1971.

DICKSON, L. *Radclyffe-Hall at the Well of Loneliness: A Sapphic Chronicle.* New York: Scribner's, 1975.

DIEDERICH, B. *Papa Doc: The Truth About Haiti Today.* New York: McGraw-Hill, 1969.

DIEHL, G. *Miró.* New York: Crown, 1974.

DIXON, J., and NOORBERGEN, R. *Jeane Dixon: My Life and Prophecies.* New York: Morrow, 1969.

DORNBERG, J. *Brezhnev: The Masks of Power.* New York: Basic Books, 1974.

DOYLE, P. A. *Sean O'Faolain.* Boston: Twayne, 1968.

DRINNON, R. *Rebel in Paradise.* Chicago: University of Chicago Press, 1971.

DRUXMAN, M. B. *Paul Muni: His Life and His Films.* New York: Barnes & Noble, 1974.

DU BOIS, S. G. *His Day Is Marching On.* Philadelphia: Lippincott, 1971.

DU BOIS, W. E. B. *Autobiography of W. E. B. Du Bois.* New York: International Publishers, 1968.

DUNHAM, K. *A Touch of Innocence.* New York: Harcourt Brace Jovanovich, 1959.

DUNHAM, K. *Island Possessed.* New York: Doubleday, 1969.

DUPEE, F. W. (Ed.). *Selected Letters of E. E. Cummings.* New York: Harcourt Brace Jovanovich, 1969.

DYKSHOORN, M. B., and FELTON, R. H. *My Passport Says Clairvoyant.* New York: Hawthorn Books, 1974.

EBAN, A. S. *Abba Eban: An Autobiography.* New York: Random House, 1977.

ECKNAN, F. M. *Curious Passage of James Baldwin.* Philadelphia: Lippincott, 1966.

EDWARDS, A. *Judy Garland: A Mortgaged Life.* New York: Simon & Schuster, 1975.

EELLS, G. *The Life That Late He Led: A Biography of Cole Porter.* New York: Putnam's, 1967.

EHRENBURG, I. *People and Life, 1891–1921.* New York: Knopf, 1962.

EHRENBURG, I. *The Post-War Years, 1945–1954.* New York: World, 1967.

EINSTEIN, C. *Willie Mays: Coast to Coast Giant.* New York: Putnam's, 1963.

EISELE, A. *Almost to the Presidency: A Biography of Two American Politicians.* Blue Earth, Minn.: Piper, 1972.

ELGAR, F. *Mondrian.* New York: Praeger, 1968.

EPSTEIN, J. *Epstein: An Autobiography.* New York: Arno Press, 1975.

EVANS, O. W. *The Ballad of Carson McCullers.* New York: Coward, McCann & Geoghegan, 1966.

EVANS, O. W. *Anaïs Nin.* Carbondale: Southern Illinois University Press, 1968.

EVANS, R. *Dialogue with Erikson.* New York: Harper & Row, 1967.

EWEN, D. *Leonard Bernstein.* New York: Bantam Books, 1961.

FALK, R. *Bufano.* Millbrae, Calif.: Celestial Arts, 1975.

FANON, FRANTZ. *The Wretched of the Earth.* New York: Grove Press, 1963.

FANON, F. *Black Skin, White Masks.* New York: Grove Press, 1968.

FARRAR, D. *For God Almighty: A Personal Memory.* New York: Stein & Day, 1969.

FEELEY, K. *Flannery O'Connor: Voice of the Peacock.* New Brunswick, N.J.: Rutgers University Press, 1972.

FERBER, E. *A Kind of Magic.* New York: Doubleday, 1963.

FERBER, E. *A Peculiar Treasure.* (rev. ed.) New York: Doubleday, 1973.

FERRIS, P. *The House of Northcliffe: A Biography of an Empire.* New York: World, 1972.

FIELD, A. *Nabokov: His Life in Art.* Boston: Little, Brown, 1967.

FIELDING, D. *Those Remarkable Cunards: Emerald and Nancy.* New York: Atheneum, 1968.

FINLER, J. W. *Stroheim.* Berkeley: University of California Press, 1968.

FIORI, G. *Antonio Gramsci: Life of a Revolutionary.* New York: Dutton, 1971.

FLEISCHMAN, H. *Norman Thomas.* New York: Norton, 1964.

FLORENCE, R. *Fritz: The Story of a Political Assassin.* New York: Dial Press, 1972.

FONTEYN, M. *Margot Fonteyn.* New York: Knopf, 1976.

FORD, A. *The Life Beyond Death.* New York: Putnam's, 1971.

404 References

FOSTER, M. *Joyce Cary: A Biography.* Boston: Houghton Mifflin, 1968.

FOUERE, R. *Krishnamurti: The Man and His Teaching.* Bombay, India: Chetana, 1964.

FOX, L. *Broadway Joe and His Super Jets.* New York: Coward, McCann & Geoghegan, 1969.

FRADY, M. *Wallace.* New York: World, 1968.

FREEDLAND, M. *Jolson.* New York: Stein & Day, 1972.

FREWIN, L. *Dietrich: The Story of a Star.* New York: Stein & Day, 1967.

FRIEDAN, B., and BEAUVOIR, S. DE. "Sex, Society and the Female Dilemma." *Saturday Review,* June 14, 1975.

FRIEDLANDER, S. *Kurt Gerstein: The Ambiguity of Good.* New York: Knopf, 1969.

FRIEDMAN, B. H. *Jackson Pollock: Energy Made Visible.* New York: McGraw-Hill, 1972.

FRIEDMAN, M. *Buried Alive: The Biography of Janis Joplin.* New York: Morrow, 1973.

FRISCH, K. VON. *A Biologist Remembers.* Elmsford, N.Y.: Pergamon Press, 1967.

FULLER, R. B. *Ideas and Integrities: A Spontaneous Autobiographical Disclosure.* New York: Collier, 1969.

GADEA, H. *Ernesto: A Memoir of Ché Guevara.* New York: Doubleday, 1972.

GALLAGHER, M. B. *My Life with Jacqueline Kennedy.* New York: McKay, 1969.

GAMOW, G. *My World Line: An Informal Autobiography.* New York: Viking Press, 1970.

GANANTE, P. *Mademoiselle Chanel.* Chicago: Regnery, 1973.

GARRETT, E. J. *Many Voices: The Autobiography of a Medium.* New York: Putnam's, 1968.

GARWOOD, D. *Artist in Iowa.* New York: Norton, 1944.

GEHRIG, E. *My Luke and I.* New York: Crowell, 1976.

GEISMAR, M. D. *Ring Lardner and the Portrait of a Family.* New York: Crowell, 1972.

GEISMAR, P. *Fanon.* New York: Dial Press, 1974.

GELLER, U. *Uri Geller: My Story.* New York: Praeger, 1975.

GENDZIER, I. *Frantz Fanon.* New York: Pantheon, 1973.

GERBER, A. B. *Bashful Billionaire: The Story of Howard Hughes.* New York: Stuart, 1967.

GERSON, N. B. *Because I Loved Him: The Life and Loves of Lillie Langtry.* New York: Morrow, 1971.

GILES, F. L. *Norma Jean.* New York: McGraw-Hill, 1969.

GILLIAM, D. B. *Paul Robeson: All American.* New York: New Republic, 1976.

GOERTZEL, V., and GOERTZEL, M. G. *Cradles of Eminence.* Boston: Little, Brown, 1962.

GOLDMAN, E. *Living My Life.* (2 vols.) New York: Dover, 1970.

GOLDMAN, P. L. *The Death and Life of Malcolm X.* New York: Harper & Row, 1973.

GOODRICH, L. *John Sloan, 1871–1951.* New York: Whitney Museum, 1952.

GOOLD-ADAMS, R. J. M. *John Foster Dulles: A Reappraisal.* New York: Appleton-Century-Crofts, 1962.

GORDON, H. *The Mind and Art of Henry Miller.* Baton Rouge: Louisiana State University Press, 1967.

GORMAN, J. B. *Kefauver: A Political Biography.* New York: Oxford University Press, 1971.

GOURLAY, L. *Olivier.* New York: Stein & Day, 1974.

GRAHAM, F. *Lou Gehrig: A Quiet Hero.* New York: Putnam's, 1942.

GREBSTEIN, S. N. *John O'Hara.* Boston: Twayne, 1966.

GREEN, M. B. *The von Richtofen Sisters: The Triumphant and the Tragic Modes of Love.* New York: Basic Books, 1974.

GREEN, M. *Children of the Sun.* New York: Basic Books, 1976.

GREEN, S. *Starring Fred Astaire.* New York: Dodd, Mead, 1973.

GREENBERG, H. *Quest for the Necessary: W. H. Auden and the Dilemma of Divided Consciousness.* Cambridge, Mass.: Harvard University Press, 1968.

GREENE, G. *A Sort of Life.* New York: Simon & Schuster, 1971.

GREENFIELD, J. *Wilhelm Reich vs. the USA.* New York: Norton, 1974.

GREY, M. *Song and Dance Man.* New York: Dutton, 1972.

GRUEN, J. *The Private World of Leonard Bernstein.* New York: Viking Press, 1968.

GUHIN, M. A. *John Foster Dulles: A Statesman and His Time.* New York: Columbia University Press, 1972.

HAHN, O. *My Life: The Autobiography of a Scientist.* New York: Herda, 1970.

HALBERSTAM, D. *Ho.* New York: Random House, 1971.

HALL, D. *Henry Moore: The Life and Work of a Great Sculptor.* New York: Harper & Row, 1966.

HAMBLETON, R. *Mazo De La Roche of Jalna.* New York: Hawthorn Books, 1966.

HAMILTON, V. *Paul Robeson: The Life and Times of a Free Black Man.* New York: Harper & Row, 1974.

HAMMARSKJÖLD, D. *Markings.* New York: Knopf, 1964.

HANNAH, D. *"Isak Dinesen" and Karen Blixen: The Mask and the Reality.* New York: Random House, 1971.

HANO, A. *Sandy Koufax: Strikeout King.* New York: Putnam's, 1964.

HARRIS, L. A. *Upton Sinclair: American Rebel.* New York: Crowell, 1975.

HARWOOD, R. *Lyndon.* New York: Praeger, 1973.

HASKINS, J. *Shirley Chisholm.* New York: Dial Press, 1975.

HATCH, A. *Pope Paul VI.* New York: Random House, 1966.

HATCH, A. *The Lodges of Massachusetts.* New York: Hawthorn Books, 1973.

HAYES, H., and DODY, S. *On Reflection: An Autobiography.* New York: Evans, 1968.

HAYES, H., and FUNKE, L. *A Gift of Joy.* Philadelphia: Lippincott, 1965.

HAYES, P. M. *Quisling: The Career and Political Ideas of Vidkun Quisling, 1887–1945.* Bloomington: Indiana University Press, 1972.

HEALY, P. F. *Cissy: The Biography of Eleanor M. "Cissy" Patterson.* New York: Doubleday, 1966.

HELLER, D., and HELLER, D. *John Foster Dulles: Soldier for Peace.* New York: Holt, Rinehart and Winston, 1960.

HELLMAN, L. *An Unfinished Woman: A Memoir.* Boston: Little, Brown, 1969.

HELLMAN, L. *Pentimento: A Book of Portraits.* Boston: Little, Brown, 1973.

HELLMAN, L. *Scoundrel Time.* Boston: Little, Brown, 1976.

HEMMINGS, R. *Children's Freedom: A. S. Neill and the Evolution of the Summerhill Idea.* New York: Schocken Books, 1973.

HENDIN, J. *The World of Flannery O'Connor.* Bloomington: Indiana University Press, 1970.

HERSEY, J. R. *The President.* New York: Knopf, 1975.

HERZOG, A. *McCarthy for President.* New York: Viking, 1969.

HEYERDAHL, T. *Kon-Tiki.* Chicago: Rand McNally, 1950.

HEYERDAHL, T. *The Ra Expeditions.* New York: Doubleday, 1971.

HEYERDAHL, T. *Fatu-Hiva: Back to Nature.* New York: Doubleday, 1974.

HIGHAM, C. *Kate.* New York: Norton, 1975.

HILL, C. *Bertolt Brecht.* Boston: Twayne, 1975.

HODES, A. *Martin Buber: An Intimate Portrait.* New York: Viking Press, 1971.

HODIN, J. P. *Oskar Kokoschka: The Artist and His Times—A Biographical Study.* New York: New York Graphic Society, 1966.

HOFFA, J. R. *The Trials of Jimmy Hoffa.* Chicago: Regnery, 1970.

HOFFER, E. *An American Odyssey.* Minneapolis, Minn.: Dillon, 1968.

HOGE, A. A. *Cissy Patterson.* New York: Random House, 1966.

HOLROYD, M. *Lytton Strachey: A Critical Biography.* (2 vols.) New York: Holt, Rinehart and Winston, 1968.

HOLROYD, M. *Augustus John: A Biography.* New York: Holt, Rinehart and Winston, 1975.

HOLT, R. *Mary McLeod Bethune.* New York: Doubleday, 1964.

HOOPES, T. *The Devil and John Foster Dulles.* Boston: Little, Brown, 1973.

HOWARD, P. *The Operas of Benjamin Britten: An Introduction.* New York: Praeger, 1969.

HOYT, E. P. *Marilyn: The Tragic Venus.* Radnor, Pa.: Chilton, 1965.

HSU KAI-YU. *Chou En-lai: China's Gray Eminence.* New York: Doubleday, 1968.

HUMPHREY, H. H. *The Education of a Public Man: My Life and Politics.* New York: Doubleday, 1976.

HUTHESSING, K. *Dear to Behold: An Intimate Biography of Indira Gandhi.* New York: Macmillan, 1967.

HUXLEY, J. *Memories.* New York: Harper & Row, 1970.

INGLIS, B. *Roger Casement: A Ghost in England's Haunted House.* New York: Harcourt Brace Jovanovich, 1973.

ISHERWOOD, C. *Kathleen and Frank.* New York: Simon & Schuster, 1971.

ISHERWOOD, C. *Christopher and His Kind, 1929–1939.* New York: Farrar, Straus & Giroux, 1977.

JAMES, D. *Ché Guevara: A Biography.* New York: Stein & Day, 1969.

JASEN, D. A. *P. G. Wodehouse: Portrait of a Master.* New York: Mason/Charter, 1974.

JELLINEK-MERCÉDÈS, G. *My Father, Mr. Mercédès.* Radnor, Pa.: Chilton, 1966.

JENKINS, R. *Asquith: Portrait of a Man and an Era.* New York: Chilmark Press, 1964.

JESSUP, J. K. *The Ideas of Henry Luce.* New York: Atheneum, 1969.

JOFFROY, P. *A Spy for God: The Ordeal of Kurt Gerstein.* New York: Harcourt Brace Jovanovich, 1971.

JOHNPOLL, B. K. *Pacifist's Progress: Norman Thomas and the Decline of American Socialism.* New York: Quadrangle, 1970.

JOHNSON, H. B. *Fulbright, the Dissenter.* New York: Doubleday, 1968.

JOHNSON, S. *My Brother Lyndon.* New York: Cowles, 1970.

JUNG, C. G. *Memories, Dreams, Reflections.* New York: Pantheon, 1963.

JURMAN, P. *Moshe Dayan: A Portrait.* New York: Dodd, Mead, 1968.

KAHNWEILER, D. H. *Gris: His Life and Work.* New York: Abrams, 1967.

KALB, M., and KALB, B. *Kissinger.* Boston: Little, Brown, 1974.

KALLIR, O. *Grandma Moses.* New York: Abrams, 1973.

KANIN, G. *Tracy and Hepburn: An Intimate Memoir.* New York: Viking Press, 1971.

KATCHER, L. *Earl Warren: A Political Biography.* New York: McGraw-Hill, 1967.

KATOV, G. *The Trial of Bukharin.* New York: Stein & Day, 1969.

KAZANTZAKIS, H. *Nikos Kazantzakis: A Biography Based on His Letters.* New York: Simon & Schuster, 1968.

KEARNS, D. *Lyndon Johnson and the American Dream.* New York: Harper & Row, 1976.

KENNEDY, R. F. *Times to Remember.* New York: Doubleday, 1974.

KENNER, H. *The Pound Era.* Berkeley: University of California Press, 1971.

KENNER, H. *Bucky: A Guided Tour of Buckminster Fuller.* New York: Morrow, 1973.

KIERNAN, T. *Jane: An Intimate Biography.* New York: Putnam's, 1973.

KIMBALL, R. (Compiler.) *Cole.* New York: Holt, Rinehart and Winston, 1971.

KIRK, R. *Eliot and His Age.* New York: Random House, 1971.

KISTLER, R. *I Caught Flies for Howard Hughes.* Chicago: Playboy Press, 1976.

KLEIN, M. C. *Käthe Kollwitz: Life in Art.* New York: Holt, Rinehart and Winston, 1972.

KLURFELD, H. *Behind the Lines: The World of Drew Pearson.* Englewood Cliffs, N. J.: Prentice-Hall, 1968.

KNAPP, B. L. *Jean Genet.* Boston: Twayne, 1968.

KNAPP, R. H., and GOODRICH, H. B. *Origins of American Scientists.* Chicago: University of Chicago Press, 1952.

KOBLER, J. *Luce: His Time, Life, and Fortune.* New York: Doubleday, 1968.

KOERNER, J. D. *Hoffer's America.* La Salle, Ill.: Library Press, 1973.

KOKOSCHKA, O. *My Life.* New York: Macmillan, 1974.

KOUFAX, S., and KOUFAX, L. *Koufax.* New York: Viking Press, 1966.

KOWET, D. *Pelé.* New York: Atheneum, 1976.

KRAMER, J. *Ginsberg in America.* New York: Random House, 1969.

KUCHARSKY, D. *The Man from Plains: The Mind and Spirit of Jimmy Carter.* New York: Harper & Row, 1976.

KULIK, K. *Alexander Korda: The Man Who Could Work Miracles.* New Rochelle, N.Y.: Arlington House, 1975.

LACOUTURE, J. *Ho Chi Minh: A Political Biography.* New York: Random House, 1968.

LACOUTURE, J. *André Malraux.* New York: Pantheon, 1975.

LAING, M. I. *Edward Heath, Prime Minister.* New York: Third Press, 1973.

LAMAITRE, G. *Jean Giraudoux: The Writer and His Work.* New York: Ungar, 1971.

LANDAU, D. *Kissinger: The Uses of Power.* Boston: Houghton Mifflin, 1972.

LARDNER, R., JR. *The Lardners: My Family Remembered.* New York: Harper & Row, 1976.

LASH, J. P. *Dag Hammarskjöld.* New York: Doubleday, 1961.

LASH, J. P. *From the Diaries of Felix Frankfurter.* New York: Norton, 1975.

LASSAIGNE, J. *Miró: A Biographical and Critical Study.* New York: Skira, 1972.

LASSON, F. *The Life and Destiny of Isak Dinesen.* New York: Random House, 1970.

LAWRENCE, J. *Actor: The Life and Times of Paul Muni.* New York: Putnam's, 1974.

LEAKEY, L. S. B. *By the Evidence: Memoirs, 1932–1951.* New York: Harcourt Brace Jovanovich, 1974.

LEDUC, V. *La Bâtarde.* New York: Farrar, Straus & Giroux, 1965. (Introduction by S. de Beauvoir.)

LEEK, S. *Diary of a Witch.* Englewood Cliffs, N.J.: Prentice-Hall, 1968.

LEEK, S. *My Life in Astrology.* Englewood Cliffs, N.J.: Prentice-Hall, 1972.

LEGGE, J. D. *Sukarno: A Political Biography.* New York: Praeger, 1972.

LEHMANN, J. *In My Own Time: Memoirs of a Literary Life.* Boston: Little, Brown, 1969.

LEIBHOLTZ-BONHOEFFER, S. *The Bonhoeffers: Portrait of a Family.* New York: St. Martin's Press, 1971.

LEIGHTON, J. S. *Simone de Beauvoir on Women.* Cranbury, N.J.: Fairleigh Dickinson University Press, 1975.

LEITCH, D. *God Stand Up for Bastards.* Boston: Houghton Mifflin, 1973.

LESLIE, A. *Francis Chichester: A Biography.* New York: Walker, 1975.

LESSING, D. M. *A Small Personal Voice: Essays, Reviews, Interviews.* New York: Knopf, 1974.

LEVINE, S. A. *Evangeline Booth: Daughter of Salvation*. New York: Dodd, Mead, 1970.

LEVY, J. *Cesar Chavez: Autobiography of La Causa*. New York: Norton, 1975.

LEWIS, A. *Miss Elizabeth Arden: An Unretouched Portrait*. New York: Coward, McCann & Geoghegan, 1972.

LILLIE, B. *Every Other Inch a Lady*. New York: Doubleday, 1972.

LINDBERGH, A. *Bring Me a Unicorn, 1922–1928*. New York: Harcourt Brace Jovanovich, 1972.

LINDBERGH, A. *The Hour of Gold, 1929–1932*. New York: Harcourt Brace Jovanovich, 1973.

LIPCHITZ, J. *Jacques Lipchitz: Sketches in Bronze*. New York: Praeger, 1969.

LIPCHITZ, J. *My Life in Sculpture*. New York: Viking Press, 1972.

LIPPMAN, T., JR. *Senator Ted Kennedy*. New York: Norton, 1976.

LIPPMAN, T. JR., and HANSEN, D. C. *Muskie*. New York: Norton, 1971.

LOCKWOOD, L. *Castro's Cuba, Cuba's Fidel*. New York: Macmillan, 1967.

LOGSDON, G. *Wyeth People: A Portrait of Andrew Wyeth as He Is Seen by His Friends and Neighbors*. New York: Doubleday, 1971.

LUCAS, J. *Agnew: Profile in Conflict*. New York: Scribner's, 1970.

LUCAS, R. *Frieda Lawrence: The Story of Frieda von Richtofen and D. H. Lawrence*. New York: Viking Press, 1973.

LUTYENS, J. *Krishnamurti: The Years of Awakening*. New York: Farrar, Straus & Giroux, 1975.

LYONS, E. *David Sarnoff: A Biography*. New York: Harper & Row, 1966.

MCCARRY, C. *Citizen Nader*. New York: Saturday Review Press, 1972.

MCCARTHY, P. *Céline*. New York: Viking Press, 1976.

MCCLANATHAN, R. *The Brandywine Heritage: Howard Pyle, N. C. Wyeth, Andrew Wyeth, James Wyeth*. New York: New York Graphic Society, 1971.

MCCLELLAND, D. C., and OTHERS. *Talent and Society*. New York: D. Van Nostrand, 1958.

MCDONAUGH, D. *Martha Graham: A Biography.* New York: Praeger, 1973.

MCGOVERN, E. S. *Uphill: A Personal Story.* Boston: Houghton Mifflin, 1974.

MACLAINE, S. *Don't Fall Off the Mountain.* New York: Norton, 1970.

MACLAINE, S. *You Can Get There From Here.* New York: Norton, 1975.

MCNEAL, R. H. *Bride of the Revolution: Krupskaya and Lenin.* Ann Arbor: University of Michigan Press, 1972.

MCNEISH, J. *Fire Under the Ashes: The Life of Danilo Dolci.* Boston: Beacon Press, 1966.

MADDEN, D. *Remembering James Agee.* Baton Rouge: Louisiana State University Press, 1974.

MAILER, N. *Marilyn: A Biography.* New York: Grosset & Dunlap, 1973.

MALKOFF, K. *Theodore Roethke: An Introduction to His Poetry.* New York: Columbia University Press, 1966.

MALRAUX, A. *Antimemoirs.* New York: Farrar, Straus & Giroux, 1967.

MANKIEWICZ, F. *With Fidel: A Portrait of Castro and Cuba.* Chicago: Playboy Press, 1975.

MANN, P. *Golda: The Life of Israel's Prime Minister.* New York: Coward, McCann & Geoghegan, 1971.

MASSERMAN, J. H. *A Psychiatric Odyssey.* New York: Science House, 1970.

MATTHEWS, H. L. *Fidel Castro.* New York: Simon & Schuster, 1969.

MATTHEWS, T. S. *Great Tom: Notes Toward the Definition of T. S. Eliot.* New York: Harper & Row, 1973.

MAUGHAM, R. *Somerset and All the Maughams.* New York: New American Library, 1966.

MAUGHAM, R. *Escape from the Shadows.* New York: McGraw-Hill, 1973.

MAXWELL, G. *Tennessee Williams and Friends.* New York: World, 1965.

MAY, J. *Mickey Mantle Slugs It Out.* Mankato, Minn.: Crestwood House, 1972a.

MAY, J. *Willie Mays: Most Valuable Player*. Mankato, Minn.: Crestwood House, 1972b.

MAY, R. *Paulus: Reminiscences of a Friendship*. New York: Harper & Row, 1973.

MAYAKOVSKY, V. V. *Mayakovsky*. New York: Hill & Wang, 1965.

MAYFIELD, S. *Exiles from Paradise*. New York: Delacorte Press, 1971.

MEAD, M. *Blackberry Winter: A Memoir*. New York: Morrow, 1972.

MEAD, M., and BALDWIN, J. *A Rap On Race*. Philadelphia: Lippincott, 1971.

MEIR, G. M. *My Life*. New York: Putnam's, 1975.

MENDELSON, W. (Ed.). *Felix Frankfurter: A Tribute*. New York: Reynal, 1964.

MEREDITH, S. *George S. Kaufman and His Friends*. New York: Doubleday, 1974.

METCALF, G. R. *Up from Within*. New York: McGraw-Hill, 1971.

MEYNELL, F. *My Lives*. New York: Random House, 1971.

MIGEO, M. *Saint-Exupéry*. New York: McGraw-Hill, 1960.

MILFORD, N. *Zelda: A Biography*. New York: Harper & Row, 1970.

MILLER, H. *Air-Conditioned Nightmare*. New York: New Directions, 1945.

MILLER, H. *Letters to Anaïs Nin*. New York: Putnam's, 1965.

MILLER, W. J. *Henry Cabot Lodge: A Biography*. New York: Heineman, 1967.

MOHAN, A. *Indira Gandhi: A Personal and Political Biography*. Des Moines, Iowa: Meredith, 1967.

MOLLENHOFF, C. *Tentacles of Power*. New York: World, 1965.

MONROE, M. *My Story*. New York: Stein & Day, 1974.

MONTGOMERY, R. *Mrs. L.B.J.* New York: Holt, Rinehart and Winston, 1964.

MOORE, R. E. *Niels Bohr: The Man, His Science, and the World They Changed*. New York: Knopf, 1966.

MORAES, D. F. *My Son's Father: A Poet's Autobiography*. New York: Macmillan, 1968.

MOREAU, G. *The Restless Journey of James Agee*. New York: Morrow, 1977.

MORELLA, J., and EPSTEIN, E. Z. *Brando: The Unauthorized Biography*. New York: Crown, 1973.

MORRELL, O. *Memoirs.* (2 vols.) New York: Knopf, 1974.

MORSBERGER, R. E. *James Thurber.* Boston: Twayne, 1964.

MOSES, A. M. *Grandma Moses: My Life's History.* New York: Harper & Row, 1952.

MOSLEY, L. *Haile Selassie: The Conquering Lion.* Englewood Cliffs, N.J.: Prentice-Hall, 1964.

MOSS, H. A., and KAGAN, J. "Maternal Influences on Early I. Q. Scores." *Psychological Reports,* 1959, *14,* 655–661.

MURRAY-BROWN, J. *Kenyatta.* New York: Dutton, 1973.

MYRDAL, J. *Confessions of a Disloyal European.* New York: Pantheon, 1968.

NADELSON, R. *Who Is Angela Davis? The Biography of a Revolutionary.* New York: McKay, 1972.

NAGEL, O. *Käthe Kollwitz.* New York: New York Graphic Society, 1972.

NAMATH, J. W. *I Can't Wait Until Tomorrow.* New York: Random House, 1969.

NARAYAN, R. K. *My Days.* New York: Viking Press, 1974.

NATHAN, J. *Mishima.* Boston: Little, Brown, 1974.

NEARY, J. *Julian Bond, Black Rebel.* New York: Morrow, 1971.

NEGRI, P. *Memoirs of a Star.* New York: Doubleday, 1970.

NEILL, A. S. *Neill, Neill, Orange Peel: An Autobiography of the Headmaster of Summerhill School.* New York: Hart, 1972.

NEVIN, D. *Muskie of Maine.* New York: Random House, 1972.

NEWLON, C. *L.B.J.: The Man from Johnson City.* New York: Dodd, Mead, 1966.

NEWMAN, P. C. *A Nation Divided: Canada and the Coming of Pierre Trudeau.* New York: Knopf, 1969.

NICOLSON, N. (Ed.). *Diaries and Letters of Harold Nicolson.* (3 vols.) New York: Atheneum, 1966.

NICOLSON, N. *Portrait of a Marriage.* New York: Atheneum, 1973.

NIN, A. *The Diary of Anaïs Nin, 1931–1934.* Chicago: Swallow, 1966. (See also five additional vols. for 1934–1966.)

NORMAN, C. *E. E. Cummings: The Magic-Maker.* Indianapolis, Ind.: Bobbs-Merrill, 1972.

NUREYEV, R. *Nureyev: An Autobiography with Pictures.* New York: Dutton, 1962.

O'CONNOR, F. V. *Jackson Pollock.* New York: Museum of Modern Art, 1967.

O'CONNOR, R. *John Steinbeck.* New York: McGraw-Hill, 1970.

ODINGA, O. *Not Yet Uhuru: The Autobiography of Oginga Odinga.* New York: Hill & Wang, 1967.

O'DONOVAN, M. *An Only Child.* New York: Knopf, 1961.

O'DONOVAN, M. *My Father's Son.* New York: Knopf, 1968.

O'FAOLAIN, S. *Vive Moi!* Boston: Little, Brown, 1964.

O'HIGGINS, P. *Madame: An Intimate Biography of Helena Rubinstein.* New York: Viking Press, 1971.

O'KEEFFE, G. *Georgia O'Keeffe.* New York: Viking Press, 1976.

OSTROVSKY, E. *Céline and His Vision.* New York: New York University Press, 1967.

OSTROVSKY, E. *Voyeur Voyant: A Portrait of Louis-Ferdinand Céline.* New York: Random House, 1971.

OUELLETTE, F. *Edgard Varèse.* New York: Orion, 1968.

PARKINSON, C. S. *The Life and Times of Horatio Hornblower.* Boston: Little, Brown, 1970.

PAYNE, P. S. R. *A Portrait of André Malraux.* Englewood Cliffs, N.J.: Prentice-Hall, 1970.

PAYNE, R. *The Rise and Fall of Stalin.* New York: Simon & Schuster, 1965.

PERCIVAL, J. *Nureyev: Aspects of the Dancer.* New York: Putnam's, 1975.

PERLIS, V. *Charles Ives Remembered: An Oral History.* New Haven, Conn.: Yale University Press, 1974.

PETERS, H. F. *My Sister, My Spouse.* New York: Norton, 1962.

PETRE, D. *The Secret Orchard of Roger Ackerley.* New York: Braziller, 1975.

PEYRE, H. *French Novelists of Today.* New York: Oxford University Press, 1967.

PILAT, O. R. *Drew Pearson: An Unauthorized Biography.* New York: Harper & Row, 1973.

PITRONE, J. *Man of the Migrants.* Staten Island, N.Y.: Alba, 1972.

PLATH, S. *Letters Home: Correspondence, 1950–1963.* New York: Harper & Row, 1975.

POMEROY, W. B. *Dr. Kinsey and the Institute for Sex Research.* New York: Harper & Row, 1972.

PRITCHETT, V. S. *A Cab at the Door.* New York: Random House, 1968.

PRITCHETT, V. S. *Midnight Oil.* New York: Random House, 1972.

PRITTIE, T. *Willy Brandt: Portrait of a Statesman.* New York: Schocken Books, 1974.

PRYCE-JONES, D. *Evelyn Waugh and His World.* Boston: Little, Brown, 1973.

QUINN, A. *The Original Sin: A Self-Portrait.* Boston: Little, Brown, 1972.

QUIRK, L. J. *Ingrid Bergman.* New York: Citadel, 1970.

RACHEWILTZ, M. DE. *Discretions.* Boston: Little, Brown, 1971.

RASMUSSEN, A.-M. *There Was Once a Time.* New York: Harcourt Brace Jovanovich, 1975.

READ, H. *Henry Moore: A Study of His Life and Work.* New York: Praeger, 1966.

REAGAN, R., and HUBLER, R. C. *Where's the Rest of Me?* New York: Duell, Sloan & Pearce, 1965.

RECK, M. *Ezra Pound: A Close-up.* New York: McGraw-Hill, 1967.

REICH, I. O. *Wilhelm Reich: A Personal Biography.* New York: St. Martin's Press, 1969.

REICH, P. *A Book of Dreams.* New York: Harper & Row, 1973.

REICH, W. *Schoenberg: A Critical Biography.* New York: Praeger, 1971.

REID, C. *John Barbirolli: A Biography.* New York: Taplinger, 1971.

RENOIR, J. *Renoir, My Father.* Boston: Little, Brown, 1962.

RESHETOVSKAIA, N. A. *Sanya: My Life With Alesandr Solzhenitsyn.* Indianapolis, Ind.: Bobbs-Merrill, 1975.

RHODES, A. *Louis Renault: A Biography.* New York: Harcourt Brace Jovanovich, 1969.

RICHTOFEN, M. VON. *The Red Baron.* New York: Doubleday, 1969.

RIOU, R. *The Island of My Life: From Petty Crime to Priestly Mission.* New York: Delacorte Press, 1975.

ROAZEN, P. *Erik H. Erikson: The Power and Limits of a Vision.* New York: Free Press, 1976.

ROBINSON, E. G., and SPIGELGAS, L. *All My Yesterdays: An Autobiography.* New York: Hawthorn Books, 1973.

ROE, A. *Making of a Scientist.* New York: Dodd, Mead, 1953.

ROSEN, S. *Wizard of the Dome: R. Buckminster Fuller, Designer for the Future.* Boston: Little, Brown, 1969.

ROSENTHAL, D. *Genetic Theory and Abnormal Behavior.* New York: McGraw-Hill, 1970.

ROSSI, A. S. *The Feminist Papers: From Adams to de Beauvoir.* New York: Columbia University Press, 1973.

ROSSITER, F. R. *Charles Ives and His America.* New York: Liveright, 1975.

RUBINSTEIN, A. *My Young Years.* New York: Knopf, 1973.

RUTH, C. M. *The Babe and I.* Englewood Cliffs, N.J.: Prentice-Hall, 1959.

RYCROFT, C. *Wilhelm Reich.* New York: Viking Press, 1971.

RYSKIND, A. H. *Hubert: An Unauthorized Biography of the Vice President.* New Rochelle, N.Y.: Arlington House, 1968.

SACHS, M. *Witches' Sabbath.* New York: Stein & Day, 1964.

SACKVILLE-WEST, V. *Pepita.* New York: Doubleday, 1938.

SAINT-EXUPÉRY, A. *Airman's Odyssey.* New York: Harcourt Brace Jovanovich, 1942.

ST. JOHN, B. *John Sloan.* New York: Praeger, 1971.

ST. JOHN, R. *Eban.* New York: Doubleday, 1970.

SALTER, E. *Daisy Bates.* New York: Coward, McCann & Geoghegan, 1972.

SANDERS, M. K. *Dorothy Thompson: A Legend in Her Time.* Boston: Houghton Mifflin, 1963.

SARTRE, J.-P. *Saint Genet: Actor and Martyr.* New York: Braziller, 1963.

SARTRE, J.-P. *Les Mots.* New York: Braziller, 1964.

SAYRE, A. *Rosalind Franklin and DNA.* New York: Norton, 1975.

SCHOOR, G. *Young Robert Kennedy.* New York: McGraw-Hill, 1969.

SCHULBERG, B. W. *Loser and Still Champion.* New York: Doubleday, 1972.

SCHUR, E. M. *The Awareness Trap: Self-Absorption Instead of Social Change.* New York: Quadrangle, 1976.

SCOTT-STOKES, H. *The Life and Death of Yukio Mishima.* New York: Farrar, Straus & Giroux, 1974.

SEAGER, A. *The Glass House: The Life of Theodore Roethke.* New York: McGraw-Hill, 1968.

SEIB, K. *James Agee: Promise and Fulfillment.* Pittsburgh, Pa.: University of Pittsburgh Press, 1968.

SEIDLER, M. B. *Norman Thomas: Respectable Rebel.* Syracuse, N.Y.: Syracuse University Press, 1967.

SENCOURT, R. *T. S. Eliot: A Memoir.* New York: Dodd, Mead, 1973.

SERRANO, M. *C. G. Jung and Hermann Hesse: A Record of Two Friendships.* New York: Schocken Books, 1966.

SHANKAR, R. *My Music, My Life.* New York: Simon & Schuster, 1968. (Introduction by Y. Menuhin.)

SHAW, A. *Sinatra: Twentieth-Century Romantic.* New York: Holt, Rinehart and Winston, 1968.

SHAWCROSS, W. *Dubček.* New York: Simon & Schuster, 1970.

SHEEAN, V. *Dorothy and Red.* Boston: Houghton Mifflin, 1963.

SHEPPARD, D. *Elizabeth: The Life of Elizabeth Taylor.* New York: Doubleday, 1974.

SHERIDAN, W. *The Fall and Rise of Jimmy Hoffa.* New York: Saturday Review Press, 1972.

SHERRILL, R. *The Last Kennedy.* New York: Dial Press, 1976.

SHIPTON, E. E. *That Untravelled World: An Autobiography.* New York: Scribner's, 1969.

SHNEIDMAN, E. S. *Suicidology: Contemporary Developments.* New York: Grune & Stratton, 1976.

SIEBEN, P. *The Immortal Jolson: His Life and Times.* New York: Fell, 1962.

SIMENON, G. *When I Was Old: Simenon on Simenon.* New York: Harcourt Brace Jovanovich, 1971.

SIMENON, G. *Letter to My Mother.* New York: Harcourt Brace Jovanovich, 1976.

SINCLAIR, A. *Ché Guevara.* New York: Viking Press, 1970.

SINCLAIR, U. B. *The Autobiography of Upton Sinclair.* New York: Harcourt Brace Jovanovich, 1962.

SINGER, I. B. *In My Father's Court.* New York: Farrar, Straus & Giroux, 1969.

SKIDELSKY, R. *Oswald Mosley.* New York: Holt, Rinehart and Winston, 1975.

SLATER, L. *Aly: A Biography.* New York: Random House, 1965.

SMITH, M. *The President's Lady.* New York: Random House, 1964.

SNOW, P. J. *Hussein: A Biography.* Washington, D.C.: Luce, 1972.

SOBY, J. T. *Joan Miró.* New York: Doubleday, 1959.

SOLZHENITSYN, A. *Solzhenitsyn: A Pictorial Autobiography.* New York: Farrar, Straus & Giroux, 1974.

SORELL, W. *Three Women: Lives of Sex and Genius.* Indianapolis, Ind.: Bobbs-Merrill, 1975.

SORENSEN, T. C. *The Kennedy Legacy.* New York: Macmillan, 1969.

SOYER, R. *Self-Revealment: A Memoir.* New York: Random House, 1969.

SOYER, R. *Moses Soyer.* New York: Barnes & Noble, 1970. (Introduction by A. Werner; memoir by D. Soyer.)

SPEARS, M. K. (Ed.). *Auden: A Collection of Critical Essays.* Englewood Cliffs, N.J.: Prentice-Hall, 1964.

SPENDER, S. (Compiler.) *W. H. Auden: A Tribute.* New York: Macmillan, 1975.

SPRAGGETT, A., and RAUSCHER, W. V. *Arthur Ford: The Man Who Talked with the Dead.* New York: New American Library, 1973.

SPRIGGE, E. *Gertrude Stein: Her Life and Work.* New York: Harper & Row, 1975.

SPRINGER, J. S. *The Fondas: The Films and Success of Henry, Jane, and Peter Fonda.* New York: Citadel, 1970.

STEARN, J. *A Prophet in His Own Country: The Story of Young Edgar Cayce.* New York: Morrow, 1974.

STEEGMULLER, F. *Cocteau.* Boston: Little, Brown, 1970.

STEICHEN, E. *A Life in Photography.* New York: Doubleday, 1963.

STEICHEN, P. *My Connemara.* New York: Harcourt Brace Jovanovich, 1969.

STEINBECK, E., and WALLSTEN, R. (Eds.). *Steinbeck: A Life in Letters.* New York: Viking Press, 1975.

STEINBERG, A. *Sam Johnson's Boy: A Close-up of the President from Texas.* New York: Macmillan, 1968.

STEINER, N. H. *A Closer Look at Ariel: A Memory of Sylvia Plath.* New York: Harper & Row, 1972. (Introduction by G. Slade.)

STEINER, S. *The Female Factor: A Study in Five Western European Societies.* New York: Putnam's, 1977.

STERLING, P. *Sea and Earth.* New York: Crowell, 1970.

STERN, P. J. *C. G. Jung: The Haunted Prophet.* New York: Braziller, 1976.

STERNE, E. G. *Mary McLeod Bethune.* New York: Knopf, 1957.

STEWART, W. *Trudeau in Power.* New York: Outerbridge, 1971.

STOESSINGER, J. G. *Henry Kissinger: The Anguish of Power.* New York: Norton, 1976.

STREENE, B. *Ingmar Bergman.* Boston: Twayne, 1968.

STUART, D. *Alan Watts.* Radnor, Pa.: Chilton, 1976.

SUGRUE, T. *There Is a River: The Story of Edgar Cayce.* New York: Dell, 1970.

SUKARNO (as told to Adams, C.). *Sukarno: An Autobiography.* Indianapolis, Ind.: Bobbs-Merrill, 1965.

SUYIN, H. *A Many Splendored Thing.* Boston: Little, Brown, 1952.

SUYIN, H. *The Crippled Tree.* New York: Putnam's, 1965.

SUYIN, H. *A Mortal Flower.* New York: Putnam's, 1966.

SWADOS, H. *Standing Up for the People: The Life and Work of Estes Kefauver.* New York: Dutton, 1972.

SWANBERG, W. A. *Luce and His Empire.* New York: Scribner's, 1972.

SWEET, F. A. *Miss Mary Cassatt.* Norman, Okla.: University of Oklahoma Press, 1966.

SYKES, C. *Nancy: The Life of Lady Astor.* New York: Harper & Row, 1972.

SYKES, C. *Evelyn Waugh: A Biography.* Boston: Little, Brown, 1975.

SYLVESTER, D. *Henry Moore.* New York: Praeger, 1968.

SZIKNOKI, R. N. *Namath, My Son Joe.* Birmingham, Ala.: Oxmoor House, 1975.

TAYLOR, A. J. P. *Beaverbrook.* New York: Simon & Schuster, 1972.

TAYLOR, R. B. *Chavez and the Farm Workers.* Boston: Beacon Press, 1975.

TEBBEL, J. W. *David Sarnoff: Putting Electrons to Work.* Chicago: Encyclopaedia Britannica, 1963.

TEICHMANN, H. *George S. Kaufman: An Intimate Portrait.* New York: Atheneum, 1972.

TER HORST, J. F. *Gerald Ford and the Future of the Presidency.* New York: Third Press, 1974.

TEVETH, S. *Moshe Dayan: The Soldier, the Man, the Legend.* Boston: Houghton Mifflin, 1973.

THAYER, M. *Jacqueline Kennedy: The White House Years*. Boston: Little, Brown, 1971.

THODY, P. *Jean Genet*. New York: Haimish-Hamilton, 1968.

THODY, P. *Sartre: A Biographical Introduction*. New York: Scribner's, 1971.

THOMAS, B. *Marlon: Portrait of the Rebel as an Artist*. New York: Random House, 1974.

THOMPSON, H. *Fred Astaire*. Los Angeles: Falcon, 1970.

THOMPSON, T. *Positively Main Street: An Unorthodox View of Bob Dylan*. New York: Coward, McCann & Geoghegan, 1971.

THOMPSON, V. D. "Family Size: Implicit Policies and Assumed Psychological Outcomes." *Journal of Social Issues*, 1974, *30* (4), 93–123.

TILLICH, H. *From Time to Time*. New York: Stein & Day, 1973.

TILLICH, H. *From Place to Place: Travels with Paul Tillich and Without Paul Tillich*. New York: Stein & Day, 1976.

TOBIAS, R. C. *The Art of James Thurber*. Columbus: Ohio State University Press, 1969.

TORRANCE, E. P. *Status of Knowledge Concerning Education and Creative Scientific Talent*. Minneapolis: University of Minnesota Press, 1961.

TORRES, J. *Sting Like a Bee*. New York: Abelard-Schuman, 1971.

ULAM, S. M. *Adventures of a Mathematician*. New York: Scribner's, 1976.

USTINOV, N. B. *Klop and the Ustinov Family*. New York: Okpaku, 1973.

VALJEAN, N. *John Steinbeck, the Errant Knight: An Intimate Biography of His California Years*. San Francisco: Chronicle Books, 1975.

VAN DER POST, L. *Jung and the Story of Our Time*. New York: Pantheon, 1975.

VARÈSE, L. M. *Varèse: A Looking Glass Diary*. New York: Norton, 1972.

VESTAL, B. *Jerry Ford Up Close: An Investigative Biography*. New York: Coward, McCann & Geoghegan, 1974.

VINING, E. G. *Windows for the Crown Prince*. Philadelphia: Lippincott, 1952.

VINING, E. G. *Return to Japan*. Philadelphia: Lippincott, 1960.

VINING, E. G. *Quiet Pilgrimage.* Philadelphia: Lippincott, 1970.

WAAGENAAR, S. *Mata Hari.* New York: Appleton-Century-Crofts, 1965.

WALEN, R. J. *The Founding Father.* New York: World, 1964.

WALLACE, G., JR. (as told to Gregory, J.). *The Wallaces of Alabama: My Family.* Chicago: Follett, 1975.

WARNER, S. T. *T. H. White: A Biography.* New York: Viking Press, 1968.

WATERBURY, R. *Elizabeth Taylor.* New York: Appleton-Century-Crofts, 1964.

WATERS, E. *His Eye Is on the Sparrow: An Autobiography.* New York: Doubleday, 1951.

WATERS, E. *To Me It's Wonderful.* New York: Harper & Row, 1972.

WATSON, J. *The Double Helix.* New York: Atheneum, 1969.

WATTS, A. *In My Own Way: An Autobiography, 1915–1965.* New York: Pantheon, 1972.

WAUGH, A. *My Brother Evelyn and Other Portraits.* New York: Farrar, Straus & Giroux, 1967.

WAUGH, E. *The Early Years.* Boston: Little, Brown, 1964.

WEATHERBY, W. J. *Conversations with Marilyn.* New York: Mason/Charter, 1976.

WEAVER, J. D. *Warren: The Man, the Court, the Era.* Boston: Little, Brown, 1967.

WEBB, B. L. *The Basketball Man: James Naismith.* Lawrence: University of Kansas Libraries, 1973.

WEHR, G. *Portrait of Jung.* New York: Herder & Herder, 1971.

WEISGAL, M. W. *Meyer Weisgal . . . So Far.* New York: Random House, 1971.

WELK, L. *Wunnerful, Wunnerful! The Autobiography of Lawrence Welk.* Englewood Cliffs, N.J.: Prentice-Hall, 1971.

WELK, L. *Ah-One, Ah-Two: Life with My Musical Family.* Englewood Cliffs, N.J.: Prentice-Hall, 1974.

WEST, J. *To See the Dream.* New York: Harcourt Brace Jovanovich, 1957.

WEST, J. *Hide and Seek: A Continuing Journey.* New York: Harcourt Brace Jovanovich, 1973.

WEST, J. *The Woman Said Yes: Encounters with Life and Death— Memoirs.* New York: Harcourt Brace Jovanovich, 1976.

WHEELER, L. *Jimmy Who? An Examination of Presidential Candidate Jimmy Carter: The Man, His Career, His Stand on the Issues.* Woodbury, N.Y.: Barron's Educational Series, 1976.

WHITE, E. W. *Benjamin Britten: His Life and Operas.* Berkeley: University of California Press, 1970.

WIDMER, K. *Henry Miller.* New York: Grosset & Dunlap, 1963.

WIJSENBEEK, L. *Piet Mondrian.* New York: New York Graphic Society, 1968.

WILLIAMS, C. J., and WEINBERG, M. S. *Homosexuals and the Military: A Study of Less than Honorable Discharge.* New York: Harper & Row, 1971.

WILLIAMS, E. *George: An Early Autobiography.* New York: Random House, 1962.

WILLIAMS, E. *Emlyn: An Early Autobiography, 1927–1935.* New York: Viking Press, 1974.

WILLIAMS, R. M. *The Bonds: An American Family.* New York: Atheneum, 1971.

WILLIAMS, T. *Memoirs.* New York: Doubleday, 1975.

WILSON, E. *Sinatra: An Unauthorized Biography.* New York: Macmillan, 1976.

WIND, H. W. *The World of P. G. Wodehouse.* New York: Praeger, 1971.

WITCOVER, J. *White Knight: The Rise of Spiro Agnew.* New York: Random House, 1972.

WOOD, R. *Ingmar Bergman.* New York: Praeger, 1969.

WOOLF, L. S. *Sowing: An Autobiography of the Years 1880–1904.* New York: Harcourt Brace Jovanovich, 1960.

WOOLF, L. S. *Growing: An Autobiography of the Years 1904–1911.* New York: Harcourt Brace Jovanovich, 1961.

WOROSZYLSKI, W. *The Life of Mayakovsky.* New York: Grossman, 1971.

WYETH, N. C. *The Wyeths: The Letters of N. C. Wyeth, 1901–1945.* Boston: Gambit, 1971.

YEVTUSHENKO, Y. *A Precocious Autobiography.* New York: Dutton, 1963.

YODER, J. A. *Upton Sinclair.* New York: Ungar, 1975.

YOGANANDA, P. *Autobiography of a Yogi.* Los Angeles: Self-Realization Fellowship, 1969.

ZABLOCKI, B. *The Joyful Community.* New York: Penguin Books, 1974.

ZELLER, B. *Portrait of Hesse.* New York: Herder & Herder, 1971.

ZHUKOV, G. K. *The Memoirs of Marshall Zhukov.* New York: Delacorte Press, 1971.

ZIEROLD, N. J. *Garbo.* New York: Stein & Day, 1969.

ZIOLKOWSKI, T. (Ed.). *Hermann Hesse: Autobiographical Writing.* New York: Farrar, Straus & Giroux, 1972.

ZORACH, W. *Art Is My Life: The Autobiography of William Zorach.* New York: World, 1967.

Index